Microcomputer Software: Step by Step

TED KALMON
NANCY LONG
LARRY LONG

PRENTICE HALL, Englewood Cliffs, New Jersey 07632

Library of Congress Cataloging-in-Publication Data

```
Kalmon, Ted.
    Microcomputer software : step by step / Ted Kalmon, Nancy Long,
Larry Long.
       p.   cm.
    ISBN 0-13-824699-8
    1. Computer software.  2. MS-DOS (Computer operating system)
3. WordPerfect (Computer program) 4. dBase III plus (Computer
program)  5. Lotus 1-2-3 (Computer program)  I. Long, Nancy
.  II. Long, Larry E.  III. Title.
QA76.754.K35  1990
005.36--dc20                                          90-30075
                                                         CIP
```

WordPerfect® is a registered trademark of WordPerfect
Corporation. Lotus® 1-2-3® are registered trademarks of Lotus
Development Corporation. dBASE III PLUS® and dBASE
IV® are registered trademarks of Ashton-Tate Corporation.

Cover design: Wanda Lubelska
Manufacturing buyer: Mary Ann Gloriande

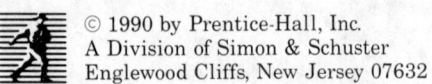

© 1990 by Prentice-Hall, Inc.
A Division of Simon & Schuster
Englewood Cliffs, New Jersey 07632

All rights reserved. No part of this book may be
reproduced, in any form or by any means,
without permission in writing from the publisher.

Printed in the United States of America
10 9 8 7 6 5 4 3 2

ISBN 0-13-824699-8 01

Prentice-Hall International (UK) Limited, *London*
Prentice-Hall of Australia Pty. Limited, *Sydney*
Prentice-Hall Canada Inc., *Toronto*
Prentice-Hall Hispanoamericana, S.A., *Mexico*
Prentice-Hall of India Private Limited, *New Delhi*
Prentice-Hall of Japan, Inc., *Tokyo*
Simon & Schuster Asia Pte. Ltd., *Singapore*
Editora Prentice-Hall do Brasil, Ltda., *Rio de Janeiro*

Contents

Preface xi

How to Use This Book xiii

Chapter 1   Introduction to the Computer   1

The Personal Computer Revolution 2
What Is a Microcomputer? 4
Inside the Computer 6
Input/Output Devices 10
Data Storage Devices and Media 13
Configuring a Microcomputer System 16
Microcomputer Operation 18
User Friendly Software 23

Chapter 2   DOS   25

DOS Fundamentals 26

Step 1	The Disk Operating System	26
Step 2	Running a Software Package	27
Step 3	Files and Filenames	28
Step 4	Directories and Paths	29

Session One   Loading DOS 31

Step 1	Turning On the Computer	31
Step 2	Entering the Date and Time	32
Step 3	Entering a DOS Command	32
Step 4	Entering Commands with User-Supplied Data	34
Step 5	Practice	34
Step 6	Turning Off the Computer	35
Step 7	Summary	35

Session Two   Files and Filenames (DIR) 36

Step 1	Displaying a Filename List	36
Step 2	Displaying Individual Filenames	38
Step 3	Practice	39
Step 4	Ending the Session	39

	Session Three (Commands: FORMAT and DISKCOPY)	**....40**
Step 1	Write Protecting a Diskette	41
Step 2	Formatting a Diskette	42
Step 3	Copying a Diskette using DISKCOPY	43
Step 4	Changing the Active Drive	44
Step 5	Labeling and Storing Diskettes	44
Step 6	Practice	45
Step 7	Ending the Session	45

Session Four	**Introduction to Hard Drives and Directories**	**46**
Step 1	Creating a Directory	46
Step 2	Changing Directories	47
Step 3	Removing a Directory	47

Session Five	**The Powerful COPY Command**	**....49**
Step 1	Creating a Practice Subdirectory	49
Step 2	Copying a File from the Hard Drive to a Diskette	50
Step 3	Making a Second Copy of a File on a Diskette	53
Step 4	Using COPY to Create a Short Text File	54
Step 5	Practice	56
Step 6	Removing the Practice Directory and Ending the Session	59

Session Six	**Using Wildcard Characters**	**....60**
Step 1	The Asterisk (*)	60
Step 2	The Question Mark (?)	61
Step 3	Using Wildcard Characters with Other Commands	62
Step 4	Practice	67

Session Seven	**Edlin**	**....68**
Step 1	Using the PATH Command	68
Step 2	Creating a File Using EDLIN	69
Step 3	Modifying a File Using EDLIN	70
Step 4	Practice	72

Session Eight	**DOS Batch Files**	**....74**
Step 1	Creating a Batch File	74
Step 2	Practice	76
Step 3	Removing the Practice Directory and Ending the Session	77

Chapter 3   WordPerfect   79

Session One	**Using WordPerfect to Create a Memo**	**....80**
Step 1	Loading WordPerfect	80

Step 2	Entering Text	85
Step 3	Moving Text	86
Step 4	Adding Text	89
Step 5	Saving a Document	90
Step 6	Displaying the Reveal Codes Screen	91
Step 7	Search and Replace	92
Step 8	Centering, Boldfacing, Underlining Text	94
Step 9	Retrieving a Document	96
Step 10	Printing a Document	97
Step 11	Practice	98
Step 12	Exiting WordPerfect and Terminating the Session	100

Session Two — Margins, Tabs and Line Draw 101

Step 1	Preparing the Heading	101
Step 2	Using Tabs and Adjusting Margins	104
Step 3	Saving and Printing the Party Invitation	107
Step 4	Practice	108
Step 5	Exiting WordPerfect and Terminating the Session	108

Session Three — Spell-check and Thesaurus 109

Step 1	Spell-checking a Document	109
Step 2	Using the On-Line Thesaurus	111
Step 3	Creating Footnotes	112
Step 4	Practice	115
Step 5	Exiting WordPerfect and Terminating the Session	116

Session Four — Merging 117

Step 1	Creating the Name and Address File	117
Step 2	Creating the Letter File	119
Step 3	Merging Two Files	122
Step 4	Printing the Documents	123
Step 5	Practice	124
Step 6	Exiting WordPerfect and Terminating the Session	125

Session Five — Columns, Math and Sorting 126

Step 1	Defining and Using Newspaper Columns	128
Step 2	Using the Math Feature	130
Step 3	Sorting by Line	134
Step 4	Sorting a Secondary Merge File	136
Step 5	Combining Files	139
Step 6	Practice	140
Step 7	Terminating the Session	142

Session Six — Macros 143

Step 1	Creating a Simple ALT-Letter Macro	144
Step 2	Using an ALT-Letter Macro	145
Step 3	Creating a Simple Named Macro	146

Step 4	Executing a Named Macro	147
Step 5	Creating and Executing a Temporary Macro	148
Step 6	Editing Macros	149
Step 7	Creating an Interactive Macro	153
Step 8	Using an Interactive Macro	158
Step 9	Chaining Macros	158
Step 10	Practice	160
Step 11	Exiting WordPerfect	161

Session Seven Desktop Publishing Capabilities 162

Step 1	Preparing the Newsletter Format	162
Step 2	Assigning a Style	167
Step 3	Creating a Graphics Text Box	168
Step 4	Creating a User-Defined Box	169
Step 5	Changing a User-Defined Box Definition	171
Step 6	Importing Clip-Art into a Graphics Box	173
Step 7	Combining Graphics Boxes	175
Step 8	Practice	177
Step 9	Exiting WordPerfect	178

Chapter 4 dBASE III PLUS 179

Session One Creating a Data Base 180

Step 1	Using dBASE III PLUS	180
Step 2	Creating a Data Base	182
Step 3	Adding Data Base Records	187
Step 4	Modifying Records in a Data Base	188
Step 5	Creating and Adding Records to the TRAINING Data Base	190
Step 6	Printing a Record Listing	191
Step 7	Practice	192
Step 8	Saving and Retrieving a Data Base	193
Step 9	Terminating a Session	193

Session Two Understanding dBASE Command Structure 194

Step 1	Retrieving a Data Base	194
Step 2	Displaying the Help Screen	195
Step 3	The Expression List Parameter	196
Step 4	Appending Records from Another Data Base	199
Step 5	The SCOPE Parameter	200
Step 6	The FOR Condition Parameter	202
Step 7	The WHILE Condition Parameter	205
Step 8	The OFF and TO PRINT Parameters	205
Step 9	Combining Parameters	205
Step 10	Using Command Parameters to Make Data Base Inquiries	206
Step 11	Practice	208
Step 12	Terminating the Session	209

Session Three	**Introduction to Sorting and Indexing**	**210**
Step 1	Sorting	210
Step 2	Indexing	212
Step 3	Practice	214
Step 4	Terminating the Session	215
Session Four	**Reports (and More on Indexing)**	**216**
Step 1	Creating a Data Base and Adding Data Base Records	217
Step 2	Single Field Indexing and Creating a Summary Report	218
Step 3	Multiple Field Indexing and Modifying a Report	221
Step 4	Copying a File's Structure and Appending Selected Records to a New File	223
Step 5	Deleting Records from a Data Base	224
Step 6	Practice	226
Step 7	Terminating the Session	226
Session Five	**Introduction to Programming**	**227**
Step 1	Creating a Program	231
Step 2	Running a Program	232
Step 3	Modifying a Program	233
Step 4	Practice	233
Step 5	Terminating the Session	233
Session Six	**More Programming**	**234**
Step 1	Creating Data Bases and Adding Data Base Records	234
Step 2	Entering Repetitive Data	236
Step 3	Building a Multiple Field Index Expression Using Nested Functions	237
Step 4	Planning a Program	239
Step 5	Entering the Program Code	242
Step 6	Running the INVOICE Program	242
Step 7	Practice	246
Step 8	Terminating the Session	248

Chapter 5   Lotus 1-2-3   249

Session One	**Creating a Spreadsheet**	**250**
Step 1	Using Lotus 1-2-3	251
Step 2	Creating a Simple Income Statement	253
Step 3	Formatting the Column Width	257
Step 4	Entering Labels	258
Step 5	Entering Values	260
Step 6	Entering Formulas	260
Step 7	Saving a Spreadsheet	261

Step 8	Using Predefined Functions	261
Step 9	Formatting the Cell Entries	262
Step 10	Saving a Previously Saved Spreadsheet	264
Step 11	Printing a Document	264
Step 12	Retrieving a Spreadsheet	265
Step 13	Practice	265
Step 14	Terminating a Session	265

Session Two   What if... Analysis 266

Step 1	Inserting a Column	266
Step 2	Creating a Forecast Variable Template	268
Step 3	Adding "What if" Formulas to Column B	269
Step 4	Performing "What if..." Analysis	270
Step 5	Saving Incremental Versions of a Spreadsheet	272
Step 6	Practice	272
Step 7	Terminating the Session	275

Session Three   Modifying a Spreadsheet 276

Step 1	Inserting a Column	276
Step 2	Creating Absolute Cell Addresses	277
Step 3	Using Absolute Cell Addresses	279
Step 4	Adding a Template to an Existing Template	281
Step 5	Modifying the "R&G1" Template to Create Another Template	282
Step 6	Using Windows	283
Step 7	Practice	285
Step 8	Terminating the Session	286

Session Four   The Database Side of Spreadsheets 287

Step 1	Understanding Spreadsheet Data Bases	287
Step 2	Creating a Spreadsheet Data Base	289
Step 3	Extracting Data	290
Step 4	Finding Data	292
Step 5	Sorting a Spreadsheet Data Base	293
Step 6	Practice	295
Step 7	Terminating the Session	296

Session Five   Graphics Capabilities 297

Step 1	Starting the Lotus Access System	298
Step 2	Entering the Data	299
Step 3	Producing a Bar Graph	300
Step 4	Saving and Printing/Plotting a Graph	302
Step 5	Producing Stack-Bar and Clustered-Bar Graphs	305
Step 6	Producing a Pie Graph	308
Step 7	Producing a Line Graph	309
Step 8	Practice	311
Step 9	Terminating the Session	312

Session Six	**Introduction to Macros** 313
Step 1	Creating a Macro 314
Step 2	Invoking a Macro 316
Step 3	Creating a Print Macro 316
Step 4	Editing a Macro 317
Step 5	Creating a Macro Menu 318
Step 6	Creating a Goto Macro 319
Step 7	Practice 321
Step 8	Terminating a Session 322

Session Seven	**Dates and More on Macros** 323
Step 1	Using Lotus Add-in Features with Release 2.01 324
Step 2	Entering and Formatting Dates 328
Step 3	Entering Spreadsheet Data and Aligning Column Headings 328
Step 4	Practice 330
Step 5	Terminating the Session 331

Session Eight	**Printing with Allways** 332
Step 1	Preparing the SUMMARY Template 332
Step 2	Invoking Allways and Formatting the Template 334
Step 3	Printing and Saving an Allways Version of the Template 335
Step 4	Printing Graphs with Allways 336
Step 5	Practice 339
Step 6	Terminating the Session 341

Session Nine	**New Features in Release 3** 342
Step 1	Activating Multiple Spreadsheets 343
Step 2	Linking Multiple Files 345
Step 3	Updating Linked Files 347
Step 4	Connecting to an External Data Base 349
Step 5	Using UNDO 350
Step 6	Practice 351
Step 7	Terminating the Session 352

Appendices   353

Appendix A	MS-DOS Command Summary 354
Appendix B	WordPerfect 5.0 Command Summary 359
Appendix C	dBASE III PLUS Command Summary 371
Appendix D	Lotus 1-2-3 Command Summary (Release 2.01) 375

Index   381

Preface

Every day microcomputers become more important in our working lives. Many companies have announced that microcomputer skills are not only desirable but sometimes requirements for employment. This integration of microcomputers into society's mainstream means that what you learn from this book will surely help you in your academic pursuits and your career.

This book presents concepts and enables hands-on experience in the IBM-compatible environment. The software covered includes the operating system and the three most widely used software productivity tools in the business environment: word processing, database management and electronic spreadsheets. The software presented in each category is the best-selling software of its type.

Just as driving a car and playing a musical instrument are developed skills, using a microcomputer is a skill that evolves with practice. The step-by-step approach used in this book will help you develop the skills to become an effective user of microcomputers and microcomputer software.

How This Book Is Structured

This book is divided into five chapters.

- ◆ **Chapter 1** describes the components that together make up a computer system.
- ◆ **Chapter 2** introduces and illustrates the use of DOS, the operating system that orchestrates the integration of a computer system's various elements.
- ◆ **Chapter 3** introduces and illustrates the use of WordPerfect 5.0 while presenting word processing concepts.
- ◆ **Chapter 4** introduces and illustrates the use of dBASE III PLUS while presenting database management concepts.
- ◆ **Chapter 5** introduces and illustrates the use of Lotus 1-2-3 while presenting electronic spreadsheet concepts.

Why This Book?

- ◆ Each software application (DOS, WordPerfect, dBASE, and Lotus) is presented step by step, keystroke by keystroke. Each chapter is divided into several sessions. Each session is a complete unit that discusses software concepts, guides the student through step-by-step examples, and includes practice questions based on the material covered. Each successive session introduces concepts of greater complexity.

- ◆ The presentation of each concept and the accompanying keystroke examples have been thoroughly "classroom tested." This book is based on actual courses taught to over 1000 professionals in a variety of careers.

- ◆ Over 200 "screen shots" help students know if they are performing the keystrokes correctly.

- ◆ Many "problem solving" boxes provide solutions to commonly made mistakes.

- ◆ An Example Files Diskette is supplied to the instructor of each class that adopts this book. The Example Files Diskette contains files that have been prepared by the authors to facilitate keystroke entry and expedite the learning process. The Example Files Diskette is referred to throughout the book.

Production Notes

The text of this book was created and edited in WordPerfect 5.0 and formatted in Ventura Publisher 2.0. The book was printed on a Hewlett-Packard LaserJet Series II enhanced by a LaserMaster LX-6 controller. Each page was supplied "camera ready" to the publisher.

Acknowledgments

A book is never created by the authors alone, and so we wish to thank a few of the many people who made this book a reality. At Prentice Hall, ideas and patient help were available from Ted Werthman, Nancy DeWolfe, Elaine Rusoff, Crystal Waters, and Dolores Kenney. We would also like to thank Gary June for giving this project its initial boost.

Many professionals at the New York City Department of Environmental Protection contributed to this project. In particular, thanks to Mike Schultz and Al Leidner for recognizing the importance of microcomputers and their commitment to microcomputer training. In addition, thanks to the DEP teaching staff, especially Steven Fried for his useful critiques, and Phyllis Fisher, our "secretary *extraordinaire*," who made sure that each class was filled and every memo arrived as intended. Also, thanks to the DEP students who knew they were testing a book-in-progress and rather enjoyed picking it apart.

Finally, special thanks to Valerie Grant, whose support and suggestions helped Mr. Kalmon immeasurably.

How to Use This Book

Using the Step-by-Step Sessions

In learning to use a computer, your major activity should be using the computer. Throughout this book, concepts are not only explained but also are presented keystroke by keystroke to familiarize students with computer concepts through actual experience.

Because the acquisition of new skills requires time and practice, all keystroke sessions are designed to be used more than once. Students should not expect to understand new concepts the first time through. In actual use, students find that second and third "workthroughs" greatly enhance their understanding.

General Format of the Sessions

Each session begins with a general description of the material to be covered followed by a listing of the concepts that will be introduced. Each step appears in the following format:

Step #: Descriptive Title

Overview description of this step, if needed.

- ☐ Brief description of the current activity.

  * **Actual keystroke entries** ↵

  Follow-up clarification and additional remarks regarding commands and idiosyncrasies of the package.

- ☐ A sequence of activities is continued until the step is completed.

The Use of Bullets, Boxed Keys, and Italic

All keystroke entries are preceded by a star:

* **This is a sample keystroke entry** ↵

In most cases, you should type exactly what you see. Exceptions occur when arrows or text within a box appears. For example:

* [F1] ↑ ↵

In the foregoing, you should tap function key F1, tap the up cursor control key and then tap the ENTER key.

Italics are used in the keystroke entry area to include additional information. For example:

* → *(4 times)*

In the foregoing, you should tap the right cursor control key 4 times.

Summary of Keystroke Conventions

Keystroke(s)	Action
↵	Tap ENTER, RETURN, CR(carriage return).
← → ↑ ↓	Tap the left, right, up, or down cursor control key, as indicated.
[F1]	Tap function key number 1 (or the number indicated).
[ESC]	Tap the ESCAPE key (or the key indicated).
/FS	Tap the "/" key, then tap the "F" and "S" keys.
[ALT]-C	Press and hold the ALT key, tap the "C" key, then release the ALT key.
[SHIFT]-[F7]	Press and hold the SHIFT key, tap function key F7, then release the SHIFT key.

Effective Learning

It is possible to breeze through the steps, jumping from keystroke entry to keystroke entry. Doing so will complete the task but will not help you understand the importance of each keystroke. We suggest that you read the activity's summary before you tap any keys. We also suggest that you glance at the screen during keystroke entry to see what effect the keystrokes are creating. Your goal should be to understand WHY you are tapping each key so that, ultimately, you will be able to make your own keystroke choices based on the needs of the task at hand.

About the Authors

Ted Kalmon is the Microcomputer Training Coordinator for over 5000 employees of the New York City Department of Environmental Protection. At DEP, Mr. Kalmon planned and built a state-of-the-art microcomputer training facility and authored training materials used in DEP courses. In addition to his work with DEP, Mr. Kalmon is owner of Step by Step, Inc., a microcomputer training corporation that specializes in software development and training for New York City area businesses.

Dr. Larry Long and **Dr. Nancy Long,** both of Long and Associates, are lecturers, authors, consultants, and educators in the computer and information services fields. Their many books cover a broad spectrum of computer- and MIS-related topics from micros to programming to MIS strategic planning.

Chapter 1

Introduction to the Computer

The Personal Computer Revolution

Personal Computers

The computer revolution is upon us. This unprecedented technical revolution has made computers a part of life. With the rapid growth in the number and variety of computer applications, they are rapidly becoming a way of life. This book will enable you to experience the adventure of computers and, at the same time, learn skills that will make you an active participant in the computer revolution, both at work and at home.

This book is about **microcomputers** and their application to your computing needs. Of the four categories of computers--**supercomputers**, **mainframe computers**, **minicomputers**, and **microcomputers**-- only **micros**, as they are often called, are designed primarily for use by one person at a time. Because of their single-user orientation micros are also called **personal computers**, or **PCs** for short. Personal computers are everywhere, from kindergartens to corporate boardrooms. You can see them at work, at school, and possibly in your own home. The personal computer boom of the 1980s has made it possible for people in every walk of life to see first hand the usefulness of personal computers. Each passing month brings more power at less expense and an expansion to the seemingly endless array of microcomputer **software**. Software is a collective reference to computer programs that cause the computer to perform desired functions (for example, word processing).

A personal computer is an electronic version of a scratch pad, a file cabinet, a drawing board, a typewriter, a worksheet, a musical instrument, and even a friend. It can help you to think logically, to improve your spelling, to select the right word, to learn, to expand your memory, to organize data, to add numbers, and much more.

Personal Computing

Most uses of the personal computer, called **personal computing**, revolve around using microcomputers in conjunction with productivity software. Microcomputer-based productivity software is a series of commercially available programs that can help end users save time and obtain the information they need to make more informed decisions. Easily the most popular productivity tools are the word processing, integrated electronic spreadsheet (includes spreadsheet, database, and presentation graphics capabilities), and database software. These three applications software categories are the foundation of personal computing in the business world.

Word Processing. Word processing is using the computer to enter text, to store it on magnetic storage media, to manipulate it in preparation for output, and to produce a hard copy. Numerous applications involve written communications: letters, reports, memos, and so on.

Integrated Electronic Spreadsheet. A popular microcomputer application is the integrated electronic spreadsheet. These packages enable three capabilities: electronic spreadsheet, presentation graphics, and database. The electronic spreadsheet capability enables you to manipulate a tabular structure of rows and columns. The presentation graphics capability permits you to create a variety of presentation graphics (bar graphs, for example) based on data in a data base or a spreadsheet. The integrated electronic spreadsheet also has limited database capabilities.

Database. Database software permits you to create and maintain a data base, and also to extract information from the data base.

This text is designed to help you acquire the knowledge and skills that you will need to become proficient in the use of the market leader productivity tools in each of the three major categories--WordPerfect, Lotus 1-2-3, and dBASE. However, before learning about these packages you will need to familiarize yourself with microcomputers and DOS (the microcomputer operating system). This chapter provides an overview of general microcomputer **hardware** (computing equipment composed of the computer and its peripheral devices) and software concepts. The focus of Chapter 2, DOS is the **operating system**. Operating system software provides the interface or link between the micro and an applications software package. Chapters 3, 4, and 5 present WordPerfect 5.0, dBASE III PLUS, and Lotus 1-2-3. Chapters 2 through 5 contain conceptual discussions, step-by-step instructions, and exercises.

What Is a Microcomputer?

Micro Components

All computer systems have only four fundamental components: **input**, **processing**, **output**, and **storage**. Note that a computer system, not a computer, has four components. The actual computer is the processing component and is combined with the other three to form a **computer system** (see Figure 1-1).

In the microcomputer-based application, data are entered (input) on a typewriterlike **keyboard** and displayed (output) on a televisionlike (video) screen, called a **monitor**. Permanent or **hard copy** output is produced on a device called a **printer**. Data are stored for later recall on **magnetic disk**. There are a wide variety of input/output (**I/O**) and storage devices. The variety of hardware devices that make up a microcomputer system are discussed in detail later in this chapter.

The Motherboard

The **microprocessor** is sometimes confused with its famous offspring, the microcomputer. The microprocessor is a product of the microminiaturization of electronic circuitry; it is literally a "computer on a chip." A keyboard,

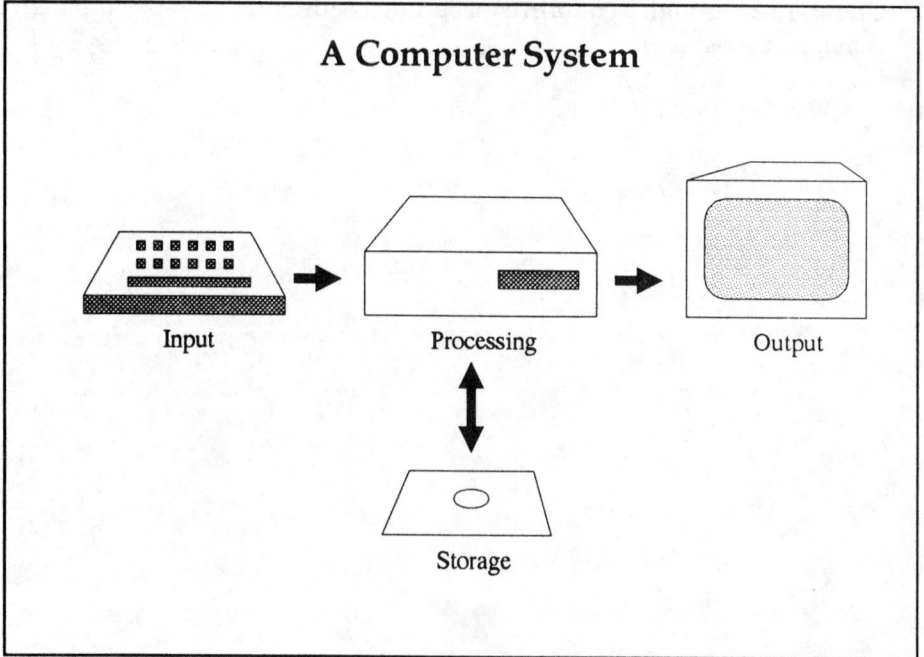

Figure 1-1 The four components of a computer system

video monitor, and memory were attached to the microprocessor and the microcomputer was born!

In a microcomputer, the microprocessor, electronic circuitry for handling input/output signals from the peripheral devices, and memory chips are mounted on a single circuit board, called a **motherboard**. The motherboard, the "guts" of a microcomputer, is what distinguishes one microcomputer from another.

Pocket, Lap, and Desktop PCs

Personal computers come in three different physical sizes: pocket PCs, lap PCs, and desktop PCs. The pocket and lap PCs are light (a few ounces to 8 pounds), compact, and can operate without an external power source; so they earn the "portable" label as well. There are also a number of "transportable" desktop PCs on the market, but they are more cumbersome to move. They fold up to about the size of a small suitcase, weigh about 25 pounds, and usually require an external power source. Desktop PCs are not designed for frequent movement and are therefore not considered portable.

The power of a PC is not necessarily in proportion to its size. A few lap PCs can run circles around some of the desktop PCs. Some user conveniences, however, must be sacrificed to achieve portability. For instance, the miniature keyboards on pocket PCs make data entry and interaction with the computer difficult and slow.

What Can a Personal Computer Do?

Input/Output Operations. The computer reads from input and storage devices. The computer writes to output and storage devices. Before data can be processed, they must be "read" from an input device or data storage device. Input data are usually entered by a user via a keyboard or some other input device or retrieved from a data storage device, such as a magnetic disk drive. Once data have been processed, they are "written" to an output device, such as a printer, or to a data storage device.

Processing Operations. The computer is totally objective. That is, any two computers instructed to perform the same operation will arrive at the same result. This is because the computer can perform only computation and logic operations.

The computational capabilities of the computer include adding, subtracting, multiplying, and dividing. Logic capability permits the computer to make comparisons between numbers and between words, and, based on the result of the comparison, perform appropriate functions.

Inside the Computer

Representing Data in a Computer

The computer's seemingly endless potential is, in fact, based on only two electrical states, on and off. The physical characteristics of the computer make it possible to combine these two electronic states to represent letters and numbers. An "on" or "off" electronic state is represented by a **bit**. Bit is short for binary digit. The presence or absence of a bit is referred to as on-bit and off-bit, respectively. In the **binary** numbering system (base 2) and in written text, the on-bit is a 1 and the off-bit is a 0.

Physically, these states are achieved in a variety of ways. In the micro's solid-state memory (memory chips), the two electronic states are represented by the direction of current flow. Another approach is to turn the circuit on or off. In rotating memory (disks), the two states are made possible by the magnetic arrangement of the iron oxide coating on magnetic disks.

Bits may be fine for computers, but human beings are more comfortable with letters and decimal numbers (the base-10 numerals 0 through 9). Therefore, the letters and decimal numbers that we input to a computer system must be translated to 1s and 0s for processing and storage. The computer translates the bits back to letters and decimal numbers on output. This translation is performed so that we can recognize and understand the output, and it is made possible by encoding systems.

Computers do not talk to each other in English, Spanish, or French. They have their own languages that are better suited to electronic communication. In these languages, bits are combined according to an **encoding system** to represent letters (**alpha** characters), numbers (**numeric** characters), and special characters (such as *, $, +, and &). One such encoding system is the seven-bit **ASCII** (American Standard Code for Information Interchange, pronounced AS-key), which is used primarily in micros and for data communications. In ASCII a B and a 3 are represented by 1000010 and 0110011, respectively. Letters, numbers, and special characters are collectively referred to as **alphanumeric** characters. Alphanumeric characters are encoded to a bit configuration on input so that the computer can interpret them. The characters are decoded on output so that we can interpret them. This coding, which is based on a particular encoding system, equates a unique series of on-bits and off-bits with a specific character.

The Processor and RAM

Each computer, or processor, has only two fundamental sections: the control unit and the arithmetic and logic unit. **Random access memory**, or **RAM** (rhymes with ham), also plays an integral part in the internal operation of a processor. These three (RAM, the control unit, and the arithmetic and logic unit) work together. Their functions and the relationships between them are described in the following discussions and illustrated in Figure 1-2.

Random Access Memory (RAM). Unlike **secondary storage** devices such as magnetic disk and tape, RAM, or **primary storage**, is solid state and has no moving parts. With no mechanical movement, data can be accessed from RAM at electronic speeds, close to the speed of light. RAM provides the processor with temporary storage for programs and data.

All programs and data must be transferred to RAM from an input device (such as a keyboard) or from magnetic storage (such as a disk) before programs can be executed or data can be processed. RAM space is always at a premium; therefore, after a program has been executed, the storage space occupied by it is reallocated to another program that is awaiting execution.

A program instruction or a piece of data is stored in a specific primary storage location called an **address**. Addresses permit program instructions and data to be found, accessed, and processed. The content of each address is constantly changing as different programs are executed and new data are processed.

A special type of RAM called **read-only memory (ROM)** cannot be altered by the programmer. The contents of the ROM are hard-wired (designed

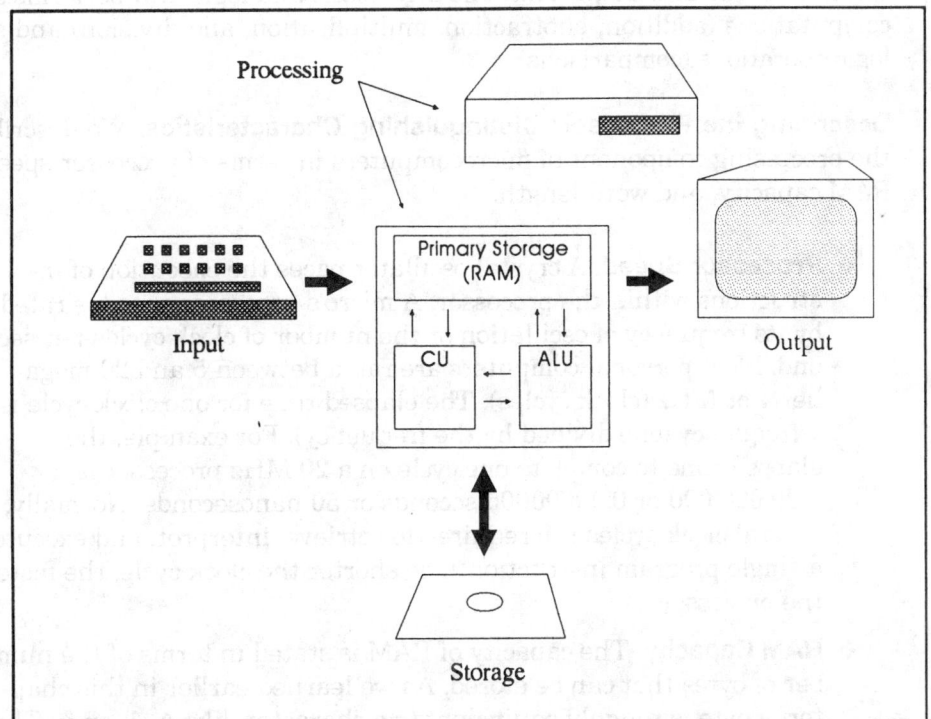

Figure 1-2 Interaction between Primary Storage and Computer System Components

into the logic of a memory chip) by the manufacturer and can be "read only." When you turn on a microcomputer system, a program in ROM automatically performs diagnostic functions such as checking RAM and readies the computer system for use. Then, a ROM program loads the operating system into RAM. Some micros can be purchased with word processing software and other applications software that can be loaded from ROM rather than disk.

The Control Unit. Just as the processor is the nucleus of a computer system, the control unit is the nucleus of the processor. The control unit has three primary functions:

- To read and interpret program instructions.
- To direct the operation of internal processor components.
- To control the flow of programs and data in and out of RAM.

Any program (word processing or database, for example) must first be loaded to RAM before it can be executed. During execution, the first in a sequence of program instructions is moved from RAM to the control unit where it is **decoded** and interpreted. The control unit then directs other processor components to carry out the operations necessary to execute the instruction.

The Arithmetic and Logic Unit. The arithmetic and logic unit performs all computations (addition, subtraction, multiplication, and division) and all logic operations (comparisons).

Describing the Processor: Distinguishing Characteristics. We describe the processing component of microcomputers in terms of processor speed, RAM capacity, and word length.

- **Processor Speed.** A crystal oscillator paces the execution of instructions within the processor. A micro's processor speed is rated by its frequency of oscillation or the number of clock cycles per second. Most personal computers are rated between 5 and 20 megahertz or MHz (clock cycles). The elapsed time for one clock cycle is 1/frequency (one divided by the frequency). For example, the elapsed time to complete one cycle on a 20 MHz processor is 1/20,000,000 or 0.00000005 seconds or 50 nanoseconds. Normally, several clock cycles are required to retrieve, interpret, and execute a single program instruction. The shorter the clock cycle, the faster the processor.

- **RAM Capacity.** The capacity of RAM is stated in terms of the number of bytes that can be stored. As we learned earlier in this chapter, a byte is roughly equivalent to a character, like A, 1, or &. The memory capacity of microcomputers is usually stated in terms of **Kb** (kilobytes, 1024 bytes) and **Mb** (megabytes, 1,048,576 bytes).

These numbers are commonly rounded off to thousands (Kb) and millions (Mb) when used to describe the number of bytes of storage. For example, RAM capacities in micros range from 256Kb (or 256,000 bytes) in small micros to 16Mb (or 16,000,000 bytes) in the more powerful multiuser micros.

- **Word Length.** A word is the number of bits that are handled as a unit for a particular computer system. The word size of modern microcomputers is normally 16 or 32 bits. The newer 16- and 32-bit micros are as much as 10 times faster than the early 8-bit PCs.

Input/Output Devices

Data are created in many places and many ways. Before data can be processed and stored, they must be translated to a form that the computer can interpret. For this we need input devices. Once the data have been processed, they must be translated back to a form that we can understand. For this we need output devices. These **peripheral** input/output (I/O) devices enable communication between us and the computer.

Input Devices

The Keyboard. All micros come equipped with a keyboard for input. The typical key-driven data entry device has a standard alphanumeric keyboard with an optional numeric keyboard, called a 10-key pad. Some keyboards also have special-function keys, which can be used to instruct the computer to perform a specific operation that may otherwise require several keystrokes.

Random Cursor Control. For some applications the keyboard is too cumbersome. For example, you might need to "draw" a line to connect two points on the micro's display screen. Such applications call for devices that go beyond the capabilities of keyboards. These devices permit random movement of the cursor to create the image. A cursor, or blinking character (usually an underscore or a rectangle), indicates the location on the screen of the next input. The joystick, digitizing tablet (or pad) and pen, and mouse are among the most popular cursor movement and input mechanisms.

The **joystick** is a single vertical stick that moves the cursor in the direction in which the stick is pushed. The **digitizing tablet and pen** is a pressure-sensitive tablet with the same X-Y coordinates as the screen and a pen. The outline of an image drawn on a tablet is reproduced on the display screen. The **mouse**, sometimes called the "pet peripheral," is now standard equipment on some micros. The mouse, attached to the computer by a cable, is a small device that, when moved across a desktop, causes comparable movement of the cursor.

Voice Data Entry. Voice data entry, or voice recognition, devices can be used to enter limited kinds and quantities of data. Despite being limited to the ability to interpret relatively few words, voice data entry has a number of applications. The use of voice data entry is valuable for those who require "hands-free" operation such as, for example, quality control inspectors.

Optical Scanners. Optical scanners bounce a beam of light off an image, and then measure the reflected light to determine the value of the image. Optical scanners can recognize printed characters and various types of codes. These scanners can "learn" to read almost any typeface, including this book! The "learning" takes place when the structure of the character set is described to the optical scanning device. One primary application for optical scanners on microcomputers is to read printed material into a word processing document file.

Output Devices

Monitors. Alphanumeric and graphic output are displayed on the micro's video monitor. Because display on the monitor's screen is temporary it is sometimes referred to as soft copy. The three primary attributes of monitors are the size of the display screen, whether the display is color or monochrome (usually white, green, or amber), and the resolution or detail of the display. The size of the screen varies from 5 to 25 inches (diagonal dimension).

In RGB monitors, the colors of red, green, and blue are combined to produce up to 64 colors. If you are willing to compromise on the quality of the display and amount of information that can be displayed, you can use an RF modulator to adapt a color television for use with microcomputers.

Some PC monitors have a much higher **resolution**, or quality of output. Resolution refers to the number of **pixels**, or addressable points on the screen, that is, the number of points to which light can be directed under program control. A strictly alphanumeric monitor has about 65,000 such points. A PC monitor used primarily for computer graphics may have over 250,000 points. The high-resolution monitors project extremely clear images that look almost like photographs.

Most PCs are equipped with flat panel monitors use liquid crystal technology. Since liquid crystal monitors display the image by reflecting light, you must have some light to read the display. Those flat panel monitors that use gas plasma technology are easier to read in situations with poor lighting.

Printers and Plotters. The most common "output only" devices are printers and plotters. **Printers** produce hard-copy output, such as management reports, payroll checks, and program listings. Microcomputer printers are generally classified as character printers or page printers. Printers are rated by their print speed. Print speeds for character printers are measured in characters per second (cps), and for page printers, they are measured in pages per minute (ppm). The print-speed ranges for the two types of printers are 40 to 450 cps and 8 to 20 ppm, respectively.

Character printers are the primary hard-copy output unit for microcomputers. Impact character printers rely on **dot-matrix** and **daisy-wheel** technology. Nonimpact character printers employ **ink-jet** and **thermal** technology. Regardless of the technology, the images are formed one character at a time as the print head moves across the paper.

The dot-matrix printer configures printed dots to form characters and all kinds of images in much the same way as lights display time and temperature on bank signs. One or several vertical columns of small print hammers are contained in a rectangular print head. The hammers are activated independently to form a dot character image as the print head moves horizontally across the paper. Dot-matrix printers can produce graphic output as well as text output.

The daisy-wheel printer produces high-quality output for word processing applications. An interchangeable daisy wheel containing a set of fully formed characters is spun to the desired character. A print hammer strikes the embossed character on the print wheel to form the image.

Ink-jet printers squirt "dots" of ink on the paper to form images in a manner similar to that of the dot-matrix printer. The heat elements of thermal printers are activated to produce dot-matrix images on heat-sensitive paper. The big advantage that these two nonimpact character printers have over the impact printers is that they can produce multicolor output.

Microcomputer page printers, often called **desktop laser printers**, use laser technology to achieve high-speed hard-copy output by printing a page at a time. The nonimpact laser printers have many inviting characteristics: They are quiet; they can print near-typeset-quality text and graphics; they can mix type styles and sizes on the same page, and they are much faster than character printers.

A pen **plotter** is a device that converts computer-generated graphs, charts, and line drawings to high-precision hard-copy output. The plotter that is commonly used with micros has one or more pens that move concurrently with the paper to produce the image. Several pens are required to vary the width and color of the lines. Pens are selected and manipulated under computer control.

Printer or Plotter Drivers. The various kinds of printers and plotters differ markedly in capabilities. Because of these differences, the electronic signals passed between the processor and the printer or plotter are unique for each printer and plotter. Because of this, a **driver set** for a particular printer or plotter must be used in conjunction with an applications software package (for example, an electronic spreadsheet package). The driver set is software that enables communication between the processor and the printer or plotter. Essentially, the driver set receives signals from the processor and relays these signals in a format that can be interpreted by the printer or plotter (or vice versa). Commercial software packages are distributed with driver sets for most of the popular printers and plotters.

Sound and Speech. One of the standard capabilities of most micros is the ability to output sounds of varying duration and frequency. This micro output feature is used for everything from warning users of a keying error to playing the melodies of popular songs. **Speech synthesizers** convert raw data to electronically produced speech.

Data Storage Devices and Media

Secondary Storage

Within a computer system, programs and data are stored in RAM and in secondary storage. Programs and data are stored permanently for periodic retrieval in secondary storage. Programs and data are retrieved from secondary storage and stored temporarily in high-speed RAM for processing.

The various types of **magnetic disk drives** and their respective storage media are the overwhelming choice of micro users for secondary storage. In the microcomputer environment, **magnetic tape drives** are used exclusively to backup and store disk files.

Magnetic Disks

Magnetic disk drives are secondary storage devices that provide a computer system with **random** and **sequential processing** capabilities. In random processing, the desired programs and data are accessed directly from the storage medium.

A variety of magnetic disk drives (the hardware device) and magnetic disks (the media) are manufactured for different user requirements. The two most popular types of interchangeable magnetic disks for micros are the **diskette** and the **microdisk**.

- **Diskette.** The diskette is a thin, flexible disk that is enclosed within a 5 1/4-inch square jacket. Because the diskette is flexible, like a page in this book, it is also called a **flexible disk** or a **floppy disk**.
- **Microdisk.** The microdisk is also called a floppy disk but is housed within a 3 1/2 inch square rigid compartment.

Once inserted in a **disk drive**, the programs and data on the diskette or microdisk are said to be **on-line**. This means that the programs and data on the disk are accessible to and under the control of a computer system. Once the programs and data are no longer needed for processing, the disks can be removed for **off-line** storage. The storage capacity of diskettes and microdisks ranges from about 320K to 1.4M bytes.

Not all disk storage media are interchangeable. In fact, the trend is toward permanently installed **hard** or **fixed disks**. Most of the newer personal computers are configured with at least one diskette drive and one hard disk. The storage capacity of hard disks ranges from about 20M to 330M bytes.

A hard disk, which may have several disk platters, spins continuously at a high speed. The floppy, however, is set in motion only when a command is issued to read from or write to disk. An indicator light near the disk drive is illuminated only when the disk is spinning. The rotational movement of the disk passes all data under or over a **read/write head**, thereby making all data available for access on each revolution of the disk.

The manner in which data and programs are stored and accessed is very similar for both hard and floppy disks. The disk storage medium has a thin film coating of cobalt or iron oxide. The thin film coating on the disk can be electronically magnetized by the read/write head to represent the absence or presence of a bit (0 or 1). Data are recorded **serially** in concentric circles called **tracks** or **cylinders** by magnetizing the surface to represent bit configurations.

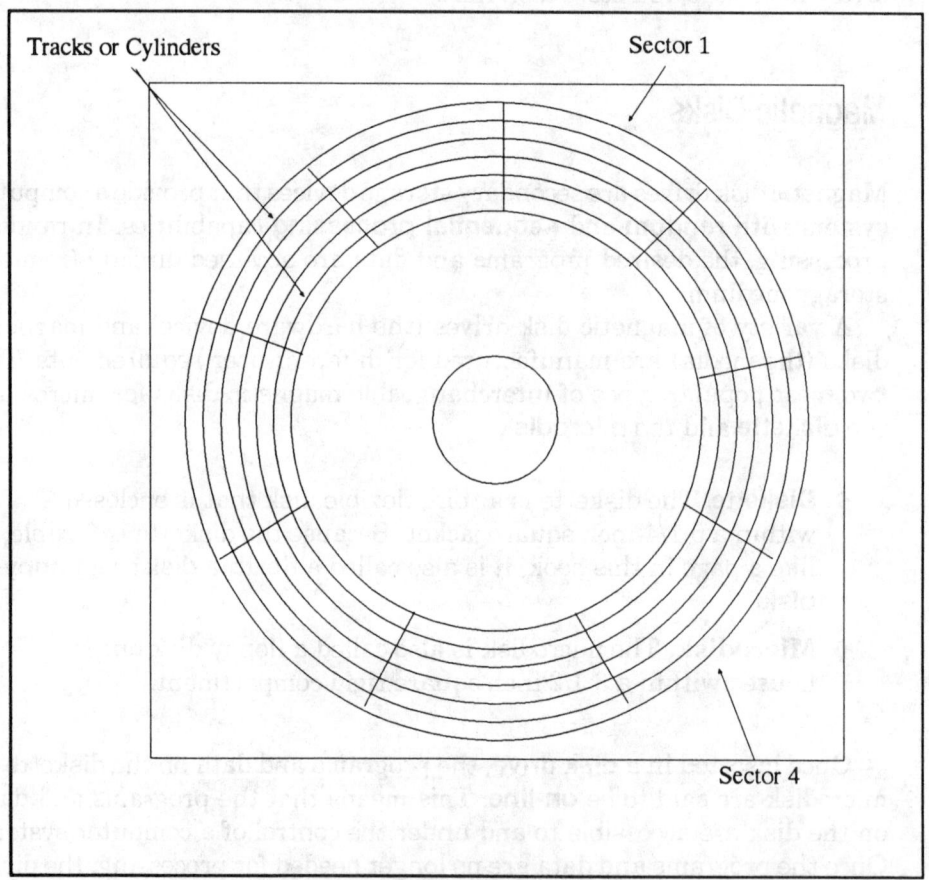

Figure 1-3 Facsimile of the electronic grid placed on a floppy diskette to create unique disk addresses (i.e., Sector 4, Cylinder 37)

PC disk storage uses **sector organization** to store and retrieve data. In sector organization, the recording surface is divided into pie-shaped sectors. Each sector is assigned a unique number; therefore, the sector number and track number are all that is needed to comprise a **disk address** (the physical location of data or a program -- see Figure 1-3). To read from or write to a disk, an **access arm** containing the read/write head is moved under program control to the appropriate track. When the appropriate sector passes under or over the read/write head the data are read or written.

Magnetic Tape

The primary use of magnetic tape storage for micros is as a backup medium for the hard disk. For backup, a **tape cassette** is taken from off-line storage, mounted into a tape drive, and the contents of a disk file are "dumped" from the disk to the tape. The tape is removed and placed in off-line storage as a backup to the operational disk. A single tape cassette can store from 20M to 60M bytes. Approximately 60 diskettes would be needed to backup a 20M byte hard disk, but only one tape cassette would be needed.

Configuring a Microcomputer System

A Typical Microcomputer Configuration

The computer and its peripheral devices are called the computer system **configuration**. The configuration of a microcomputer can vary. The most typical micro configuration consists of the following:

- A computer
- A keyboard for input
- A monitor for soft copy (temporary) output
- A printer for hard copy (printed) output
- One or two disk drives for permanent storage of data and programs

Linking Micro Components

Micro components are linked via a common electrical **bus**. Just as the brain sends and receives signals through the central nervous system, the processor sends and receives electrical signals through the bus. The bus is the path through which the processor sends data and commands to RAM and all peripheral devices. Data and commands are transmitted between the processor and its peripheral devices in the form of electronic signals. In short, the bus is the vehicle by which the processor communicates with its peripherals and vice versa. The processor, RAM, and expansion slots are usually connected directly to the bus, that is, without cables.

External input/output devices (that is devices external to the processor cabinet) and some storage devices are plugged into the bus in much the same way that you would plug a lamp into an electrical outlet. The receptacle, called a **port**, provides a direct link with the micro's common electrical bus.

External peripheral devices are linked or interfaced with the processor through either a **serial port** or a **parallel port**. Serial ports facilitate the serial transmission of data, one bit at a time. Serial ports provide an interface for low-speed printers and modems. The defacto standard for micro serial ports is the **RS-232C port**. Parallel ports facilitate the parallel transmission of data, usually one byte (eight bits) at a time. Parallel ports provide the interface for devices like high-speed printers (e.g., laser printers), magnetic tape backup units, and other computers.

Also connected to the common electrical bus are **expansion slots**, which are usually housed in the processor cabinet. These slots enable a micro owner to enhance the functionality of a basic micro configuration with a wide variety of special-function add-on boards, also called **add-on cards**. These "add-ons" contain the electronic circuitry for a wide variety of computer-related functions. The number of available expansion slots varies from computer to computer. Some of the more popular add-on boards are listed below.

- RAM. Expands memory, usually in increments of 64K bytes.
- Color and graphics adapter. Permits the interfacing of video monitors that have graphics and/or color capabilities. The EGA or enhanced graphic adapter board enables the interfacing of high resolution monitors (e.g., 640x350). The EGA boards usually come with at least 256K bytes of dedicated RAM or RAM that is not available to the user.
- Modem. Permits communication with remote computers via a telephone line link.
- Internal battery-powered clock/calendar. Provides continuous and/or on-demand display of, or access to, the current date and time (e.g., Wednesday, Dec. 18, 1991, 9:35 a.m.).
- Serial port. Installation of the board provides access to the bus via another serial port.
- Parallel port. Installation of the board provides access to the bus via another parallel port.
- Printer spooler. Enables data to be printed while the user continues with other processing activities. The data are transferred (spooled) at high speed from RAM to a print buffer (an intermediate storage area) and then routed to the printer from the buffer.
- Hard disk. Hard disks with capacities of as much as 40M bytes can be installed in expansion slots.
- Coprocessor. These "extra" processors, which are under the control of the main processor, help to relieve the main processor of certain tasks, such as arithmetic functions. This sharing of duties helps to increase system **throughput**, the rate at which work can be performed by the microcomputer system.
- VCR backup. This board enables an ordinary Beta or VHS video cassette recorder to be used as a tape backup device. One ordinary video cassette tape can hold up to 80M bytes of data.

Most of the add-on boards are multifunction: that is, they include two of more of these capabilities. For example, one popular **multifunction add-on board** comes with a serial port, additional RAM, and an internal battery-powered clock/calendar.

Microcomputer Operation

Getting Started

Once all micro components have been installed and connected to the processor unit, DOS has been installed (hard disk systems), and the various components are connected to an electrical power source, you are ready to begin processing. Micros are similar to copy machines, toasters, and other electrical devices--you must turn them on by applying electrical power. If you have a micro with a hard disk, all you have to do is turn on the computer and, perhaps, the monitor and printer. After a short period, a beep signals the end of the system check and DOS is loaded automatically from disk to RAM. If your micro does not have a hard disk and is configured with one or two diskette drives, you must insert the DOS diskette before turning on the system. Interaction with DOS is covered in detail in Chapter 2, DOS.

Entering Commands and Data from the Keyboard

A microcomputer's keyboard is normally the primary input and control device. You enter data and issue commands via the keyboard. Besides the standard typewriter keyboard, most micro keyboards have **function keys**, also called **soft keys**. When tapped, these function keys trigger the execution of software, thus the name "soft" key. For example, tapping a particular function key might call up a menu of possible activities that can be performed. Some function keys are permanently labeled: copy, find, save, and so on. The software packages are usually distributed with **keyboard templates** that designate which commands are assigned to which function keys. For example, "help" is often assigned to F1 or function key number 1. The templates are usually designed to be fitted over the keyboard or attached with an adhesive.

Most keyboards are equipped with a 10-key pad and cursor control keys. The 10-key pad permits rapid numeric data entry. It is normally positioned to the right of the standard alphanumeric keyboard. The cursor control keys or "arrow" keys allow you to move the cursor up and down (usually a line at a time) and left and right (usually a character at a time). To move the cursor rapidly about the screen, simply hold down the desired cursor control key.

For many software packages, you can use the cursor control keys to view parts of a document or worksheet that extend past the bottom, top or sides of the screen. This is known as **scrolling**. Use the up and down cursor control keys to scroll vertically and the left and right keys to scroll horizontally. For example, if you wish to scroll vertically through a word processing document, move the up or down cursor control key to the edge of the current screen and continue to tap the key to view more of the document, one line a time.

In summary, there are three basic ways to enter a command from the keyboard:

- Key in the command using the alphanumeric portion of the keyboard.
- Tap a function key.
- Use the cursor control keys to select a menu option from the display of a menu. Menus are discussed in detail in the next section.

Other important keys common to most keyboards are the enter or carriage return (ENTER or RETURN), home (HOME), page up and page down (PGUP and PGDN), delete (DEL), insert-overstrike toggle (INS), backspace (BKSP), escape (ESC), space (SPACE), control (CTRL), and alternate (ALT) keys.

- Normally the **ENTER** key is used to send keyed-in data or a selected command to RAM for processing. Like most of the special keys, ENTER has other meanings, depending on the type of software package you are using. In word processing, for example, you would designate the end of a paragraph by tapping the ENTER key.
- Tapping the **HOME** key results in different actions for different packages, but often the cursor is moved to the beginning of a work area (i.e., the upper left corner of the spreadsheet, or the beginning of a field in a data base).
- With most software packages, tap **END** to move the cursor to the end of the work area (i.e., the end of a line in word processing or the end of a field in a data base).
- Tap **PGUP** (page up or previous) and **PGDN** (page down or next) to scroll vertically a page at a time to view parts of the document or spreadsheet that extend past the top or bottom of the screen. PGUP and PGDN are also used to position the cursor at the previous and next record when using database software.
- Tap **DEL** to delete the character at the cursor position.
- Tap **INS** to **toggle** (switch) between the two modes of entering data and text--insert and typeover. Both modes are discussed and illustrated later in the word processing discussion. The term toggle is used to describe the action of tapping a single key to rotate between two or more modes of operation (insert and typeover), functions (underline on or off), or operational specifications (for type of database field: character, numeric, date, logic and memo).

- Tap the **BKSP,** or backspace, key to move the cursor one position to the left and delete the character in that position.
- The **ESC,** or escape, key may have many functions, depending on the software package, but in most situations you can tap the ESC key to negate the current command.
- Tap the **SPACE** bar at the bottom of the keyboard to key in a space at the cursor position.
- The **CTRL,** or control, and **ALT,** or alternate, keys are used in conjunction with another key to expand the functionality of the keyboard. You hold down a CTRL or ALT key to give another key new meaning. For example, in WordPerfect 5.0, tap BKSP to move the cursor one character to the left and delete the character in that position. When you tap CTRL and BKSP together, the word at the cursor position is deleted.

Each keystroke that you enter is first sent to an intermediate keystroke buffer that can save from 15 to 256 keystrokes. Under normal processing conditions, the keystroke is sent immediately from the buffer to the processor; however, there are many instances (such as disk reads or preparation of a graphics display) where you can key ahead.

Issuing Commands to Micro Software Packages

You can interact with software packages, such as electronic spreadsheet and database, at several different levels of sophistication: the menu level, the macro level, and the programming level. These three levels of command interaction are discussed in the following sections.

The Hierarchy of Menus. When using productivity software, you issue commands and initiate operations by selecting activities to be performed from a hierarchy of **menus**. These hierarchies are sometimes called menu trees. When you select an item from the **main menu,** you are often presented with another menu of activities, and so on. Depending on the items you select, you may progress through as few as one and as many as eight levels of menus before processing is initiated for the desired activity.

Types of Menus. A menu can appear as a **bar menu** in the user interface portion of the display, a **pull-down menu**, or a **pop-up menu**. The user interface is from one to six lines at the bottom and/or top of the screen. The menu options in a bar menu are displayed across the screen. To select an item in a bar menu, use the left and right cursor control keys to highlight the desired menu option and tap ENTER.

The result of a menu selection from a bar menu at the top of the screen is often a pull-down menu. The subordinate menu is "pulled-down" from the selected menu option and displayed as a vertical list of menu options.

The entire menu is shown in a **window** directly under the selected menu option and over whatever is currently on the screen. A window is a rectangular display that is temporarily superimposed over whatever is currently on the screen. Use the up and down cursor control keys to highlight the desired menu option and tap ENTER to select the menu option. Figure 1-4 displays a pull-down menu that appears in dBASE III PLUS.

Like the pull-down menu, the pop-up menu is superimposed over the current screen in a window. A pop-up menu can be called up in a variety of ways, including function keys or as the result of a selection from a higher-level pop-up menu.

Defaults. As you progress through a series of menus, you are eventually asked to enter the specifications for data to be graphed (graphics software), the size of the output paper (word processing software), and so on. As a convenience to the user, many of the specification options are already filled in to reflect common situations. For example, WordPerfect 5.0 sets output document size to be 8 1/2 by 11 inches. If the user is satisfied with these **default options**, no further specifications are required. The user can easily revise the default options to accommodate the less common situations. So, to print a document on legal-size paper, the default paper length of 11 inches would need to be revised to 14 inches.

Macros and Programming. At the menu level of command interaction you are initiating individual commands. At the macro and programming levels

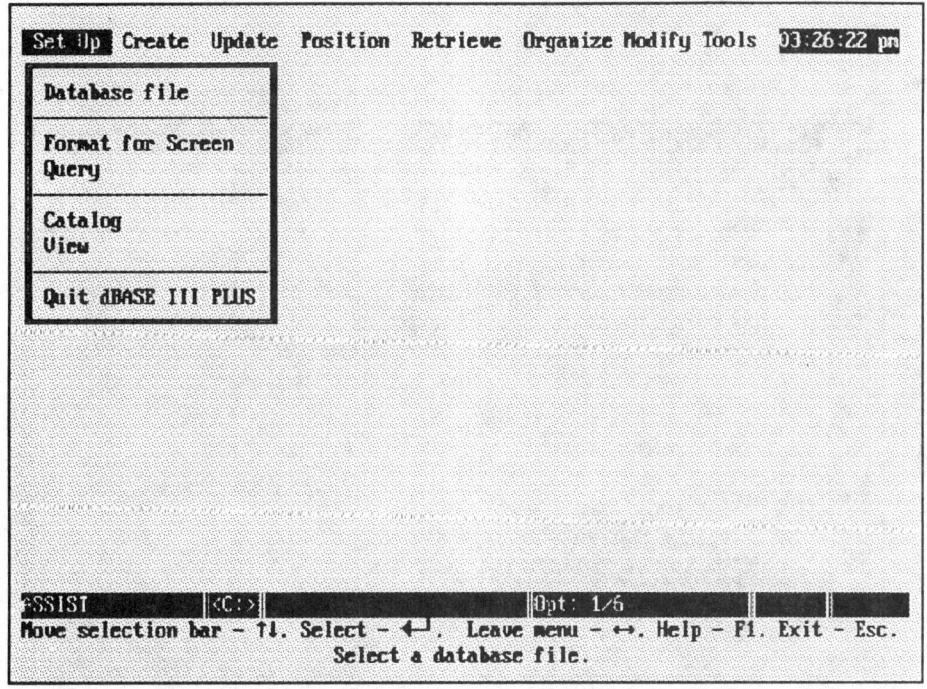

Figure 1-4 The "Set Up" pull-down menu is activated when "Set Up" is highlighted in the bar menu at the top of the screen

of interaction you can string together commands and even introduce logic operations.

A handy feature available with most micro software packages is the **macro**. A macro is a sequence of frequently used operations or keystrokes that can be recalled as you need them. You create a macro by entering the sequence of operations or keystrokes and storing them on disk for later recall. To invoke or execute the macro, you either refer to it by name (perhaps in the text of a word processing file) or enter the series of keystrokes that identify the desired macro (e.g., ALT-P). Figure 1-5 displays a macro menu created in Lotus 1-2-3. Three common user-supplied macros in word processing could be the commands necessary to format the first-, second- and third-level headings in a report. For example, the user might want the first level heading to be centered, boldfaced, and followed by two spaces; the second level to be flush left, boldfaced, and followed by an indented paragraph; and the third level to be flush left, underlined, and followed on the same line by the beginning of the first paragraph. In electronic spreadsheets, macros are commonly used to produce graphs automatically from spreadsheet data.

Some software packages permit users the flexibility to do their own **programming**. That is, micro software users can create logical sequences of instructions. For example, a database software program can be written that will retrieve records from a particular data base depending on preset criteria, process the data according to programmed instructions, and print out a report. The programming capability enables users to create microcomputer-based information systems for an endless number of applications from payroll processing to inventory control. Programming with a database software package is explained and illustrated in Chapter 4.

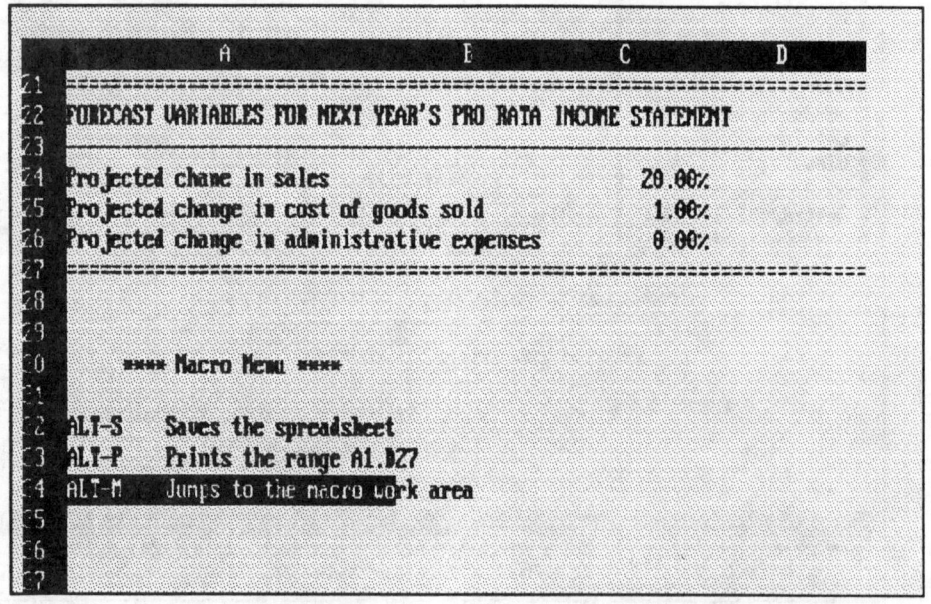

Figure 1-5 A macro menu created to remind the user which macros are available in this Lotus 1-2-3 spreadsheet.

User Friendly Software

Virtually all vendors of micro software tout their product as being **user friendly**. Software is said to be user friendly when someone with relatively little computer experience has little difficulty using the system. User-friendly software communicates easily understood words and phrases to the end user, thus simplifying the user's interaction with the computer system.

Icons and Help Commands

Some software packages use **icons** or pictographs (a graphic rendering of a file cabinet, a diskette, and so on), rather than words or phrases, to communicate with the end user.

A handy feature available on most software packages is the **help command**. When you find yourself in a corner, you can tap the help key, which is often assigned to a numbered function key, to get more explanation or instruction on how to proceed. When you are finished reading the help information, you can return to your work at the same point that you left it. Figure 1-6 displays WordPerfect's opening help screen.

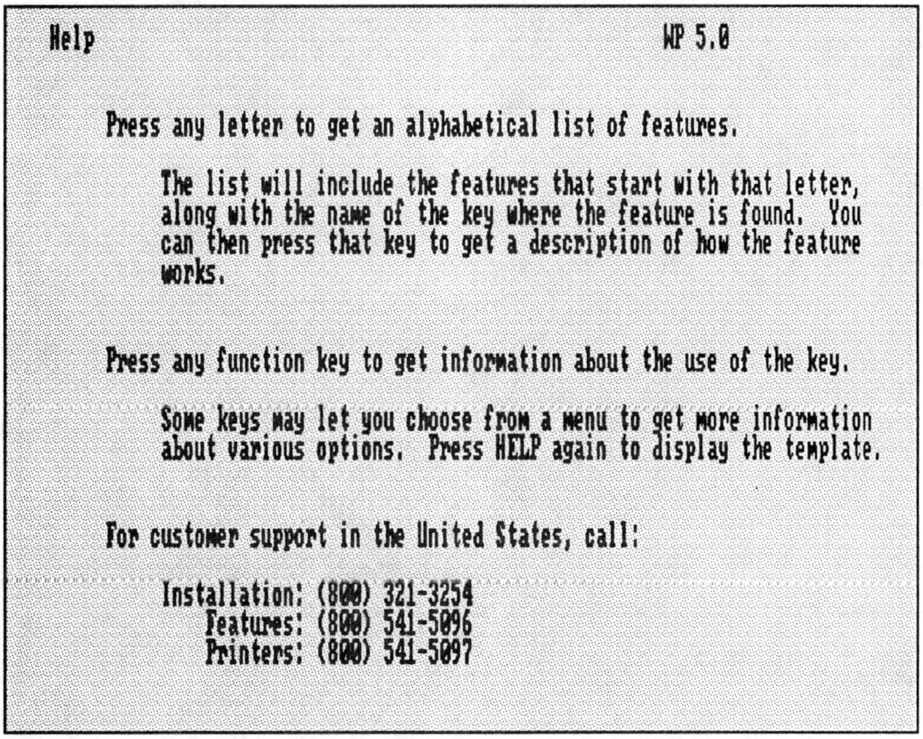

```
Help                                                    WP 5.0

     Press any letter to get an alphabetical list of features.

          The list will include the features that start with that letter,
          along with the name of the key where the feature is found. You
          can then press that key to get a description of how the feature
          works.

     Press any function key to get information about the use of the key.

          Some keys may let you choose from a menu to get more information
          about various options. Press HELP again to display the template.

     For customer support in the United States, call:

               Installation: (800) 321-3254
                   Features: (800) 541-5096
                   Printers: (800) 541-5097
```

Figure 1-6   WordPerfect's initial help screen contains instructions for the use of their help feature

Windows

Windows allow users to "look through" several windows on a single display screen; however, you can only manipulate text or data in one window at a time. This is called the current window. Windows can overlap one another on the display screen. For example, some integrated software packages permit users to view a spreadsheet in one window, a bar chart in another window, and a word processing document in a third window. With windows, you can work the way you think and think the way you work.

You can perform work in one of several windows on a display screen or you can **zoom** in on a particular window. That is, the window you select is expanded to fill the entire screen. Tap a key and you can return to a multiwindow display. A multiwindow display permits you to view how a change in one window affects another window. For example, as you change the data in a spreadsheet, you can view how an accompanying pie graph is revised to reflect the new data.

You can even create **window panes**! As you might expect, a window is divided into panes so that you can view several parts of the same window subarea at a time. For example, if you are writing a long report in a word processing window, you might wish to write the conclusions to the report in one window pane while viewing portions of the report in another window pane.

Chapter 2

DOS

```
C:\DOS>dir /w
```

DOS Fundamentals

An Overview

In this session you will learn how to:

- Describe the function and purpose of a microcomputer's disk operating system (DOS).
- Load and run both DOS and microcomputer applications software.
- Name and reference files.
- Describe the use of directories and paths.

Step 1: The Disk Operating System (DOS)

The nucleus of a microcomputer system is its operating system. The operating system monitors and controls all input/output and processing activities within a computer system. All hardware and software, including micro productivity software, are under the control of the operating system. Micro users need a working knowledge of their micro's operating system because they must use it to interface their applications programs with the microcomputer hardware.

Some of the more popular micro operating systems are MS-DOS, CP/M, UNIX, and Operating System/2. You may encounter spin-offs of these operating systems. For example, PC-DOS for the IBM PC is based on Microsoft Corporation's MS-DOS. Unfortunately, the logic, structure, and nomenclature of the different operating systems vary considerably. Our emphasis will be on PC-DOS, the operating system used with the IBM PC series of computers and the IBM Personal System/2 series of computers, and on MS-DOS, the operating system used with IBM PC-compatible computers. The discussions in this chapter apply to both MS-DOS and PC-DOS. In practice, these operating systems, which are essentially the same, are referred to simply as DOS (rhymes with boss), an acronym for disk operating system. DOS is a "disk" operating system because it was created in the late 1970's to control what was then an exciting new addition to computers, the floppy diskette.

DOS Is the BOSS

Just as the processor is the center of all hardware activity, DOS is the center of all software activity. The operating system is a family of systems software programs that are usually, though not always, supplied by the computer system vendor. Because all hardware, software, and input/output are controlled by DOS, you might even call DOS the "boss."

One of the DOS family of programs is always resident in RAM during processing. This program, called COMMAND.COM, loads other operating system and applications programs into RAM as they are needed or as directed by you, the user. COMMAND.COM is usually referred to as COMMAND "dot" COM (rhymes with mom).

Besides controlling the ongoing operation of the microcomputer systems, DOS has two other important functions.

Input/output control. DOS facilitates the movement of data between peripheral devices, the processor, RAM, and programs.

File and disk management. DOS and its file and disk management utility programs enable users to perform such tasks as making backup copies of work disks, erasing disk files that are no longer needed, making inquiries about the number and type of files on a particular diskette, and preparing new diskettes for use. DOS also handles many file and disk oriented tasks that are transparent to the end user. For example, DOS keeps track of the physical location of disk files so that we, as users, need only to refer to them by name (for example, myfile.txt) when loading them from disk to memory.

The DOS commands needed to perform user-oriented input/output tasks and file and disk management tasks are discussed and illustrated later in this chapter.

Booting the System

Before you can use a microcomputer you must load DOS, or **boot** the system. The procedure for booting the system on most micros is simply to load the operating system from disk storage into random access memory. On micros with hard disks, all you have to do is turn on the system and DOS is automatically loaded from the hard disk to RAM. On micros without hard disks, this is no more difficult than inserting a DOS disk in a disk drive, closing the disk drive door, and flipping the switch on.

Micros configured with an internal clock-calendar have time and date data available to the user and user programs at all times. If your micro is not configured with an internal clock-calendar, DOS will give you the option of entering the date and time. See Session One: Loading DOS later in this chapter.

Step 2: Running a Software Package

The system prompt or the DOS prompt is the operating system's message to you, the user, that you can enter a system command (for example, copy files from one diskette to another) or the name of the program to run an applications program, such as an electronic spreadsheet.

The form of the system prompt varies among operating systems. The system prompt for DOS is the greater than symbol prefaced by a disk drive specification (C> is the prompt when the hard disk, drive C, is the active or default drive).

Once you have loaded the operating system to memory and the system prompt is displayed on the screen, you are ready to run a graphics package, a word processing package, or any other software package. To run a software package, load the program directly from the hard disk by entering the name of the file that contains the applications software. For example, to run the Lotus 1-2-3 electronic spreadsheet package on a DOS-based micro, you would key in "123" (the name of the program file) after the DOS prompt. The next thing you see would be the opening screen, followed by Lotus's work screen.

Step 3: Files and Filenames

Naming Files. On a microcomputer, a **file** is related information that is stored to disk (from memory) or retrieved from a disk (to memory) as a unit. A file can be a payroll program, sales data for an electronic spreadsheet, a database of names and addresses, the text of a progress report, or even a game. Each file is given a name, either by a user or by someone else like a software vendor. The name of a file includes

- A rootname of up to eight characters
- An optional extension of up to three characters

The rootname and extension are separated by a period (.). Typically, the extension identifies files that are associated with a certain application. For example, Release 2.01 of Lotus 1-2-3 appends the extension WK1 to a user-supplied filename (QTR1.WK1). The extension appended to dBASE data bases is DBF.

The following are legal filenames:

    NAMEADDR.DBF
    SALES.WK1
    A

These are not legal:

    N+A.DBF   (+.=/\[]:| ;, are not allowed)
    FIRSTQUARTERSALES   (more than 8 characters)
    .OUT   (no rootname)

Referencing Files. The file specification includes the rootname, the extension, and a reference to the appropriate disk drive. A file (e.g., SALES.WK1) is associated with a particular disk drive. On a hard disk system (typically one floppy drive and one hard disk), the disk drives are labeled A and C.

One of the disk drives is designated to be the active drive, that is, DOS commands that you issue apply to the active drive unless you state otherwise in the command. The DOS prompt indicates which drive is the active drive. For example, if the DOS prompt is C, the active drive is C. If the desired file (SALES.WK1) is on drive C and the active drive is C, the drive specifier can be omitted. If the active drive is A (the DOS prompt is A>) and the desired file (SALES.WK1) is on the hard disk, the entire filename is needed to reference the file.

Active Drive	File Reference
C	SALES.WK1
A	C:SALES.WK1

There are many instances when you might wish to issue a DOS command that applies to several files. To perform these operations, you would use a **wildcard** or global character, in this case, the asterisk (*). When used in a rootname.extension combination, the * is a generic reference to any combination of legal characters. To illustrate the use of the wildcard *, consider the following directory. A directory is simply a list of the names of the files that are stored on a particular diskette (a floppy disk) or in a named area on a hard disk (a hard disk can have several logical directories). The files on the disk in the active drive for this example are:

LETTER.WP	SALES1Q.WK1	SALES3Q.WK1
MEMO2.WP	MASTER.DBF	NET.WK1
NAMES.DBF	SALES2Q.WK1	MEMO1.WP
REPORT.WP	STATEMNT.WP	EMPLHIST.DBF

Wildcard Reference	Files Referenced
*.WP	LETTER.WP REPORT.WP MEMO1.WP MEMO2.WP STATEMENT.WP
S*.WK1	SALES1Q.WK1 SALES2Q.WK1 SALES3Q.WK1
.	all files in directory

Step 4: Directories and Paths

It is not uncommon for a hard disk to contain hundreds of files. To make file management and inquiries easier for both the user and DOS, users organize their files into a hierarchy or tree of directories and subdirectories. At the highest level of the "upside-down tree" is the **root directory**. When you load DOS on a hard disk system, drive C's root directory is the active directory. The designator C:\> denotes the root directory for the hard disk drive.

The directory feature of DOS enables us to form groups of related files. For example, we can create a directory into which we would store only spreadsheet files. In practice, users seldom set up directories on diskettes. Therefore, when we talk of directory A:, we are referring to all files contained on the diskette in disk drive A:. However, establishing directories on a hard disk is common practice.

Consider the directory tree illustrated in Figure 2-1. Two managers, Jim and Marcia, share the same personal computer. To keep their programs and files separate, they established directories as shown in Figure 2-1. Jim and Marcia created the subdirectories \JIM and \MARCIA to which they could assign subordinate subdirectories. The subdirectory \JIM\LOTUS contains the software for LOTUS 1-2-3 and all of Jim's Lotus 1-2-3 data files (SALES.WK1, BOOKFILE.WK1, etc.). The subdirectories \MARCIA\WP and \MARCIA\DBASE contain the software for WordPerfect and dBASE and all of Marcia's associated data and document files (MEMO.WP, LETTER.WP, TRAINING.DBF, and so on).

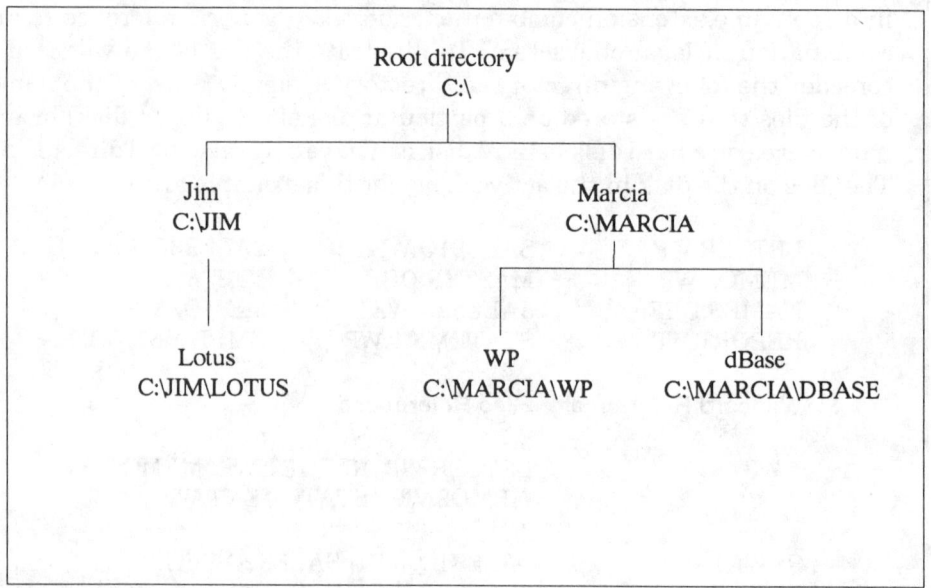

Figure 2-1 Sample hard disk directory tree

Files of any kind can be stored in the root directory or in any subdirectory. When working with files that are stored on a disk with a hierarchy of directories, you need to specify the **path**. The path is the logical route that DOS must follow in order to locate the specified file. For example, the path to Jim's SALES.WK1 file would be from the root directory (C:\>) to

    Jim's subdirectory (C:\JIM) to
    the LOTUS subdirectory (C:\JIM\LOTUS) to
    the specific file (C:\JIM\LOTUS\SALES.WK1).

The filename is always the last entry in the path.

Session One

Loading DOS

(Booting Up the System)

Assumption: the computer is ready to be turned on. The keyboard and monitor are connected to the computer. The computer is plugged in. If the terms in this paragraph are unfamiliar, read chapter one, Introduction to the Computer.

Someone has probably told you not to be afraid, that you will not break the computer. That someone is right.

Ready?

In this session you will learn how to:

- Turn on the computer
- Enter the date and time
- Enter a DOS command
- Change the appearance of the DOS prompt
- Turn off the computer

Step 1: Turning On the Computer

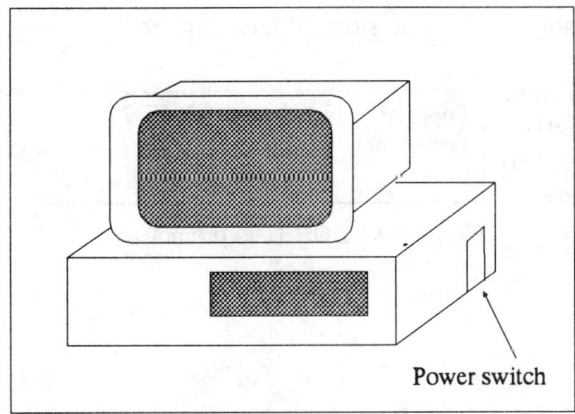

Figure 2-2 Typical power switch location

Figure 2-2 demonstrates the location of the power switch on IBM PC, XT, and AT computers. Other manufacturers may place the switch on the front or back panel.

The monitor may be plugged into the back of the computer and will turn on when the computer is turned on. If your monitor does not have a power on indicator light, wait about 30 seconds (the time it takes for the monitor to warm up) to determine if the monitor is on. If necessary, flip the monitor's power switch to the ON position.

The computer is active immediately. It is not available for use, though, until it finishes its initial check-out routine (10 to 60 seconds). Wait patiently. When check-out is complete the date prompt appears (see Figure 2-3).

```
Current date is Wed  3-06-1991
Enter new date (mm-dd-yy):
```

Figure 2-3   DOS Date prompt

> **Problem Solving**
>
> 1. If you do not see the date message, but do see "C>" or "C:\>". Your computer has been set up to by-pass Date and Time entry. You may skip Step 2: Entering the Date and Time.
>
> 2. If the monitor is blank. Make sure the monitor is on.
>
> 3. If you see "Non-System disk or disk error". First, check to see if there is a diskette in drive A. If so, remove it and tap a letter key. If the drive was empty, contact your instructor.

Step 2: Entering the Date and Time

Unless a computer contains an internal battery operated clock, the correct date and time must be entered each time the computer is turned on. This step demonstrates date and time entry.

☐ The computer is waiting for you to accept the displayed date or enter a new date. Enter a new date, September 24, 1990. Use the format displayed in the date prompt (mm-dd-yy).

* **9-24-90** ↵

Next, the computer displays the time prompt (see Figure 2-4).

☐ Enter a new time, 9:27 a.m. To enter a colon (:), press the SHIFT key and hold it, tap the colon key, then release SHIFT.

```
Current time is 10:03:05.72
Enter new time:
```

Figure 2-4   DOS Time prompt

* **9:27** ↵

Step 3: Entering a DOS Command

We use DOS commands to run applications programs, make system inquiries, and manage files. DOS is like a well trained dog that waits for your command before springing into action. Bowser is eager and ready but has a limited vocabulary. He may not understand, "Bowser, would you fetch my slippers, fetch the newspaper and then lie down on your pad in the study." But if broken into simple commands, Bowser could easily perform each of the three tasks. DOS is the same; it can perform only one task at a time.

Figure 2-5 displays a typical DOS prompt indicating that DOS is ready for a command.

```
C>
```

Figure 2-5 Typical DOS prompt

☐ Enter the CLS command to clear the monitor screen and place the DOS prompt in the screen's upper left corner (see Figure 2-6). Use the BACKSPACE key to erase typing errors before tapping the ENTER key.

* cls ↵

```
C>cls
```

Figure 2-6 First DOS command, "cls"

The command may be entered in upper case or lower case.

Your monitor screen should be completely blank, except for the DOS prompt in the upper left corner. Check your keystroke technique. If more than one DOS prompt appears on the monitor screen, you are "holding down" the enter key rather than "tapping" it.

☐ Figure 2-7 displays what happens if you enter a command that DOS does not recognize. Suppose you typed "clw" instead of "cls" and, before correcting your mistake, tapped the enter key.

* clw ↵

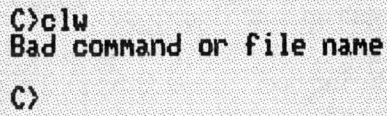

DOS could not recognize the word that was entered. It is as though we asked Bowser to "play the piano" or "go cook dinner."

Figure 2-7 DOS error message

☐ Prove that entering a mistyped command did not break the computer. Reenter the CLS command.

* cls ↵

Once again, the screen is cleared and the DOS prompt appears in the upper left corner.

Step 4: Entering Commands with User-Supplied Data

The DOS command format includes a command word followed by additional information. For example, a typical DOS command is DIR A:. DIR is the command word; it is the activity you want the computer to perform. The additional information, A:, indicates specifically which disk drive will be affected. An excellent example of this type of DOS command is the PROMPT command which is used to alter the appearance of the DOS prompt.

- Change the appearance of the DOS prompt to display the current drive and directory (see Figure 2-8). It is not necessary that you understand the concepts of current disk drive and directory at this time.

* **prompt pg** ↵

```
C>prompt $p$g
C:\>
```

Figure 2-8 Changing the DOS prompt's appearance

The additional information includes two special symbols: $p instructs DOS to display the current directory and $g instructs DOS to display the greater than symbol (>). This command will be used throughout this book. It will help you know where you are when you change from one hard drive directory to another. Session Five discusses hard drives and directories.

Step 5: Practice

This session introduced two DOS commands, CLS and PROMPT. Two other DOS commands, DATE and TIME, were automatically entered by DOS during boot up (see Step 2). This practice session utilizes all four DOS commands.

* Enter the CLS command to clear the screen.
* Use the PROMPT command to change the appearance of the DOS prompt to your name. Type PROMPT followed by a space, your name followed by another space then tap the ENTER key (example: prompt Valerie ↵).
* Clear the screen. Your name (the DOS prompt) should be in the upper left corner.
* Enter the DATE command.
* Change the date to today's date.
* Enter the TIME command.

* Change the time to the current time. Remember to use military time (i.e., 2:15 p.m. is entered 14:15).

* Clear the screen.

* Enter the command PROMPT PG (see Step 4).

* Reenter the DATE and TIME commands to check that the date and time were entered correctly. In each case, if the display is accurate, simply tap the ENTER key to return to the DOS prompt.

* Clear the screen.

Step 6: Turning Off the Computer

A computer may be safely turned off anytime the DOS prompt is present. You may turn off your computer at this point by flipping the power switch to the OFF position. If, however, you want to continue working, leave the computer on while you read the summary. Then go to Session Two.

If the monitor remains on after the computer is turned off, flip the monitor's power switch to the OFF position.

Step 7: Summary

The steps for starting a computer with a hard disk are:

1. Turn the computer on.
2. Turn the monitor on.
3. Wait for the computer to check itself out.
4. If the date prompt appears, enter the current date.
5. If the time prompt appears, enter the current time.

Computer users call this process "booting the system."

Session Two

Files and Filenames

(Command: DIR)

A computer file is a collection of related information saved to an electronic medium (i.e., a hard drive or a diskette).

When Harold Franklin, a professor in the year 4 B.C. (Before Computers), prepared a syllabus for his Writing 101 class. He typed a rough draft, made changes in pencil and typed a final draft. He filed the carbon copy in the "Syllabus- 101" folder which he kept in his "Teaching" file drawer.

Vantanee Hoontrakul, a professor in the year 15 A.D. (After Digitalization), prepares a syllabus for her Word Processing 101 class. She enters the syllabus at her computer, editing as she goes. When the syllabus is complete, she saves it on her hard drive and makes a backup copy on her "Teaching" diskette. Vantanee saves the file as "SYL101."

Computer files are electronic versions of physical files. We store them and retrieve them by using DOS commands instead of opening and closing file drawers.

Turn on your computer, boot up DOS, and enter the command "prompt pg" (see Session One). This session uses the DIR command to display the filenames contained in the DOS directory on your hard drive.

In this session you will learn how to:

- Display filename lists
- Display individual filenames

Step 1: Displaying a Filename List

The collection of separate programs that comprise DOS are found in the DOS directory. This step displays these filenames to demonstrate the use of the DIR command.

☐ Enter the following command to change to the DOS directory (see Figure 2-9).

* cd dos ↵

```
C:\>cd dos
C:\DOS>
```

Figure 2-9 Changing to the DOS directory

Notice the new appearance of the DOS prompt. Hard drive directories and the

CD command will be explained in Session Five.

❐ Use the DIR command to display the filenames in your DOS directory.

    ✱ **dir** ↵

Do not be alarmed if information was pushed off the top of the screen as new information appeared at the bottom. This is called scrolling.

❐ Add a **switch** to the DIR command to display the filenames in "page" format (i.e., one screen's worth of data at a time). The switch (display option) is /p. Tap the forward slash key, then tap p. The forward slash key is usually found just above the right end of the space bar.

    ✱ **dir /p** ↵

```
..            <DIR>       12-08-87   2:53p
ANSI     SYS       1651    3-07-85   1:43p
ASSIGN   COM       1509    3-07-85   1:43p
ATTRIB   EXE      15091    3-07-85   1:43p
BACKUP   COM       5577    3-07-85   1:43p
BASIC3   COM      17792    3-07-85   1:43p
BASICA3  COM      27520    3-07-85   1:43p
CHKDSK   COM       9435    3-07-85   1:43p
COMMAND  COM      23210    3-07-85   1:43p
COMP     COM       3664    3-07-85   1:43p
DISKCOMP COM       4073    3-07-85   1:43p
DISKCOPY COM       4329    3-07-85   1:43p
EDLIN    COM       7261    3-07-85   1:43p
FDISK    COM       8173    3-07-85   1:43p
FIND     EXE       6403    3-07-85   1:43p
FORMAT   COM       9398    3-07-85   1:43p
GRAFTABL COM       1169    3-07-85   1:43p
GRAPHICS COM       3111    3-07-85   1:43p
JOIN     EXE      15971    3-07-85   1:43p
KEYBFR   COM       2473    4-12-85   4:22p
KEYBGR   COM       2418    4-12-85   4:23p
KEYBIT   COM       2361    4-12-85   4:25p
Strike a key when ready . . .
```

Figure 2-10 Screen display resulting from "dir /p" entry

In Figure 2-10, twenty-one filenames are displayed. The last line prompts you to "strike a key" when you are ready to view the next screen. Non-printing keys (e.g., the SHIFT key) will not work.

❐ Tap the space bar to continue (a space is a character).

    ✱ SPACE *(or any character)*

The DOS prompt should reappear (if you have a large number of files in your DOS directory, you may have to tap the space bar one or two more times).

☐ Use a different switch, /w, to display filenames in "wide" format (see Figure 2-11).

* **dir /w** ↵

```
C:\DOS>dir /w

Volume in drive C is HARD DRIVE
Directory of  C:\DOS

                                    ANSI      SYS     ASSIGN   COM    ATTRIB   EXE
BACKUP   COM   BASIC3   COM    BASICA3  COM     CHKDSK   COM    COMMAND  COM
COMP     COM   DISKCOMP COM    DISKCOPY COM     EDLIN    COM    FDISK    COM
FIND     EXE   FORMAT   COM    GRAFTABL COM     GRAPHICS COM    JOIN     EXE
KEYBFR   COM   KEYBGR   COM    KEYBIT   COM     KEYBSP   COM    KEYBUK   COM
LABEL    COM   MODE     COM    MORE     COM     PRINT    COM    RECOVER  COM
RESTORE  COM   SELECT   COM    SHARE    EXE     SORT     EXE    SUBST    EXE
SYS      COM   TREE     COM    VDISK    SYS     CLKDVR   SYS    CONFIG   SYS
GWBASIC  EXE
```

Figure 2-11 Screen display resulting from "dir /w" entry

Step 2: Displaying Individual Filenames

In addition to displaying all filenames in a directory, the DIR command may also be used to display individual filenames.

☐ Clear the monitor screen before beginning this step.

* **cls** ↵

☐ Display the file information for the COMMAND.COM file (see Figure 2-12).

* **dir command.com** ↵

```
C:\DOS>dir command.com

Volume in drive C is HARD DRIVE
Directory of  C:\DOS

COMMAND  COM     23210   3-07-85   1:43p
        1 File(s)    6070272 bytes free

C:\DOS>
```

Figure 2-12 Using DIR to display a single filename

Notice in Figure 2-12 that DOS displays a filename with spaces between the rootname and the extension. Do not let that confuse you. Filename display is different from filename entry.

❏ What happens if DOS cannot find the specified file? Enter the name of a non-existent file to find out (see Figure 2-13).

    ✱ **dir bowser.dog** ↵

```
C:\DOS>dir bowser.dog

 Volume in drive C is HARD DRIVE
 Directory of  C:\DOS

File not found

C:\DOS>
```

Figure 2-13 Error statement generated by the DIR command

DOS tried to locate the file you specified and could not. DOS then issued the error message and another prompt to say, "What's next?"

Step 3: Practice

Use the DIR command to accomplish the following tasks.

✱ Display the file information for DISKCOPY.COM
✱ Display the file information for SORT.EXE
✱ Display the file information for CHKDSK.COM
✱ List all the filenames in the DOS directory.
✱ List the DOS directory filenames in "page" format.
✱ List the DOS directory filenames in "wide" format.
✱ Try several DIR commands on your own. Display a filename list and select individual filenames to display.

Step 4: Ending the Session

If you do not want to continue to the next session, refer to Session One, Step 6 to turn off the computer.

Session Three

(Commands: FORMAT and DISKCOPY)

Computing is not fool proof. Someday you will enter a command too quickly and damage important data. Prudent computer users make backup copies of critical files. That way, when you erase or destroy the contents of a file (computer users call this "trashing a file"), an electronic copy will exist on another diskette. A computer user without backup copies is like an aerialist performing without a safety net. One mistake and . . .

Always make backup copies of diskettes that contain hard to replace data. Before using the diskette, make a copy, store the original, and use the copy. This session describes the use of the FORMAT command to prepare new diskettes. Then the DISKCOPY command is used to make a backup copy of the Example Files Diskette.

Turn on your computer and boot DOS. Enter the "prompt pg" command so the DOS prompt will display the current directory. Change to the DOS directory (see Session Two, Step 1). You will need your Example Files Diskette, two additional diskettes, two blank diskette labels and a write protect tab. The additional diskettes do not have to be new diskettes, but please heed the following:

Warning

The commands in this session erase all data on diskettes. Proceed with caution.

If someone loaned you the additional diskettes needed for this session, be sure they know that the diskettes will be COMPLETELY ERASED.

Self-adhesive diskette labels are provided separately by diskette vendors. Instructions for filling out the label and affixing it to the diskette occur later in the session.

In this session you will learn how to:

- Write protect a diskette
- Use FORMAT to prepare new diskettes for use
- Use DISKCOPY to copy the contents of one diskette onto another diskette
- Change the active drive

Step 1: Write Protecting a Diskette

5 1/4" diskettes may be safeguarded from accidental erasure by placing a small adhesive tab over the write protect notch (see Figure 2-14). A box of diskettes usually includes labels and a sheet of write protect tabs. 3 1/2" diskettes are write protected when the write protect device is in the open position (see Figure 2-14).

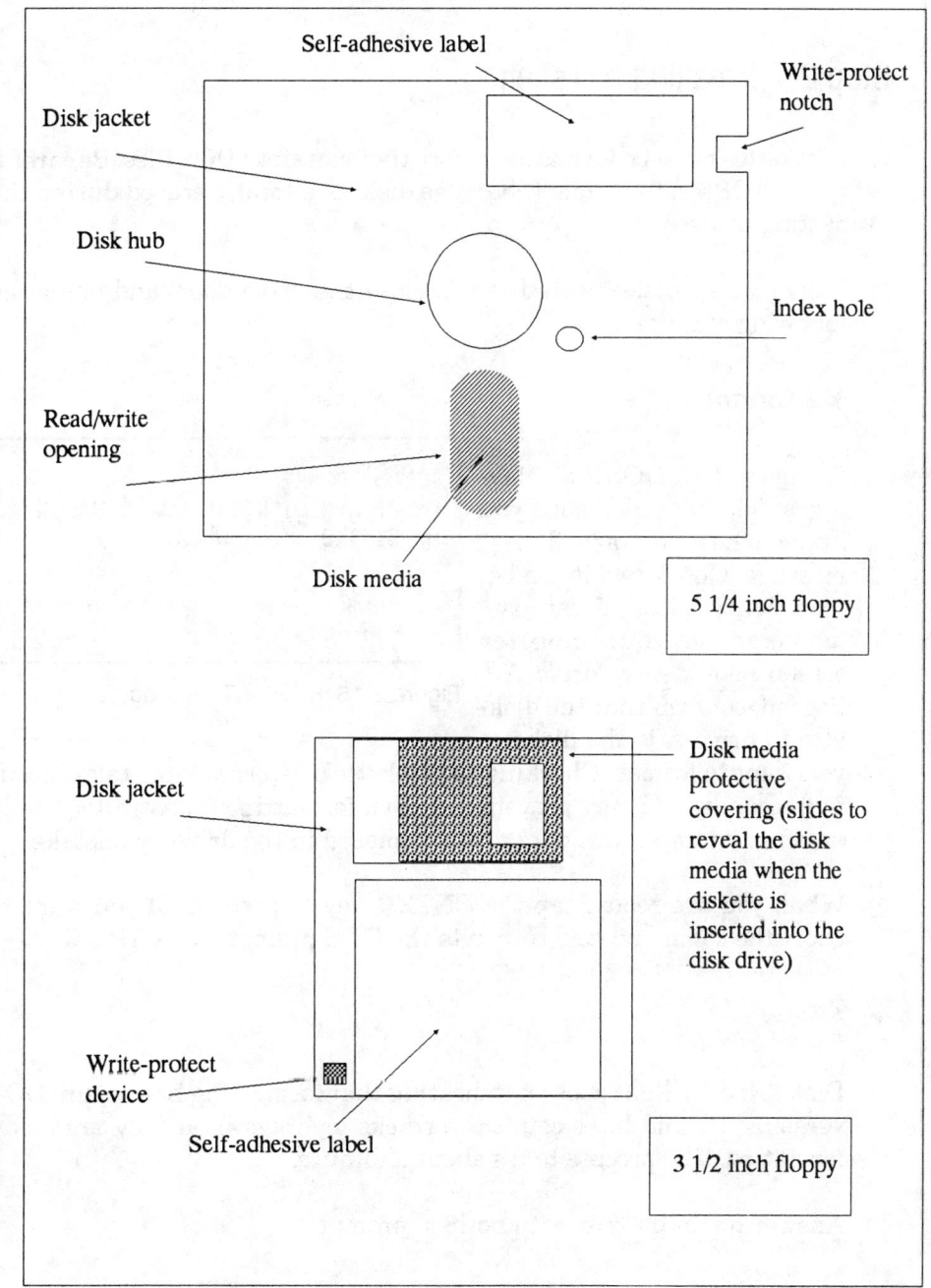

Figure 2-14 Diskette components

☐ Write protect the Example Files Diskette to prevent accidental erasure. Peel a write protect tab off its sheet, and affix it to the Example Files Diskette. One half of the tab is placed on the front of the notch, then the tab is folded around the edge of the diskette to cover the back of the notch.

Please do not proceed to the following steps until your Example Files Diskette is protected.

Step 2: Formatting a Diskette

New diskettes must be formatted before they can store DOS files. Be careful using the FORMAT command because disks are totally erased during the formatting process.

☐ Insert a new diskette in drive A, close the drive door, and enter the following command.

    * **format a:** ↵

In Figure 2-15, DOS is displaying a "please make sure you know what you are doing" message. Check two items before continuing. First, the message on your monitor screen should say "drive A:". Second, confirm that the diskette in drive A is the diskette

```
C:\DOS>format a:
Insert new diskette for drive A:
and strike ENTER when ready
```

Figure 2-15 FORMAT message

you want to format. Checking the diskette's external label takes about five seconds, and may prevent you from formatting (substitute: totally erasing) an important data diskette placed in the drive by mistake.

☐ When you are ready, tap the ENTER key to proceed. If you want to abort the command and return to the DOS prompt, tap CTRL-C.

    * ↵

Disk drive A's light goes on indicating that formatting has begun. DOS versions 3.2 and later count the tracks (cylinders) as they are being formatted. The process takes about a minute.

☐ Answer no to the "Format another" prompt.

    * **n** ↵

This diskette will be used as your data diskette. Write "Data Diskette" on a self-adhesive diskette label and affix the label to your formatted diskette. Refer to Figure 2-14 for a suggested label location.

Step 3: Copying a Diskette using DISKCOPY

Many DOS commands alter files and filenames. Be prudent and prepare for possible mistakes by making a copy of the Example Files Diskette.

Enter the DISKCOPY command to make an exact duplicate of your Example Files Diskette (see Figures 2-16 and 2-17).

* **diskcopy a: a:** ↵   *(one floppy drive)*

  or

* **diskcopy a: b:** ↵   *(two floppy drives)*

DISKCOPY involves two diskettes. The SOURCE diskette contains the data to be copied. The TARGET diskette will be transformed into an exact copy of the SOURCE diskette.

```
C:\DOS>diskcopy a: a:
Insert SOURCE diskette in drive A:
Press any key when ready . . .
```

Insert the Example Files Diskette in drive A. When prompted, insert the TARGET diskette in the appropriate drive. Use a second additional diskette as the TARGET diskette (not the diskette formatted in Step 2).

Figure 2-16 "diskcopy a: a:" prompt

```
C:\DOS>diskcopy a: b:
Insert SOURCE diskette in drive A:
Insert TARGET diskette in drive B:
Press any key when ready . . .
```

☐ When the SOURCE diskette is in place, tap a letter key to initiate the DISKCOPY process (if you have two floppy drives, insert both the SOURCE and TARGET diskettes).

Figure 2-17 "diskcopy a: b:" prompt

* **d**   *(or any letter key)*

On computers with one floppy drive, DOS reads the data into memory and prompts you to enter the TARGET diskette. You may be prompted to switch diskettes during the process.

On computers with two floppy drives, the DISKCOPY process takes from one to two minutes to complete. The disk drive activity lights signal which portion of the process is being performed. Drive A lights up as data is being read from the Example Files Diskette. Drive B lights up when data is written to the target diskette. DOS may go back and forth between the disk drives several times to copy all the information.

❏ When the process is complete, DOS asks if you want to "Copy another diskette." Answer no.

    * **n** ↵

Step 4: Changing the Active Drive

❏ Change to drive A to display the contents of the Example Files Backup Diskette. Insert the backup Example Files Diskette in drive A and close the drive door. Enter disk drive A's designator to make drive A the active drive.

    * **a:** ↵

The DOS prompt should now look like "A:\>"

❏ Display the directory of the backup diskette in drive A.

    * **dir** ↵

❏ Change back to disk drive C

    * **c:** ↵

You should be back at the original DOS prompt.

Step 5: Labeling and Storing Diskettes

Put the Example Files Diskette in its jacket and store it vertically in a box made for diskette storage. Do not use the Master Example Files Diskette again unless something happens to your backup copy.
    Next place the backup copy of the Example Files Diskette in its jacket. Write "Example Files Diskette Copy" on a label then attach the label to the diskette (see Figure 2-14 for a suggested label location).
    If you do not wish to continue to the next session, turn off your computer.

Step 6: Practice

* Use your knowledge of the DIR command (Session Three) in conjunction with the ability to change the active drive to display directories of drives A and C.
* Format several new diskettes.

Step 7: Ending the Session

If necessary, remove your diskette from drive A. Refer to Session One, Step 6 to turn off the computer.

Session Four

Introduction to Hard Drives and Directories

(Commands: MD, CD, and RD)

Turn on your computer and boot DOS before beginning this session. Enter the command "prompt pg" (see Session One, Step 4).

Like the diskette, the hard drive is secondary (permanent) storage. Program and data files are stored on the hard drive until they are needed.

DOS commands exist to create directories, change from one directory to another, and remove directories. The user creates directories as they are needed, and removes directories when they are no longer useful. See the DOS Fundamentals section for a complete discussion of hard drives and directories.

In this session you will learn how to:

♦ Create a directory

♦ Change from one directory to another

♦ Remove a directory

Step 1: Creating a Directory

The command used to create a directory is MKDIR (Make Directory). The command is more commonly used in its shorthand form, MD.

❏ Enter the two following commands to insure that you are logged onto the C drive and are in its root (or top level) directory.

* **c:** ↵
* **cd** ↵

The cd command is used to change from one directory to another and will be explained in Step 2.

> **Problem Solving**
>
> If you received the message "Invalid parameter". Reenter the command using a backslash (\) and not the forward slash (/).

☐ Create the PRACTICE directory, a subdivision of the root directory, by entering the following command.

* **md practice** ↵

The PRACTICE directory has been created. Confirm its existence by entering the DIR command and look for the listing, PRACTICE <DIR>. The <DIR> extension indicates that the listing is the name of a directory and not the name of a file.

Step 2: Changing Directories

The command used to change directories is CHDIR or more commonly CD. Directories exist in a Parent-Child relationship to one another. Any directory may have one or more subdirectories (children). The root directory, for instance, is usually "parent" to several "children" directories.

☐ Change from a parent directory to one of its children directories. Enter the CD command, a space, and the name of the directory to be changed to.

* **cd practice** ↵

```
C:\>cd practice
C:\PRACTICE>
```

The DOS prompt should now look like, C:\PRACTICE> (see Figure 2-18). You are logged onto the PRACTICE directory which is one level below the root directory.

Figure 2-18 Changing to the PRACTICE directory

☐ The symbol for the root directory is "\" by itself. Change to the root directory by entering the CD command followed by the root directory symbol.

* **cd** ↵

```
C:\PRACTICE>cd\
C:\>
```

The DOS prompt should now look like, C:\> (see Figure 2-19).

Figure 2-19 Changing to the root directory

Step 3: Removing a Directory

The command to remove a directory is RMDIR or RD. Efficient hard disk management includes removing directories that are no longer in use.

Two requirements must be met before removing a directory. First the directory must be empty. Erase all files and remove any children directories. Second, the directory you are trying to remove may not be the current directory. If you are sitting on the limb you saw off, where are you?

▢ Confirm that the PRACTICE directory is empty.

* **cd practice** ↵
* **dir** ↵

Two directory names appear in the listing (. and ..). These are null directories that have special DOS functions. They cannot be erased.

▢ Change to the root directory (the parent) then issue the command to remove the PRACTICE directory.

* **cd** ↵
* **rd practice** ↵

The PRACTICE directory is no longer on the hard drive. Confirm by entering the DIR command. The contents of the root directory appear, and PRACTICE <DIR> should not be present (see Figure 2-20).

* **dir** ↵

```
Volume in drive C is HARD DRIVE
Directory of  C:\

COMMAND  COM     23210   3-07-85   1:43p
AUTOEXEC BAT       261   3-12-89   2:58p
DOS          <DIR>        12-08-87   2:53p
CONFIG   SYS       151   4-22-89   4:53a
WP50         <DIR>         7-23-89   5:14a
LOTUS        <DIR>         1-14-90  12:23p
DBASE        <DIR>         5-05-90   8:04a
       7 File(s)    6004736 bytes free
```

Figure 2-20 Sample root directory contents after removal of the PRACTICE directory

Session Five

The Powerful COPY Command

(Command: COPY)

The COPY command is one of DOS's most functional commands. This session presents COPY command fundamentals.

Turn on the computer and log onto the root directory of drive C. Enter the "prompt pg" command.

In this session you will learn how to:

- Copy a file from a diskette to the hard drive
- Copy a file from the hard drive to a diskette
- Make a copy of a file on the file's diskette
- Use the COPY CON command to create new files

Step 1: Creating a Practice Subdirectory

Set aside an area of the hard drive for this session's work so other files and directories will not be disturbed. At the end of the session, the new directory will be removed, leaving the hard drive in its original condition.

☐ Use the MD command to create a new directory called PRACTICE. Refer to Session Four for a complete discussion of DOS directory commands.

* **md practice** ↵

☐ Insert the backup copy of the Example Files Diskette into drive A and close the drive door.

☐ Change to the PRACTICE directory (see Figure 2-21).

* **cd practice** ↵

Problem Solving

If you received the error message "Unable to create directory". The PRACTICE directory may already exist. Find out by entering DIR or DIR /P and look for PRACTICE <DIR>. Check with your instructor to find out what to do.

```
C:\>cd practice
C:\PRACTICE>
```

Figure 2-21 Changing to the PRACTICE directory

☐ Copy all the files on the Example Files Diskette into the newly created hard drive directory. The following command is an advanced COPY command that employs wildcard characters (the asterisks).

* **copy a:*.*** ↵

Each files's filename will be listed as the file is copied from drive A to the hard drive.

☐ Remove the Example Files Diskette from drive A and insert a blank formatted diskette (see Session Four).

Step 2: Copying a File from the Hard Drive to a Diskette

Use the COPY command to copy files from the hard drive to a diskette. The most common format for COPY is:

   COPY (space) What (space) Where.

Typical examples include:

   copy command.com a:
   copy qtr1.wk1 c:\lotus
   copy inventry.dbf invenbak.dbf
   copy *.* c:\wp50\files

☐ Disk drive A contains a newly formatted diskette. Confirm that the diskette is empty by displaying its directory (see Figure 2-22).

```
C:\PRACTICE>dir a:

Volume in drive A has no label
Directory of  A:\

File not found

C:\PRACTICE>
```

* **dir a:** ↵

The command displays the directory of the diskette in drive A even though drive C is the current drive.

Figure 2-22 The "dir a:" command

☐ Use the COPY command to copy MESSAGE.TXT to the diskette in drive A (see Figure 2-23).

* **copy message.txt a:** ↵

```
C:\PRACTICE>copy message.txt a:
       1 File(s) copied

C:\PRACTICE>
```

DOS should reply "1 File(s) copied". If you received any other message, check your spelling and spacing and try the command again.

Figure 2-23 Copying a file from the hard drive to a diskette in drive A

☐ Use the DIR A: command to confirm that the file was copied to drive A.

* **dir a:** ↵

☐ Copy another file from the DOS directory to your data diskette.

* **copy report.txt a:** ↵

Again, check for errors if you did not receive the "1 File(s) copied" message.

☐ Confirm the success of the copy (see Figure 2-24).

* **dir a:** ↵

```
C:\PRACTICE>dir a:

Volume in drive A has no label
Directory of  A:\

MESSAGE  TXT      304   6-20-90   6:14a
REPORT   TXT      239   6-20-90   6:33a
       2 File(s)      359663 bytes free
```

Figure 2-24 Contents of the diskette in drive A

You should see two filenames displayed, MESSAGE.TXT and REPORT.TXT.

☐ Create a new name for the copy by including a name in the "Where" portion of the command.

* **copy report.txt a:bowser.dog** ↵

This form of the command still fits the general format described above. The "Where" portion includes the disk drive designation and the new filename. Please notice that the entire "Where" portion contains no spaces.

Problem Solving

If the error message, "Invalid number of parameters", is displayed. You probably have a space between a: and bowser.dog. Enter the command again without the offending space as you mutter to yourself,"I don't think I will ever understand when to space and when not to space."

☐ As before, confirm the success of the copy.

* **dir a:** ↵

```
C:\PRACTICE>copy report.txt a:
       1 File(s) copied
C:\PRACTICE>copy report.txt a:bowser.dog
       1 File(s) copied
C:\PRACTICE>dir a:

 Volume in drive A has no label
 Directory of  A:\

MESSAGE  TXT      304    6-20-90   6:14a
REPORT   TXT      239    6-20-90   6:33a
BOWSER   DOG      239    6-20-90   6:33a
        3 File(s)     359424 bytes free

C:\PRACTICE>
```

Figure 2-25   The file BOWSER.DOG is a copy of the file REPORT.TXT

In Figure 2-25, visually compare REPORT.TXT, and BOWSER.DOG. Except for the filenames, all columns are identical.

☐ Copy another file, first without changing the name, then again with a changed name, and compare the results.

* **copy memo.txt a:** ↵
* **copy memo.txt a:lunch.yet** ↵

☐ Confirm the process.

* **dir a:** ↵

In Figure 2-26, visually compare MEMO.TXT and LUNCH.YET. They should be identical (they are the same size and were created at the same date and time).

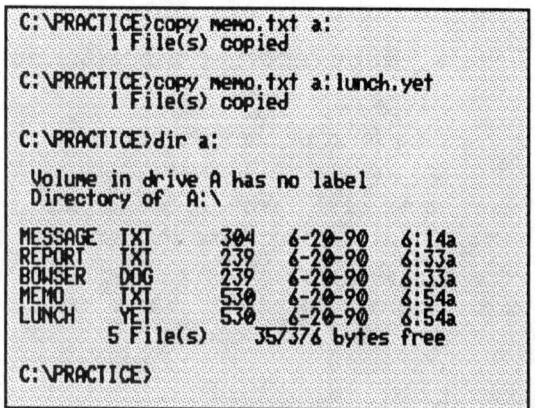

Figure 2-26   The file LUNCH.YET is a copy of the file MEMO.TXT

> **Warning**
>
> **Files may be overwritten without notice.**
>
> This happens when an existing file has the same name as the name to be used for the copy. The new file replaces the old file, completely erasing the old file. The danger is that DOS does not issue a warning notice.

☐ At this point MEMO.TXT and LUNCH.YET are copies of the same file. Enter the following commands to demonstrate a COPY command trap.

* **copy message.txt a:lunch.yet** ↵
* **dir a:** ↵

```
C:\PRACTICE>copy message.txt a:lunch.yet
        1 File(s) copied

C:\PRACTICE>dir a:

 Volume in drive A has no label
 Directory of A:\

MESSAGE  TXT      304   6-20-90   6:14a
REPORT   TXT      239   6-20-90   6:33a
BOWSER   DOG      239   6-20-90   6:33a
MEMO     TXT      530   6-20-90   6:54a
LUNCH    YET      304   6-20-90   6:14a
        5 File(s)     357376 bytes free
```

Figure 2-27   The file LUNCH.YET was changed without warning

Look at the listing displayed in Figure 2-27. LUNCH.YET is now the same file as MESSAGE.TXT. DOS erased the old LUNCH.YET file and replaced it with the new LUNCH.YET. All this happened without any warning from DOS that the old file was being overwritten.

Step 3: Making a Second Copy of a File on a Diskette

The COPY command is also used to make multiple file copies on one diskette. Each new copy must be given a new filename since DOS does not allow two files on a diskette to have the same name.

☐ Log onto drive A and make an additional copy of the MESSAGE.TXT file (see Figure 2-28).

* **a:** ↵

* **copy message.txt missive.txt** ↵
* **dir** ↵

```
C:\PRACTICE>a:
A:\>copy message.txt missive.txt
        1 File(s) copied
A:\>dir
 Volume in drive A has no label
 Directory of  A:\
MESSAGE  TXT      304   6-20-90   6:14a
REPORT   TXT      239   6-20-90   6:33a
BOWSER   DOG      239   6-20-90   6:33a
MEMO     TXT      530   6-20-90   6:54a
LUNCH    YET      304   6-20-90   6:14a
MISSIVE  TXT      304   6-20-90   6:14a
        6 File(s)      356352 bytes free
```

Figure 2-28 Making multiple copies of a file on the same diskette

MESSAGE.TXT and MISSIVE.TXT are different filenames, but the sizes and creation dates are the same. DOS creates the copy on the current drive when the "Where" portion of the command (missive.txt) does not contain a disk drive designation.

▢ The slightest change to a filename creates an entirely new name. MESSAGE.TXT is considered wholly different from MESSAGES.TXT or MESSAGE1.TXT. Make slight alterations to a filename when creating backup copies to show the copy's origin (see Figure 2-29).

* **copy message.txt message1.txt** ↵
* **copy message.txt message2.txt** ↵
* **dir** ↵

The two new files are relatives of the original MESSAGE.TXT file. Use this procedure before making alterations to a file. The copy will be available in case something happens to the original.

Step 4: Using COPY to Create a Short Text File

As you will learn in Session Eight, experienced computer users automate many computer tasks by creating batch files. A batch file is a text file that contains DOS commands. When the batch file is loaded, these commands are executed one after another in the order they appear in the batch file.

```
A:\>copy message.txt message1.txt
        1 File(s) copied

A:\>copy message.txt message2.txt
        1 File(s) copied

A:\>dir

 Volume in drive A has no label
 Directory of  A:\

MESSAGE  TXT      304    6-20-90   6:14a
REPORT   TXT      239    6-20-90   6:33a
BOWSER   DOG      239    6-20-90   6:33a
MEMO     TXT      530    6-20-90   6:54a
LUNCH    YET      304    6-20-90   6:14a
MISSIVE  TXT      304    6-20-90   6:14a
MESSAGE1 TXT      304    6-20-90   6:14a
MESSAGE2 TXT      304    6-20-90   6:14a
        8 File(s)    354304 bytes free

A:\>
```

Figure 2-29 Making multiple copies of MESSAGE.TXT

It is not uncommon for computer users to create several batch files during a working session.

The command most often used to create a batch file "on the fly," is the COPY CON command, which is a special version of the COPY command. COPY CON is used to create short text files. The "con" in the "What" portion of the COPY command instructs DOS to copy keyboard input to a named file. Con is short for console, or keyboard.

This step demonstrates the use of COPY CON to create short text files.

☐ Use COPY CON to create a one line file (see Figure 2-30).

* **copy con first.txt** ↵

The cursor moved down one line just below the DOS prompt. The computer is waiting for you to type the text to be included in the file.

```
A:\>copy con first.txt
_
```

Figure 2-30 The COPY CON command

☐ Type the following text onto the screen.

* **I am not quite sure what I am doing.** ↵

☐ Next, signal DOS that you are finished typing and are ready to copy the file. The signal involves two keys: function key six (F6) and the ENTER key.

* **F6** ↵

❏ Confirm that the file FIRST.TXT is on your data diskette.

    ✳ **dir** ↵

The file should be listed. Notice that the file's creation date and time are the same as the system date and time. DOS stamped the file at its moment of creation.

❏ Use COPY CON to create a multi-line file (see Figure 2-31).

    ✳ **copy con second.txt** ↵
    ✳ **The concept is still fuzzy,** ↵
    ✳ **but it makes a little more sense.** ↵
    ✳ **F6** ↵

```
A:\>copy con second.txt
The concept is still fuzzy,
but it makes a little more sense.
^Z
        1 File(s) copied

A:\>
```

Figure 2-31 Using COPY CON to create a multi-line text file

❏ Display the contents of the PRACTICE directory to confirm the successful creation of SECOND.TXT.

    ✳ **dir** ↵

Notice that its creation time is slightly later and its size is slightly larger than FIRST.TXT.

Step 5: Practice

1. Copy files from the PRACTICE directory to your data diskette.

    ✳ If necessary, insert your data diskette in drive A.
    ✳ List the files in the PRACTICE directory.

* Copy any of the files to your data diskette, keeping the name the same.

* Copy any of the files to your data diskette and rename the file as you make new copies. Remember that the limitation on file names is one to eight characters in the rootname and one to three characters in the extension.

* Log onto drive A.

* Make an additional copy of FIRST.TXT (you will have to supply a new name).

2. Use the COPY CON command to create a text file and the COPY + CON command to add to an existing text file (see Figure 2-32).

* Use the COPY CON command (see Step 4) to create the following text file. Name the file FLIRTS.

    * ↵
    * **HE** ↵ ↵
    * **I sit at computer #16. My name is George. What's yours?** ↵
    * F6 ↵

* Use the command COPY FLIRTS + CON FLIRTS to add the following text to the file. The command adds any data entered from the keyboard (CON) to the end of FLIRTS and writes the new file to FLIRTS.

    * ↵
    * **SHE** ↵ ↵
    * **You have to guess.** ↵
    * F6 ↵

```
HE
I sit at computer #16. My name is George. What's yours?
^Z
        1 File(s) copied
A:\>copy flirts + con flirts
FLIRTS
CON
SHE
You have to guess.
^Z
        1 File(s) copied
A:\>type flirts
HE
I sit at computer #16. My name is George. What's yours?
SHE
You have to guess.
```

Figure 2-32 Creating the FLIRTS text file

* Use the TYPE command to display the contents of the file FLIRTS on the monitor.
* Make sure your printer is on and use SHIFT-PRTSC to print the contents of the monitor screen.
* Use the COPY FLIRTS + CON command from above to add the following text to the file.

* " ↵
* **HE** ↵
* **May I have a hint?** ↵ ↵
* **SHE** ↵
* **If your last name is Washington, you know my first name.** ↵ ↵
* **HE** ↵
* **Would you like to get a soda with me after lab, MARTHA?** ↵
* F6 ↵

* Use the TYPE command to display the contents of the file on the monitor (see Figure 2-33).
* Use SHIFT-PRTSC to print the contents of the monitor screen.

```
A:\>type flirts

HE
I sit at computer #16. My name is George. What's yours?

SHE
You have to guess.

HE
May I have a hint?

SHE
If your last name is Washington, you know my first name.

HE
Would you like to get a soda with me after lab, MARTHA?

A:\>
```

Figure 2-33 The completed FLIRTS text file

Step 6: Removing the Practice Directory and Ending the Session

☐ This step saves your work to your data diskette and returns the hard drive to its condition before the session began. This allows other students to use the same computer to work through these sessions. Insert your data diskette in drive A. Enter the following commands to copy your work to your data diskette and remove the PRACTICE directory. See Session Four for a complete discussion.

* **c:** ↵
* **cd \practice** ↵
* **copy *.* a:** ↵
* **erase *.*** ↵
* **y** ↵
* **cd ** ↵
* **rd practice** ↵

Session Six

Using Wildcard Characters

Turn on your computer and boot DOS. Enter the command, "prompt pg". Log onto the DOS directory (cd \dos).

DOS has two wildcard characters, the asterisk (*) and the question mark (?). Both wildcard characters may be used to enhance the power of selected DOS commands. Steps 1 and 2 use the DIR command to demonstrate the use of wildcard characters. The remaining steps explore wildcard characters with the COPY, DIR and ERASE commands.

In this session you will learn how to:

- ◆ Use the asterisk (*) wildcard character
- ◆ Use the question mark (?) wildcard character
- ◆ Use F3 to retype the most recently entered command

Step 1: The Asterisk (*)

The asterisk represents the remaining valid characters in the rootname or the extension of a filename. The best way to understand the asterisk is to use it, so...

☐ Use the asterisk to display only those files which have an EXE extension. Enter the following command. Notice that the only space in the command is between DIR and the asterisk (see Figure 2-34).

* **dir *.exe** ↵

The common element in the listing is each filename's EXE extension. The asterisk was placed in the rootname position of the filename making any rootname a legal match.

☐ Display only those files which have a SYS extension.

* **dir *.sys** ↵

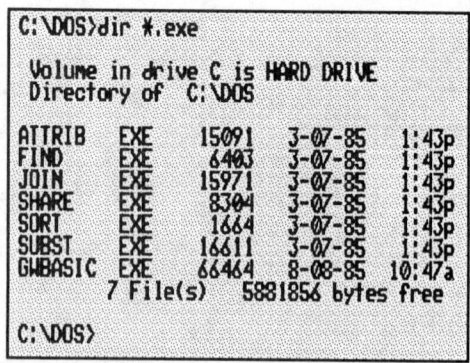

Figure 2-34 Display any file with an ".EXE" extension

❏ Give yourself a little test. Imagine what the following command will display before you enter the command.

* **dir *.*** ↵

Were you correct? The command displayed every filename in the DOS directory because each filename matched the specification "any valid rootname followed by any valid extension."

❏ Use the Asterisk to display a particular rootname with any extension. Insert an asterisk in the extension portion of the filename and the filename will be displayed no matter what the extension is.

* **dir diskcopy.*** ↵

The filename DISKCOPY.COM should now be displayed.

❏ Display any filename that begins with the letter "s" (see Figure 2-35).

* **dir s*.*** ↵

Figure 2-35 Display filenames that start with "s"

Step 2: The Question Mark

The question mark wildcard character represents one valid character in a DOS filename.

❏ Display any DOS filename that has a rootname which is four characters or less (see Figure 2-36).

* **dir ????.???** ↵

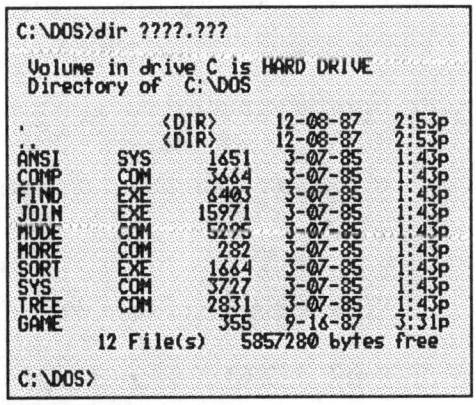

Figure 2-36 Using the question mark wildcard character

❐ Which files would be displayed if the there were only three question marks in the rootname portion?

* **dir ???.???** ↵

❐ Which files would be displayed if there were only two question marks in the extension portion?

* **dir ????.??** ↵

All the files in the example DOS directory have three characters in their extensions, so no filenames qualified as matches (see Figure 2-37). How about your listing?

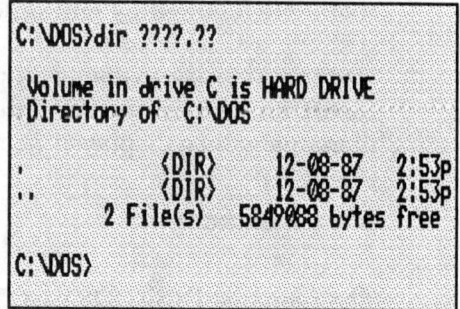

Figure 2-37 No files in the directory match the wildcard request

❐ Although this example may not be used often in real computer work, it helps clarify the question mark. Display any filename that contains the letter "S" as the third letter of the rootname.

* **dir ??s*.*** ↵

Step 3: Using Wildcard Characters with Other Commands

The DIR command is safe, it does not create, alter or erase files. Let's be more adventuresome and use wildcard characters with "live" commands such as COPY and ERASE.

In this step, we will use COPY CON and COPY to create several files on your data diskette. Then we will use DIR to display the filenames and finally, we will erase the files.

❐ Insert a formatted diskette in drive A and log onto drive A.

* *(insert a formatted diskette in drive A)*
* **A:** ↵

Your DOS prompt should read "A:\>".

❐ Use COPY CON to create a short text file (see Figure 2-38).

* **copy con banner.txt** ↵
* ******+****+****+****+****+** ↵
* **Ta Da !!!!!** ↵
* ******+****+****+****+****+** ↵
* **F6** ↵

You should see the response "1 File(s) copied".

```
A:\>copy con banner.txt
****+****+****+****+****+****+
        Ta Da !!!!!
****+****+****+****+****+****+
^Z
        1 File(s) copied

A:\>
```

Figure 2-38 Creating BANNER.TXT

☐ Make two copies of the "banner.txt" batch file.

* **copy banner.txt banner1.txt** ↵

☐ Recall the previous command and modify it to make the second copy of the file. Tap function key F3 to retype the most recently entered DOS command.

* **F3**
* **BKSP** *(5 times)* **2.txt** ↵

☐ Confirm the existence of the 3 banner files.

* **dir** ↵

☐ Make three more copies of the "banner.txt" batch file by using one command that contains the question mark wildcard character (see Figure 2-39).

* **copy banner?.txt banner?.blu** ↵

The question mark allows any of the three existing banner files to be recognized by the COPY command. The "blu" extension is used to create three more distinct copies. Each file is listed as it is copied.

DOS: Session Six 63

```
A:\>copy banner?.txt banner?.blu
BANNER.TXT
BANNER1.TXT
BANNER2.TXT
        3 File(s) copied

A:\>dir

 Volume in drive A has no label
 Directory of  A:\

.            <DIR>       3-12-91   5:33a
..           <DIR>       3-12-91   5:33a
BANNER   TXT       86    3-12-91   4:42p
BANNER1  TXT       86    3-12-91   4:42p
BANNER2  TXT       86    3-12-91   4:42p
BANNER   BLU       86    3-12-91   4:42p
BANNER1  BLU       86    3-12-91   4:42p
BANNER2  BLU       86    3-12-91   4:42p
       8 File(s)    305360 bytes free
```

Figure 2-39 Using the question mark wildcard with the COPY command

☐ List all the files.

  *   dir ↵

The date, time, and number of characters per file will vary depending on your system date and the size of the banner in your file. However, the banner filenames should be the same as the list displayed in Figure 2-39.

☐ Create six more files.

  *   copy banner*.* emblem*.* ↵

☐ List all the files.

  *   dir ↵

☐ List any file with the name "banner" followed by any extension.

  *   dir banner.* ↵

Two files are listed (see Figure 2-40).

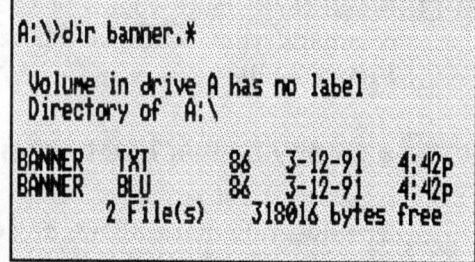

Figure 2-40 Wildcard extension display

☐ List any file with the extension "txt" preceded by any name.

* **dir *.txt** ↵

Six files are listed (see Figure 2-41).

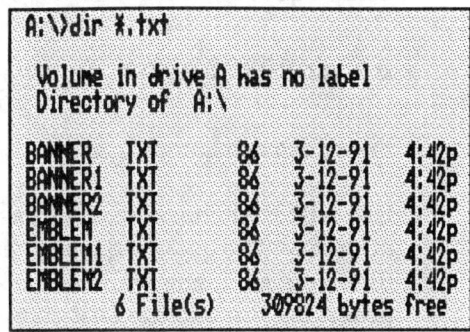

Figure 2-41 Wildcard rootname display

☐ List any file whose name is six or seven characters long, the first six characters being equal to "banner" and followed by the ".txt" extension.

* **dir banner?.txt** ↵

Three files are listed.

☐ List any file whose name is six or seven characters long, the first six characters being equal to "banner" and followed by any extension.

* **dir banner?.*** ↵

Six files are listed.

☐ List any file whose name begins with "b" and is any length from one to eight characters followed by any extension (see Figure 2-42).

* **dir b*.*** ↵

```
A:\>dir b*.*

Volume in drive A has no label
Directory of  A:\

BANNER   TXT        86   3-12-91   4:42p
BANNER1  TXT        86   3-12-91   4:42p
BANNER2  TXT        86   3-12-91   4:42p
BANNER   BLU        86   3-12-91   4:42p
BANNER1  BLU        86   3-12-91   4:42p
BANNER2  BLU        86   3-12-91   4:42p
       6 File(s)    301632 bytes free
```

Figure 2-42 Using the * to fill in the rootname

☐ List any file whose name is seven characters long, the seventh character being equal to 2 and followed by any extension.

* **dir ??????2.*** ↵

Four files are listed.

☐ Use wildcard characters to erase unwanted files from the PRACTICE directory. The use of wildcard characters can be very dangerous because files you may not want to be erased might be erased. Experienced programmers use the DIR command to see which files will be affected. For example, before erasing all files with the extension "blu", first list the files.

* **dir *.blu** ↵
* **erase *.blu** ↵

☐ Confirm that all six "blu" files are erased.

* **dir** ↵

☐ Use the asterisk wildcard character as a keystroke saver. The following command erases one file because only one file named "banner1" remains in the directory. The asterisk is used in place of the "txt" extension.

* **erase banner1.*** ↵

☐ Erase all remaining "banner" files.

* **dir b*.*** ↵
* **erase b*.*** ↵

☐ Erase all remaining EMBLEM files.

* **dir emblem*.*** ↵
* **erase emblem*.*** ↵

The PRACTICE directory should be empty. Leave the PRACTICE directory on the diskette, it will be used in the next step.

DOS: Session Six 66

Step 4: Practice

Create a text file, make multiple copies then erase the files.

* If necessary, insert a formatted diskette in drive A, log onto drive A, create a PRACTICE directory, then change to the PRACTICE directory. Your DOS prompt should read "A:\PRACTICE".
* Clear the screen.
* Use COPY CON to create a one line text file named "one.ref". Include the following text in the file: "I really am enjoying this exercise!!"
* Confirm that one.ref was created.
* Print the screen image (SHIFT-PRTSCRN) and clear the screen.
* Create a duplicate copy of "one.ref" and call it "two.ref".
* Confirm that the copy was successful.
* Make another copy of "one.ref" and call it "three.ref".
* Confirm all three files' existence.
* Print the screen image.
* Clear the screen.
* Use one command (with a wildcard reference) to create three more files and change the extension of the new files to ".grn".
* List the files (see Figure 2-43).
* Print the screen image.
* Clear the screen.
* Display all files with the ".ref" extension.
* Use one command to erase all files with an ".ref" extension.
* List the files in the directory.
* Print the screen image.
* Clear the screen.
* Display all files with the ".grn" extension.
* Use one command to erase all files with an ".grn" extension.
* List the files in the directory.
* Print the screen image.
* Change to the root directory of the A drive and remove the PRACTICE directory (see Session Four).

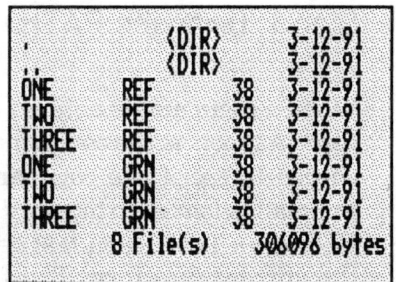

Figure 2-43 Files created in Step 4: Practice

Session Seven

Edlin

Session Five demonstrated how to use COPY CON to create short text files. As you may have discovered, COPY CON has a major disadvantage: if you make a mistake, you have to type the whole file over again. To solve this problem, DOS includes a line editor called EDLIN. EDLIN allows you to edit text files one line at a time. EDLIN does not contain many of the features found in word processing programs, but is sufficient for its designed task: modifying small batch and system files that usually contain between 4 and 30 lines of text.

This session shows you how to create and modify text files using EDLIN. If necessary, turn on your computer and boot DOS. Enter the "prompt pg" command. Insert your data diskette in drive A and log onto drive A.

In this session you will learn how to:

- Use the PATH command to load programs that are not in the current directory
- Use EDLIN to create a text file
- Modify text files with EDLIN

Step 1: Using the PATH Command

When a command is entered at the DOS prompt, DOS performs a series of tests. As soon as the command passes a test, it is loaded and run. DOS first checks to see if the command is an internal command (i.e., one of the commands loaded to memory when the computer is turned on: COPY, DIR, CLS, etc.). The second test determines if the command is a program file in the current directory. The final test searches any directory listed by a previously entered PATH command for the named program file.

For example, entering the command PATH C:\DOS makes any program file in the DOS directory available no matter which drive or directory is current.

☐ Enter the PATH command to allow DOS to find and run any program file in the DOS directory.

* **path c:\dos** ↵

☐ Confirm that your DOS prompt looks like "A:\>".

Step 2: Creating a File Using EDLIN

Create a text file using EDLIN, the line editor supplied with MS-DOS and PC-DOS.

❏ Load EDLIN and name the file to be created (see Figure 2-44).

* **edlin practice.txt** ↵

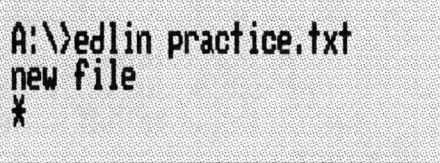

If EDLIN does not find the file named in the command line (see Figure 2-44), it will create a new file with the filename specified. The * indicates that EDLIN is ready to accept your input.

Figure 2-44 Using EDLIN to create a new file

❏ Activate insert-line mode.

* **I** ↵

When DOS is ready to insert or modify a text line, the line number is indented and marked with an asterisk.

❏ Enter the following lines of text.

* **This file was created in Session Seven to demonstrate** ↵
* **DOS's line editor, EDLIN. It is a small file, but** ↵
* **should be sufficient.** ↵

❏ Leave insert-line mode and return to command mode.

* **CTRL -C** *(exit insert-line mode)*

❏ List the lines that have been entered (see Figure 2-45).

* **L** ↵

❏ Save the lines you have entered and exit EDLIN. EDLIN files are saved as ASCII files.

* **E** ↵

```
A:\>edlin practice.txt
New file
*i
        1:*This file was created in Session Seven to demonstrate
        2:*DOS's line editor, EDLIN. It is a small file, but
        3:*should be sufficient.
        4:*^C

*l
        1: This file was created in Session Seven to demonstrate
        2: DOS's line editor, EDLIN. It is a small file, but
        3: should be sufficient.
*
```

Figure 2-45 Text "insert" and "listing" in EDLIN

Step 3: Modifying a File Using EDLIN

☐ Load EDLIN and name the file to be edited. The last command entered at the DOS prompt was "edlin practice.txt". Tap function key F3 to retype the most recently entered DOS command.

* F3 ↵

The appearance of the phrase "End of input file" indicates that the file named on the command line (practice.txt) exists and is ready to be modified.

☐ List the lines that are in the file.

* L ↵

☐ Edit the first line to insert the word "text" before the word "file" (see Figure 2-46).

* 1 *(edit line 1)* ↵
* F1 *(5 times--recreates the line one character at a time)*
* INS *(toggle to insert mode)*
* text SPACE
* F3 *(recreates the remainder of the line)*
* ↵

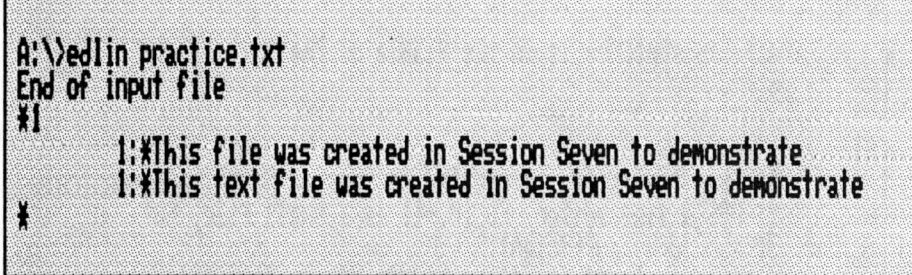

Figure 2-46 Inserting text into an existing text line

☐ Create a duplicate copy of lines 1 through 3, beginning at line 4.

* **1,3,4C** ↵

The parameters are: beginning line number, ending line number, destination line number. With the exception of the beginning line number, the destination line number may not be one of the lines to be copied. In this example, the destination line number may not be either line 2 or line 3, but may be line 1.

☐ List the lines that are now in the file.

* **L** ↵

☐ Insert a line of text before line 4 and exit the insert-line mode.

* **4I** ↵
* **This sentence is in the middle of the text file.** ↵
* **CTRL -C**

☐ List the lines that are now in the file (see Figure 2-47).

* **L** ↵

☐ Replace all occurrences of the word "small" with "little".

* **1,7Rsmall F6 little** ↵

☐ List the lines that are now in the file (see Figure 2-47).

* **L** ↵

☐ Delete the first four lines of the file.

```
*4i
        4:*This sentence is in the middle of the text file.
        5:*^C
*l
        1: This text file was created in Session Seven to demonstrate
        2: DOS's line editor, EDLIN. It is a small file, but
        3: should be sufficient.
        4: This sentence is in the middle of the text file.
        5:*This text file was created in Session Seven to demonstrate
        6: DOS's line editor, EDLIN. It is a small file, but
        7: should be sufficient.
*1,7rsmall^Zlittle
        2: DOS's line editor, EDLIN. It is a little file, but
        6: DOS's line editor, EDLIN. It is a little file, but
*l
        1: This text file was created in Session Seven to demonstrate
        2: DOS's line editor, EDLIN. It is a little file, but
        3: should be sufficient.
        4: This sentence is in the middle of the text file.
        5: This text file was created in Session Seven to demonstrate
        6:*DOS's line editor, EDLIN. It is a little file, but
        7: should be sufficient.
```

Figure 2-47 Edlin's INSERT and REPLACE features

* 1,4d ↵

▢ List the lines that are now in the file.

* L ↵

▢ Save the lines you have entered and exit EDLIN.

* E ↵

Step 4: Practice

Use EDLIN to revise the FLIRTS file created in the Session Five, Step 5. The revised file is displayed in Figure 2-48.

* Copy FLIRTS from your data disk to the PRACTICE directory.
* Use the TYPE command to display the contents of the file FLIRTS on the monitor.

* Use SHIFT-PRTSC to print the contents of the monitor screen.
* Add a reply to the FLIRTS file (a blank line, a "SHE" line, another blank line, and Martha's reply). Use the replay displayed in Figure 2-48 or make up your own reply.
* Add the title THE FLIRTATION at the beginning of the file. (Hint: use EDLIN's insert-line mode.)
* Save, display and print (SHIFT-PRTSC) the revised file.

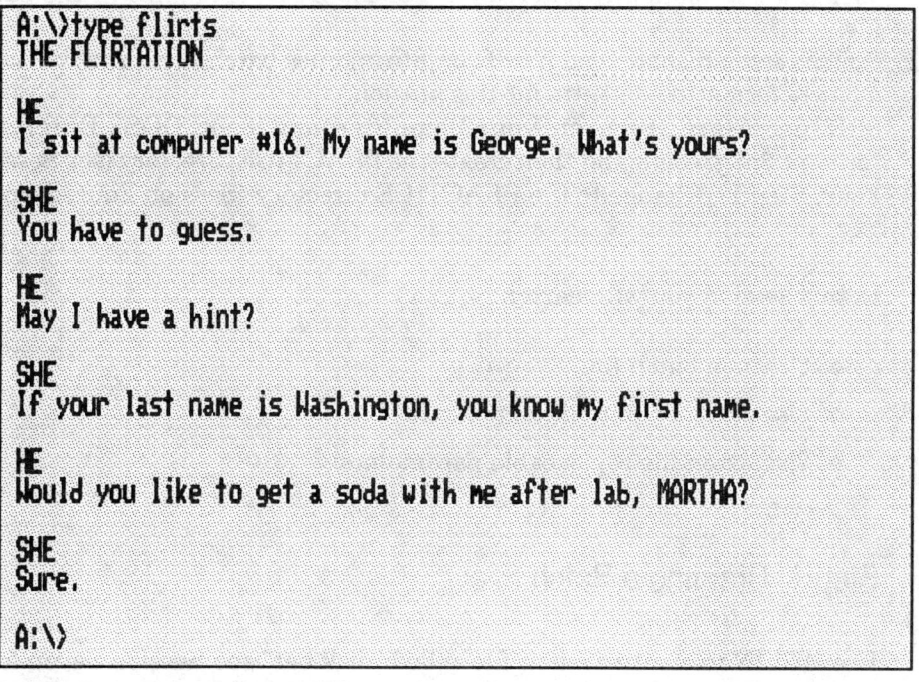

Figure 2-48 Revised FLIRTS file

Session Eight

DOS Batch Files

Batch files are files that contain DOS commands and have a .BAT filename extension. These files are executed by entering the file's rootname without the extension at the DOS prompt. The result is the same as if you had manually entered each of the DOS commands in the batch file.

This session shows you how to create and use batch files. You will need a newly formatted diskette for this session.

If necessary, turn on your computer and boot DOS. Enter the "prompt pg" command then create the PRACTICE directory (see Session Four, Step 1). Change to the PRACTICE directory (Session Four, Step 2).

In this session you will learn how to:

- Create a batch file
- Use special batch file commands
- Use batch file replaceable parameters

Step 1: Creating a Batch File

Use EDLIN to create a batch file called "disk.bat"(see Session Seven for a complete EDLIN discussion). After disk.bat is created, it will be used to copy all files in the PRACTICE directory to a diskette in drive A.

☐ Enter the following to create the batch file disk.bat (see Figure 2-49).

```
* c:\dos\edlin disk.bat ↵
* I ↵
* echo off ↵
* echo This is an example batch file that will copy all ↵
* echo files from the PRACTICE directory to the disk in ↵
* echo drive A, and then display a directory of the files ↵
* echo on the disk in drive A. ↵
* echo Insert a newly formatted diskette in drive A: ↵
* pause ↵
* cd \practice ↵
```

* **copy *.* a:** ↵
* **echo Here is a directory of the new disk:** ↵
* **dir a:/p** ↵
* **CTRL -C**

```
C:\PRACTICE>edlin disk.bat
New file
*i
        1:*echo off
        2:*echo This is an example batch file that will copy all
        3:*echo files from the PRACTICE directory to the disk in
        4:*echo drive A, and then display a directory of the files
        5:*echo on the disk in drive A.
        6:*echo Insert a newly formatted diskette in drive A:
        7:*pause
        8:*cd \practice
        9:*copy *.* a:
       10:*echo Here is a directory of the new disk:
       11:*dir a:/p
       12:*^C

*
```

Figure 2-49 Complete batch file, "DISK.BAT"

The batch file displayed in Figure 2-49 contains several DOS commands that are used primarily in batch files. The first line, "echo off" instructs DOS to suppress the display of each command as it is entered. The next 5 lines each display a comment line on the monitor. The "echo" command (not "echo off") instructs DOS to display the text that follows it on the monitor. The last special command is the "pause" command, which displays the message "Strike a key when ready . . ." and halts batch file execution until a key is tapped.

☐ Save "disk.bat".

* **E** ↵

☐ Insert a newly formatted disk in drive A. Execute the batch file.

* **disk** ↵
* *(follow the instructions that appear on the monitor)*

DOS: Session Eight 75

Step 2: Practice

Use COPY CON to create a text file and EDLIN to revise the file. Create a batch file to call EDLIN for you.

* Use COPY CON to create the following text file. Name the file SPEECH and save it (see Figure 2-50).

* **Well, howdy folks. I am very glad to be here today. I** ↵
* **consider it an honor to be able to come to your fair city** ↵
* **and talk about some of the important issues facing our** ↵
* **country today.** F6 ↵

* Use COPY CON to create the following batch file. Name the file EDIT.BAT (see Figure 2-50).

* **echo off** ↵
* **c:\dos\edlin %1** ↵
* **cls** ↵
* **type %1** ↵
* F6 ↵

```
C:\PRACTICE>copy con speech
Well, howdy folks. I am very glad to be here today. I
consider it an honor to be able to come to your fair city
and talk about some of the important issues facing our
country today. ^Z
        1 File(s) copied

C:\PRACTICE>copy con edit.bat
echo off
c:\dos\edlin %1
cls
type %1
^Z
        1 File(s) copied

C:\PRACTICE>
```

Figure 2-50 Using COPY CON to create SPEECH and EDIT.BAT files

The command "echo off" suppresses the display of DOS commands. The command "c:\dos\edlin %1" calls the program EDLIN from the DOS directory on drive C. The "%1" is explained below. The command "cls" clears the screen, and the command "type %1" displays the contents of the edited file.

* Enter EDIT SPEECH. (EDIT calls the batch file. SPEECH is a parameter that is assigned to the character combination "%1" within the batch file. For example, line 2 is effectively "c:\dos\edlin speech" and line 4 becomes "type speech".)
* Replace "very" in line 1 of the speech with "powerfully" (see Figure 2-51).
* Exit EDLIN and save the revised file.
* Use SHIFT-PRTSC to print the display of the revised file.

```
Well, howdy folks. I am powerfully glad to be here today. I
consider it an honor to be able to come to your fair city
and talk about some of the important issues facing our
country today.

C:\PRACTICE>
```

Figure 2-51 Final version of the edited SPEECH file

Step 3: Removing the Practice Directory and Ending the Session

Follow the instructions listed in Session Five, Step 6 to save your work and remove the PRACTICE directory.

Chapter 3

WordPerfect

5.0

Doc 1 Pg 1 Ln 1" Pos 1"

Session One

Using WordPerfect to Create a Memo

Word processing is using the computer to enter, store, manipulate, and print text for letters, reports, books, and so on. Once you have used word processing, you will probably wonder (like a million others before you) how in the world you ever survived without it!

Word processing, now the number one application for microcomputers, has virtually eliminated the need to rekey revised letters and reports. Revising a hard copy is time consuming and cumbersome, but revising the same text that is in an electronic format is quick and easy. You simply make corrections and revisions to the computer-based text before the document is displayed or printed in final form. Beginning a word processing session is as simple as booting DOS and loading the word processing software.

Word processing packages are generally categorized by the manner in which the user interacts with the system. WordPerfect is a menu-driven word processing package. The user interacts with the software by selecting options from a hierarchy of menus.

In this session you will learn how to:

- Allow entered text to "wrap around"
- Enter additional text in insert mode
- Edit text in typeover mode
- Save a document
- Display the Reveal Codes screen
- Search and replace
- Center text
- Boldface text
- Underline text
- Retrieve a document
- Print a document

The Keystroke Conventions box in the preface explains and illustrates the keystroke format used in the following sessions.

Step 1: Loading WordPerfect

☐ Boot the system if necessary (see DOS, Session One).

❏ Insert your data diskette in drive A and make drive A the active drive.

* *(insert your data diskette in drive A)*
* **a:** ↵

Your DOS prompt should look like A> or A:\>.

❏ Load WordPerfect to memory. In the next command, use the name of your WordPerfect drive and directory in place of "c:\wp50" if it is different.

> **Problem Solving**
>
> If you received the error message: "Not ready error reading drive A". You may have forgotten to close the drive door, or you may have inserted an unformatted diskette. Tap A to abort, correct your mistake and try again.

* **c:\wp50\wp** ↵

When the WordPerfect work screen appears you will see a blank screen with the cursor in the top left corner. WordPerfect calls this screen their Clean Screen (see Figure 3-1). The cursor position indicators are in the bottom right corner: document 1 (Doc 1), page 1 (Pg 1), line 1 inch (Ln 1"), and position 1 inch (Pos 1").

Figure 3-1 WordPerfect's "Clean Screen"

The line designator (Ln 1") indicates the current distance from the top of the printed page (not the top of the monitor). The position designator (Pos 1") indicates the current distance from the left side of the printed page (not the left side of the monitor). WordPerfect automatically sets all margins (top, bottom, left and right) at one inch (see Figure 3-2). The default page size is 8½ by 11 inches. Therefore, when the cursor is

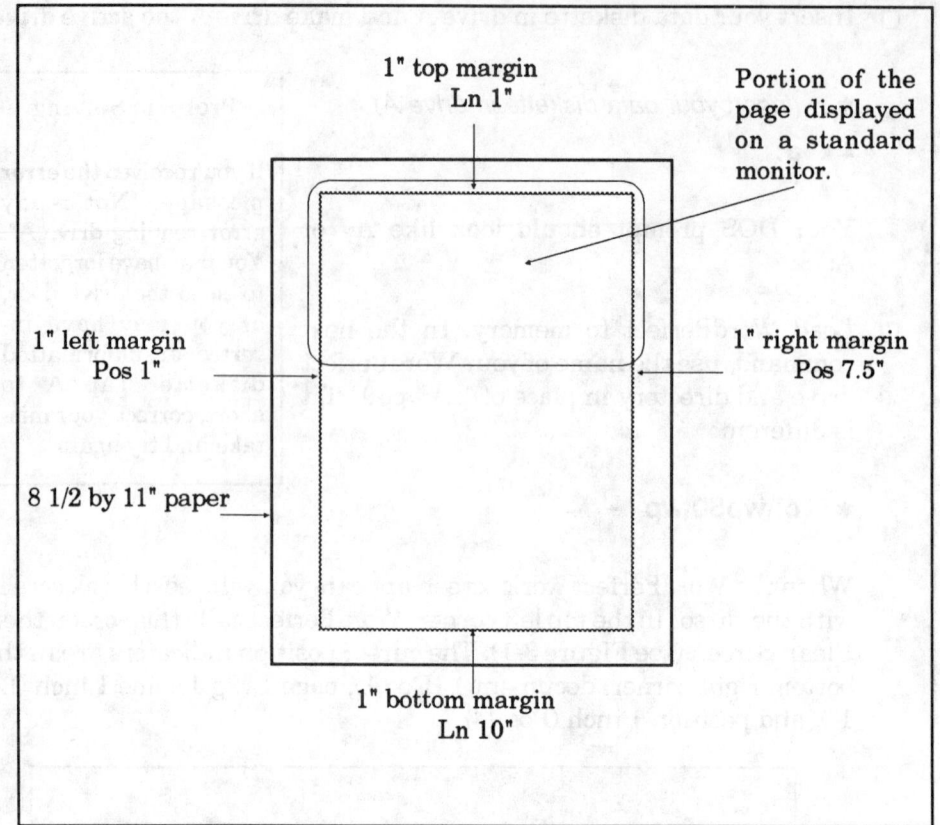

Figure 3-2 WordPerfect's default settings: page size 8 1\2" by 11" and all margins set to 1" each

at the right margin the position indicator reads Pos 7.5" and when the cursor is at the bottom of the page the line indicator reads Ln 10". The Pos indicator blinks when Num Lock is on.

❐ Most WordPerfect commands are entered using the function keys. WordPerfect supplies a handy template for quick reference that fits over the function keys. Ask your instructor if there is one available or refer to the key assignments presented in the Quick Reference Guide. WordPerfect also displays a command template in HELP. Tap function key F3 to activate help.

* ☐ F3

Study WordPerfect's help screen (see Figure 3-3). You may tap any letter to display that letter's portion of the features index. You may also tap a command's function key sequence to display information about the command.

```
Help                                              WP 5.0

    Press any letter to get an alphabetical list of features.

        The list will include the features that start with that letter,
        along with the name of the key where the feature is found. You
        can then press that key to get a description of how the feature
        works.

    Press any function key to get information about the use of the key.

        Some keys may let you choose from a menu to get more information
        about various options. Press HELP again to display the template.


    For customer support in the United States, call:

        Installation: (800) 321-3254
            Features: (800) 541-5096
            Printers: (800) 541-5097
```

Figure 3-3   The "help" screen

☐ Display the thesaurus activation keystroke sequence by tapping "t" and looking up thesaurus in the listing (see Figure 3-4).

  *   T


```
-->|         Tab                                   Tab
Ctrl-F6      Tab Align                             Tab Align
Ctrl-F3      Tab Ruler                             Screen,1,23
Shft-F8      Tab Set                               Format,1
Alt-F5       Table of Authorities (Block On)       Mark Text
Shft-F1      Table of Authorities, Default         Setup,5
Alt-F5       Table of Contents, Mark (Block On)    Mark Text
Alt-F5       Target                                Mark Text,1
Alt-F9       Text Box                              Graphics
Alt-F7       Text Columns                          Math/Columns
Ctrl-F5      Text In/Out                           Text In/Out
Shft-F7      Text Quality                          Print; Setup,5,7
Ctrl-F5      Text to Comment (Block On)            Text In/Out
Alt-F1       Thesaurus                             Thesaurus
Shft-F8      Thousands' Separator                  Format,4
Shft-F5      Time/Date                             Date/Outline
Shft-F1      Timed Document Backup                 Setup,1
Shft-F8      Top and Bottom Margin                 Format,2
Shft-F7      Type Through (to printer)             Print
Hm, Ins      Typeover, Forced                      Home, Ins
Ins          Typeover Mode                         Ins
```

Figure 3-4   Topical index displayed by tapping "t" while in help mode

☐ Display information about the thesaurus by tapping its activation keys (ALT-F1).

* `ALT` - `F1`

☐ Tap F3 to display the command template (see Figure 3-5).

* `F3`

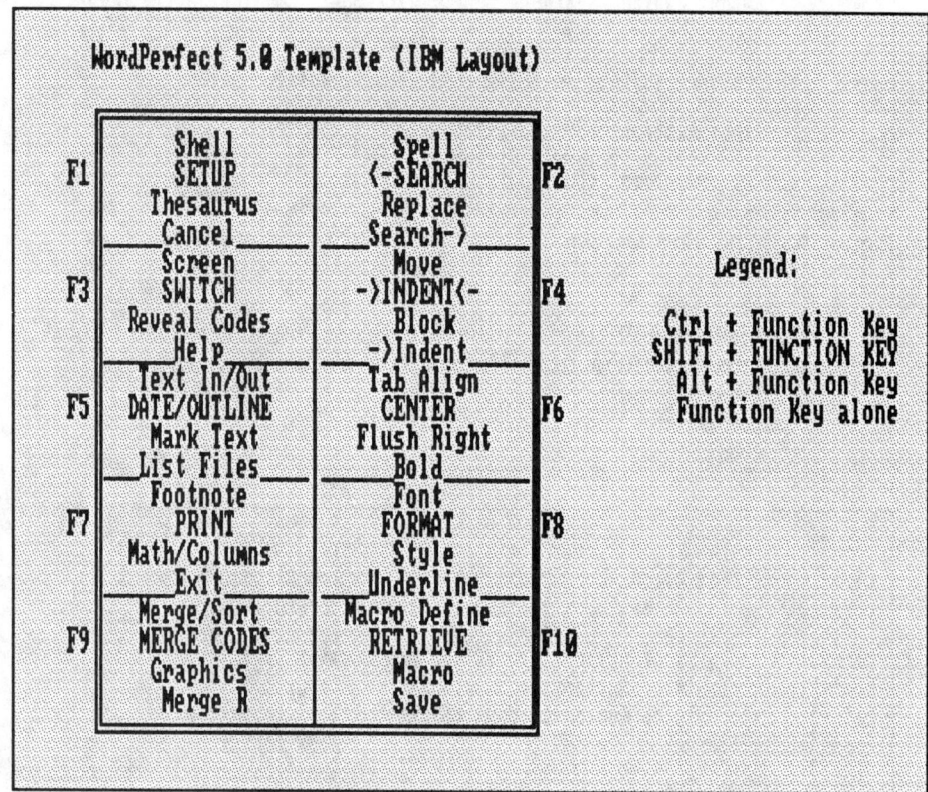

Figure 3-5 WordPerfect's command template. Displayed by tapping F3 twice

☐ Tap the ENTER key or the space bar to exit help.

* ↵

You are now ready to begin your word processing session. In the next step, we will enter the first draft of a memo. Then in subsequent steps we will move text, add text, add a heading, include boldface and underlining, reveal codes and finally print the memo.

Step 2: Entering Text

When WordPerfect's "clean screen" appears, the program is ready to start a new document. To begin, just start typing. As you type, text that extends past the defined margins automatically wraps around to the next line. That is, words that are pushed past the right margin are moved into the next line, and so on, to the end of the paragraph. This capability is known as word wrap. To end a paragraph and begin another, tap ENTER. Each time you tap ENTER you insert a hard carriage return in your document.

☐ Enter the first three lines of the text of the memo (Figure 3-6). To correct typographical errors, use the cursor control keys in combination with the DEL and BKSP keys.

* **To:** |TAB| |TAB| **All personnel** ↵
* **From:** |TAB| **Stephen Garrity, VP Administration** ↵
* **Re:** |TAB| |TAB| **Computer training and OA** ↵ ↵

The second ENTER adds a blank line. The status line should indicate Ln 1.67", Pos 1".

```
To:     All personnel
From:   Stephen Garrity, VP Administration
Re:     Computer training and OA
```

Figure 3-6 First three lines of the memo

☐ Key in the text of the memo in Figure 3-7. Since the lines wrap automatically, tap ENTER only at the end of the paragraph!

* |TAB| **A computer training program ...** *(see Figure 3-7)*
* **further information.** ↵

```
To:     All personnel
From:   Stephen Garrity, VP Administration
Re:     Computer training and OA

        A computer training program has been established to teach OA
skills. The implementation of OA is changing the working
environment and challenging us all to become more computer
literate. Contact Marion Reyes in personnel for further
information.
```

Figure 3-7 First draft of Mr. Garrity's memo

☐ Save the current document to secondary storage (your data diskette). At this point, your document exits only in RAM (see Chapter One). If your computer lost power, all your work would be lost. Develop the habit of saving your work often during a session. That way, if something happens, you will have a recent version to retrieve. Occasionally say to yourself, "Do I want to reenter all of this?" If not, save it.

* F10
* memo ↵

Since you are logged onto drive A, the document is saved as "memo" on your diskette. The saving method just used works for documents that have not been saved before. A complete discussion of saving is presented in Step 5. If at anytime you cannot continue with the session, save your work so that you can pick up where you left off.

Step 3: Moving Text

The block operations are among the handiest of word processing features. They are the block **move**, the block **copy**, and the block **delete** commands. These commands are the electronic equivalent of "cut and paste."

Moving Blocks. With the move block feature, you can select a block of text (a word, a sentence, a paragraph, a section of a report, or as much contiguous text as you desire) and move it to another portion of the document. To do this, follow these steps.

- Indicate the start and end positions of the block of text to be moved (mark the text).
- Select the "move" menu option.
- Move the cursor to the destination location (where the text is to be moved).
- Tap the ENTER key to complete the move operation.

At the end of the move procedure, the marked block of text is moved to the location that you designate, and the original is deleted. The text is adjusted accordingly.

Copying Blocks. The copy block command works similarly to the move block command, except that the text block you select is copied to the designated location (the original is not affected). To perform a copy operation, follow these steps:

- Indicate the start and end positions of the block of text to be copied (mark the text).
- Select the "copy" option from the "move" menu.
- Move the cursor to the destination location (where the copied text is to be placed).
- Tap the ENTER key to complete the copy operation.

At the completion of the operation, two exact copies of the text are present in the document.

Deleting Blocks. The delete block command works similarly to the move and copy block commands. To perform a delete operation, follow these steps:

- Indicate the start and end positions of the block of text to be deleted (mark the text).
- Select the "delete" menu option or tap the "delete" key.

Of the three block commands (move, copy, and delete), the delete command is potentially the most dangerous. If you make an error when performing a move or copy block operation, the marked text is still in the document. However, if you accidentally delete the wrong block of text, that text is removed from the document. Unless you tap the Cancel key (F1) before making two more deletions, the text will be permanently lost. When you tap the Cancel key, either of the last two lines (or blocks) of text that were added to the delete stack (text that has been deleted) may be retrieved from intermediate buffer area in memory and restored to the document.

```
To:       All personnel
From:     Stephen Garrity, VP Administration
Re:       Computer training and OA

     The implementation of OA is changing the working environment
and challenging us all to become more computer literate. A computer
training program has been established to teach OA skills. Contact
Marion Reyes in personnel for further information.
```

Figure 3-8 Memo after moving the second sentence to the beginning

In this step, we will move the second sentence in the current memo to be the first sentence in a revised memo (see Figures 3-7 and 3-8).

☐ Position the cursor anywhere in the second sentence and mark the sentence to be moved.

* *(position cursor anywhere in the second sentence)*
* [CTRL]-[F4]

```
Move: 1 Sentence; 2 Paragraph; 3 Page; 4 Retrieve: 0
```

Figure 3-9   The "Move" command's block selection menu

The block selection menu appears at the bottom of the screen (see Figure 3-9). Menu options may be chosen by tapping the appropriate number or by tapping the highlighted letter in the menu option name. For instance, to choose the Sentence option, tap either "1" or "s". These sessions feature the mnemonic selection method.

* S

Now that the text to be moved (or copied or deleted) has been marked, WordPerfect displays an action selection menu (see Figure 3-10). Select the move option.

```
1 Move; 2 Copy; 3 Delete; 4 Append: 0
```

Figure 3-10   The "Move" command's action selection menu

* M

Swoosh! The sentence has been stored in memory.

☐ Indicate the block's move destination by positioning the cursor at the beginning of the first sentence. Execute the move (retrieve and insert the stored sentence).

* *(position cursor on the "A" of "A computer...")*
* ↵

The keystroke sequence presented works as long as the text to be moved is a sentence, paragraph or page. Any other text length (i.e., several sentences within a paragraph) must first be marked using ALT-F4 (see Step 8). Once the text is marked, tap CTRL-F4 (Move) and select the "Block" menu option.

Step 4: Adding Text

Text is entered in **insert** mode or **typeover** mode. WordPerfect's default setting, insert mode, allows additional text to be inserted anytime, anywhere in a document. The user toggles between insert and typeover mode by tapping the INS key. When in typeover mode, the character that you enter overstrikes the character at the cursor position. For example, suppose that you typed the word "the" but you wanted to type "and". To make the correction in typeover mode, you would position the cursor at the "t" and type "and", thereby replacing "the" with "and".

Mr. Garrity continues editing his memo by adding "Therefore" to the beginning of the second sentence and adding a new third sentence. This step uses both insert and typeover modes to add text to the memo.

☐ Add "Therefore" to the beginning of the second sentence.

* *(position cursor on the "A" of "A computer...")*
* **Therefore,** SPACE

☐ Shift to typeover mode to replace the uppercase "A" with a lowercase "a". "Typeover" appears in the lower left corner of the monitor when you are in typeover mode.

* INS a INS

The second INS returns to insert mode.

☐ Add the sentence "Please take advantage of this excellent opportunity." (see Figure 3-11).

* *(position cursor on the "C" of "Contact")*
* **Please take advantage of this excellent opportunity.**
* SPACE

```
To:        All personnel
From:      Stephen Garrity, VP Administration
Re:        Computer training and OA

       The implementation of OA is changing the working environment
and challenging us all to become more computer literate. Therefore,
a computer training program has been established to teach OA
skills. Please take advantage of this excellent opportunity.
Contact Marion Reyes in personnel for further information.
```

Figure 3-11 Memo with inserted text

☐ When text extends beyond the right margin, as it does in this instance, move the cursor and the document will be reformatted to fit the defined margins.

* →

Step 5: Saving a Document

As stated at the end of Step 2, you should save often during a working session. After you tap F10 to start the save sequence, WordPerfect's response varies depending on whether the document is being saved for the first time, or has been saved before.

If a document is being saved for the first time, WordPerfect displays the save prompt. If the document has been saved before, the document's name (including the drive and path) is displayed as part of the save prompt (see Figure 3-12).

This step demonstrates the procedure for saving a document that has been saved before.

☐ Save the current version of the memo to secondary storage.

* [F10]

Notice that the document's name is displayed as part of the save prompt. Tap the ENTER key to save the document under the same name. A new name could be entered at this point to retain the old version.

```
Document to be saved: A:\MEMO
```

Figure 3-12 The save a document prompt

* ↵

When a name is entered, WordPerfect searches for a similarly named file. If one exists, WordPerfect displays the replace prompt (see Figure 3-13). You must decide whether the current version in RAM should replace the version on secondary storage. Answer yes (Y) to erase the old version and save the new version.

* Y

```
Replace A:\MEMO? (Y/N) No
```

Figure 3-13 The document replace option

Step 6: Displaying the Reveal Codes Screen

WordPerfect does not place formatting codes on the screen. They are inserted into the document in the "background" and are viewed by entering the Reveal Codes command (ALT-F3). This step reveals and describes the codes in the current document.

☐ Use WordPerfect's HOME-HOME-Arrow sequence to place the cursor at the top of the document.

* HOME HOME ↑

Other HOME-arrow key sequences are:

- ◆ HOME ↑ jumps the cursor to the top of the screen
- ◆ HOME ↓ jumps the cursor to the bottom of the screen
- ◆ HOME ← jumps the cursor to the left margin
- ◆ HOME → jumps the cursor to right end of the current line
- ◆ HOME HOME ↓ jumps the cursor to the end of the document

☐ Enter the Reveal Codes command to study the codes included in the current document.

* ALT - F3

Figure 3-14 displays the reveal codes screen. The lower portion of the split screen contains the document with visible format codes. For example, the first line includes two [Tab] codes and one [Hrt] code. Each [Tab] indicates that the tab key was tapped once. The [Hrt] code is entered when the ENTER key is tapped.

When word wrap occurs, WordPerfect automatically inserts soft carriage returns. These soft carriage returns are placed after the last full word that is within the right margin in all but the last line in a paragraph. In Figure 3-14, soft carriage returns have been automatically placed after "environment", "Therefore," "OA" and "opportunity." If text is inserted or deleted, the paragraph is automatically reformatted to fit within the prescribed margins. In reformatting the memo, WordPerfect removes and inserts soft carriage returns as necessary. The insertion and deletion of soft carriage returns is transparent to the end user; that is, it is done automatically without any action on the part of the user.

```
To:        All personnel
From:      Stephen Garrity, VP Administration
Re:        Computer training and OA

    The implementation of OA is changing the working environment
and challenging us all to become more computer literate. Therefore,
a computer training program has been established to teach OA
skills. Please take advantage of this excellent opportunity.
Contact Marion Reyes in personnel for further information.




A:\MEMO                                         Doc 1 Pg 1 Ln 1" Pos 1"
{    ▲    ▲   ▲   ▲   ▲   ▲   ▲   ▲   ▲   ▲   ▲   }   ▲    ▲
To:[Tab][Tab]All personnel[HRt]
From:[Tab]Stephen Garrity, VP Administration[HRt]
Re:[Tab][Tab]Computer training and OA[HRt]
[HRt]
[Tab]The implementation of OA is changing the working environment[SRt]
and challenging us all to become more computer literate. Therefore,[SRt]
a computer training program has been established to teach OA[SRt]
skills. Please take advantage of this excellent opportunity.[SRt]
Contact Marion Reyes in personnel for further information.
```

Figure 3-14   The Reveal Codes screen

- Tap the reveal codes keys again to return to the document.

* ALT - F3

The Reveal Codes screen may be used to add and remove codes from your document. Ask your instructor or refer to the WordPerfect manual for more information.

Step 7: Search and Replace

Just as Stephen Garrity's memo was about to be printed, his secretary pointed out that many people do not know what "OA" means. Mr. Garrity instructed his secretary to change each "OA" to "office automation". His secretary can make the necessary revisions to the memo by using any of several word processing features.

One option is to use the **search** feature. This feature permits Mr. Garrity's secretary to search forward (F2) or backward (SHIFT-F2) through the document and identify all occurrences of a particular character string. For example, to search for all occurrences of "OA" in the memo of Figure 3-11, simply initiate the search command and type in the desired **search string**, "OA" in this example. The cursor is immediately positioned at the first occurrence of the character string "OA" so it can be edited. From there, "search" for other occurrences of "OA" by entering the command again.

As an alternative approach to making the OA-to-office automation change, use the **search and replace** feature. This feature enables Mr. Garrity's secretary to selectively replace occurrences of "OA" (the search string) in the memo with "office automation" (the replacement string). Since all occurrences of "OA" are to be replaced by "office automation", his secretary performs a search without confirmation.

Since a search and replace without confirmation automatically replaces occurrences of the search string with the replacement string throughout the entire document, you should check your work carefully before selecting the global option. For example, if you accidentally replaced all commas with periods in a long report, you would have to read through the entire report to identify and then change the erroneous periods back to commas.

This step follows Mr. Garrity's secretary's steps to replace all occurrences of the letters "OA" in the memo with the words "office automation".

☐ Search and replace proceeds from the current cursor position to the end of the document. To search and replace an entire document, position the cursor at the beginning of the document before activating search and replace.

* `HOME` `HOME` ↑

☐ Enter the search and replace command and answer "no" to the "w/confirmation" prompt.

* `ALT` - `F2`
* N

> w\Confirm? (Y/N) No

Figure 3-15 Search and replace confirmation

Answering "N" or No to the prompt causes all occurrences of the search string to be replaced without waiting for confirmation at each occurrence (see Figure 3-15).

☐ Enter the search and replace patterns. The result should be similar to Figure 3-16.

* OA `F2`
* office automation `F2`

WordPerfect uses the F2 key, not the ENTER key, to signify the end of the search pattern. This allows the user to include a hard carriage return in the search string, if necessary. If lower case characters are entered, WordPerfect matches both lower and upper case occurrences.

If upper case characters are entered, WordPerfect matches upper case occurrences only. To search for a word, tap the space bar before and after both the search and replace strings.

```
To:        All personnel
From:      Stephen Garrity, VP Administration
Re:        Computer training and office automation

        The implementation of office automation is changing the
working environment and challenging us all to become more computer
literate. Therefore, a computer training program has been
established to teach office automation skills. Please take
advantage of this excellent opportunity. Contact Marion Reyes in
personnel for further information.
```

Figure 3-16   After replacing "OA" with "office automation"

Step 8: Centering, Boldfacing, Underlining Text

WordPerfect provides two methods to boldface and/or underline parts of the text for emphasis. Which method you use depends on whether the text already exists or is about to be entered.

If text is already present, you must first mark the text to be underlined or boldfaced. After the text is marked (using the BLOCK command, ALT-F4), tap the appropriate function key to add bold or underline. This is the marked text method.

To boldface or underline text that is about to be entered, first tap the appropriate function key, enter the text then tap the function key again. For example, to boldface the title MEMORANDUM, tap F6, type MEMORANDUM and tap F6 again. The first F6 turns boldface on, the second F6 turns boldface off. This is called the in-line method.

Mr. Garrity decides to add a title to his memo and underline the name of the contact person, Marion Reyes. He uses the in-line method to center and boldface the title and the marked text method to underline Marion Reyes.

❐   Position the cursor at the top of the document, add a blank line, then reposition the cursor at the top again.

   * | HOME | | HOME | ↑
   *   ↵   ↑

❐   Use the in-line method to center and boldface the title.

* SHIFT - F6
* F6

The cursor moves to the center of the line and boldface is turned on (the Pos indicator changes color or intensity to signify that bold is on). Enter the title "MEMORANDUM".

* **MEMORANDUM**

Turn boldface off then tap the ENTER key to add a blank line beneath the heading.

* F6 ↵

The Pos indicator returns to its original color or intensity.

☐ Use the marked text method to underline "Marion Reyes". To mark text, first place the cursor at the beginning or one character to the right of the text to be marked. Next, tap ALT-F4 to activate the block marker and use the cursor control keys to pass the cursor through the text. If the cursor is placed at the beginning of the text, once blocking is activated, the cursor will jump to the first occurrence of the next key that is tapped. In the following example, the cursor is placed at the beginning of Marion Reyes's name and blocking is activated. When the "s" key is tapped, the cursor jumps to the end of her name (the first occurrence of "s"). Note: make sure that Caps Lock is not on when tapping the "s" in the next activity. After "Marion Reyes" is blocked, F8 is tapped to underline the marked text.

* *(position cursor on the "M" of "Marion")*
* ALT - F4
* s *(cursor moves to the s at the end of "Reyes")*
* F8

☐ Save the current version of the memo (see Step 5).

* F10
* ↵
* Y

Figure 3-17 displays the completed memo.

```
                    MEMORANDUM


    To:         All personnel
    From:       Stephen Garrity, VP Administration
    Re:         Computer training and office automation

       The implementation of office automation is changing the
    working environment and challenging us all to become more computer
    literate.  Therefore, a computer training program has been
    established to teach office automation skills. Please take
    advantage of this excellent opportunity. Contact Marion Reyes in
    personnel for further information.
```

Figure 3-17 Vice President Garrity's completed memo

Step 9: Retrieving a Document

When a document is retrieved, WordPerfect enters the document at the current cursor position. That means that if the cursor is currently in another document, WordPerfect will place the retrieved document within the document currently on the screen. Unless you want to use retrieve to combine two documents, always clear the screen before retrieving a document.

In this step, we will clear the screen, then retrieve the saved version of the memo. To clear the screen, use WordPerfect's exit routine.

☐ Clear the screen before retrieving "memo". "Exit" from the current document to clear the screen (see Figure 3-18).

* F7
* N

Figure 3-18 "Save" option in the exit routine

The text has not been modified since the last save, therefore you do not need to save the memo. Tap ENTER to answer "no" to the "Exit WP?" prompt (see Figure 3-19).

* ↵

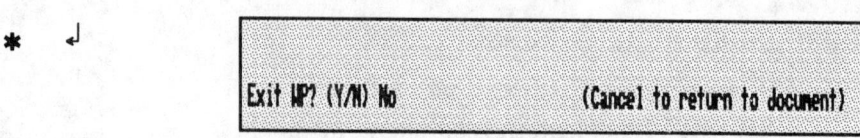

Figure 3-19 "Exit" option in the exit routine

Since you did not exit WordPerfect, you are returned to a "clean screen."

☐ Retrieve "memo" (see Figure 3-20).

* ⌈SHIFT⌉ - ⌈F10⌉
* memo ↵

The "memo" document should now be on the screen with its name listed in the lower left corner. Again, notice that the screen was cleared before document retrieval. Otherwise the retrieved document becomes part of the old document.

```
Document to be retrieved:
```

Figure 3-20 "Retrieve a document" prompt

Step 10: Printing a Document

WordPerfect is a "what you see is what you get" or WYSIWYG (pronounced WIZ-e-wig) package; that is, at any given point in a word processing session, **what you see** displayed on the screen is very similar in appearance to **what you get** when the document is printed. WordPerfect's work screen display is not exact because some print features, such as underlining and proportionately spaced print, cannot be displayed on the monitor. To compensate, WordPerfect 5.0 includes a new feature that accurately displays WYSIWYG, the View Document feature.

This step uses the "view" feature to display the document, then produces a printed version of the memo.

☐ Open the print menu and preview the printed version of the memo by using the "view" feature (see Figure 3-21).

* ⌈SHIFT⌉ - ⌈F7⌉
* v

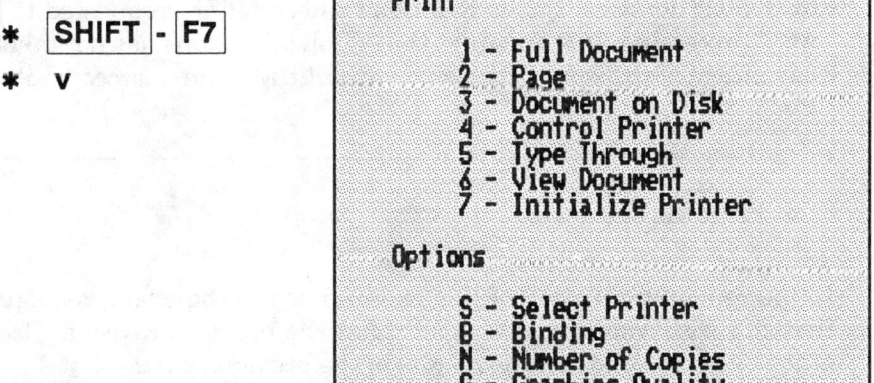

Figure 3-21 Print menu

Tap 1, 2 or 3 to view the a 100% enlargement, a 200% enlargement or the entire page. The view document display is very close to what will actually appear on the printout.

☐ Tap the CANCEL key to return to the Print Menu.

✴ F1

If you want to return directly to the document from the view document screen, tap the EXIT key (F7).

☐ Print a hardcopy of the memo.

✴ F

Notice that although the right justification does not appear on the screen, the view screen and the printed document are right justified. To print a document without first viewing the document, tap SHIFT-F7 then F.

Step 11: Practice

Exercise A: Create and edit the following memo.

✴ Clear the screen (F7 N N) then enter the following text:

Too Much Paper!

Last year, the Public Relations Department's paper budget was overrun by $350. Therefore, Public Relations personnel are requested to learn word processing. It is apparent that Public Relations has not taken full advantage of the word processing capabilities of its microcomputers.

✴ Print the document.

In the remaining portion of this exercise, make the changes cumulative; that is, revise whatever text is left after the previous revision. Each part of the exercise builds on the results of the previous part.

✴ Insert the word "all" before "Public" in the second sentence.

✴ Center the title.

* At the end of the second sentence, add "by the end of the month". Use the move command to move the second sentence to the end of the document. Print the document.

* Underline "all" and boldface the title.

* Use the Page option of the move command to produce another copy of the entire document just below the original. Place a required page break (CTRL- ↵) between the two copies of the document. Print the document.

* Use the search and replace command to replace all occurrences of "Public Relations" in the second document with "Research and Development". Revise $350 in the second document to be $525.

* Save the document as PAPER.

* Print the document.

Exercise B: Create a memo to the faculty.

* Enter the following memo from Professor Gladstone.

To: Faculty
From: Professor Gladstone, Chairperson
Re: Coffee breaks

It has been brought to my attention that the secretarial coffeepot in the main office has become a popular meeting place for faculty members. In fact, so many faculty now participate in these coffee breaks that the secretaries' working area is overrun 15 minutes out of every hour.

I am pleased that you get along with each other so well, but we must consider our hard-working secretaries. Therefore, I have set up a new coffeepot in room A143 and encourage you to meet there.

---

* At the beginning of the memo add the heading TOP PRIORITY and make it boldfaced and centered. Insert two blank lines between the heading and the line "To: Faculty".

* Underline "room A143" in the last line of the memo.

* Save the memo as COFFEE.

* Print the memo.

* Use the search and replace feature to replace all occurrences of "coffee" with "tea".

* Save the revised memo as TEA.

* Print the revised memo.

Step 12: Exiting WordPerfect and Terminating the Session

☐ If necessary, save your current document.

☐ Exit WordPerfect.

    ✱ F7

As a safety precaution, you are prompted to save the document on which you are working. If any revisions have been made since the document was last saved, answer "Y" to the prompt; otherwise the revisions will be lost.

    ✱ **N**
    ✱ **Y**

☐ Take your data diskette out of drive A and turn off the computer.

Session Two

Margins, Tabs and Line Draw

The application of word processing software is limited only by your imagination. Sally Marcio is known for her parties. She recently moved into a new home, and what a great opportunity to celebrate. To announce her party, she uses word processing software to create an invitation (see Figure 3-22). This session demonstrates the procedure that Sally follows to create the invitation.

If WordPerfect is not currently running, refer to Session One, Step 1 in this chapter to start your computer and load WordPerfect. Confirm that your data diskette is in drive A and that drive A is the active drive.

In this session you will learn how to:

- ◆ Use ESC to repeat keystrokes
- ◆ Use line draw to create graphics
- ◆ Delete and add tab markers
- ◆ Use the format menu
- ◆ Reset margins within a document

Step 1: Preparing the Heading

Sally begins her invitation with an eye-catching heading. She uses line draw to create a box and typeover mode to enter text inside the box and on either sides of the box. Sally uses the ESC repeat feature to save keystrokes while drawing the box. WordPerfect allows all characters and certain features to be repeated a specified number of times using ESC.

❐ Tap ESC to display the message "n =", enter the number of repetitions desired, and select the character or WordPerfect feature to be repeated. The default number of repetitions is 8, but other numbers may be entered as demonstrated below. Use the ESC feature to position the cursor at the upper left corner of the box.

* ESC
* 22 SPACE

The cursor should be at position Ln 1", Pos 3.2".

```
                          IT'S
           Yea!!         PARTY              Whoopee!!
                          TIME
```

"Can it possibly be as good as the last one?"
                              -Lester Rich, Noted Party Critic

"Any Marcio party is a MUST ATTEND!!"
                              -Veronica Sensatia, Society Editor

"I mean, wow."
                              -Sheila Valley, Party Goer

"Sally Marcio's parties definitely belong in the big leagues."
                              -Playbill Magazine

           Where: Sally Marcio's **NEW** Residence
                          5426 Maple Avenue

           Date: Saturday, May 9th

           Time: 8:00 p.m. to whenever

                             RULES
     +-+-++-+-++-+-++-+-++-+-++-+-++-+-++-+-++-+-++-+-++-+-+
     Become your favorite fantasy character. The character
     may be real or fictional but you must **be** the character.
     Dress like, walk like, talk like, eat like, behave like
     your fantasy for a night!
     +-+-++-+-++-+-++-+-++-+-++-+-++-+-++-+-++-+-++-+-++-+-+

          What to bring: An active imagination

               * * * * All refreshments provided * * * *

RSVP: 555-7312

Figure 3-22   Sally Marcio's party flyer

☐ Open the Screen menu and select the Line Draw option.

* `CTRL` - `F3` L

☐ Select single line.

* 1

Other border settings are available.

☐ The box is twenty characters wide and six characters high. Use the ESC feature to help draw the box.

* `ESC`
* 20 → *(draw top)*
* `ESC`
* 6 ↓ *(draw right side)*
* `ESC`
* 20 ← *(draw bottom)*
* `ESC`
* 6 ↑ *(draw left side)*

☐ Return to text-entry mode.

* `F7`

☐ After drawing the box, change from insert to typeover mode to add words on each side of the box. Typeover mode does not disturb the position of the box or the heading.

* `INS`
* *(position cursor in Ln 1.33", Pos 4")*
* IT'S ↓ ← ← ← ←
* PARTY ↓ ← ← ← ← ←
* TIME
* *(position cursor in Ln 1.5", Pos 2")*
* Yea!!
* `HOME` → *(position cursor at end of line, Pos 5.3")*
* `SPACE` *(6 times to Pos 5.9")*

* **Whoopee!!** HOME ↓ ↵

☐ Leave four blank lines below the box and return to insert mode.

* ↵ *(4 times)*
* INS

Step 2: Using Tabs and Adjusting Margins

Tab settings represent the character positions to which the cursor will move when you tap the TAB key. For a given line, the cursor will be positioned at the first setting (e.g., the 1.5" column) the first time you tap TAB and at the second setting (e.g., the 2" column) the second time, and so on. The default TAB settings are preset at .5" (half-inch) intervals.

Sally adds comments from fictitious critics. Reset the tabs twice while creating this invitation--once before entering the four critics' reviews and again before entering the date and time information.

☐ Delete the existing tab settings by displaying the tab ruler and tapping the delete-to-end-of-line keystroke sequence (CTRL-END).

* SHIFT - F8

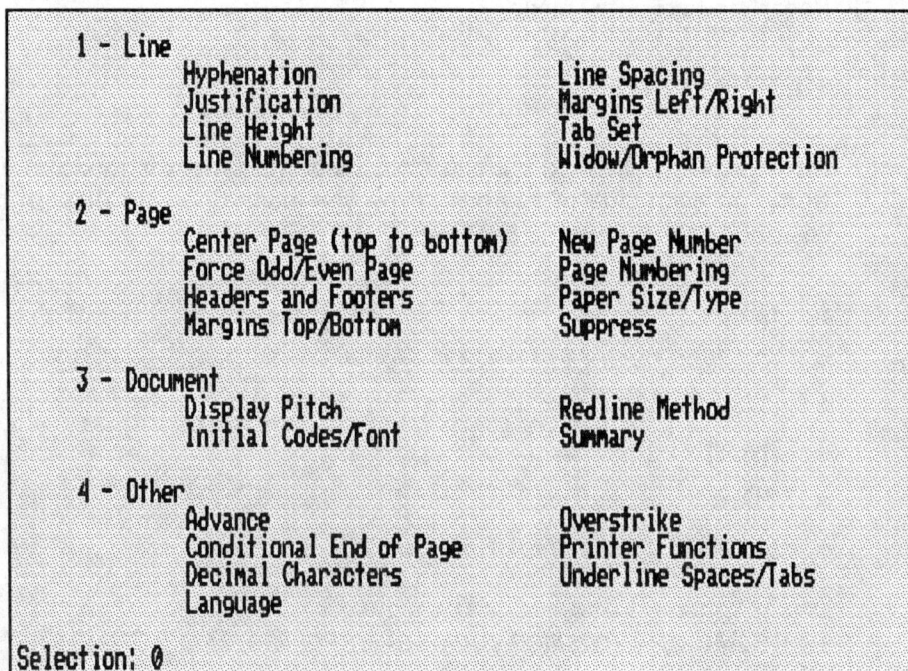

Figure 3-23 WordPerfect's Format Menu, a collection of four sub-menus

WordPerfect 5.0 combines several menus that appeared individually in earlier WordPerfect versions. The keystroke combination SHIFT-F8 displays a full screen format menu (see Figure 3-23). The menu is divided into four submenus: 1 Line, 2 Page, 3 Document, and 4 Other.

* **L T**
* **CTRL** - **END**

☐ Set the tab stop for entering the critics' names.

* **4** ↵
* **F7** **F7**

☐ Enter the comments.

* **"Can it possibly be as good as the last one?"** ↵
* **TAB** **-Lester Rich, Noted Party Critic** ↵ ↵

Follow the same procedure to enter the other comments (see Figure 3-22).

☐ Follow the reviews with four blank lines.

* ↵ *(4 times)*

☐ Add another tab setting to the format line.

* **SHIFT** - **F8** **L T 2** ↵ **F7** **F7**

☐ Key in the location, date, and time information. Use the in-line text enhancement method to underline and boldface "NEW".

* **TAB** **Where:** **TAB** **Sally Marcio's** **SPACE**
* **F6** **F8** **NEW** **F8** **F6** **Residence** ↵
* **TAB** **TAB** **5426 Maple Avenue** ↵ ↵

Follow the same procedure to key in the date and time (see Figure 3-22).

☐ Add three blank lines below the time entry.

* ↵ *(3 times)*

☐ Sally wants to have a theme party so she includes rules in the invitation. To set the rules section apart from the invitation section, narrow the margins and identify the rules section with visually distinctive lines. Begin by centering the subheading "RULES".

* SHIFT-F6 **RULES** ↵

☐ Reset the margins to left equals 1.5" and right equals 1.55".

* SHIFT-F8 **L M**
* **1.5** ↵
* **1.55** ↵ F7

☐ Use the search and replace feature to place two rows of alternating plus (+) and minus (-) signs in the document (see Figure 3-25). The rules section will be entered between these lines. Repeat the +-+-+ pattern eleven times to fill a line. Save keystrokes by keying in the letter "x" eleven times on each line (see Figure 3-24) and then replacing each x with the pattern. Use the ESC feature to enter the eleven x's.

* ESC
* **11 x** ↵ ↵
* ESC
* **11 x**

Move the cursor to the first x of the first row.

* HOME ← ↑ ↑

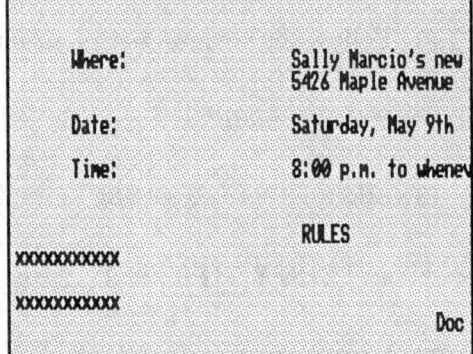
Figure 3-24 Party "rules" boundary entry

Replace each x with the pattern. Notice that the minus sign appears as [-] in a search pattern.

* ALT-F2
* **N**
* **x** F2
* **+-+-+** F2

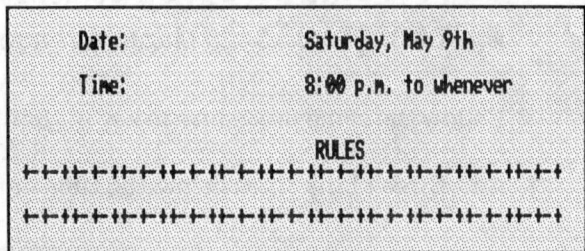
Figure 3-25 "Rules" boundaries after search and replace

☐ Move the cursor to the line between the plus-and-minus lines.

* ↑

☐ Enter the rules. Do not tap the ENTER key because the sentences wrap automatically. Use the in-line text enhancement method to underline "be".

* **Become your favorite fantasy character. The character may be real or fictional but you must** [F8] **be** [F8] **the character. Dress like, walk like, talk like, eat like, behave like your fantasy for a night!**

☐ Move the cursor to the line below the last patterned line.

* ↓ [HOME] → ↵

☐ Reset the margins again before entering the remainder of the invitation.

* [SHIFT]-[F8] L M
* 1 ↵
* 1 ↵ [F7]

The tabs remain set to 2" and 4".

☐ Add three blank lines below the **rules** section.

* ↵ *(3 times)*

☐ Enter the remainder of the text to complete the invitation.

* [TAB] What to bring: [TAB] An active imagination ↵ ↵
* [TAB] **** All refreshments provided ****
* ↵ *(5 times)*
* RSVP: 555-7312 ↵

Step 3: Saving and Printing the Party Invitation

☐ Save the document.

WP: Session Two 107

* ⬚F10⬚ **party** ↵

☐ Print the invitation.

* ⬚SHIFT⬚ - ⬚F7⬚ F

Step 4: Practice

Exercise A: Use WordPerfect to design and compile a personal resume.

* Use appropriate word processing features to enhance the presentation of the resume. At a minimum, include these elements: your name, address, telephone number, education history (dates, school, degree), work history (dates, position title and brief description of work, employer, employer address), and a personal section (interests, special achievements, and so on).

* Print the resume.

Step 5: Exiting WordPerfect and Terminating the Session

Save your current document and exit WordPerfect (see Session One, Step 12).

☐ If necessary, save your current document.

☐ Exit WordPerfect.

* ⬚F7⬚

As a safety precaution, you are prompted to save the document on which you are working. If any revisions have been made since the document was last saved, answer "Y" to the prompt; otherwise the revisions will be lost.

* N
* Y

☐ Take your data diskette out of drive A and turn off the computer.

Session Three

Spell-check and Thesaurus

WordPerfect can check your spelling and suggest alternate words. These features are called the spell-checker and the thesaurus. Use both features to edit the end-of-semester remarks of Professor Phred Verbose.

WordPerfect also has an excellent footnote creation feature which facilitates the creation and maintenance of footnotes and endnotes. Professor Verbose uses the footnote feature to document his idea sources.

If WordPerfect is not currently running, refer to Session One, Step 1 in this chapter to start your computer and load WordPerfect. Confirm that your data diskette is in drive A and that drive A is the active drive.

In this session you will learn to:

- ❖ Use the spell-checker
- ❖ Use the thesaurus
- ❖ Save a file under a new name (preserving the original)
- ❖ Create and edit footnotes
- ❖ Select italics text appearance

Step 1: Spell-checking a Document

> On this gala ocassion of our last class meeting, before you beat an ignminious retreat to the beaches immacullately atired, breathing a sigh of relief at at your narrow escape from the fatefull scene of the great learning that has occurred, let me take this opportuneity to offer a floral tribute witha few well chosan words about a class, obviously second to none, that disspelled the idea that ignorence is bliss and hastily summoned their infinate capacity to marshall their resources and by hook or crook conquered in due course everything computer that with brute force was thrown at, sometimes amidst a veil of tears sometimes picked up in a twinkaling of an eye but often -- particullarly on Mondey mornings -- moved from the sublime to the ridiculaus as I, your unempeacheble authority, against overwhellming odds shifted into high gear and part and parcal and with the patience of Job said "Keepp all options open, for in the nick of time your will find your knowladge inextricabaly linked to the auspiciaus moments that lie ahead."

Figure 3-26 Professor Verbose's unedited end-of-semester comments

Professor Phred Verbose prepared a rough draft of remarks that he plans to deliver to his students on the last day of class before summer vacation.

- ☐ Professor Verbose is notorious for his bad spelling and inadequate typing ability; therefore, there may be spelling mistakes in this draft. Enter the draft (see Figure 3-26), even with mistakes. (Alternative: retrieve the file VERBOSE.TXT from the Example Files Diskette, but make sure to re-insert your data diskette before continuing to the next activity.)

- ☐ Save the document twice, once as VERBOSE .TXT and once as VERBOSE1.TXT.

  * [F10] verbose.txt ↵
  * [F10] verbose1.txt ↵

Notice that the name of the document (lower left corner of the monitor screen) is now VERBOSE1.TXT. We will edit this copy to retain the original.

- ☐ Initiate the spell-checker to spell-check VERBOSE1.TXT (see Figure 3-27).

  * [CTRL]-[F2]

```
Check: 1 Word; 2 Page; 3 Document; 4 New Sup. Dictionary; 5 Look Up; 6 Count: 0
```

Figure 3-27 Spell-check menu

- ☐ Select the "Document" option from the spell-check menu (see Figure 3-27).

  * D

WordPerfect highlights the first unrecognized word (probably "ocassion"), suggests optional spellings, and displays a menu.

- ☐ Tap the letter next to the correct spelling to replace "ocassion" with "occasion".

  * B *(occasion)*

Spell-Checking Options

As you spell-check the remainder of the document, you may need to select options from the spell menu. The options are:

1) **Skip once:** Spell-checking continues; the Speller stops at the next occurrence of the word.
2) **Skip:** Spell-checking continues; the word is ignored for the rest of the document.
3) **Add:** The word is saved in the supplementary dictionary and spell-checking continues (do not use this option at this time).
4) **Edit:** You can correct the spelling, then tap F7 (exit) to continue spell-checking.
5) **Look up:** You can look up a word in the main dictionary that matches a pattern and replace the word not found with the correct spelling.

Continue the above procedure for each misspelled word until you reach the end of the document. The five spell check options are described in the box at the top of the next page.

❐ Save the edited version of VERBOSE1.TXT, replacing the unedited version.

* F10
* ↵
* y

Step 2: Using the On-Line Thesaurus

Professor Verbose is not satisfied with the word "gala" in the last sentence of the memo and wants to examine other voluble possibilities.

❐ Employ the on-line thesaurus feature to find another word for "gala". The cursor must be on the desired word before opening the thesaurus (see Figure 3-28).

* ALT - F1

WordPerfect reads the word at the cursor (i.e., gala) and suggests alternative synonyms (see Figure 3-28).

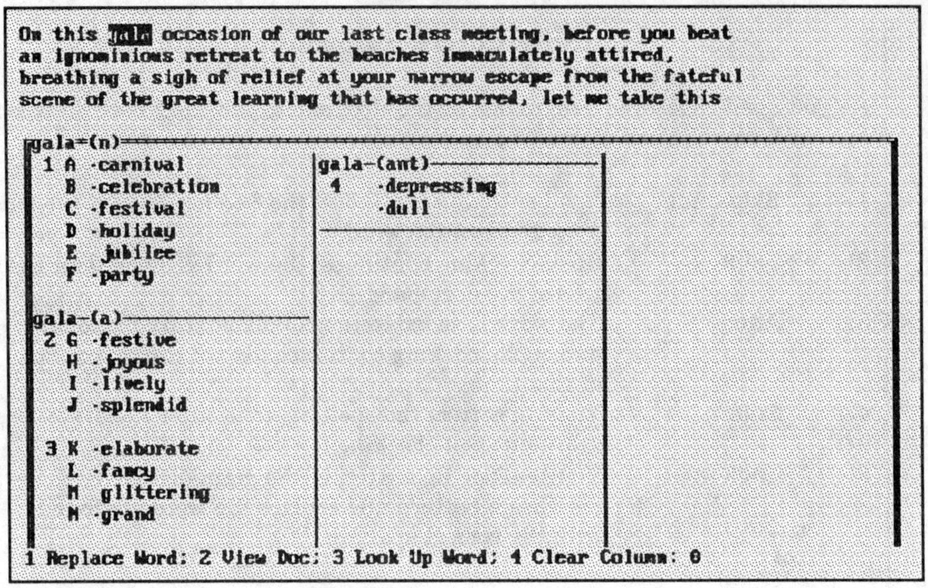

```
On this gala occasion of our last class meeting, before you beat
an ignominious retreat to the beaches immaculately attired,
breathing a sigh of relief at your narrow escape from the fateful
scene of the great learning that has occurred, let me take this
┌gala-(n)─────────────────┬─────────────────────────────────
│  1 A ·carnival          │gala-(ant)───────
│    B ·celebration       │  4   ·depressing
│    C ·festival          │      ·dull
│    D ·holiday           ├─────────────────
│    E ·jubilee
│    F ·party
├gala-(a)─────────────────
│  2 G ·festive
│    H ·joyous
│    I ·lively
│    J ·splendid
│
│  3 K ·elaborate
│    L ·fancy
│    M ·glittering
│    N ·grand
│
1 Replace Word; 2 View Doc; 3 Look Up Word; 4 Clear Column: 0
```

Figure 3-28 WordPerfect's Thesaurus screen

▢ Not satisfied with the options, the Professor wants to see more. Select the adjective "lively".

∗   I   *(select the adjective "lively")*

▢ After examining the new set of options, Prof. Verbose decides to replace "gala" with the word "spirited".

∗   1   *(word replacement key)*
∗   H

You are returned to the work screen.

Step 3: Creating Footnotes

Footnotes are often used to indicate the source of facts and quotes. Footnotes may also be used to provide additional material that, though relevant, would interrupt the smooth flow of the main text.

To create a footnote, place the cursor at the location where the footnote number should appear, tap CTRL-F7, type the footnote text and tap F7. Footnote numbering is handled automatically by WordPerfect. WordPerfect also devotes suitable space at the bottom of each page for footnotes and automatically renumbers when footnotes are deleted or new footnotes are added.

Professor Verbose's favorite book is *Advanced Prolixity, Ideas and Phrases for Dynamic Communication* by Randolph K. Noitall. The professor meticulously footnotes every idea borrowed from the Noitall tome. In this step we follow Professor Verbose's procedure as he creates three footnotes: two book footnote references and one additional material reference. This step demonstrates footnote creation, insertion and editing.

☐ Professor Verbose creates a footnote to reference the idea "ignorance is bliss."

* *(position the cursor immediately to the right of "bliss")*
* |CTRL| - |F7|
* F
* C

The footnote editing screen appears. Type the footnote text, selecting italics for the book's name and tap F7 to return to the document.

* **Randolph K. Noitall,** |SPACE|
* |CTRL| - |F8| A I
* **Expanded Prolixity, Ideas and Phrases for Dynamic Communication,** |SPACE|
* |CTRL| - |F8| N
* **2d ed. (Englewood Cliffs, N.J.; Prentice-Hall, 1990), p. 542.**
* |F7|

The "in-line" method was used to italicize the book's title. Italics was chosen, the title was entered then the text was returned to "normal."

☐ The quoted phrase at the end of the remarks is also from Mr. Noitall's book so Professor Verbose creates a second footnote to reference the quote. Enter and italicize "ibid" to reference the same book cited in the immediately preceding footnote.

* *(position the cursor at the end of the document)*
* |CTRL| - |F7|
* F
* C
* |CTRL| - |F8| A I
* **ibid,** |SPACE|

* ☐ CTRL - F8 N
* p. 351.
* F7

☐ As he reads his speech, Professor Verbose notices that his students need "further elucidation" about the phrase "sublime to the ridiculous". Since he will be handing out autographed copies of his remarks, he decides to include another footnote.

* *(position the cursor immediately to the right of "ridiculous")*
* CTRL - F7 F C

Notice that the current footnote is number two. WordPerfect will automatically renumber the previous number two footnote to become number three.

* **Leaping the generation gap, I was aware that the vast majority arrived terror-stricken when being placed in close proximity with advanced computational technology. But we took the bull by the horns, engaged in an epic struggle and for the most part were eminently successful.**
* F7

When you first return to the document, both the new footnote and the last footnote will appear to be numbered "2." Move the cursor to the end of the document to change the appearance of the last footnote to "3."

☐ "op. cit" is used in footnotes to reference a previously cited book that does not appear in the footnote immediately preceding. Since a new footnote has been placed between the two book reference footnotes, the second book footnote must be edited to delete the "ibid" reference and replace it with "op. cit."

* CTRL - F7 F
* E 3 ↵
* →
* Noitall, SPACE →
* op. cit.
* DEL *(4 times)*
* F7

Endnotes are created and edited in the same way as footnotes. Endnote placement codes are placed in the document to signify the printing location of all previous endnotes. If no endnote placement code is present or endnotes exist between the last placement code and the end of the document, endnotes that have not been printed will be printed at the end of the document.

❐ Save then print the document.

* `F10` ↵ y
* `SHIFT` - `F7` F

Step 4: Practice

Exercise A: Write a cover letter to accompany the resume you created in Session Two, Step 4.

* Address the letter to Mrs. Peggy Peoples, VP of Personnel, Ellis Enterprises, P.O. Box 923481, Dallas, TX, 75208. In the letter, inform Mrs. Peoples of your availability, describe the type of work you are seeking, mention that your resume is enclosed, and state that references will be supplied upon request.
* Use the thesaurus function to enhance your letter.
* Use the spell-checker to check your cover letter for misspelled words and typographical errors.
* Print the cover letter.

Exercise B: Create a multi-page note to be sent to Professor Verbose from his assistant.

* Retrieve the uncorrected version of Professor Verbose's remarks, VERBOSE.TXT (see Session Four).
* Insert five blank lines at the top of the page, position the cursor at the beginning of the document, and add the following note from his assistant.

Dear Professor Verbose:
As I typed this, my word processor detected a few spelling errors. I took the liberty of fixing these errors (I hope you do not mind). The corrected version is on page 2.
These are the most moving comments I have ever read. Your students are indeed lucky.
Your Assistant,

* Add your name below the words "Your Assistant" and save the document, replacing the previous version of VERBOSE.TXT.
* Print both VERBOSE.TXT and VERBOSE1.TXT, each on a separate page.

Exercise C: With the help of the thesaurus function, edit Professor Phred Verbose's remarks. Make the remarks more understandable or less understandable, as you wish. Just have fun with it.

* Retrieve the spell-checked version of the speech (that is, VERBOSE1.TXT) from your data disk (see Session Four) and edit it using the thesaurus function.
* Save your vastly improved version of the speech as VERBOSE2.TXT.
* Print VERBOSE2.TXT.

Step 5: Exiting WordPerfect and Terminating the Session

Save your current document and exit WordPerfect (see Session One, Step 12).

☐ If necessary, save your current document.

☐ Exit WordPerfect.

* `F7`

As a safety precaution, you are prompted to save the document on which you are working. If any revisions have been made since the document was last saved, answer "Y" to the prompt; otherwise the revisions will be lost.

* N
* Y

☐ Take your data diskette out of drive A and turn off the computer.

Session Four

Merging

Often called mail-merge, merging is the ability to type one letter and create numerous personalized copies by reading data from a separate name and address file. Merging requires the creation of two files. The primary file is the letter (memo, contract, boilerplate, etc.) that directs the merging process. The primary file contains codes that call for data from the separate secondary merge file.

For example, George Chew, Chief Executive Officer of Chew & Chew, Inc., dictates a letter to his secretary, Alyson Peabody, announcing the upcoming board of directors meeting. Alyson uses word processing software to create the letter. Instead of typing a separate letter to each board member, though, she creates one letter placing merge codes at the location in the letter where each board member's name, company name, and address will appear. The names and addresses of the board members are permanently saved in a second file (the secondary merge file). Alyson merges the primary file (the letter) with the secondary file (the board members' names and addresses), and creates a separate personalized letter for each board member.

This session demonstrates the procedure that Alyson follows. Figure 3-34 displays the completed letter sent to Robert Petersen.

If WordPerfect is not currently running, refer to Session One, Step 1 in this chapter to start your computer and load WordPerfect. Confirm that your data diskette is in drive A and that drive A is the active drive.

In this session you will learn to:

- Create a primary and secondary merge file
- Use merge codes
- Merge two documents
- Print individual pages of a document

Step 1: Creating the Name and Address File

Alyson will merge a name and address file with a letter file, which is created in "Step 2: Creating the Letter File." The name and address file contains a separate record for each board member. Each record contains these fields: name field, company field, address field, and salutation field. When creating this file, function keys are used to enter merge codes at the end of each field and each record. This address file becomes the secondary merge file when the final letters are produced.

☐ Enter the name for record one (see Figure 3-29).

* **Robert Petersen** F9

Tapping F9 places the end-of-field merge code at the end of Mr. Petersen's name and positions the cursor at the beginning of the next line.

```
Robert Petersen^R
```

Figure 3-29 First entry to the name and address file

☐ Next, enter the company name.

* **Petersen, Lawson & Pritchard** F9

☐ Enter the address.

* **470 Fifth Avenue, Suite 1124** ↵
* **New York, NY 10021** F9

Notice that a field may contain more than one line of text.

☐ Enter the fourth and final field, the salutation, and enter the end of record merge code (see (Figure 3-30).

* **Bob** F9

* SHIFT - F9 E

```
Robert Petersen^R
Petersen, Lawson & Pritchard ^R
470 Fifth Avenue, Suite 1124
New York, NY 10021^R
Bob^R
^E
=====================================
```

Figure 3-30 Robert Petersen's record

Tapping SHIFT-F9 displays the merge code menu. Merge code ^E marks the end of the record. When it is chosen, WordPerfect enters the merge code followed by a required page break (designated by a line of equals signs).

☐ See Figure 3-31 for a listing of the other board members, and use the preceding steps to add their records to the file. Remember to tap ENTER and not F9 after the first line of the address field. Dr. Dolgin's record contains an additional line in field number 2, so tap ENTER there as well.

WP: Session Four 118

```
Liduina Marcellus^R
Arthur Rindow Products, Inc.^R
1400 Holly Street
Denver, CO 80205^R
Liduina^R
^E
================================================
Edmond Dolgin, M.D.^R
Radiology Department
Mt. Hope Hospital^R
325 Center Avenue
Evanston, IL 60202^R
Ed^R
^E
================================================
Valerie Hamilton^R
Unified Pictures, Inc.^R
4785-32 Paseo Drive
Hollywood, CA 90023^R
Valerie^R
^E
```

Figure 3-31 Additional name and address file entries

❐ Save the file and clear the screen.

* **F7** Y
* **address.sf** ↵
* **N**

The .sf is a user-added extension that identifies "address.sf" as a secondary file. The extension is not required by WordPerfect, it is merely a good working habit. When you view a list of files you have created, any file with an .sf extension will immediately be recognized as a secondary merge file.

Step 2: Creating the Letter File

Alyson creates a new file that contains the letter that is to be sent to each member of the board. She includes merge commands in the heading and the salutation to call in text from the address file that was created in Step 1.

❐ The date insertion merge code (^D) causes the current date to be inserted in the letter (see Figure 3-32). Because Alyson is planning to use Chew & Chew, Inc. letterhead stationery, no other heading information is needed.

* **SHIFT** - **F6**
* **SHIFT** - **F9** *(call up merge code menu)*
* **D** *(select merge code)* ↵

The ENTER positions the cursor at the beginning of the next line.

☐ Insert four blank lines.

* ↵ *(4 times)*

☐ Enter the merge code that will retrieve information from the first field of each record, that is, the person's name (see Figure 3-32).

* **SHIFT** - **F9**
* **F 1** ↵ ↵

The last ENTER positions the cursor at the beginning of the next line.

```
                              ^D



^F1^
```

Figure 3-32 "Date" and "Field 1" merge code entries

☐ Repeat the preceding two steps to insert ^F2^ on the second line and ^F3^ on the third line (see Figure 3-33).

☐ Insert a blank line before the salutation and then enter the salutation and its respective field-number merge code (see Figure 3-33).

* ↵
* *(cursor should be on line 2.5)*
* **Dear** **SPACE**
* **SHIFT** - **F9** **F 4** ↵
* **:** ↵
* ↵

The last ENTER inserts a
blank line after the salutation.

```
^F1^
^F2^
^F3^

Dear ^F4^:
```

Figure 3-33 "Letter" heading showing the field merge codes

☐ Enter the body of the letter. The style is a modified block form.

* **It is time again for our annual planning meeting. We will convene in the boardroom at corporate headquarters at 10:00 a.m. on the 22nd.** ↵ ↵
* **Accommodations have been arranged for you at the Windsor Hotel. You are invited to stay an extra day if you wish to view our Dallas operations.** ↵ ↵
* **The following topics will appear on the agenda:** ↵ ↵
* **TAB - A proposed 2-for-1 stock split.** ↵ ↵
* **TAB - First year domestic sales of the Tough Turkey.** ↵ ↵

Because the final topic has several lines, use the indent feature (F4) to indent the left margin to the next tab and wrap characters automatically to the new setting. Do not tap ENTER until the end of the sentence. The indent feature remains active until ENTER is tapped.

☐ You will need to add an additional tab marker at position 1.7" so that the characters can be made to wrap to this second tab setting.

* SHIFT - F8 L T 1.7 ↵ F7
* ↵ ↵

☐ Enter the third point on the agenda. F4 is tapped once after the hyphen causing word wrap to indent to this temporary left margin.

* **TAB - F4 Strong foreign sales of Chocolate Leather suggest the possibility of building a CL manufacturing plant in France.** ↵ ↵
* **I look forward to seeing you at the meeting.** ↵ ↵
* **Sincerely,**
* ↵ *(4 times)*

* **George Chew, CEO** ↵
* **Chew & Chew Enterprises** ↵

☐ Save the letter and clear the screen.

* [F7] Y
* **letter.pf** ↵
* N

Like the .sf extension, the .pf is a user-added extension that identifies "letter.pf" as a primary file.

Step 3: Merging Two Files

To create a finished letter for each board member, Alyson merges the "letter.pf" and "address.sf" files into a "merge.ltr" file. Figure 3-34 illustrates the printed letter sent to Robert Petersen.

☐ Start the merge process.

* [CTRL] - [F9]
* M
* **letter.pf** ↵
* **address.sf** ↵

The merge creates a new document that is four pages long. Each page contains a board member's name and address followed by the letter.

☐ Position the cursor at the beginning of the document and view the heading of each letter by tapping PGDN.

* [HOME] [HOME] ↑
* [PGDN] *(3 times)*

PGDN moves the cursor to the top of each successive page in the document. Use the up or down arrow keys to examine portions of the letters not shown on the screen.

☐ Name and save the new file as "merge.ltr".

* [F10] **merge.ltr** ↵

```
                    September 30, 1990


Robert Petersen
Petersen, Lawson & Pritchard
470 Fifth Avenue, Suite 1124
New York, NY 10021

Dear Bob:

It is time again for our annual planning meeting. We will convene
in the boardroom at corporate headquarters at 10:00 a.m. on the
22nd.

Accommodations have been arranged for you at the Windsor Hotel.
You are invited to stay an extra day if you wish to view our Dallas
operations.

The following topics will appear on the agenda:

     - A proposed 2-for-1 stock split

     - First year domestic sales of the Tough Turkey.

     - Strong foreign sales of Chocolate Leather suggest the
       possibility of building a CL manufacturing plant in France.

I look forward to seeing you at the meeting.

Sincerely,



George Chew, CEO
Chew & Chew Enterprises
```

Figure 3-34 Merge file's first page (this is too long for most monitors)

Step 4: Printing the Documents

Alyson uses Chew & Chew letterhead stationery to print the four letters. She uses the "Page" option in the print menu to print one page at a time, inserting the stationery as needed.

☐ Select the Page option of the print menu. This causes one page of a multipage document to be printed. The page that is printed is the one that contains the cursor. Print Dr. Dolgin's letter, the third page, by moving the cursor to page 3, calling up the print menu, and selecting the Page option.

   * `CTRL` - `HOME` 3
   * `SHIFT` - `F7` P

Step 5: Practice

Exercise A: Use merging to address the cover letter created in Session Three, Step 4 to three additional companies.

* Create an employer name and address file that contains Ellis's address (see Session Three, Step 4) and the addresses of three companies in your local area.

* Modify the cover letter so that the salutation reads "To the Director of Personnel:" and so that it can be merged with the employer name and address file.

* Use the merge capability to print a cover letter to each company in the employer name and address file.

Exercise B: Use the WordPerfect's merge feature to create a personalized memo to employees of Nomlak, Inc. (see Session Five).

* Create a data file by entering the following list of employees. Each employee record contains three fields.

Jerry Jolly Customer Relations Jerry	Delores Delightful Personnel Delores
Alison Aggressive Marketing Alison	Ingrid Intelligencia Research and Development Ingrid
George Grump Purchasing George	Sam Specific Accounting Sam

* Save the list as EMPLYS.SF

* Enter the memo that appears at the top of the following page and create a letter file. Replace the name in parentheses with the correct merge field representation.

* Save the letter file as BONUS.PF

* Use the merge feature to create a personalized memo for each of the six employees listed in EMPLYS.SF. Use BONUS.PF as the primary file and EMPLYS.SF as the secondary file in the merge. Name the created merge file ALLMEMOS.

> To: (name)
> From: Det Nomlak, President
> Re: Surprise
>
> As you know, (salutation), this past year was an excellent year for Nomlak, Inc. Our sales tripled after we launched our newest products.
>
> None of this would have been possible without the help of the (department) Department. Therefore the Board of Directors has declared a bonus equal to 37% of each employee's salary. Congratulations (salutation) and thank you.

Step 6: Exiting WordPerfect and Terminating the Session

Save your current document and exit WordPerfect (see Session One, Step 12).

☐ If necessary, save your current document.

☐ Exit WordPerfect.

* `F7`

As a safety precaution, you are prompted to save the document on which you are working. If any revisions have been made since the document was last saved, answer "Y" to the prompt; otherwise the revisions will be lost.

* N
* Y

☐ Take your data diskette out of drive A and turn off the computer.

Session Five

Columns, Math and Sorting

As you may have noticed, WordPerfect includes an abundance of features. This session discusses three advanced document enhancement features: columns, math and sorting.

The columns feature allows the user to create multiple columns on one page. Columns are used in either of two styles: newspaper or parallel. **Newspaper** columns contain text that flows from the bottom of one column to the top of the next column (see Figure 3-35). Newspaper columns are often used in newsletter style documents. **Parallel** columns allow information to flow across columns. A parallel columns example is a personnel list that contains the columns: name, address, department, family members, education and salary. Each employee's information flows across the six columns. If any of the columns (i.e., the address column) contains more than one line, WordPerfect adjusts the next employee's listing accordingly.

The math feature performs mathematical operations on columns of numbers. WordPerfect can add sub-totals, totals and grand totals within the same column. The user can also set up formulas to perform calculations across columns.

The sorting feature lets the user reorder lines, paragraphs and secondary merge documents. For example, Alyson Peabody uses the sorting feature to alphabetize the board member list contained in ADDRESS.SF (the secondary merge file created in Session Four).

In Session Four, Alyson Peabody used the merge feature to create personalized letters for each of Chew & Chew's board members. To complete her task, Alyson retrieves and edits a file detailing the company's third quarter activity. She uses columns and the math feature to enhance the document, then combines it with the board members' letter. Finally, Alyson sorts the board member secondary file and regenerates the letters in alphabetical order based on the board members' last names.

If WordPerfect is not currently running, refer to Session One, Step 1 in this chapter to start your computer and load WordPerfect. Confirm that your data diskette is in drive A and that drive A is the active drive.

In this session you will learn to:

- Define and activate newspaper columns
- Select "Ragged Right" justification
- Retrieve one document into another document
- Center text vertically
- Use the math feature to sum a numeric column

- Use the sort feature to sort a marked block
- Use the sort feature to sort a secondary merge file
- Use the block command to print a portion of a file

Once again, Chew & Chew, Inc. has enjoyed a profitable quarter. Sales during the third quarter are up 20% over last year's third quarter and up by 5% when compared with our second quarter sales. We believe several trends are responsible for our continued success and also believe that these trends will benefit Chew & Chew, Inc. into the fourth quarter and beyond.

As before, our association with the B&R Stores chain serves as our foundation. B&R is the first store to display our products and they sold so well that B&R has steadily expanded our representation beyond our initial southern regional basis. B&R now includes our products in its southern stores, its northern stores and its midwestern stores. Starting this quarter, B&R has also begun selling our products in its central stores. Of course, we are very pleased with our association with B&R and are actively pursuing options to expand into other B&R outlets.

As you know, B&R is not our only outlet. We also are represented in stores throughout the south. Our solid southern base continues to bolster our profits.

Possibly the most interesting sales trend this year is that sales of our newest product, Tough Turkey, are remaining steady from month to month. We expected a surge in Tough Turkey chewing last year at Thanksgiving and a seasonal drop thereafter. What did take place, to the wonderment of all, was continued steady sales through December and into the beginning of this calendar year. In January, when the sales trend became clear, we began to increase our Tough Turkey advertising. You may recall seeing our advertisements in February, March and April based on the theme, "Tough Turkey Equals Tough Teeth." We still are waiting for the results of a market research study which will indicate exactly which age category is buying Tough Turkey. In any event, we expect sales of Tough Turkey to increase during the fourth quarter's holiday season.

Naturally we are pleased with the steady success of Tough Turkey, but our flagship product, Chocolate Leather, is still our best selling and most successful product. Each new store that places Chocolate Leather on its shelves, soon places reorders and becomes a Chocolate Leather steady customer.

We are a young, growing company. Each product is successful. We believe that the next calendar year will bring continued expansion as we focus on adding greater manufacturing capabilities and increasing our sales staff.

Chew & Chew, Inc. headquarters are always open to stock holders and you are encouraged to visit. We hope to see you soon chewing Chocolate Leather and chewing Tough Turkey.

Figure 3-35   Text to be used in the Third Quarter Activity Report. This text is displayed in Newspaper Column format.

Step 1: Defining and Using Newspaper Columns

Newspaper columns allow text to flow from one column to another. Creating columns involves two steps. First the columns must be defined, then column use must be turned on. Define columns by selecting the number of columns to be used, then setting the width of each column and the amount of space between each column. Column creation sounds more difficult than it is in practice. WordPerfect computes column widths based on the number of columns selected. You may either use the computed column widths or enter new column widths.

The default column setting is two 3" wide columns separated by a half inch trough (the empty space between the columns). This step creates the "Third Quarter Activity Report" using WordPerfect's default column setting to define two columns (Figure 3-35 displays the first page of the completed report). First we will enter the report's heading and define the columns. Then the text of the report (3RDQTR.TXT) will be retrieved from the Example Files Diskette into the defined columns.

❏ Center and boldface the heading "Third Quarter Activity Report."

* SHIFT - F6
* F6 Third Quarter Activity Report F6 ↵ ↵

The second ENTER places a blank line between the heading and the body of the letter.

❏ Define the type and number of columns to be used (see Figure 3-36).

* ALT - F7
* D

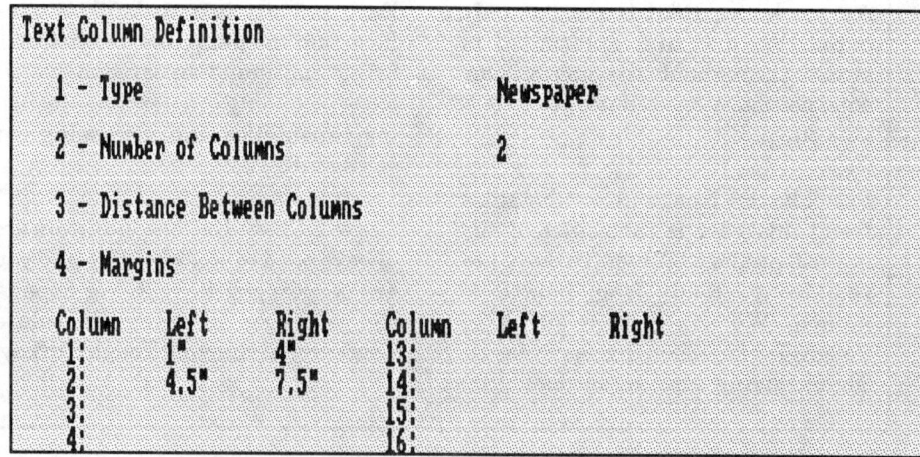

Figure 3-36 Text Column Definition screen showing WordPerfect's default column settings

The text column definition screen displays WordPerfect's default column selections. The column type is Newspaper, the number of columns is 2 and the default width of each column is 3" (the column margin settings are 1" to 4" and 4.5" to 7.5"). Tapping the ENTER key selects the default settings.

* ↵

WordPerfect returns to the Math/Column menu.

❏ Now that the columns have been defined, column use must be activated.

* C

❏ Before retrieving the report text, set justification off to create columns with "ragged right" borders.

* SHIFT - F8 L J N F7

If you wish, use Reveal Codes (ALT-F3) to display the column and justification codes that have been entered into your document (see Figure 3-37).

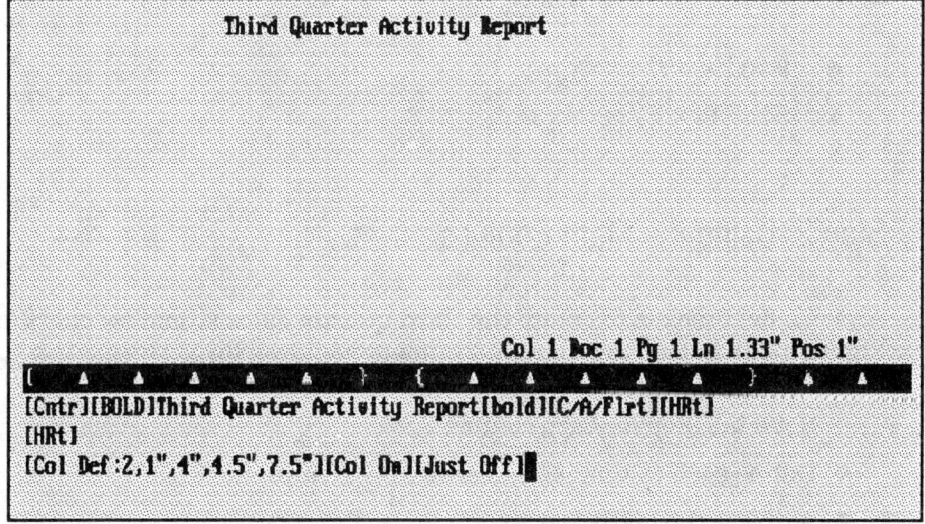

Figure 3-37 Column definition, column on and justification off codes entered to format the Activity Report

❏ Save the current document.

* F10
* report.3qt ↵

☐ The text of the report exists in the 3RDQTR.TXT file on the Example Files Diskette. Retrieve the text into the current document (option: manually enter the text while squinting at Figure 3-35).

* *(insert the Example Files Diskette into drive A)*
* [SHIFT] - [F10]
* **3rdqtr.txt**
* *(reinsert your data diskette into drive A)*

WordPerfect reads the 3RDQTR.TXT file into the current document starting at the current cursor position.

☐ Position the cursor at the end of the report and turn column use off.

* [HOME] [HOME] ↓
* [ALT] - [F7] C

A page break is inserted and the cursor is positioned at the beginning of page 2. If text is entered at this point, it would not be displayed in columns. Columns may be redefined and turned on and off as needed.

☐ Save and print the report.

* [F10] ↵ Y
* [SHIFT] - [F7] F

Step 2: Using the Math Feature

Alyson's next task is to create the third quarter sales summary chart (see Figure 3-38). Setting up a math document requires three steps:

◆ Set a tab stop for each column

◆ Define each column as either "text" or "numeric"

◆ Activate the math feature

Alyson follows the three steps to set up the sales summary chart. She sets three tab stops, then defines the first two columns as text and the third column as numeric. Next, Alyson activates the math feature and enters each store's data. When all data is entered, she uses the math feature to sum the Sales Total column. This step demonstrates Alyson's procedure.

```
        Third Quarter Sales Summary

Store Name              Regional Location        Sales

B&R Stores              Southern                 3,400
Marcy's                 Southern                 2,100
Radiccio & Sons         Southern                 4,500
B&R Stores              Northern                 6,200
Rudy's Rudiments        Southern                 3,700
Food Galore             Southern                 1,800
B&R Stores              Midwestern               5,700
Salacious Sensations    Southern                 2,400

                        Total:                  29,800+
```

Figure 3-38 Completed Sales Summary chart demonstrating WordPerfect's MATH feature

☐ Enter the vertical page centering code to place the chart in the center of the page. WordPerfect determines the top and bottom margins to center the chart vertically.

* [SHIFT]-[F8] P C [F7]

☐ Center (horizontally) and boldface the chart's heading.

* [SHIFT]-[F6]
* [F6] Third Quarter Sales Summary [F6] ↵ ↵

☐ Before activating the math feature, reset the tabs for the report. Create three tab stops, one for each of the report's columns (see Figure 3-38).

* [SHIFT]-[F8] L T
* [CTRL]-[END]
* 1.5 ↵ 4 ↵ 7 ↵
* [F7] [F7]

☐ Display the math definition screen and define each of the three columns (see Figure 3-39). Each tab stop is a column. In this report, tab 1.5" is column A, tab 4" is column B and tab 7" is column C.

* [ALT]-[F7] E

```
Math Definition        Use arrow keys to position cursor
Columns                A B C D E F G H I J K L M N O P Q R S T U V W X
Type                   2 2 2 2 2 2 2 2 2 2 2 2 2 2 2 2 2 2 2 2 2 2 2 2
Negative Numbers       ( ( ( ( ( ( ( ( ( ( ( ( ( ( ( ( ( ( ( ( ( ( ( (
Number of Digits to    2 2 2 2 2 2 2 2 2 2 2 2 2 2 2 2 2 2 2 2 2 2 2 2
  the Right (0-4)
Calculation     1
  Formulas      2
                3
                4

Type of Column:
     0 = Calculation    1 = Text      2 = Numeric     3 = Total

Negative Numbers
     ( = Parentheses (50.00)        - = Minus Sign  -50.00
```

Figure 3-39 MATH definition screen

Since the first two columns are for text entry, they must be defined as "text." The cursor is currently at the column definition position for column A. The default setting for each column is 2 or Numeric. Change the column definition for columns A and B to Text by tapping 1 twice. After defining a column, the cursor automatically positions itself at the next column's definition.

* 1 1

☐ Change the number of decimal positions displayed in column C from the default value of 2 to 0.

* ↓ ↓ 0

☐ Exit the Math Definition screen.

* [F7]

WordPerfect returns to the Math/Columns menu.

☐ Activate the math feature by selecting the "Math On" option.

* M

"Math" appears in the lower left corner of the screen indicating that the math feature is on.

☐ Enter the column headings.

* [TAB] **Store Name**
* [TAB] **Regional Location**
* [TAB] **Sales** ↵ ↵

Notice that when you tabbed to the third column, "Align char = . Math" appeared in the lower left corner of the screen. WordPerfect treats a numeric column as though the tab setting is a decimal tab. All numbers and/or characters will be entered to the left of the tab position (right aligned) until the period (.) is tapped. At that point, numbers and/or characters will be entered to the right of the period. The alignment character is the period (.).

☐ Enter the first store's data.

* [TAB] **B&R Stores**
* [TAB] **Southern**
* [TAB] **3,400** ↵

Refer to Figure 3-38 and enter the next seven lines of data (the remaining stores).

☐ Enter a blank line, then enter the "Total:" line. Place a plus sign (+) in the third column to indicate where WordPerfect should calculate the total (see Figure 3-40).

* ↵
* [TAB][TAB] **Total:**
* [TAB] **+**

```
B&R Stores            Midwestern              5,700
Salacious Sensations  Southern                2,400

                      Total:                      +
```

Figure 3-40 The "+" in the third column indicates column summation display

☐ Display the Math/Columns menu and select the "Calculate" option to enter the column total.

* ALT - F7 A

The result should be the same as Figure 3-38. The plus sign next to the total will not appear when the page is printed.

☐ Save the document and print the current page.

* F10 ↵ Y
* SHIFT - F7 P

Step 3: Sorting by Line

Alyson showed the completed sales summary chart to her boss and he asked Alyson to rearrange the stores so they would appear in alphabetical order. Alyson knows that WordPerfect can sort a block of text by line so she said, "No problem." To sort the chart, Alyson:

♦ Marks the lines containing the stores' data
♦ Enters the sort command
♦ Defines the sort "type" and the sort "key"
♦ Performs the sort

This step demonstrates the sorting by line procedure.

☐ Position the cursor at the beginning of the line which contains the first store's data (see Figure 3-41).

* *(position the cursor at the beginning of the first store's data line, Ln 1.67" Pos 1")*

```
B&R Stores            Southern         3,400
Marcy's               Southern         2,100
Raddiccio & Sons      Southern         4,500
```

Figure 3-41 Cursor position before marking the store data lines

☐ Mark the eight lines containing the sales data.

* ALT - F4
* HOME →
* ↓ *(7 times)*

☐ Enter the sort command.

* CTRL - F9

```
B&R Stores              Southern            3,400
Marcy's                 Southern            2,100
Radiccio & Sons         Southern            1,500
B&R Stores              Northern            6,200
Rudy's Rudiments        Southern            3,700
Food Galore             Southern            1,800
B&R Stores              Midwestern          5,700
Salacious Sensations    Southern            2,400


                                         Doc 2 Pg 1 Ln 1" Pos 1"
[       ▲               ▲                   ▲    ]
─────────────────────── Sort by Line ──────────────────────

Key Typ Field Word    Key Typ Field Word    Key Typ Field Word
 1   a    1    1       2                     3
 4                     5                     6
 7                     8                     9
Select


Action                Order                 Type
Sort                  Ascending             Line sort

1 Perform Action; 2 View; 3 Keys; 4 Select; 5 Action; 6 Order; 7 Type: 0
```

Figure 3-42 The sort definition screen. "Sort by Line" is the selected sort type

Figure 3-42 displays the Sort by Line screen. Your current display may not read Sort by Line. If necessary, select the "Type" option and choose "Line."

* *(if necessary)* **T L**

☐ The "Typ" selection in the sort key determines which data type to sort (alphanumeric or numeric). The "Field" and "Word" selections define which column and which word within that column shall determine the alphabetized order of the lines. For example, the store names are in column 2 (for sorting, the first column is the left margin and each successive column is defined when the tab key is tapped). The store's name is the first word within column 2. Therefore, the sort key to alphabetize the eight marked lines is: Type = alphanumeric, Field = 2 and Word = 1. Select the "Key" option to define the sort key.

* K
* A 2 ↵ 1 F7

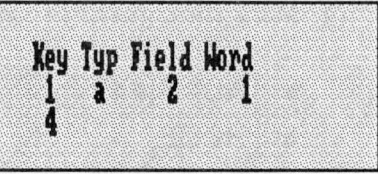

Figure 3-43 Sort key selecting the Store Name column

Your sort key should look like Figure 3-43.

❐ Perform the sort (see Figure 3-44).

* P

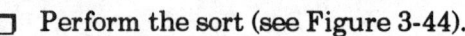

Figure 3-44 Sorted display based on the Store Name column

If needed, it is possible to define multiple keys and perform multilevel sorts. For example, to sort on region within store name, key number 2 would be defined: key = alphanumeric, Field = 3 and Word = 1. In this sort, the B&R Stores would be grouped together as in the current sort, but within the B&R listing the stores would alphabetized by region.

❐ Save the file and print the sorted sales chart.

* F10 ↵ Y
* F7 P

Step 4: Sorting a Secondary Merge File

Secondary merge files are set aside as a special sorting category because they contain defined records which in turn contain defined fields. This allows us to reorder the records in a secondary merge file based on the contents of one or several fields within each record. For example, when Alyson showed her boss the sorted sales summary chart, he said, "That's great. Can you reorder the Board of Director's file so the merged letters print in alphabetical order based on the board members' last names?" Once again, Alyson said, "No problem, be right back."

This step demonstrates Alyson's procedure as she sorts the secondary merge file, ADDRESS.SF.

☐ If necessary, clear the screen.

* F7 N N

☐ Retrieve the ADDRESS.SF file from your data diskette (ADDRESS.SF was created in Session Four, Step 1).

* SHIFT - F10
* **address.sf** ↵

☐ In the previous step, we marked text, entered the sort command and were taken directly to the sort definition screen. When the sort command is entered without marking text, a different sequence is initiated. Several decisions must be made before the sort definition screen can be displayed. When you tap CTRL-F9, the decisions are:

◆ Merge or Sort (assume we select sort)
◆ Input file to sort (screen or disk)
◆ Output file for sort (screen or disk)

You may sort the file currently on the screen or sort a file on disk. You may save the sort to the screen or to a disk file. When text is marked (as in the previous step), the sort is automatically performed from the screen file to the screen file. In this step, we will sort from the screen to the screen so we can see the results of the sort.

* CTRL - F9
* **S** ↵ ↵

The Sort menu appears. Notice that the most recent sort settings have been preserved.

☐ Select the sort type (merge).

* **T M**

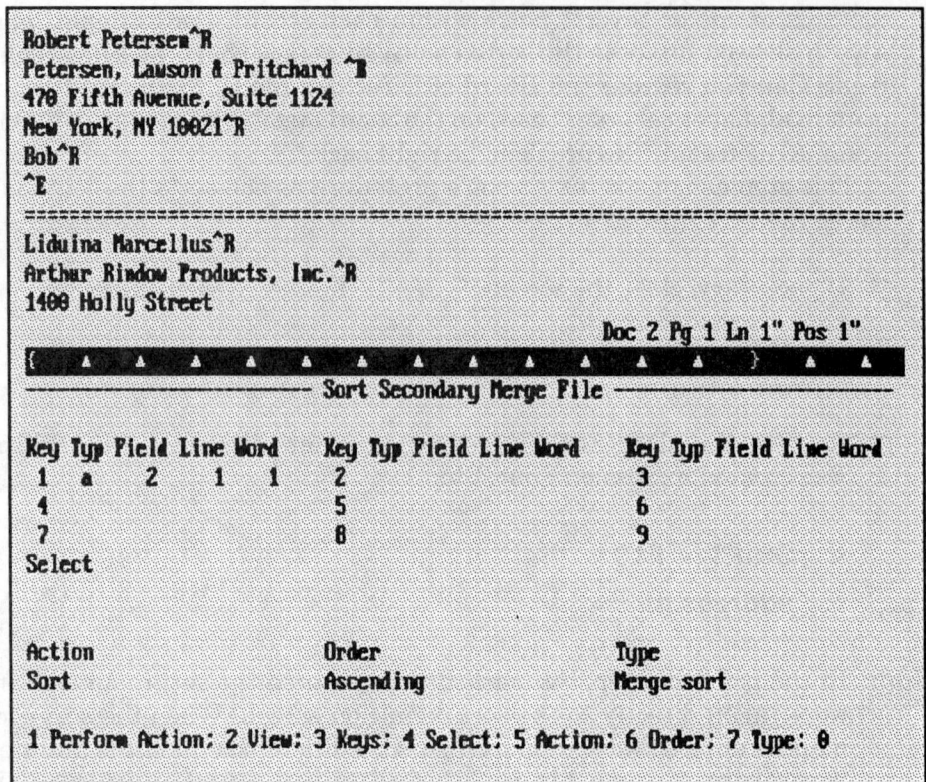

Figure 3-45 Sort definition screen. The sort type is "Secondary Marge File"

Notice that the title and the key contents have changed (see Figure 3-45).

☐ Define the sort key: Type = alphanumeric, Field = 1, Line = 1 and Word = 2.

* K
* A 1 ↵ 1 ↵ 2 F7

☐ Perform the sort.

* P

The Board of Directors should now be in alphabetical order based on their last names.

☐ Save the newly ordered secondary merge file as ADDRESS1.SF.

* F10
* **address1.sf** ↵

Step: 5 Combining Files

Alyson's final step is to combine the primary merge file cover letter (letter.pf) with the third quarter activity report (report.3qt) to create one primary file that contains three pages (the cover letter, the activity report and the sales summary chart). Alyson then merges the three page primary file with the sorted secondary file to generate a personalized letter to each board member in alphabetical order.

☐ Clear the screen and retrieve the primary merge file created in Session Four, Step 2.

* `F7` N N
* `SHIFT` - `F10`
* **letter.pf** ↵

☐ Position the cursor at the end of the document and enter a required page break.

* `HOME` `HOME` ↓
* `CTRL` - ↵

☐ Retrieve the activity report without clearing the screen to combine the two documents. The retrieved document will be read in at the current cursor position.

* `SHIFT` - `F10`
* **report.3qt** ↵

Tap PGUP and PGDN as you wish to confirm that all three pages are present.

☐ Save the three page file under the name LETTER1.PF

* `F10`
* **letter1.pf** ↵

☐ Clear the screen and merge LETTER1.PF and ADDRESS1.SF.

* `F7` N N
* `CTRL` - `F9` M
* **letter1.pf** ↵

* **address1.pf** ↵

Use PGUP and PGDN to examine the merged file.

☐ Save the merged file as MERGE1.LTR.

* F10
* **merge1.ltr**

☐ Print the first three pages of the MERGE1.LTR file (Edmond Dolgin's complete letter). Use the block command in conjunction with the print command to print the three pages.

* HOME HOME ↑
* ALT - F4
* PGDN PGDN PGDN

The cursor is currently at the beginning of page 4. Tap the left arrow key once to move the cursor to the end of page 3 to prevent a blank fourth page from being printed.

* ←
* SHIFT - F7

Alyson takes the completed letters to her boss, who looks at them and says, "WordPerfect can do all this? The training we sent you to was really worthwhile. Thank you, Mrs. Peabody, good job."

Step 6: Practice

Exercise A: Sort the EMPLYS.SF file created in Session Four, Step 5.

* Retrieve the EMPLYS.SF file.
* Use the sort feature to reorder EMPLYS.SF by employee last name. Use the name EMPLYS1.SF to save the new order.
* Use the sort feature to reorder EMPLYS.SF by department. Use the name EMPLYS2.SF to save the new order.
* Print the two new files.

Exercise B: Create a letter written by a student.

> Wow hi there. I mean I just had to tell you about this class I'm taking. It's like a computer class. Wow I mean I think I finally decided to join the twentieth century you know.
>
> Well today I learned something totally cosmic. I mean it is really like you know out there. TA DA!! PC-DOS limits the main name of a file to eight characters. (Wow, didn't that last sentence sound SO computer?)
>
> Remember when we heard the guru InterBeingMantra say that like you have to know limits to like know the infinite. Well get this. My prof said that every computer program that runs on PC-DOS (DOUBLE WOW that is such a computer name -- I mean what does it mean anyway) has to deal with that limitation, OK? I think there is something you know really universal about the whole thing, don't you?
>
> Well, computer lab is almost over (like I wrote this on the computer). So you know write when you get chance, OK?

* Enter the above letter (Option: retrieve ROOMATE.TXT from the Example Files Diskette).
* Use the name ROOMATE1.TXT to save the letter.
* Add a salutation at the beginning, a closing, and your name at the end. Print the document.
* Boldface "SO" in the second paragraph and "DOUBLE WOW" in the third paragraph.
* Underline "TA DA" in the second paragraph. Print the document.
* Save the file.

Exercise C: Edit the previous letter to create an alternative version:

* Use the name ROOMATE2.TXT to save the file.
* Edit the file ROOMATE2.TXT by deleting all occurrences of the words "you know," "I mean," "like," "double," and "wow" in the first, second, and fourth paragraphs (do not edit the third paragraph). Hint: use search and replace with confirm.
* Print the document.
* Delete "Well " in the second paragraph and capitalize the "t" of "today."
* Replace "totally cosmic" with "important".
* Delete what remains of the second sentence of the second paragraph.

* Move the last two sentences of the third paragraph to the end of the second paragraph.
* Replace the first sentence of the fourth paragraph with "Must run."
* Delete what remains of the third paragraph.
* Delete all phrases within parentheses and the accompanying parentheses.
* Place quotations around the last sentence of paragraph two. Print the document.
* Replace ", OK?" with "." in the fourth sentence of the second paragraph.
* Add the characters "As my roommate says, " at the beginning of the last sentence of paragraph two.
* Capitalize the "h" of "hi" and add or delete spaces as needed to clean up the document.
* Save the revised letter and print it, OK?

Exercise D: Create a third file that places the two roommate's letters side by side on the page.

* Start with a clean screen.
* Enter the heading (centered) "Letters to Friends".
* Define double columns and turn columns on.
* Add three blank lines.
* Retrieve ROOMATE1.
* Move the cursor to the bottom of the document.
* Enter a Hard Page (CTRL- ↵) to force the cursor to the top of the second column.
* Retrieve ROOMATE2.
* Save the document as ROOMATES.
* Print ROOMATES.

Step 7: Terminating the Session

Save your current document and exit WordPerfect (see Session One, Step 12). Remove your data diskette from drive A and turn off the computer.

Session Six

Macros

WordPerfect has two types of macros: simple and advanced. Simple macros record keystrokes and play them back in the exact order they were entered. Simple macros are created to perform often repeated tasks such as:

- Entering long names
- Underlining a word
- Saving and printing files
- Typing standard letter headings and closings
- Inserting often used format changes

In fact, anytime you find yourself repeating a series of keystrokes during a session, create a simple macro and let WordPerfect do the typing for you.

Advanced macros include recorded keystrokes and programming features (i.e., variables, subroutines, conditional choices and waiting for keyboard input). Advanced macros allow the user to make decisions during macro execution. Examples of advanced macros are:

- An interactive memo heading that pauses for user input
- A menu display of boilerplate phrases to be used in letter creation
- A menu of letter closings (Sincerely yours, Very truly yours, etc.)
- An edit macro that continually repeats until the end of a document is encountered

For example, Emilie Pierrel is at her father's office helping him catch up on his work. Christian (the father) has bought new stationery and must adjust all his unsent letters to the new format. He shows Emilie what to do: change the top margin, change the left and right margins, move the date from the left margin to the right margin, remove the beginning indent from each paragraph and add a blank line between paragraphs.

Christian apologizes to Emilie for giving her a repetitious task that will occupy her most of the morning. He doesn't know that Emilie is a WordPerfect whiz. She creates macros to accomplish each task, combines them into a macro menu and reformats all the letters within an hour.

This session demonstrates the creation of simple macros and an advanced menu macro. It also demonstrates macro chaining.

If WordPerfect is not currently running, refer to Session One, Step 1 in this chapter to start your computer and load WordPerfect. Confirm that your data diskette is in drive A and that drive A is the active drive.

In this session you will learn how to:

- Name a macro
- Describe a macro
- Record keystrokes to create a macro
- Playback a macro
- Edit a macro
- Create an interactive macro
- Chain macros

Step 1: Creating a Simple ALT-Letter Macro

Christian's marketing research company is named "Christian Pierrel's Certified Product Characterization Profiles, Inc.", or CP3 for short. He lost six good secretaries before Emilie showed him how to create a macro that would type the name automatically. This is what Emilie taught her father.

Five operations are involved in creating a simple macro.

- Turn on macro define
- Name the macro
- Describe the macro
- Perform the activity (each keystroke is being recorded)
- Turn off macro define

☐ First, activate WordPerfect's macro definition mode (see Figure 3-46).

* CTRL - F10

```
Define macro:
```

Figure 3-46 This prompt appears after tapping CTRL-F10. Enter the macro name

☐ Next, name the macro. A macro may be named in one of three ways: 1) By typing a name that includes from one to eight characters, 2) By pressing the ALT key and tapping a letter key, or 3) By tapping the ENTER key by itself. Each method will be presented during this session. Use the ALT letter key method for this macro.

* [ALT] - C

☐ In operation 3, describe the macro. The description may include up to 39 characters (see Figure 3-47).

* **Company name entry** ↵

Description: Company name entry

Figure 3-47   Describing the macro's function

☐ The flashing words "Macro Def" signify that WordPerfect is ready to record keystrokes. Type the company name, followed by a space. Do not tap the ENTER key. If you make a mistake while entering the name, correct it the way you normally would. Every keystroke is being recorded.

* **Christian Pierrel's Certified Product Characterization Profiles, Inc.** [SPACE]

☐ Tap CTRL-F10 again to turn off macro definition.

* [CTRL] - [F10]

The keystrokes required to enter the company name have been recorded and saved on your data diskette under the name ALTC.WPM.

☐ Clear the screen before continuing to Step 2.

* [F7] N N

Step 2: Using an ALT-Letter Macro

Macros named with an ALT-letter combination are executed by using that combination.

WP: Session Six 145

☐ Play back the recorded keystrokes that type the company's name by pressing and holding the ALT key and tapping "c". The following sentences demonstrate how to execute an ALT-letter macro (see Figure 3-48).

* ALT -C
* is a marketing research company. SPACE
* ALT -C
* employs highly trained market research personnel. When you need product information, call SPACE
* ALT -C

> Christian Pierrel's Certified Product Characterization Profiles, Inc. is a marketing research company. Christian Pierrel's Certified Product Characterization Profiles, Inc. employs highly trained market research personnel. When you need product information, call Christian Pierrel's Certified Product Characterization Profiles, Inc.

Figure 3-48 Screen display after using the ALT-C macro to enter Mr. Pierrel's company name

☐ Clear the screen.

* F7 N N

Step 3: Creating a Simple Named Macro

A named simple named macro works just like a simple ALT-letter macro. The only difference between the two types of macros occurs in operation two, naming the macro. A named macro is assigned a name that is one to eight characters long.

Emelie creates a named macro to help her reformat her father's letters. The macro resets the top, left and right margins. She uses the same five operations outlined above. In operation two (naming the macro), she names her macro, FORM.

☐ Create a named macro that automatically adjusts the top, left and right margins.

* **CTRL** - **F10**

☐ Enter the macro name.

* **form** ↵

☐ Describe the macro's function.

* **Resets the top and side margins** ↵

☐ Perform the activity while WordPerfect records your keystrokes.

* **SHIFT**-**F8** **L M 1.5** ↵ **1.5** ↵
* ↵
* *(in the format menu)*
* **P M 2** ↵ ↵ **F7**

☐ Turn off macro definition.

* **CTRL** - **F10**

☐ Clear the screen and all code settings before continuing to the next step.

* **F7** N N

Step 4: Executing a Named Macro

Emilie uses the FORM macro to reformat each of her father's letters. She executes the macro by tapping ALT-F10 and entering the macro's name at the resulting prompt.

☐ Execute a named macro by tapping ALT-F10 (Macro) and entering the name of the macro.

* **ALT** - **F10**
* **form** ↵

☐ Activate reveal codes to see the format change codes entered by the macro (see Figure 3-49).

*

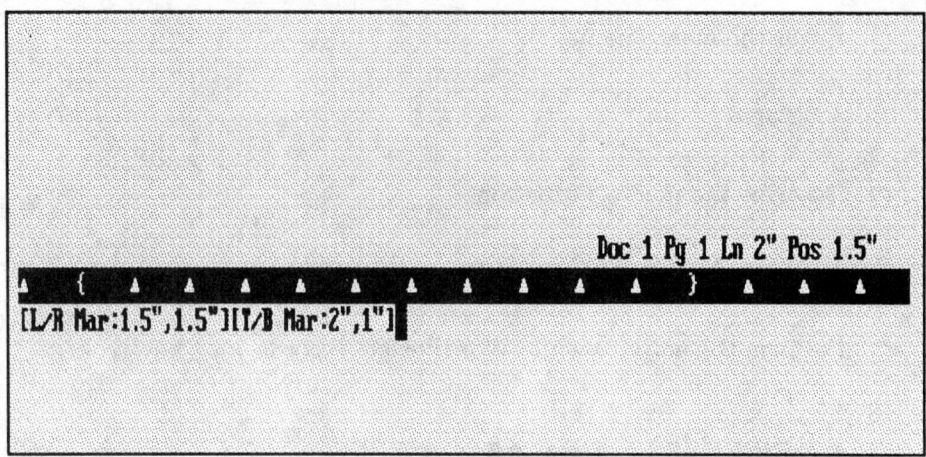

Figure 3-49 Formatting codes entered by the FORM macro

The current document contains codes that supersede the default settings. Any document can be formatted to these settings by executing the "form" macro.

☐ Deactivate reveal codes and clear the screen before continuing to the next step.

* ALT - F3

Step 5: Creating and Executing a Temporary Macro

As you work with macros, you will discover that you want to create a "one-session" macro. This temporary macro is used only during the current session and is erased when you exit WordPerfect. Temporary macros differ from their more permanent relatives in the following ways:

- ◆ No name is entered at the macro define prompt
- ◆ No permanent .WPM file is created
- ◆ The macro description option is by-passed

Create a temporary macro by activating macro definition and tapping the ENTER key. This step demonstrates the creation and use of a temporary macro to type a person's name several times while creating a congratulatory letter.

Mr. Antreas Ghebreigzabher is this week's lottery winner. Allie Marcellus is typing the congratulatory letter and does not want to type Mr. Ghebreigzabher's name more than once (can you blame her?). So the first time Allie types Mr. Ghebreigzabher's name she creates a temporary macro to memorize her keystrokes. Each subsequent time Allie must type Mr. Ghebreigzabher's name, she uses the temporary macro to type the name for her.

❒ Allie begins typing the letter, then creates the temporary macro the first time she types Mr. Ghebreigzabher's name.

* **Dear** `SPACE`
* `CTRL` - `F10`
* ↵
* **Mr. Antreas Ghebreigzabher**
* `CTRL` - `F10`

❒ Continue typing the letter and use the temporary macro each time Mr. Ghebreigzabher's name is to be included.

* **This letter is confirmation that** `ALT` - `F10` ↵ `SPACE`
* **is the sole winner of last week's $4,000,000 dollar lottery. Congratulations** `ALT` - `F10` ↵ **, you should receive the first of your twenty annual payments in approximately three weeks.** ↵

❒ Clear the screen before continuing to the next step.

* `F7` N N

Step 6: Editing Macros

WordPerfect 5.0 includes a macro editing feature. Once a macro is created, it may be fine tuned through the macro editor. Keystrokes may be added or removed as needed. This feature allows macros to be modified without having to recreate the macro.

To demonstrate macro editing, this step creates a simple ALT-letter macro that centers the cursor and types the date. Then the macro is edited to display the date flush right and add two blank lines beneath the date.

❒ Create the following macro which moves the cursor to the center and enters the current date.

> ### Comparing Macro Naming Methods
>
> Each naming method has a unique strength:
>
> * An ALT-letter macro is easy to execute (hold the ALT key and tap a letter key)
> * Named macros can use their name to reveal the macro's function
> * Temporary macros are used during the current session and forgotten
>
> Of course the strength of each naming method implies a weakness:
>
> * Only twenty-six ALT-letter macros may be created.
> * Named macros require several keystrokes to be executed (ALT-F10, enter the name)
> * Temporary macros are not automatically saved

* **CTRL** - **F10**
* **ALT** -D
* **Enters current date, centered** ↵
* **SHIFT** - **F6** **SHIFT** - **F5** C ↵
* **CTRL** - **F10**

☐ Execute the macro to test it (see Figure 3-50).

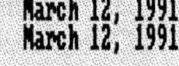

* **ALT** -D

The date should appear centered and the cursor should be at the beginning of the next line.

Figure 3-50 Screen display after creating (line 1) and invoking (line 2) the ALT-D macro

☐ After looking at the result, you decide you would rather have the date aligned flush right and have two more empty lines between the date and the cursor placement. Activate the macro editor to modify the macro (see Figure 3-51).

* **CTRL** - **F10**
* **ALT** -D

    ALTD.WPM is Already Defined. 1 Replace; 2 Edit: 0

Figure 3-51   Macro editor activation prompt

When an existing macro name is entered, WordPerfect displays a Replace/Edit message. Selecting "Replace" erases the old macro and continues macro definition as before. Selecting "Edit" activates the macro editor.

* E

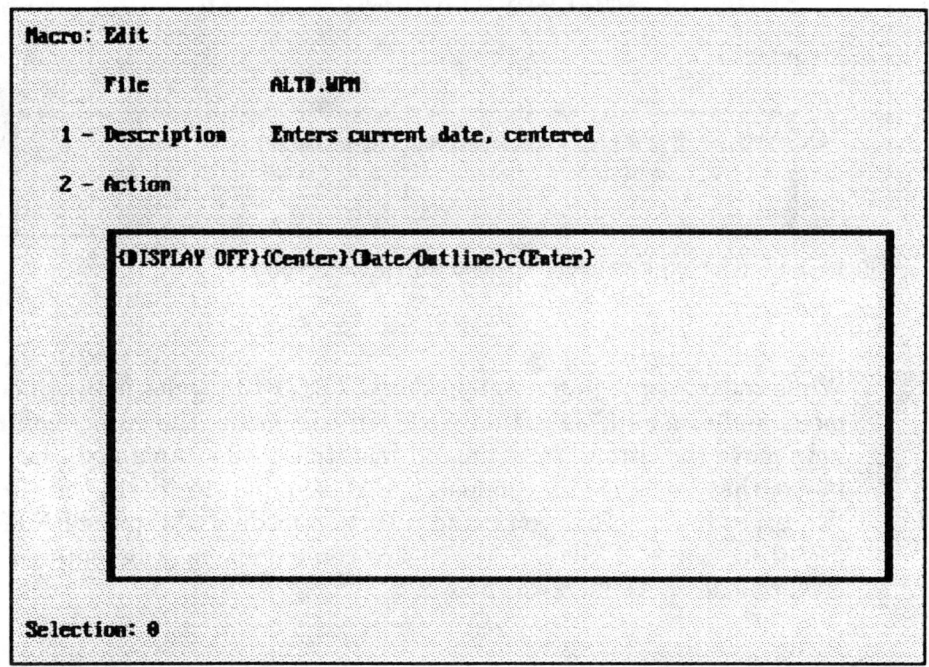

Figure 3-52 Macro editing screen

Take a moment to look at the macro editor screen (see Figure 3-52). The macro's filename and description appear at the top of the screen, and the macro's "Action" appears in the box. The action contains four code entries and one keystroke entry. The first code entry, {DISPLAY OFF}, freezes the monitor display until macro execution is completed. This code is entered automatically when a macro is created. If you want to watch macro execution, you must delete the {DISPLAY OFF} code. Macro code deletion and addition will be explained later.

The next two codes are WordPerfect keystroke combination commands ({Center} and {Date/Outline}). These are followed by the "c" keystroke which selects the Date Code option from the Date/Outline menu. The last code represents tapping the ENTER key to move the cursor to the next line.

❏ First, edit the "action." Change the {Center} code to {Flush Right} and then add two more {Enter} codes (see Figures 3-53 and 3-54).

WP: Session Six 151

* A
* → DEL
* ALT - F6
* → →

Figure 3-53 {Center} has been replaced with {Flush Right}

While the cursor is in the Action Box, CTRL-F10 toggles between edit mode and command insertion mode. In edit mode, the cursor control keys move the cursor. In command insertion mode, tap an edit key to insert that key's macro command. For example, to insert the three {Enter} codes, toggle to command insertion mode and tap the ENTER key three times. Function key macro commands may be entered in either mode as ALT-F6 was above.

* CTRL - F10
* ↵ ↵
* CTRL - F10
* F7

Figure 3-54 Final version of the edited macro's action

Always return to edit mode to exit the Action Box.

☐ Next, edit the macro's description. Change the final word from "centered" to "flush right" (see Figure 3-55).

* D
* **END**
* **BKSP** *(8 times)*
* **flush right**
* **F7**

```
Macro: Edit

     File        ALTD.WPM

1 - Description  Enters current date, flush right

2 - Action


     {DISPLAY OFF}{Flush Right}{Date/Outline}c{Enter}{Enter}{Enter}
```

Figure 3-55 The macro's action and description have been edited

☐ Exit the macro editor.

* **F7**

☐ Clear the screen then execute the modified macro.

* **F7** N N
* **ALT**-D

☐ Clear the screen before continuing to the next step.

* **F7** N N

Step 7: Creating an Interactive Macro

WordPerfect macros can do more than just memorize keystrokes. Commands are available to allow macros to make decisions based on user input. Create a macro that lets you decide whether the current date will be entered left aligned, flush right or centered. The macro's completed action is displayed in Figure 3-56.

```
{DISPLAY OFF}
{CHAR}0~Date entry: {^]}1 L{^\}eft; {^]}2 R{^\}ight; {^]}3 C{^\}entered: 0{Left}~

{CASE}{VAR 0}~
    1~left~l~left~L~left~
    2~right~r~right~R~right~
    3~center~c~center~C~center~
~

{QUIT}

{LABEL}left~
    {Home}{Home}{Left}{GO}date~
{LABEL}right~
    {Flush Right}{GO}date~
{LABEL}center~
    {Center}
```

Figure 3-56 The DATE macro's complete action

☐ All commands will be entered through the macro editor. Since WordPerfect must find an existing macro before calling the macro editor, create an empty macro named "date".

* **CTRL** - **F10**
* **date** ↵
* **left, right, centered or no date** ↵
* **CTRL** - **F10**

☐ Activate the macro editor.

* **CTRL** - **F10**
* **date** ↵
* **E**

The macro editor appears and the macro is empty except for the {DISPLAY OFF} code.

☐ When the cursor is in the Action Box, tap CTRL-PGUP to display a list of macro programming commands (see Figure 3-57).

* **A**
* **→ ↵**
* **CTRL - PGUP**

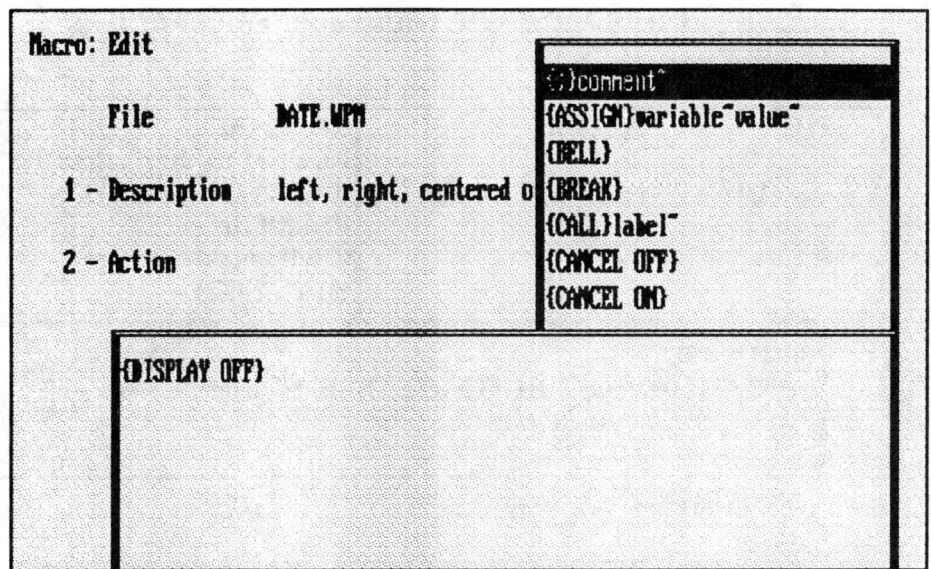

Figure 3-57 The macro command menu

All macro commands must be selected from the macro command menu. If the command is typed into the action box it will be treated as a text string and not as a macro command. Select commands from the menu by highlighting the command and tapping the ENTER key. You can move the highlight bar to a command by using the cursor control keys or by typing the necessary letters in the command's name. For example, to move the highlight bar to the CHAR command type C to move the highlight bar to the first "C" command, then H to move the bar to the first "CH" command, etc.

☐ Type "CHAR" to move the highlight bar to the CHAR command then tap the ENTER key to place the CHAR command code in the action box.

* **CHAR ↵**

Complete the following to enter the first command line (see Figure 3-58). Each command will be explained after it is entered. In the following command, enter zeroes (0), not an uppercase O. To enter the

WP: Session Six 155

{Left} cursor control code, tap CTRL-V and tap the left arrow key. CTRL-V tells WordPerfect that the next keystroke should be entered as a macro command.

* 0~Date entry: [SPACE]
* [CTRL]-] 1 [SPACE] L [CTRL]-\eft; [SPACE]
* [CTRL]-] 2 [SPACE] R [CTRL]-\ight; [SPACE] ↵
* [CTRL]-] 3 [SPACE] C [CTRL]-\entered: [SPACE] 0
* [CTRL]-V ← ~ ↵ ↵

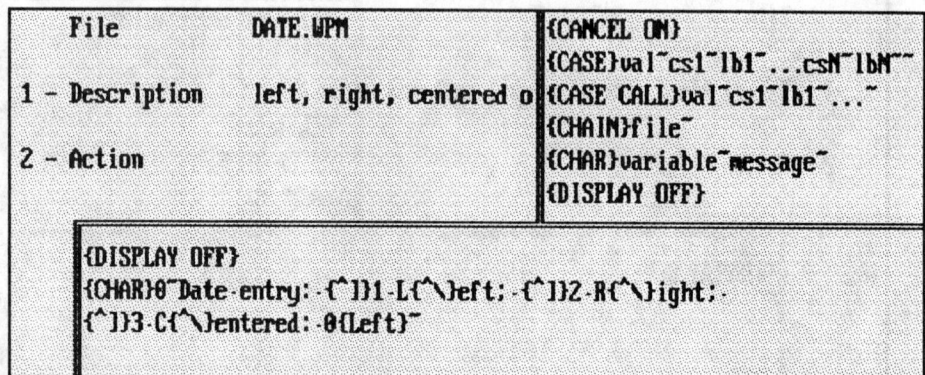

Figure 3-58 CHAR command entry

The {CHAR}variable~message~ command displays the entered "message" on the bottom monitor line then waits for a user response. When the user taps a key, it is assigned to the variable named in the command line. In the current command, the variable's name is "0". Variables may be named any number from 0 to 9. WordPerfect marks the end of variable entry and message entry with a tilde (~ rhymes with filled). The {^]} command turns on bold and {^\} turns off bold. The {Left} command places the cursor under the 0. All ENTERs are for formatting only. They are not required by the macro.

☐ Enter the {CASE} command (refer to Figure 3-56). As before, enter zero and not an uppercase O.

* [CTRL]-[PGUP]
* CAS ↵
* [CTRL]-V [ALT]-0 ~↵
* [TAB] 1~left~l~left~L~left~ ↵
* [TAB] 2~right~r~right~R~right~ ↵
* [TAB] 3~center~c~center~C~center~ ↵
* [TAB] ~ ↵ ↵

The {CASE} command reads the designated variable and tries to match its value against the listed choices. If a match is made the program jumps to the named label. If no match is made, the program continues at the line following the completion of the {CASE} command (the final tilde). In our command, the designated variable is {VAR 0}, which must be entered CTRL-V ALT-0. If you simply type the characters, the macro will treat the entry as a text entry. The second command line (1~left~l~left~L~left~) contains three possible matches: 1, l, and L. When the menu is displayed, if the user taps number 1, a lower case l or an upper case L, the program will jump to the line that contains {LABEL}left~. This allows the menu to be both numeric and mnemonic. The TABs are for formatting only and do not affect the operation of the macro.

☐ Enter the macro {QUIT} command.

* **CTRL** - **PGUP**
* **Q** ↵ ↵

The {QUIT} command terminates macro execution. It is placed here in case the user taps a key that is not one of the nine designated choices.

☐ Enter the {LABEL}left~ command and its corresponding instructions.

* **CTRL** - **PGUP**
* **L** ↵
* **left~** ↵
* **TAB** **CTRL** - **F10** **HOME** **HOME** ← **CTRL** - **F10**
* **CTRL** - **PGUP**
* **G** ↵
* **date~** ↵

The {LABEL}left~ command names this line "left". The program jumps to this line if the user taps 1, l or L. The program then continues to the next command line. The commands {Home}{Home}{Left} move the cursor to the left margin. The command {GO}date~ causes the program to jump to the line {LABEL}date~ (bypassing the "right" and "center" command lines).

☐ Refer to Figure 3-41 to enter the remainder of the macro. Use ALT-F6 to enter {Flush Right} and SHIFT-F6 to enter {Center}. Notice that the command line following {LABEL}center~ does not contain the {GO}date~ command. From there, the program does not have to jump to get to the {LABEL}date~ line.

Include a blank line before the {LABEL}date~ line. Use SHIFT-F5 to enter {Date/Outline} and toggle to command insertion mode (CTRL-F10) for the three {Enter} commands. Toggle back to edit mode before continuing.

☐ Complete the macro.

* `F7` `F7`

Step 8: Using an Interactive Macro

The interactive menu macro created in the previous step works just like a WordPerfect menu. The formatted menu is displayed and the user may select options by number or letter.

☐ Execute the date macro (see Figure 3-59).

* `ALT` - `F10`
* **date** ↵

```
Date entry: 1 Left; 2 Right; 3 Centered: 0
```

Figure 3-59 DATE macro menu

☐ Select the "Right" option by tapping "r".

* **r**

The current date should appear flush right and the cursor should be two lines below. Try the other options. Also try keys that are not options (the macro should terminate without doing anything). If your menu does not behave correctly, activate the macro editor and check your code. Look for missing tildes and commands that were entered as text. In the macro editor, all commands appear in boldface and text appears in normal typeface.

Step 9: Chaining Macros

One macro may activate another macro. A macro may be "chained" to the end of another macro by tapping ALT-F10 and naming the second macro during the creation of the first macro.

This step demonstrates the creation of a macro that enters a standard letter heading and then calls the DATE macro created in Step 7. The DATE macro is chained to the letter head macro.

❏ Create a macro named HEADING that types a standard letter heading.

* `CTRL` - `F10`
* heading ↵
* **standard letter heading** ↵
* `SHIFT` - `F6` *(enter your name)* ↵
* `SHIFT` - `F6` *(enter your address)* ↵
* `SHIFT` - `F6` *(enter your city and state)* ↵ ↵
* `SHIFT` - `F6` *(enter your telephone number)* ↵ ↵

Do not close the macro yet.

❏ Chain the DATE macro onto the HEADING macro.

* `ALT` - `F10`
* date ↵
* `CTRL` - `F10`

Notice that the DATE macro was not executed when it was called. When the HEADING macro is played back, execution will flow from one macro to the other.

❏ Clear the screen and execute the HEADING macro.

* `F7` N N
* `ALT` - `F10`
* heading ↵

❏ Select the centered date option from the date menu.

* c

Because the display was turned off ({DISPLAY OFF}) at the beginning of the macro, the heading does not appear until a choice is made from the date menu.

- Clear the screen.

* ⌴F7⌴ N N

Step 10: Practice

Create the following simple macros.

* **Purpose**: Delete the current line (no matter where the cursor is on the line). **Name**: ALT-L. **Keystrokes**: HOME HOME HOME LEFT CTRL-END DEL

* **Purpose:** Reverse the two letters at the current cursor position. **Name:** ALT-R. **Keystrokes:** DEL → F1 R ← ←

* **Purpose:** Underline a word (the cursor is anywhere in the word). **Name:** ALT-U. **Keystrokes:** → CTRL-← ALT-F4 CTRL-→ ← F8

* **Purpose:** Delete from the current cursor position to the end of the sentence (but keep the period). **Name:** ALT-E. **Keystrokes:** ALT-F4 . (period) ← DEL Y

* **Purpose:** Save the current document (assume it has been saved at least once). **Name:** ALT-S. **Keystrokes:** F10 ↵ Y

Edit the HEADING macro (see Step 8) to allow you to watch the letter heading being created.

* Clear the screen.
* Activate the macro editor (CTRL-F10 HEADING ↵).
* Delete the {DISPLAY OFF} code in the Action Box.
* Exit the macro editor.
* Execute the macro.

Create an advanced macro that displays a three choice menu. Each of the three choices is a different letter closing: 1) Sincerely, 2) Very truly yours, and 3) Most graciously and lovingly yours. This menu is exactly the same format as the DATE menu. The menu should look like Figure 3-60.

* Create an empty macro named CLOSE.
* Use CLOSE to activate the macro editor.
* Enter the {CHAR} command to display the formatted menu.

```
Letter closing: 1 Sincerely; 2 Very; 3 Most: 0
```

Figure 3-60 CLOSE macro menu

* Enter the {CASE} command to match the nine possible user entries (1,s,S,2,v,V,3,m,M). Use the labels "sincere", "very" and "most".
* Enter the {QUIT} command.
* Enter the {LABEL}sincere~ line.
* Enter its associated keystrokes and commands (Sincerely, CTRL-PGUP G signature~).
* Enter the {LABEL}very~ line.
* Enter its associated keystrokes and commands (Very truly yours, CTRL-PGUP G signature~).
* Enter the {LABEL}most~ line.
* Enter its associated keystrokes (Most graciously and lovingly yours,).
* Enter the {LABEL}signature~ line.
* Enter its associated commands (CTRL-F10 {Enter}{Enter}{Enter}{Enter}{Enter} CTRL-F10 type your name).
* Exit the macro editor.
* Execute the macro.

Step 11: Exiting WordPerfect

Save your current document and exit WordPerfect (see Session One, Step 12). Remove your data diskette from drive A and turn off the computer.

Session Seven

Desktop Publishing Capabilities

Desktop publishing features allow users to control a document's printed appearance. WordPerfect 5.0 includes features such as columns, font control, graphics, styles, macros, text formatting, and extensive printer support to help users create sophisticated documents.

Laura Grant, Publications Director for the Department of Environmental Protection (DEP), creates a bi-weekly newsletter. She edits articles from DEP personnel and uses her artistic talent to arrange them in newsletter format.

This session combines three articles and one piece of clip art to create a one page newsletter (see Figure 3-61). The session begins by creating three styles (remembered code combinations that are assigned to text blocks). Since text size and graphics box placement vary according to the selected printer, instructions are included for a laser printer (the HP LaserJet Series II) and a dot matrix printer (the Epson LQ1050). Once the styles exist, the newsletter is created by defining five graphics boxes, retrieving text and clip art into the boxes, and formatting the text by applying the created styles.

If WordPerfect is not currently running, refer to Session One, Step 1 in this chapter to start your computer load WordPerfect. To complete the newsletter, you will need four files that are on the Example Files Diskette: DEPACS.WP, FAMILY.WP, TR-FACIL.WP and APPLAUSE.WPG. At appropriate times in this session you will be asked to insert your backup copy of the Example Files Diskette into drive A and retrieve one of the four files.

In this session you will learn how to:

- ◆ Define graphics boxes
- ◆ Type text into a graphics box
- ◆ Import an existing text file into a graphics box
- ◆ Use styles to control text formatting
- ◆ Import clip art into a graphics box
- ◆ Overlap two graphics boxes

Step 1: Preparing the Newsletter Format

Use styles to help format the newsletter. WordPerfect styles are code combinations that can be assigned to a text block. For example, Laura Grant creates three styles (text body, newslet head and article head) to

DEP NEWS

The Department of Environmental Protection's Bi-Weekly Newsletter Vol 22 No. 4   Laura Grant, Editor

DEPACS backup is bug free
by Cheri Louis

The MIS department reports that the DEPACS backup system passed a stress test six months ago and has operated bug free since that time. DEPACS, the Department of Environmental Protection's Automated Complaint System, was setup to insure that citizens' complaints are routed quickly to the correct maintenance yard for correction. DEPACS is usually run by our mainframe. Since the mainframe is taken off line at least 4 hours every day for servicing, a backup system is required.

Until last year, backup complaints were sent by teletype machines from the complaint center to each yard. In a procedural review two years ago, complaint center personnel pointed out that the teletypes were expensive (over $50,000 per year for phone lines alone). They also noted that each complaint sent via teletype had to be reentered into the mainframe when the system came back up, or no record of the complaint would exist in DEPACS.

Most parties participating in the review agreed that a better system should be used. Currently, a study is being conducted to define the new system.

MIS suggested an interim solution. Install three personal computers in the complaint center and one personal computer in each maintenance yard. Dedicate each complaint center personal computer to a specific type of complaint (water related, sewer related and air related). Enter complaints into each complaint center computer. The computer then sends the complaints to a national electronic message service which dials the correct yard and reads the message to the yard's computer. At the yard, the message is printed on DEPACS forms and stored electronically. Therefore, copies of the message are retained electronically at the complaint center, in the national message service and in a history file on the yard's computer. When the mainframe goes back on line, all new messages entered into the backup system are uploaded so the complaint center operators do not have to rekey the complaints.

Over a year ago, computers were installed at the complaint center and programs were written to facilitate complaint input. Computers were ordered for each of the yards and installed as they arrived. A program was developed for the yard computers. Both programs were revised and fine tuned during preliminary testing. When the interactive programs worked, they were installed and the first stress tests began. Further refining occurred until the last successful stress test was completed six months ago.

Hats off to MIS for a job well done. Now, when do we get the new system?

Announcement:

The in-house training facility is open for business.

After only a year, we have the basic components necessary to have an operating in-house personal computer training facility. "It is still bare bones," says Reginald White, DEP's PC-Training Coordinator, "but we are going to start classes anyway." Reginald reports that the facility contains 10 custom designed student workstations that are connected together through a Local Area Network. Reginald also pointed out that the training facility is enclosed by four of the handsomest walls in DEP (the grapevine says they were painted by Reginald himself one weekend).

At first, classes in WordPerfect 5.0, Lotus 1-2-3 and dBASE IV will be taught by MIS personnel. Soon, LAN and Office Automation classes will be added. Classes should begin within a month and schedules will be sent to each bureau's training liaison.

A bid has been awarded for the final element of the training room, an instructor's console that will give the instructor complete control of the room's teaching environment.

DEP expects to save over $60,000 dollars a year by having our own training facility. So wish our instructional staff "bon chance" and we'll see you in class.

DEP Family News

A Family on the Run

A Special Report by Frank Thomason

Recently, in one of our northeastern suburbs, an entire family was on the run at the same time. You see, most of the Grant family (Jennifer, Bryan, Laura, and papa George) entered a ten mile relay race sponsored by the local road runners club. The other fifth of the family (mama Barbara) was there to cheer them on. Jennifer, a lawyer who ran track and cross country in highschool, showed that she has not lost her form. She averaged less than 7 minutes/mile in the opening 4-mile leg. When she handed the sash to her brother Bryan, a fighter pilot home on leave for the holidays, the Grant family team was near the front of the pack.

Bryan, the "energetic one", turned in a brilliant second leg. At the end of his 3 miles, the Grants were in first place. He handed the sash to Laura, the youngest of the Grant children, who is best known for her vivid imagination and artistic talent. To keep up with her siblings, Laura trained intensively for a month by eating lots of spaghetti and buying her first pair of running shoes. "Isn't that what runners do?" she asked breathlessly during her post race interview. Luckily, Laura inherited running talent from her father. So, at the end of Laura's leg, as she stated later, the Grants were "strategically placed for a strong finish". They were now in fifth place.

It was time for papa George to take over. George is locally famous for his strong kick. He ran the 220 and 440 in highschool and college and has been a member of the running club for 20 years. His anchor leg was two miles. He caught the leaders at the end of the first mile, running a 5:50 mile. He must have gone out too fast though because he was not able to pass the leader in the last mile and the Grants finished second.

In all, they were pleased with their outing, and glad to be together as a family again.

Figure 3-61   DEP Newsletter printed on a laser printer

format various portions of the newsletter. Once created, styles may be used to format successive newsletters.

In this step, instructions are included for the Hewlett-Packard Laser Jet Series II laser printer and the Epson LQ1050 dot matrix printer. Follow the instructions that are appropriate for your printer and ignore the other set of instructions.

☐ Create the newsletter heading style.

* ALT - F8
* C
* N newslet head ↵

☐ Activate the codes screen (see Figure 3-62).

* C

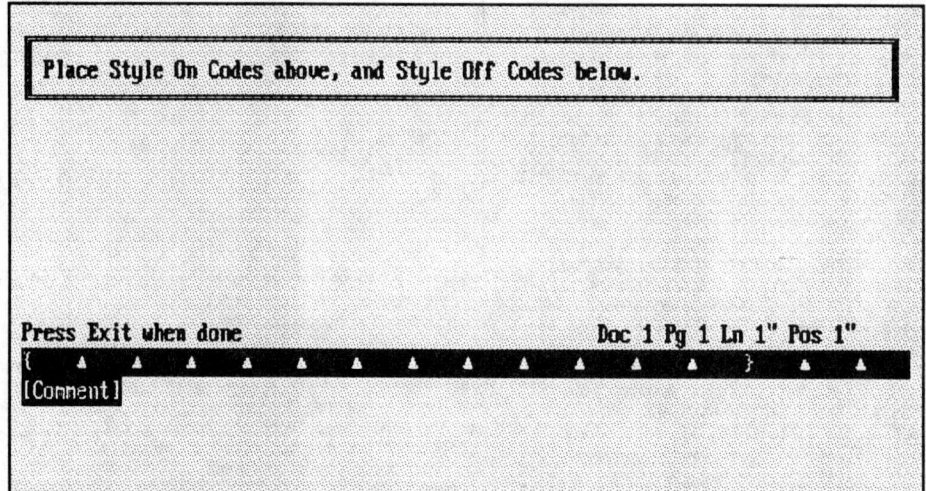

Figure 3-62 Graphics editing screen

☐ If you are using a laser printer, enter the following codes.

* SHIFT - F6
* CTRL - F8 F
* (highlight "Courier Bold 10 pitch") ↵
* F7 F7

The second code entry (CTRL-F8) selects the style's base font. This font is applied to all text that the style affects. Figure 3-63 displays the Hewlett-Packard Laser Jet Series II internal fonts.

```
* Courier 10 pitch
  Courier Bold 10 pitch
  Line Draw 10 pitch
  Line Printer 16.66 pitch
```

Figure 3-63 "APPLAUSE" box definition

☐ If you are using a dot matrix printer, enter the following codes.

* SHIFT - F6
* CTRL - F8 F
* *(highlight "San Serif 12 Pt")* ↵
* F7 F7

What Is a Font?

A font is a particular typeface in a specified typestyle and typesize. For example, this box contains two fonts. The box's title is New Century Schoolbook Bold 11 point. The box's text is New Century Schoolbook Normal 10 point. Both fonts are the same typeface (New Century Schoolbook). The fonts have different typestyles (Bold and Normal) and different typesizes (11 and 10 point).

Another font typeface is used on this page to present keystrokes and activities (see the bullets above). The SHIFT-F6 keystrokes are printed in Swiss Bold 12 point and the activity (highlight....) is printed in Swiss Italics 12 point.

Printers include a set of default fonts called internal fonts. Figure 3-64 displays a partial listing of the Epson LQ1050's internal fonts.

```
  Roman 12pt (PS) Dbl-Wide
  Roman 12pt (PS) Italic
  Roman Italic ( 5 CPI)
  Roman Italic ( 6 CPI)
  Roman Italic ( 7 CPI)
  Roman Italic (10 CPI)
  Roman Italic (12 CPI)
  Roman Italic (15 CPI)
  Roman Italic (17 CPI)
  Roman Italic (20 CPI)
  San Serif ( 5 CPI)
  San Serif ( 6 CPI)
  San Serif ( 7 CPI)
  San Serif (10 CPI)
  San Serif (12 CPI)
  San Serif (15 CPI)
  San Serif (17 CPI)
  San Serif (20 CPI)
* San Serif 12pt (PS)
  San Serif 12pt (PS) Condensed
  San Serif 12pt (PS) Dbl-Wide
```

Figure 3-64 Partial listing of the Epson LQ1050's internal fonts

Like the HP LaserJet, the Epson LQ1050 is sold with a selection of internal fonts. Enter CTRL-F8 to select the style's base font (see Figure 3-64).

There are two style types, paired and open. A paired style returns the document to the settings in effect before the style was activated. An open style is not turned off after it is activated; its codes remain in effect.

☐ Create the other two styles (laser printers).

* *(in the Style menu)*
* C
* N article head ↵
* C
* CTRL - F8 F
* *(highlight "Courier Bold 10 pitch")* ↵
* F7 F7
* *(in the Style menu)*
* C
* N article body ↵
* C
* CTRL - F8 F
* *(highlight "Line Printer 16.66")* ↵
* F7 F7 F7

☐ Create the other two styles (dot matrix printers).

* *(in the Style menu)*
* C
* N article head ↵
* C
* CTRL - F8 F
* *(highlight "Roman 12 Pt")* ↵
* F6 F7 F7
* *(in the Style menu)*
* C
* N article body ↵
* C
* CTRL - F8 F
* *(highlight "Roman 20 CPI")* ↵
* F7 F7 F7

☐ From this point on, all activities are for both laser and dot matrix printer users. The newsletter requires that the margins be reset.

Change the left, right and bottom margins to .75" and the top margin to .5".

* [SHIFT] - [F8]
* P M .5 ↵
* .75 ↵ ↵
* L M .75 ↵
* .75 ↵

☐ Before leaving the Line Menu, change the tab settings. The tab settings will be used to indent each of the newsletter's articles.

* T
* [HOME] [HOME] ←
* [CTRL] - [END]
* 0.84 ↵
* 3.85 ↵
* 4.2 ↵
* [F7][F7]

Step 2: Assigning a Style

Styles are assigned by activating the style menu and selecting a style name.

☐ Use a style to create the newsletter heading.

* [ALT] - [F8]
* *(highlight "newslet head")* ↵
* D [SPACE] E [SPACE] P [SPACE] [SPACE] [SPACE]
* N [SPACE] E [SPACE] W [SPACE] S
* [ALT] - [F8] F ↵

The style is turned off after the text is entered.

Step 3: Creating a Graphics Text Box

Graphics boxes may contain text, clip art, graphics created by other programs (i.e., Lotus 1-2-3) or images captured from graphics screens. Four graphics types appear as options in the graphics menu (see Figure 3-65). Three are predefined types (Figure, Table and Text Box) and the fourth is user-defined. All graphics boxes may be redefined as needed.

☐ Create a graphics text box to enter the publishing information box.

* ALT - F9

```
1 Figure; 2 Table; 3 Text Box; 4 User-defined Box; 5 Line; 0
```

Figure 3-65 Graphics menu options

* **B C**

The box's horizontal placement is "B"oth left and right sides of the page and its size is 7" across by .6" high. Enter the box definitions (see Figure 3-66).

* **H L**
* **S B 7 ↵ .60 ↵**
* **E**

☐ Enter the text to be included in the box.

* ALT - F8
* *(highlight "article body")* ↵
* **The Department of Environmental Protection's Bi-weekly Newsletter Vol 22 No 4**

The remainder of the text (the editor's name) is entered flush right. When ALT-F6 is tapped, the cursor jumps to the "e" of "newsletter" and Laura's name seems to overwrite the existing text. Do not be alarmed, it will look correct when printed and viewed.

* ALT - F6
* **Laura Grant, Editor** F7 F7

```
1 - Filename                (Text)
2 - Caption
3 - Type                    Paragraph
4 - Vertical Position       0"
5 - Horizontal Position     Left & Right
6 - Size                    7" wide x 0.6" high
7 - Wrap Text Around Box    Yes
8 - Edit
```

Figure 3-66   Text box definition screen

☐ View the current document.

* SHIFT - F7
* V
* F7

Step 4: Creating a User-Defined Box

User-defined boxes begin with neutral box definition settings. They are usually defined before they are created.

☐ Create a user-defined box that will contain the DEPACS article. First, define the user options (for this box, we will accept the default options, see Figure 3-67).

* ALT - F9
* U O

Accept the default options.

* ↵

The chosen options remain in effect for all user-defined boxes until a new set of options is entered.

```
1 - Border Style
        Left                              None
        Right                             None
        Top                               None
        Bottom                            None
2 - Outside Border Space
        Left                              0.17"
        Right                             0.17"
        Top                               0.17"
        Bottom                            0.17"
3 - Inside Border Space
        Left                              0"
        Right                             0"
        Top                               0"
        Bottom                            0"
4 - First Level Numbering Method          Numbers
5 - Second Level Numbering Method         Off
6 - Caption Number Style                  [BOLD]1[bold]
7 - Position of Caption                   Below box, Outside borders
8 - Minimum Offset from Paragraph         0"
9 - Gray Shading (% of black)             0%
```

Figure 3-67   User-defined box default options

☐ Define the graphics box itself (see Figure 3-68). Import an existing text file (DEPACS.WP) into the box. Select the type "page" which allows us to set the box's position precisely on the page (vertical = 1.2 and horizontal = left margin). The size of the box is 2.5" wide by 9.2 " tall. The final selection (wrap text = no) allows other boxes and text to share the same page.

* ALT - F9
* U C
* F DEPACS.WP ↵
* T A
* V S 1.2 ↵
* H M L
* S B 2.5 ↵ 9.2 ↵
* W N

```
1 - Filename                DEPACS.WP (Text)
2 - Caption
3 - Type                    Page
4 - Vertical Position       1.2"
5 - Horizontal Position     Margin, Left
6 - Size                    2.5" wide x 9.2" high
7 - Wrap Text Around Box    No
8 - Edit
```

Figure 3-68   Box definitions for the DEPACS article

Your screen should resemble Figure 3-68.

☐ Edit the imported text file (DEPACS.WP) by adding the predefined styles.

* E

Assign the "article head" style to the article's title.

* [ALT] - [F4] [END]
* [ALT] - [F8]
* *(highlight "article head")* ↵

Assign the "article body" style to the remaining text.

* [↓] [HOME] [←]
* [ALT] - [F4]
* [HOME] [HOME] [↓]
* [ALT] - [F8]
* *(highlight "article body")* ↵
* [F7] [F7]

☐ View the current document.

* [SHIFT] - [F7] V
* [F7]

Step 5: Changing a User-Defined Box Definition

Box definitions may be changed as needed. Laura decides she wants a border and gray background as part of the box that contains the in-house training announcement.

☐ Change the user-defined box definition to create the training facility announcement box (see Figure 3-69).

* [ALT] - [F9]
* U O

☐ Assign a single line border to all four box borders.

* B S S S S

☐ Redefine the inside border space.

* I .2 ↵ .2 ↵ .2 ↵ .2 ↵

❑ Reset the gray shading percentage.

* G 10 ↵
* ↵

As before, the new options remain in effect for all subsequent user-defined boxes until a another set is entered.

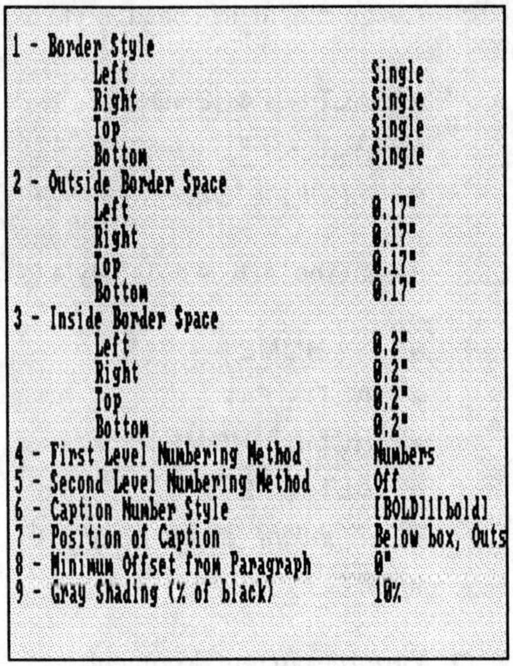

❑ Define the graphics box itself.

* ALT - F9
* U C
* F TR-FACIL.WP ↵
* T A
* V S 1.2 ↵
* H S 3.75 ↵
* S B 4 ↵ 3.9 ↵
* W N

Figure 3-69 Revised user-defined box definitions

❑ Assign predefined styles to the imported text file (TR-FACIL.WP).

* E

Center and assign the "article head" style to the article's title. Use CTRL-HOME CTRL-HOME to reassign the block highlighting to the previously defined block.

* ALT - F4 END
* SHIFT - F6 Y
* ALT - F4 CTRL - HOME CTRL - HOME
* ALT - F8
* *(highlight "article head")* ↵

❑ Center and bold the article's subheading.

* *(position the cursor on the "T" of "The in-house...")*

* ALT - F4 ↵
* SHIFT - F6 Y
* ALT - F4 CTRL - HOME CTRL - HOME
* F6

Assign the "article body" style to the subheading and the remaining text.

* *(reposition the cursor on the "T" of "The in-house...")*
* ALT - F4
* HOME HOME ↓
* ALT - F8
* *(highlight "article body")* ↵
* F7 F7

☐ View the current document.

* SHIFT - F7 V
* F7

Step 6: Importing Clip-Art into a Graphics Box

Existing clip art (line drawings) may be imported into WordPerfect graphics boxes. WordPerfect includes 30 sample images created by Publisher's PicturePaks. These clip-art files all have an .WPG extension and should be in the WP50 directory. Pictures of each image may be found in the appendix of WordPerfect 5.0's manual.

☐ Create a third user-defined box (see Figure 3-70). Do not redefine the box options. The new box will use the same options defined for the training facility announcement box.

* ALT - F9
* U C
* F \WP50\APPLAUSE.WPG ↵
* T A
* V S 5.25 ↵
* H S 3.75 ↵

* **S B 1 ↵ 1 ↵**
* **W N**

The path is included in the filename (\wp50\applause.wpg) since the file is not in the default directory.

```
1 - Filename              APPLAUSE.WPG (Gra
2 - Caption
3 - Type                  Page
4 - Vertical Position     5.25"
5 - Horizontal Position   3.75"
6 - Size                  1" wide x 1" high
7 - Wrap Text Around Box  No
8 - Edit
```

Figure 3-70 "APPLAUSE" box definition

☐ Look at the graphics editing screen (see Figure 3-71).

* **E**

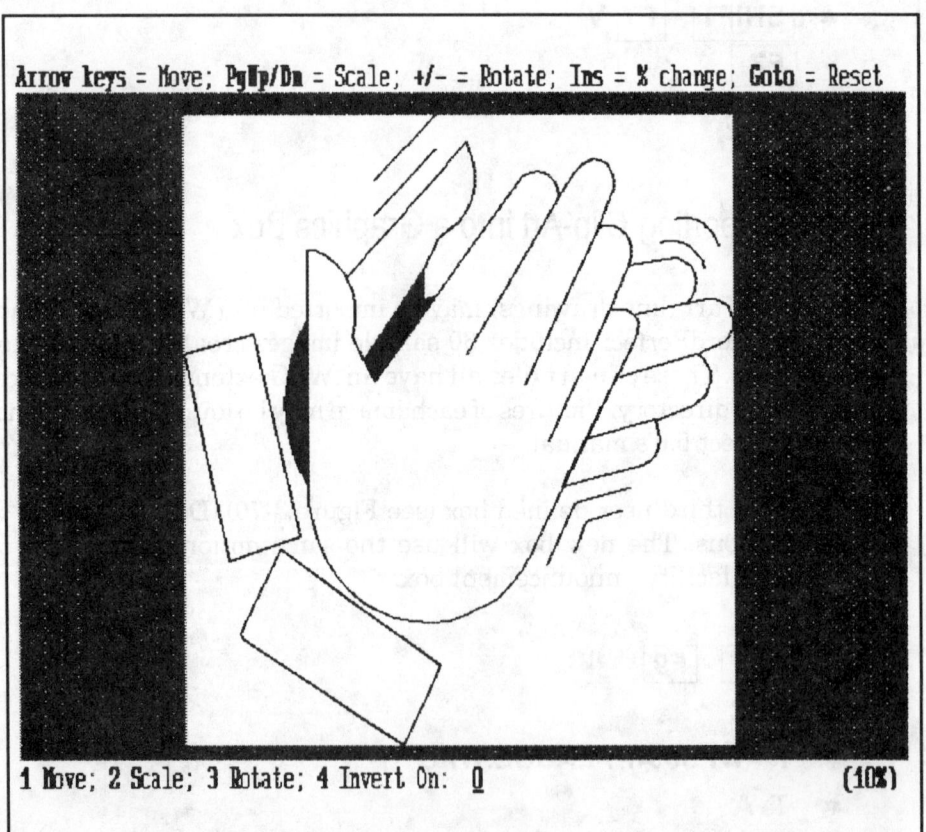

Figure 3-71 WordPerfect's graphics editing screen

- [ ] A graphic may be sized, moved, scaled, inverted and rotated. Perform the following to discover graphics editing possibilities.

    * + + +
    * [PGDN] [PGDN]
    * ↑ ↑ ↑ ↑
    * S 40 ↵ 100 ↵

- [ ] Return the graphics to its default setting.

    * [CTRL] - [HOME]

- [ ] Return to the document.

    * [F7] [F7]

Step 7: Combining Graphics Boxes

Images and text may be combined by overlapping graphics boxes.

- [ ] Create another user-defined box that overlaps the applause graphics box. Redefine the box settings.

    * [ALT] - [F9]
    * U O

- [ ] Reset the border style.

    * B N N N N

- [ ] Redefine the inside border space. Change all inside borders to 0" except the top margin which is set to .15".

    * I 0 ↵ 0 ↵ .15 ↵ 0 ↵

- [ ] Reset the gray shading percentage.

    * G 0 ↵
    * ↵

☐ Define the graphics box (see Figure 3-72).

* ALT - F9
* U C
* F FAMILY.WP ↵
* T A
* V S 5.25 ↵
* H S 3.75 ↵
* S B 4 ↵ 5 ↵
* W N

```
1 - Filename            FAMILY.WP (Text)
2 - Caption
3 - Type                Page
4 - Vertical Position   5.25"
5 - Horizontal Position 3.75"
6 - Size                4" wide x 5" high
7 - Wrap Text Around Box  No
8 - Edit
```

The applause box and the family box have the same upper left corner position.

Figure 3-72 "FAMILY" box definition

☐ Edit the imported text file (FAMILY.WP).

* E

Assign the "article head" style to the article's titles and align the headings flush right.

* ALT - F4 END
* ALT - F6 Y
* ALT - F4 CTRL - HOME CTRL - HOME
* ALT - F8
* (highlight "article head") ↵
* (position the cursor on the "A" of "A Family on...")
* ALT - F4 END
* ALT - F6 Y
* ALT - F4 CTRL - HOME CTRL - HOME
* ALT - F8
* (highlight "article head") ↵

☐ Align the author's byline flush right.

* (position the cursor on the "A" of "A Special Report....")

* ALT - F4 END
* ALT - F6 Y

Assign the "article body" style to the byline and the remaining text.

* *(reposition the cursor on the "A" of "A Special Report....")*
* ALT - F4
* HOME HOME ↓
* ALT - F8
* *(highlight "article body")* ↵
* F7 F7

☐ View the current document.

* SHIFT - F7 V
* F7

☐ Save and print the document.

* F10
* NEWSLTR ↵
* SHIFT - F7 F

Step 8: Practice

This practice assignment combines tasks explained in both the previous session and this session. Create a simple memo macro (one that only records keystrokes) that enters a memo heading complete with a graphics box containing the picture of a pencil.

* Activate macro definition
* Name the macro "memo"
* Enter the description "Memo form with graphics"
* Reset the top margin to 2.25"
* Activate graphics (ALT-F9)
* Select Figure
* Select Create
* Enter the filename (\WP50\PENCIL.WPG)

* Check the following settings: Type = Paragraph, Vertical Position = 0" and Horizontal Position = Right
* Set the size to 1" by 1"
* Change the Wrap Text Around Box option to No
* Return to the document
* Center and bold the heading "M E M O R A N D U M"
* Enter the memo heading: To: TAB TAB ↵ ↵ , From: TAB ↵ ↵ , Re: TAB TAB ↵ ↵
* Enter "Date: TAB" and the date code (SHIFT-F5 C)
* Reposition the cursor to the "To:" line ready to enter the name (tap the up arrow six times)
* Turn off macro definition
* Clear the screen and use the memo macro to create a short memo of your choice
* Print the completed memo

Step 9: Exiting WordPerfect

Save your current document and exit WordPerfect (see Session One, Step 12). Remove your data diskette from drive A and turn off the computer.

Chapter 4

dBASE III PLUS

```
. SET DEFAULT TO A
Command Line    <C:>
```

Enter a dBASE III PLUS command.

Session One

Creating a Data Base

dBASE III PLUS, a product of Ashton-Tate, is a relational database management system that enables users to create, maintain, and manipulate a data base. It also provides users with the flexibility to make inquiries and generate reports. User commands can be combined in files and run like a program to create unique data management applications.

There are many applications for database software. Some of the more popular applications of database software include mailing lists, inventory management, customer accounting, sales reporting, general office filing, business accounting, and personnel record keeping.

This session demonstrates the creation of two data bases, both of which will be used in later sessions. The two data bases are a COURSE data base which contains a record for each training course offered to employees, and a TRAINING data base which contains a record for each employee who has taken a course. These data bases will be explained fully when they are created.

In this session you will learn to:

- Load and run dBASE III PLUS
- Use dBASE III PLUS's function key assignments
- Define the structure of a data base
- Create a data base
- Add data base records
- Use BROWSE and EDIT to alter data
- Save your work and terminate a session

Step 1: Using dBASE III PLUS

☐ Boot the system (see DOS, Session One).

☐ Change to the dBASE directory, then load dBASE III PLUS to memory. In the following command, substitute the name of your dBASE directory. For instance if the dBASE directory name is DB3 instead of DBASE, the command would be: cd \db3.

* **cd \dbase** ↵
* **dbase** ↵

☐ Tap ENTER when dBASE III PLUS's license agreement screen appears.

* ↵

You have the option of using dBASE III PLUS as a **menu-driven** or a **command-driven** software package. You may alternate between the two modes depending on which best suits your immediate operational needs. The difference between the two approaches is implied in their names. When you opt for the menu-driven approach, you select options from a hierarchy of menus. With the command-driven approach, you key in sentence-like commands that may be composed of one or several parts. When working with the package as a command-driven system, you must be aware of the **command syntax**, or the way the commands are put together.

The default user interface is dBASE III PLUS's Assistant, a menu-driven system (see Figure 4-1). The initial work screen displays the main menu in a bar menu at the top of the screen and a pull-down menu for the "Set Up" option of the main menu. This session uses the command mode, commonly known as the "dot prompt" (see Figure 4-2).

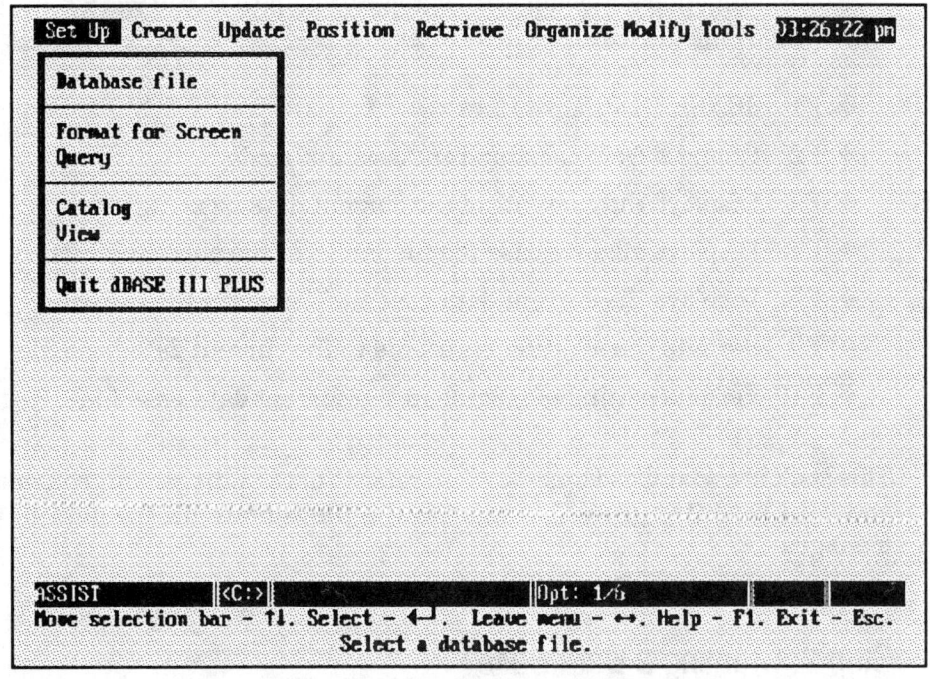

Figure 4-1   The ASSISTANT, a menu-driven user interface

☐ Tap ESC to switch from "Assistant" mode to command mode. The dBASE III PLUS dot prompt (a period) should appear at the bottom of the screen.

* ESC

☐ Insert your data diskette in drive A and enter the following command to make drive A the active drive.

* *(insert your data diskette in drive A)*
* **SET DEFAULT TO A** ↵

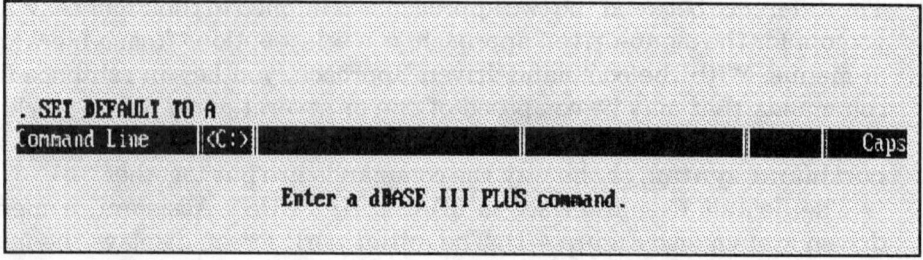

Figure 4-2 The dot prompt, a command driven user interface containing the first command to be entered

At this point you are ready to begin your dBASE III PLUS session. Several function key commands will prove helpful as you work through the following dBASE III PLUS tutorials.

- F1 dBASE III PLUS's Help key
- F2 Changes from command to Assistant mode
- F3 Displays the contents of the current data base file
- F4 Displays all data base file filenames in the current directory
- F5 Displays the current data base file's structure
- F9 Permits the addition of records to the current data base file
- F10 Permits editing of records in the current data base file

This book uses database (one word) to refer to data management software, and data base (two words) to refer to the file containing the data to be managed.

Step 2: Creating a Data Base

To create a data base, we have to know what data elements are to be included in the data base. This is done by breaking the data to be managed by dBASE into its basic elements. For instance, a name and address data base might contain the basic elements: Firstname, Lastname, Address, City, State, Zip and Phone. Each of these basic elements is called a **field**.

We create the data base's structure by defining each field that is to be included in the data base. A field is defined by entering the field's name, data type and width.

Each individual entry to a data base is called a **record**. For instance, in a name and address data base, each record contains one person's data. Their last name is entered in the Lastname field, their first name is entered in the Firstname field, etc. All records contain the same fields, but the data in the fields are unique to each record.

Edwina Cool is the education coordinator at Environmental Research Institute (ERI). ERI believes that well trained employees are more productive. ERI also believes that training should continue throughout an employee's working life. To this end, ERI offers in-house and vendor taught courses to its employees. Edwina uses dBASE III PLUS to help her with her record-keeping tasks. To do this, Edwina creates two data bases. The COURSE data base (see Figure 4-3) contains a record for each course offered: in-house courses, several courses at State University and vendor taught courses.

Record#	ID	TITLE	TYPE	SOURCE	DURATION
1	100	MIS Orientation	in-house	Staff	24
2	201	Micro Overview	in-house	Staff	8
3	2535	Intro to Info. Proc.	media	Takdel Inc	40
4	310	Programming Stds.	in-house	Staff	6
5	3223	BASIC Programming	media	Takdel Inc	30
6	7771	Data Base Systems	media	Takdel Inc	30
7	CIS11	Business COBOL	college	St. Univ.	45
8	EX15	Local Area Networks	vendor	HAL Inc	30
9	MGT10	Mgt. Info. Systems	college	St. Univ.	45
10	VC10	Elec. Spreadsheet	media	VidCourse	20
11	VC44	4th Generation Lang.	media	VidCourse	30
12	VC88	Word Processing	media	VidCourse	18

Figure 4-3   The COURSE data base

Each record in the COURSE data base contains the following fields:

- Identification number (supplied by ERI for in-house courses, by vendors, and by State University; provides cross-reference to the TRAINING data base)
- Title of course
- Type of course (in-house seminar, multimedia, college or vendor seminar)
- Source of course (ERI staff or supplier of course)

Record#	ID	EMPLOYEE	DEPARTMENT	START	STATUS
1	VC10	Bell, Jim	Marketing	01/12/91	I
2	VC10	Austin, Jill	Finance	01/12/91	I
3	VC10	Targa, Phil	Finance	01/12/91	C
4	VC88	Day, Elizabeth	Accounting	03/18/91	C
5	VC88	Fitz, Paula	Finance	04/04/91	I
6	MGT10	Mendez, Carlos	Accounting	01/15/91	I
7	EX15	Adler, Phyllis	Marketing	02/10/91	W
8	100	Targa, Phil	Finance	01/04/91	C
9	100	Johnson, Charles	Marketing	01/10/91	C
10	100	Klein, Ellen	Accounting	01/10/91	C

Figure 4-4 The TRAINING data base

❖ Duration (number of hours required to complete course)

The TRAINING data base (see Figure 4-4) contains a record for each ERI employee who is enrolled in or has taken a course. Each record contains the following fields:

❖ Identification number (provides cross-reference to COURSE data base)

❖ Employee (name of ERI employee)

❖ Department (department affiliation of employee)

❖ Start (date course was begun)

❖ Status (employee's status code: I=incomplete, W=withdrawn from course, C=completed course)

Let's create the COURSE data base first. To create the COURSE data base of Figure 4-3, you need to define its structure (i.e., define each field to be included in the data base).

☐ Create the data base structure (see Figure 4-5). The following dBASE command includes two words. The first word, CREATE, is the command verb. Almost all dBASE commands begin with a command verb. The second word, COURSE, is the name of

	Field Name	Type	Width	Dec
1	ID	Character	5	
2	TITLE	Character	20	
3	TYPE	Character	8	
4	SOURCE	Character	10	
5	DURATION	Numeric	4	0
6	-	Character		

Figure 4-5 The COURSE data base's structure

the data base to be created. Entering the command calls the field definition screen.

* **CREATE COURSE** ↵

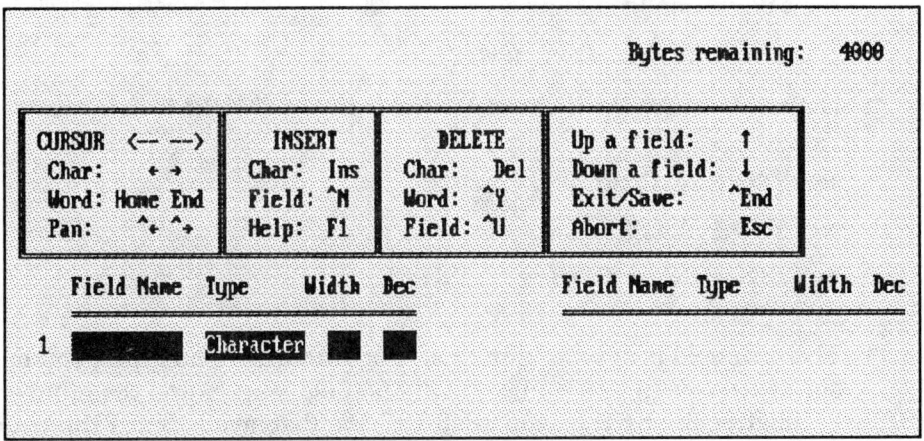

Figure 4-6 The field definition screen used to create a data base's structure. The cursor is positioned to enter the first field's name.

Study the input and editing keystroke options at the top of the screen (see Figure 4-6), the record definition work area, and the status/user-instruction interface at the bottom of the screen.

☐ Define field number 1, the ID field. Enter the Field Name. Use the backspace or delete keys to correct data entry errors.

* **ID** ↵

☐ Select the field type. The five types of fields are "character" (the default), "numeric," "date," "logical," and "memo." The COURSE data base includes four character fields and one numeric field (see Figure 4-5). The ID field will contain character data. A **character** field type can be a single word or any alphanumeric (numbers, letters, and special characters) phrase up to several hundred characters in length. To select a field type, tap the first character of the desired field type or tap the SPACE bar to toggle through the options.

* **C**

☐ Define the width of the field, sometimes called the field length, in character positions.

dBASE: Session One **185**

* 5 ↵

The cursor is automatically positioned for the next field definition because fields of type "character" do not require a "Dec" or decimal positions definition (see Figure 4-7).

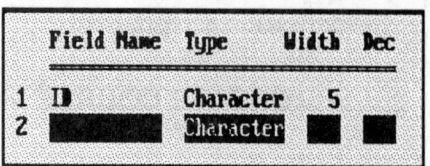

Figure 4-7 The ID field's definition

☐ Define the other three character fields in the COURSE data base.

* **TITLE** ↵ **C 20** ↵
* **TYPE** ↵ **C 8** ↵
* **SOURCE** ↵ **C 10** ↵

☐ The fifth field is of type "numeric." For **numeric** field types, you must specify the maximum number of digits (field length) and the number of decimal positions that you wish to have displayed. Since the course durations are all defined in whole hours, the number of decimal positions for the DURATION field is set at zero. Set "Dec," or the number of spaces to the right of the decimal, to zero (see Figure 4-8).

* **DURATION** ↵ **N 4** ↵ **0** ↵

☐ Tap ENTER with the cursor at the "Field Name" prompt to signify the end of the record definition for the COURSE data base file. Tap ENTER again to confirm that the definition is correct.

Figure 4-8 Five fields are defined, the cursor is positioned to name the next field

* ↵ ↵

☐ Return to the dot prompt with a "No" response.

* **N**

A "Yes" response would display the data entry screen for the COURSE data base. We selected the "No" response to be able to demonstrate the APPEND command in the next step.

Step 3: Adding Data Base Records

The screen format for entering, editing, and adding records to the COURSE data base is shown in Figure 4-9. This screen is generated automatically from the specifications outlined in the structure of the COURSE data base (see Figure 4-5). To enter data into the COURSE data base, Edwina Cool issues a command that calls up the data entry screen of Figure 4-9. Then she enters the data for the first record, then the second record, and so on. dBASE automatically assigns a number to each record as it is entered.

Edwina uses the **APPEND** command to add records to the existing COURSE data base. This command displays the format screen of Figure 4-9 (without data) so that she can enter the data for the new record(s). Each additional record is assigned a record number that is one higher than the current total.

At this point the COURSE data base has no records. Add the records, as shown in Figure 4-3, to the COURSE data base.

☐ The APPEND command displays the data entry screen (see Figure 4-9).

* **APPEND** ↵

☐ Enter the data for the first record shown in Figure 4-3. Please enter the data for this record and all records exactly as it is shown. Remember that an uppercase M is a different character from a lowercase m. In later sessions, when we extract data from the data base, the dBASE data references are case specific. If you enter the data incorrectly now, your commands will not work later. In the next step, you will be shown how to view and edit your entries.

* **100** ↵
* **MIS Orientation** ↵
* **in-house**

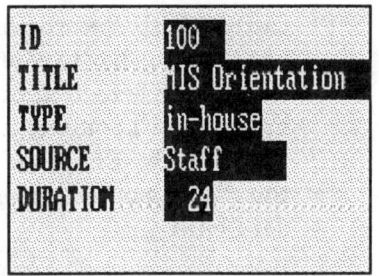

Since "in-house" is exactly as long as the field width definition, the cursor is automatically positioned at the next field. You may hear a warning beep. To turn the warning beep off, enter the command SET BELL OFF at the dot prompt.

Figure 4-9 Data entry/editing screen

☐ Complete the first record with entries for the SOURCE and DURATION fields.

* **Staff** ↵

* **24** ↵

☐ Repeat the record entry procedure described above to enter records 2 through 12 of the COURSE data base (Figure 4-3). After entering the last record, you should be at the end-of-file (EOF) and record number 12 (see the indicators, EOF/12, in the status bar).

☐ Return to the dot prompt.

* **CTRL** - **END**

☐ List the data base to view your work. If you see entry mistakes, the next step describes how to correct the errors.

> **Problem Solving**
>
> If you return to the dot prompt unintentionally, enter the APPEND command to continue record entry. Returning to the dot prompt prematurely happens if the cursor is in the first field (ID) of a new record and you tap the ENTER key before entering any data.

* **LIST** ↵

Step 4: Modifying Records in a Data Base

Unfortunately, entry errors occur. dBASE III PLUS has several commands that allow record editing. The three record modification commands discussed in this step are BROWSE, EDIT and APPEND. BROWSE displays data base records in table format. EDIT and APPEND display one record at a time. All three commands allow the user to modify the data. First, we will discuss the BROWSE command.

☐ Currently the record pointer is pointing to the end of the data base (look at the status bar to confirm). When the BROWSE command is entered, the browse screen appears and the current record (the one pointed to by the record pointer) is positioned at the top of the browse window (see Figure 4-10). Enter the "BROWSE" command, then tap PGUP to move the record pointer to the first record to display all the records in this data base.

* **BROWSE** ↵

☐ Use the Set Options menu to reposition the record pointer to the top record. Tap CTRL-HOME to open the Set Options menu, then select the "Top" option by tapping T.

* **CTRL** - **HOME**
* **T**

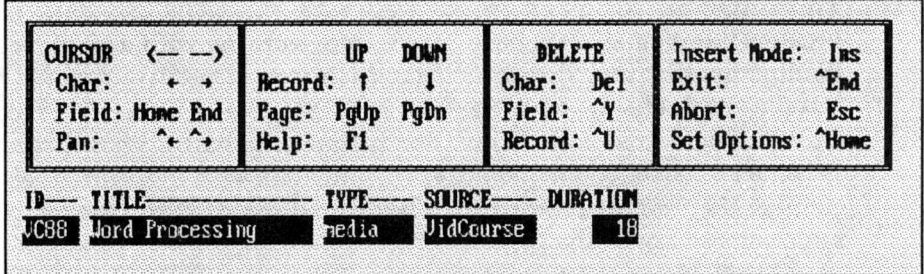

Figure 4-10   The BROWSE screen as it first appears. The record pointer is positioned at the last record in the data base

Figure 4-11 displays the BROWSE screen with the record pointer positioned at record 1. Use the four cursor control keys to browse through the records of the data base. To make corrections or modifications, position the cursor at the proper location and key in the correct data. Use the INS key to toggle between insert and replace data entry modes.

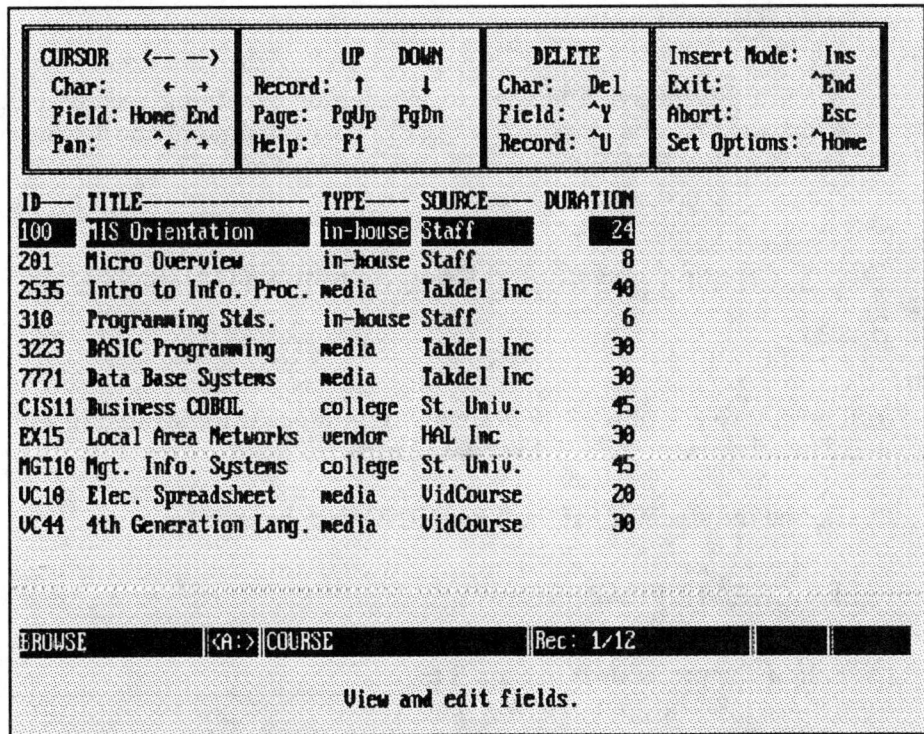

Figure 4-11   The BROWSE screen. The record pointer has been repositioned to the top record (Rec: 1/12)

Return to the dot prompt.

* `CTRL` - `END`

❏ The BROWSE command works well with the COURSE data base because it is a small data base. If you were working with a 3000 record mailing list that included 25 fields in each record, BROWSE would not be efficient. Instead, you use a command that selects a specified record from the data base for editing. For instance, to edit a known record, Edwina issues the command **edit** in conjunction with the desired record number (for example, record 10). The desired record would then appear superimposed over the format screen, as in Figure 4-9. Changes are made to fields in the format screen in much the same way that you would change text in a word processing document. For demonstration purposes, assume that record 10 needs to be modified.

* **EDIT RECORD 10** ↵

The record is available for editing. When editing is complete you may tap CTRL-END to save your changes and return to the dot prompt, or tap the ESC key to ignore your changes and return to the dot prompt.

* |CTRL| - |END|

A third alternative approach to viewing or modifying records of the active data base is to issue the "APPEND" command at the dot prompt and PGUP or PGDN to select the appropriate record.

Step 5: Creating and Adding Records to the TRAINING Data Base

You now have one of the two permanent data bases illustrated in Figure 4-1. The other is the TRAINING data base.

❏ Define the structure of the TRAINING data base.

* **CREATE TRAINING** ↵

❏ Follow the procedures in Step 2 to create the structure for the TRAINING data base (see Figure 4-12).

* **ID** ↵ **C 5** ↵
* **EMPLOYEE** ↵ **C 20** ↵
* **DEPARTMENT** ↵ **C 10** ↵

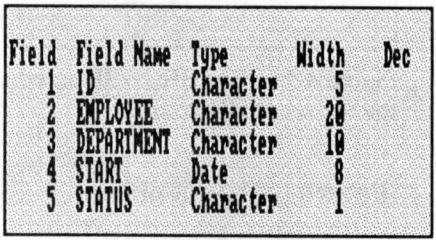

Figure 4-12   The structure for the TRAINING data base

☐ The START field is a "date" field. All date fields have a default width of 8 positions and a predefined data entry format of MM/DD/YY. Notice that the cursor immediately jumps to the next field's name entry after you tap the "d" to select type "date."

* **START ↵ D**
* **STATUS ↵ C 1 ↵**

☐ Exit the data base structure definition screen.

* **↵ ↵**

☐ Answer "Y"es to the "Input data records now" prompt to add the records, as shown in Figure 4-4, to the TRAINING data base.

* **Y**

☐ Enter the data for the each of the 10 records in the same manner as described in Step 3 and return to the dot prompt.

* **CTRL - END**

Step 6: Printing a Record Listing

Append the qualifier, TO PRINT, to the end of the LIST command to route LIST selections from the active data base file to the printer.

☐ Print the entire TRAINING data base file.

* **LIST TO PRINT ↵**

☐ Print the entire COURSE data base file. When a dBASE command is entered, it is applied to the active data base. Currently TRAINING is the active data base. To list and print the COURSE data base, it first must be made the active data base. The USE command selects a data base file to be the active data base.

* **USE COURSE ↵**
* **LIST TO PRINT ↵**

Step 7: PRACTICE

Create a data base named AUDIO to keep track of an individual's library of recordings: compact discs (CDs), long-playing (LP) records, and audio tapes.

* The data base should have the structure displayed in Figure 4-13.
* Enter the data displayed in Figure 4-14 into the audio data base.
* Use BROWSE to edit the data base.
* List and print the entire data base.

Field	Field Name	Type	Width	Dec
1	FORMAT	Character	7	
2	ARTIST	Character	17	
3	TITLE	Character	22	
4	TIME	Numeric	5	2
5	SONGS	Numeric	5	

Figure 4-13   The structure of the AUDIO data base

Record#	FORMAT	ARTIST	TITLE	TIME	SONGS
1	CD	Depeche Mode	Some Great Reward	38.59	13
2	RECORD	London Symphony	Mozart: Requiem	61.25	1
3	CD	Depeche Mode	Black Celebration	41.19	12
4	RECORD	Depeche Mode	People Are People	32.37	11
5	CD	Ofra Haza	Shaday	48.30	10
6	RECORD	Elvis Costello	Spike	50.20	15
7	CD	Des Voix Bulgares	Le Mystere	35.60	13
8	TAPE	Liz Story	Unaccountable Effect	39.70	8
9	TAPE	Various Artists	Stay Awake	58.00	23
10	TAPE	Natalie Cole	Everlasting	52.00	13
11	RECORD	Kiri Te Kanawa	Tosca (highlights)	50.00	8

Figure 4-14   Records to be entered into the AUDIO data base

Step 8: Saving and Retrieving a Data Base

Closing an active data base saves it to secondary storage. Close an active file by:

- ◆ Issuing a USE command by itself;
- ◆ Issuing the USE command for another data base file or the active data base file;
- ◆ Exiting dBASE III PLUS with a QUIT command; or
- ◆ Issuing the CLOSE DATABASE command.

☐ Use the CLOSE DATABASE command to close the current data base.

* **CLOSE DATABASE** ↵

☐ To retrieve a data base, issue the USE command. Retrieve the COURSE data base.

* **USE COURSE** ↵

If another data base is active (i.e., the TRAINING data base), the USE command first closes the active data base then retrieves the new data base.

Step 9: Terminating a Session

The QUIT command closes all dBASE files and returns the user to the DOS prompt.

☐ If you do not plan to continue to the next Session now, enter the QUIT command to terminate the current session.

* **QUIT** ↵

☐ When the DOS prompt appears, you may remove your data diskette from drive A and turn off the computer. Before turning off the computer, enter the DOS command DIR A: to display a directory of your data diskette. Look for the three files created in this session, TRAINING.DBF, COURSE.DBF and AUDIO.DBF. When you create a data base file you enter the rootname (e.g., CREATE COURSE). dBASE III PLUS adds the DBF extension to mark the file as one of its data base files.

Session Two

Understanding dBASE

Command Structure

A dBASE command includes a command verb and a list of optional parameters. The parameters help define the command by focusing its action. For instance, the command LIST displays all the records in the active data base. Add the parameter NEXT 10 (as in, LIST NEXT 10) and the command is limited to displaying only the next 10 records beginning with the current record.

This session takes a detailed look at command syntax by presenting the LIST command and its parameters. Though other dBASE commands may use different parameters, the principles learned in this session may be applied to understanding all dBASE commands.

If dBASE III PLUS is not currently running, load the program to memory (refer to Session One, Step 1). Progress to the dot prompt, insert your data diskette in drive A and enter the command SET DEFAULT TO A.

In this session you will learn to:

- ❖ Activate an existing data base
- ❖ Use the HELP screen to understand dBASE commands
- ❖ Understand and use the EXPRESSION LIST parameter
- ❖ Append records from another data base into the current data base
- ❖ Understand and use the SCOPE parameter
- ❖ Understand and use the FOR condition parameter
- ❖ Understand and use the WHILE condition parameter
- ❖ Suppress record numbers during a listing
- ❖ Use dBASE command parameters to make data base inquiries

Step 1: Retrieving a Data Base

☐ The USE command retrieves a saved data base file (see Figure 4-15).

* **USE TRAINING** ↵
* **LIST** ↵

```
. list
Record#  ID     EMPLOYEE         DEPARTMENT  START     STATUS
     1   VC10   Bell, Jim        Marketing   01/12/91  I
     2   VC10   Austin, Jill     Finance     01/12/91  I
     3   VC10   Targa, Phil      Finance     01/12/91  C
     4   VC88   Day, Elizabeth   Accounting  03/18/91  C
     5   VC88   Fitz, Paula      Finance     04/04/91  I
     6   MGT10  Mendez, Carlos   Accounting  01/15/91  I
     7   EX15   Adler, Phyllis   Marketing   02/10/91  W
     8   100    Targa, Phil      Finance     01/04/91  C
     9   100    Johnson, Charles Marketing   01/10/91  C
    10   100    Klein, Ellen     Accounting  01/10/91  C
```

Figure 4-15 Using the LIST command to display the TRAINING data base

Step 2: Displaying the Help Screen

dBASE III PLUS includes a HELP command that provides information about dBASE commands and the use of dBASE III PLUS. If the command is entered by itself, it calls the help main menu from which the user may select the area of help required. If the user requires information about a specific command, entering HELP plus the command name (i.e., HELP LIST) will display a screen containing the command's syntax and a description of the command.

When you make a command entry error (incorrect spelling or syntax), dBASE III PLUS prompts "Do you need help?". If you respond "Y"es to the prompt, dBASE will display a relevant help screen. To suppress the help request, enter SET HELP OFF at the dot prompt.

This step displays and discusses the LIST command's help screen.

☐ Display the LIST command help screen (see Figure 4-16).

   *   **HELP LIST** ↵

```
                              LIST
                              ════

Syntax      : LIST [<scope>] [<expression list>] [FOR <condition>]
              [WHILE <condition>] [OFF] [TO PRINT]

Description : Displays the contents of a database file.
              Used alone, it displays all records. Use the scope and
              FOR/WHILE clauses to list selectively.  The expression
              list can be included to select fields or a combination
              of fields, such as Cost * Rate.  OFF suppresses the record
              numbers.
```

Figure 4-16 dBASE III PLUS help screen describing the LIST command

The help screen displayed in Figure 4-16 includes the LIST command's syntax:

> LIST [<scope>] [<expression list>] [FOR <condition>]
> [WHILE <condition>] [OFF] [TO PRINT]

The LIST command has six optional parameters. Optional parameters are displayed within square brackets (i.e., [OFF]). Within each parameter, required words are capitalized and user supplied data are enclosed within less than - greater than symbols(< >). For example, the [<Scope>] parameter is entirely user supplied, whereas the [TO PRINT] parameter requires no user supplied data.

Each of the LIST command's six optional parameters adds greater power and precision to the command. When optional parameters are included with the command verb, neither the square brackets nor the <> signs are typed as part of the command. The following steps discuss the expression list parameter, then additional records are appended from another data base to the TRAINING data base before examining the remaining parameters.

☐ Return to the dot prompt.

∗ ESC

Step 3: The Expression List Parameter

Expression lists may include one or more expressions separated by a comma. An expression is created by combining any of the following elements:

- ◆ Field names
- ◆ Memory variables
- ◆ Constants
- ◆ Functions
- ◆ Operators

All elements within an expression must be the same type (e.g., all character or all numeric). The expression list may contain expressions of different types.

For example, the command LIST ID, START lists the ID and START fields for all records in the data base. The ID field is a character field and the START field is a date field. Each is an expression. When the two expressions are separated by a comma, they create an expression list.

This step uses field names, constants, functions and operators to build expressions and combine them in expression lists. As you will discover, expressions are used in many dBASE commands. They are incredibly powerful and, though you may not believe it now, they can be fun.

☐ The default listing includes all data base fields. Include field names in an expression list to limit the listing to the specified fields. List the EMPLOYEE field by itself.

* **LIST EMPLOYEE** ↵

☐ List the DEPARTMENT and EMPLOYEE fields. Separate multiple fields with a comma (see Figure 4-17).

* **LIST DEPARTMENT, EMPLOYEE** ↵

Notice that the two fields are not in the order they appear when the LIST command is entered alone. Entering field names causes the fields to be displayed in the order specified. DEPARTMENT is an expression. EMPLOYEE is an expression. Together, separated by a comma, they make up an expression list.

```
. list department, employee
Record#  department  employee
     1   Marketing   Bell, Jim
     2   Finance     Austin, Jill
     3   Finance     Targa, Phil
     4   Accounting  Day, Elizabeth
     5   Finance     Fitz, Paula
     6   Accounting  Mendez, Carlos
     7   Marketing   Adler, Phyllis
     8   Finance     Targa, Phil
     9   Marketing   Johnson, Charles
    10   Accounting  Klein, Ellen
```

Figure 4-17 Using an expression list (department, employee) to limit the display to two fields

In addition to field names, expressions may also include functions, memory variables, operators and constants. In the following activities, we will use field names, functions, constants and operators to demonstrate expression lists.

♦ **A function** is a predefined operation. An operator can be one of four types: mathematical, relational, logical or string.

♦ **Operators** are used to join the various elements of an expression together.

♦ **Constants** are sometimes called literal strings. A constant is a character string that appears on the monitor (or print out) exactly as it appears within the expression.

Each of these elements will make more sense after you use them in the activities below.

- Use an expression to list the phrase "Employee name: " followed by each employee's name (see Figure 4-18). In the following command, "Employee name: " is a constant, EMPLOYEE is a field name and the plus sign (+) is an operator that concatenates (joins) the two character strings together.

    * **LIST "Employee's name: " + EMPLOYEE** ↵

All three elements (constant, operator and field name) are joined together to create an expression. All the elements in the expression are of type character.

```
. list "Employee's name: " + employee
Record# "Employee's name: " + employee
     1  Employee's name: Bell, Jim
     2  Employee's name: Austin, Jill
     3  Employee's name: Targa, Phil
     4  Employee's name: Day, Elizabeth
     5  Employee's name: Fitz, Paula
     6  Employee's name: Mendez, Carlos
     7  Employee's name: Adler, Phyllis
     8  Employee's name: Targa, Phil
     9  Employee's name: Johnson, Charles
    10  Employee's name: Klein, Ellen
```

Figure 4-18 The result of entering the LIST command with the expression "Employee name: " + employee

- Since all elements in an expression must be the same type (character, date, numeric or logical), dBASE III PLUS has created functions that transform data elements from one type to another. Functions were created by the authors of dBASE III PLUS to help users perform special operations that enhance the power of dBASE III PLUS commands. For example, Edwina Cool wants to list the date each employee started a course. She wants to display the information in the form "Employee: _____ Starting date: _____" for each record in the data base. She enters the following command to accomplish her task (see Figure 4-19).

    * **LIST "Employee: " + EMPLOYEE + "Starting date: " + DTOC(START)** ↵

The expression concatenates three character elements and one transformed date element. The three character elements are: "Employee: ", a constant; EMPLOYEE, a character field; and "Starting date: ", a constant. The date field, START, is transformed into a character string by using the DTOC() function (date to character).

```
. list "Employee: " + employee + "Starting date: " + dtoc(start)
Record# "Employee: " + employee + "Starting date: " + dtoc(start)
      1 Employee: Bell, Jim        Starting date: 01/12/91
      2 Employee: Austin, Jill     Starting date: 01/12/91
      3 Employee: Targa, Phil      Starting date: 01/12/91
      4 Employee: Day, Elizabeth   Starting date: 03/18/91
      5 Employee: Fitz, Paula      Starting date: 04/04/91
      6 Employee: Mendez, Carlos   Starting date: 01/15/91
      7 Employee: Adler, Phyllis   Starting date: 02/18/91
      8 Employee: Targa, Phil      Starting date: 01/04/91
      9 Employee: Johnson, Charles Starting date: 01/18/91
     10 Employee: Klein, Ellen     Starting date: 01/18/91
Command Line    <A:> TRAINING            Rec: EOF/10
```

Figure 4-19 This LIST command includes the expression "Employee: " + employee + "Starting date: " + dtoc(start)

Step 4: Appending Records from Another Data Base

Since many of the following parameters limit the number of records displayed with the LIST command, add records to the TRAINING data base to provide more data to work with. Records may be copied from one data base to another. The TRRECS.DBF data base on the Example Files Diskette contains 22 records. The structure of the TRRECS data base is identical to the structure of the TRAINING data base.

The APPEND FROM command adds records from a named file to the end of the currently active file. In this step, we will use the APPEND FROM command to copy records from the TRRECS.DBF file to the TRAINING.DBF file.

❒ Insert the Example Files Diskette in drive A and use the APPEND FROM command to copy records from the TRRECS data base into the TRAINING data base.

  * *(insert the Example Files Diskette in drive A)*
  * **APPEND FROM TRRECS** ↵
  * *(insert your data diskette in drive A)*

The data base now contains 32 records.

❒ List the entire data base (see Figure 4-20).

  * **LIST** ↵

dBASE: Session Two

```
13  345IF  Kirchner, Sandra      Marketing   03/20/91  I
14  SC445  Lewis, Barbara        Management  03/04/91  I
15  SC445  Demopolis, Chris      Sales       03/04/91  I
16  YL877  Yodashkin, Peter      Finance     01/23/91  C
17  100    Kirchner, Sandra      Marketing   01/04/91  C
18  345IF  Austin, Jill          Finance     03/20/91  I
19  SC445  Mendez, Carlos        Accounting  03/04/91  I
20  VC10   Demopolis, Chris      Sales       01/12/91  W
21  VC10   Lewis, Barbara        Management  01/12/91  C
22  MGT10  Lewis, Barbara        Management  01/15/91  C
23  SC445  Targa, Phil           Finance     03/04/91  I
24  MGT10  Finch, Rusty          Sales       01/15/91  W
25  VC10   Houston, Charles      Accounting  01/12/91  C
26  VC10   Giacomello, Antonia   Sales       01/12/91  C
27  345IF  Pfau, Amy             Management  03/20/91  I
28  MGT10  Molone, Maggie        Personnel   01/15/91  C
29  100    Reyes, Fernando       Sales       01/04/91  C
30  SC445  McGill, Annie         Marketing   03/04/91  I
31  VC88   Fisher, Phyllis       MIS/DDP     02/15/91  C
32  3223   Washington, Armindo   Finance     02/23/91  W
```

Figure 4-20   Records 13 through 32 in the TRAINING data base after appending records from the TRRECS data base

Step 5: The SCOPE Parameter

The number of consecutive records listed is controlled by the SCOPE parameter. Four SCOPEs are available: ALL, REST, NEXT N and RECORD N.

☐ List all the records in the data base.

* **LIST ALL** ↵

Notice that this listing is the same as that obtained by the LIST command. ALL is the LIST command's default scope. If the scope parameter is blank (no scope is entered) dBASE defaults to ALL and all the records are listed.

☐ The REST scope lists all records from the current pointer position to the end of the data base. Move the pointer to record 22 and list the "rest" of the data base (see Figure 4-21).

* **22** ↵
* **LIST REST** ↵

```
. 22
. list rest
Record#  ID     EMPLOYEE              DEPARTMENT  START     STATUS
    22   MGT10  Lewis, Barbara        Management  01/15/91  C
    23   SC445  Targa, Phil           Finance     03/04/91  I
    24   MGT10  Finch, Rusty          Sales       01/15/91  W
    25   VC10   Houston, Charles      Accounting  01/12/91  C
    26   VC10   Giacomello, Antonia   Sales       01/12/91  C
    27   345IF  Pfau, Amy             Management  03/20/91  I
    28   MGT10  Molone, Maggie        Personnel   01/15/91  C
    29   100    Reyes, Fernando       Sales       01/04/91  C
    30   SC445  McGill, Annie         Marketing   03/04/91  I
    31   VC88   Fisher, Phyllis       MIS/DDP     02/15/91  C
    32   3223   Washington, Armindo   Finance     02/23/91  W
```

Figure 4-21 Using the LIST REST command to display all records from the current pointer position (record 22) to the end of the data base

- The NEXT N parameter lists a specified number of records beginning with the current record. Move the pointer to record 14 and list the "next 10" records (see Figure 4-22).

  *   **14** ↵

  *   **LIST NEXT 10** ↵

```
. 14
. list next 10
Record#  ID     EMPLOYEE              DEPARTMENT  START     STATUS
    14   SC445  Lewis, Barbara        Management  03/04/91  I
    15   SC445  Demopolis, Chris      Sales       03/04/91  I
    16   YL877  Yodashkin, Peter      Finance     01/23/91  C
    17   100    Kirchner, Sandra      Marketing   01/04/91  C
    18   345IF  Austin, Jill          Finance     03/20/91  I
    19   SC445  Mendez, Carlos        Accounting  03/04/91  I
    20   VC10   Demopolis, Chris      Sales       01/12/91  W
    21   VC10   Lewis, Barbara        Management  01/12/91  C
    22   MGT10  Lewis, Barbara        Management  01/15/91  C
    23   SC445  Targa, Phil           Finance     03/04/91  I
```

Figure 4-22 Using the NEXT N scope parameter to list 10 records starting from the current pointer position (record 14)

- The RECORD N parameter is used like the NEXT N parameter except the RECORD N lists the specified record only. List record 21.

  *   **LIST RECORD 21** ↵

Enter the command HELP SCOPE when you need to remind yourself about the four scope options.

Step 6: The FOR Condition Parameter

Database software also permits you to retrieve, view, and print records based on preset conditions. You set conditions for the selection of records by composing a condition. Conditions normally compare one or more field names to numbers or character strings using **relational operators** (see Figure 4-23). Several conditions can be combined with **logical operators** (see Figure 4-23). The standard form for a condition is:

    Field Name Relational Operator Expression

Examples:

```
DEPARTMENT = "Finance"
EMPLOYEE = "Fisher, Phyllis"
DURATION >= 10
START > CTOD('01/01/91')
```

In a condition, the data types on either side of the relational operator must be the same. The last example, START > CTOD('01/01/91') matches any date after January 1, 1991. Since START is a date field, the character string '01/01/91' is transformed into a date type by using the CTOD() function (character to date).

For example, Edwina Cool wants a listing of all in-house seminars; so she issues a command to **list** the records of all courses that are of TYPE

Relational Operators	
COMPARISON	OPERATOR
Equal to	=
Less than	<
Greater than	<
Less than or equal to	<=
Greater than or equal to	>=
Not equal to	<>

Logical Operators AND and OR	
OPERATION	OPERATOR
For the condition to be true:	
Both sub-conditions must be true	.AND.
At least one sub-condition must be true	.OR.

Figure 4-23 Relational and logical operators used in dBASE III PLUS commands

in-house in the COURSE data base (see Figure 4-3). TYPE is the name of the field that holds type of course data. To retrieve these records, she sets the condition to

>   TYPE='in-house'

The **search string** must be enclosed in single or double quotes; here we use single quotes. To produce the output of Figure 4-24, Edwina keys the command

>   LIST FOR TYPE='in-house'

Use FOR statements to select records based on field matching criteria.

☐ Activate the COURSE data base and list all 'in-house' courses. In the following command, the constant 'in-house' must be entered exactly as it appears (all lowercase).

*   **USE COURSE**
*   **LIST FOR TYPE = 'in-house'** ↵

Your display should be the same as Figure 4-24.

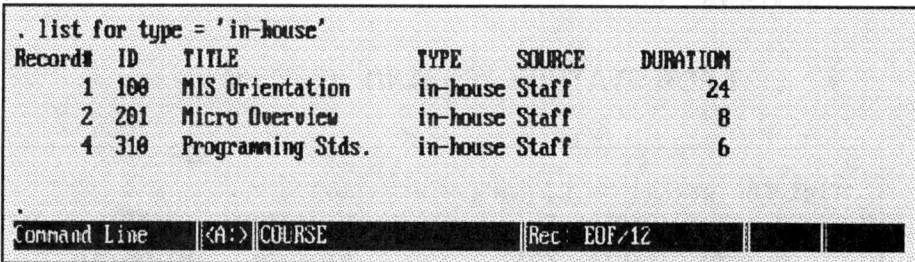

Figure 4-24 Selecting records by using a FOR condition. All records listed match the condition TYPE = 'in-house'

Problem Solving

If your display is not the same as Figure 4-24 after entering the command LIST FOR TYPE = 'in-house', check the following:

1. Is 'in-house' all lowercase in the command?
2. Is 'in-house' all lowercase in records 1, 2 and 4 (list the data base)?
3. Are the quotation symbols on either side of in-house exactly the same?

Once you have found and corrected your mistake, try the command again.

☐ Activate the TRAINING data base and list all records for which the DEPARTMENT field contains the character string "Finance" (see Figure 4-25). One last time, remember that FOR statements are case sensitive (the case of each character in the expression must match the case of each character in the field).

* **USE TRAINING**
* **LIST FOR DEPARTMENT = "Finance"** ↵

```
. list for department = 'Finance'
Record#  ID     EMPLOYEE            DEPARTMENT START    STATUS
     2   VC10   Austin, Jill        Finance    01/12/91 I
     3   VC10   Targa, Phil         Finance    01/12/91 C
     5   VC88   Fitz, Paula         Finance    04/04/91 I
     8   100    Targa, Phil         Finance    01/04/91 C
    16   YL877  Yodashkin, Peter    Finance    01/23/91 C
    18   345IF  Austin, Jill        Finance    03/20/91 I
    23   SC445  Targa, Phil         Finance    03/04/91 I
    32   3223   Washington, Armindo Finance    02/23/91 W
```

Figure 4-25 Selecting records by using a FOR condition. All records listed match the condition DEPARTMENT = 'Finance'

☐ Use a FOR statement to display records that match multiple conditions (see Figure 4-26).

* **LIST FOR STATUS = "C" .AND. ID = "100"** ↵

```
. list for status = "C" .and. id = "100"
Record#  ID    EMPLOYEE           DEPARTMENT START    STATUS
     8   100   Targa, Phil        Finance    01/04/91 C
     9   100   Johnson, Charles   Marketing  01/10/91 C
    10   100   Klein, Ellen       Accounting 01/10/91 C
    17   100   Kirchner, Sandra   Marketing  01/04/91 C
    29   100   Reyes, Fernando    Sales      01/04/91 C
```

Figure 4-26 This LIST command includes two conditions joined by a logical operator (.AND.). A record must match both conditions before being listed

The first condition (STATUS = "C") is joined to the second condition (ID = "100") with a logical operator (.AND.). Notice that FOR is not entered a second time. Also notice that 100 is enclosed with quotation marks (ID is a character field, not a numeric field). Figure 4-23 lists logical operators used in dBASE III PLUS commands.

Step 7: The WHILE Condition Parameter

WHILE conditions follow the same syntax rules as FOR conditions. The two differ in that FOR conditions list any record that matches the listed conditions, but WHILE conditions list only contiguous records as long as the listed condition(s) is matched.

☐ The first record in the data base contains VC10 in the ID field. Position the record pointer at record 1, then enter the WHILE ID = "VC10" condition to list records until the ID field no longer contains "VC10" (record 4, see Figure 4-27).

* 1 ↵
* **LIST WHILE ID = "VC10"** ↵

```
. 1
. list while id = "VC10"
Record#  ID    EMPLOYEE      DEPARTMENT START    STATUS
      1  VC10  Bell, Jim     Marketing  01/12/91 I
      2  VC10  Austin, Jill  Finance    01/12/91 I
      3  VC10  Targa, Phil   Finance    01/12/91 C
```

Figure 4-27 WHILE conditions list contiguous records as long as the condition is true.

Step 8: The OFF and TO PRINT Parameters

Include the OFF parameter (ex. LIST OFF) to suppress record number display (see Figure 4-28). Include the TO PRINT parameter (ex. LIST TO PRINT) to direct the listing to the printer as well as to the screen. Both these parameters will be demonstrated in the next step, Combining Parameters.

Step 9: Combining Parameters

dBASE command parameters can be combined to create powerful commands. After the command verb is typed (the command verb must always be first in a dBASE command), parameters may be included in any order.

☐ List the ID and STATUS fields of the first 15 records while suppressing the record number display (see Figure 4-28).

* 1 ↵
* **LIST OFF NEXT 15 ID, STATUS** ↵

This command includes the OFF parameter to suppress record number listing, the scope parameter (NEXT 15) and an expression list (ID, STATUS).

```
. 1
. list off next 15 id, status
id      status
VC10    I
VC10    I
VC10    C
VC88    C
VC88    I
MGT10   I
EX15    W
100     C
100     C
100     C
IH232   I
SC445   I
345IF   I
SC445   I
SC445   I
```

Figure 4-28 This LIST command includes three parameters

☐ List the EMPLOYEE, START and STATUS fields for Phil Targa's records (see Figure 4-29).

* **LIST EMPLOYEE, START, STATUS FOR EMPLOYEE = "Targa, Phil"** ↵

```
. list employee, start, status for employee = "Targa, Phil"
Record#  employee        start      status
      3  Targa, Phil     01/12/91   C
      8  Targa, Phil     01/04/91   C
     23  Targa, Phil     03/04/91   I
```

Figure 4-29 This command includes an expression list (EMPLOYEE, START, STATUS) and a FOR CONDITION (FOR EMPLOYEE = "Targa, Phil")

Step 10: Using Command Parameters to Make Data Base Inquiries

Many dBASE III PLUS command may be fine tuned using the same parameters discussed in the previous steps to create data base inquiries.

☐ Clear the display screen to clarify command responses.

* **CLEAR** ↵

dBASE: Session Two 206

☐ Display the entire COURSE data base.

* **USE COURSE** ↵
* **LIST** ↵

☐ Display records based on a FOR condition.

* **CLEAR** ↵
* **LIST FOR TYPE='media'** ↵

☐ Display only the ID and TITLE for the records that meet a condition.

* **CLEAR** ↵
* **LIST ID, TITLE FOR TYPE='in-house'** ↵

The display should look like Figure 4-30. As an alternative to keying in the LIST command above, you can edit the first LIST command. Use the up and down cursor control keys to scroll through previous commands. In this instance, you can simply tap the up arrow until the desired command is displayed at the dot prompt, and then edit it as needed. Tap ENTER to invoke the command. You may need to toggle between replace and insert modes with the INS key (select insert mode and insert "ID, TITLE " in the first LIST command; this creates the second).

```
. use course
. list id, title for type = "in-house"
Record#  id    title
     1   100   MIS Orientation
     2   201   Micro Overview
     4   310   Programming Stds.
```

Figure 4-30 The field used as matching criteria (TYPE='in-house') does not have to appear in the listing

☐ Display records based on a compound condition (see Figure 4-31).

* **CLEAR** ↵
* **LIST FOR TYPE='in-house' .AND. DURATION<=10** ↵

```
. list for type = "in-house" .and. duration <= 10
Record#  ID    TITLE              TYPE      SOURCE    DURATION
     2   201   Micro Overview     in-house  Staff           8
     4   310   Programming Stds.  in-house  Staff           6
```

Figure 4-31 This command includes two conditions joined by a logical operator. The first condition (TYPE = 'in-house') is of type character and the second condition (DURATION <= 10) is of type numeric

☐ Use a FOR condition with the SUM command to display the hourly total of in-house seminars made available to employees (result should be 38, see Figure 4-32). Duration is the only field displayed since it is the only numeric field in the data base.

* **CLEAR** ↵
* **SUM FOR SOURCE='Staff'** ↵

Notice that "Staff" is in upper and lower case, just as it is in the data base file.

```
. sum for source = "Staff"
      3 records summed
DURATION
   38
```

Figure 4-32 An expression list and a FOR condition used with the SUM command

☐ Display the average duration of all courses (result should be 28).

* **CLEAR** ↵
* **AVERAGE DURATION** ↵

☐ Display the total number of VidCourse courses (result should be 3).

* **CLEAR** ↵
* **COUNT FOR SOURCE='VidCourse'** ↵

Step 11: Practice

Activate the TRAINING data base and complete the following tasks.

What LIST command will display the following (use the HELP LIST screen if you need assistance):

* All records with record number display suppressed
* Record 17
* From record 25 to the end of the data base
* All records displaying only the ID and START fields
* Records 5 through 19
* All of Barbara Lewis's records (3 records should be displayed)

Use the TO PRINT parameter to print the following displays:

- * Everyone in the data base who is in Sales (6 records are displayed)
- * Everyone in the data base who is in Sales and took course SC445 (2 records are displayed)
- * The EMPLOYEE and STATUS fields for those employees who withdrew ("W") from classes (4 records are displayed)

Activate the AUDIO data base created in Session One, Step 7 and complete the following tasks.

- * List and print all CDs that were recorded by Depeche Mode
- * List and print all records and tapes with playing times in excess of 40 minutes
- * List and print the total number of songs on CD
- * List and print the average playing time for all recordings

Step 12: Terminating the Session

If you do not plan to continue to the next Session now, enter the QUIT command to terminate the current session.

- * **QUIT** ↵

When the DOS prompt appears, you may remove your data diskette from drive A and turn off the computer.

Session Three

Introduction to Sorting and Indexing

Records in a data base are displayed in the sequence in which they are stored in the data base. There are two approaches that enable the display of records in alternative sequences.

- Use the sort command and create a sorted version of the data base.
- Create an index file. **Indexing** eliminates the need to create a sorted version of the original data base.

The reordering principles used in both approaches are the same, the type of output file varies. When a data base is sorted, an entirely new data base is created to contain the reordered records. When a data base is indexed, the original data base is displayed in the requested reordering. Both approaches are explained in detail below.

If dBASE III PLUS is not currently running, load the program to memory (refer to Session One, Step 1). Progress to the dot prompt, insert your data diskette in drive A and enter the command SET DEFAULT TO A.

In this session you will learn to:

- Sort a data base
- Index a data base

Step 1: Sorting

The records in a data base can be sorted for display in a variety of formats. For example, the COURSE data base in Figure 4-1 has been sorted and is displayed in ascending order by course identification number (ID). To obtain this sequencing of the data base records, Edwina Cool selects ID as the **key field** and requests an ascending sort of the COURSE data base. In dBASE III PLUS, the **collating sequence** is set up so that numbers are considered to be less than alphabetic characters. In Figure 4-1, the numeric IDs are listed before those that begin with a letter.

☐ Edwina also wants a presentation of the COURSE data base that is sorted by ID within SOURCE. This involves the selection of a **primary** and a **secondary key field**. Secondary key fields are helpful when duplicates exist in the primary key field (for example, there are three records for SOURCE='Staff'). Edwina selects SOURCE as the primary key field, but she wants the courses offered by each source to be listed in ascending order by ID. To achieve this record sequence, she selects ID as the secondary key field. Activate the COURSE data base and enter the following command to sort the data base on ID within SOURCE.

* **SORT TO DBSORT ON SOURCE, ID** ↵

☐ The COURSE data base remains unchanged. Display the new data base that contains the sorted version of the COURSE data base file.

* **USE DBSORT** ↵
* **LIST** ↵

```
. sort to dbsort on source, id
100% Sorted        12 Records sorted
. use dbsort
. list
Record#  ID     TITLE                TYPE      SOURCE     DURATION
      1  EX15   Local Area Networks  vendor    HAL Inc          30
      2  CIS11  Business COBOL       college   St. Univ.        45
      3  MGT10  Mgt. Info. Systems   college   St. Univ.        45
      4  100    MIS Orientation      in-house  Staff            24
      5  201    Micro Overview       in-house  Staff             8
      6  310    Programming Stds.    in-house  Staff             6
      7  2535   Intro to Info. Proc. media     Takdel Inc       40
      8  3223   BASIC Programming    media     Takdel Inc       30
      9  7771   Data Base Systems    media     Takdel Inc       30
     10  VC10   Elec. Spreadsheet    media     VidCourse        20
     11  VC44   4th Generation Lang. media     VidCourse        30
     12  VC88   Word Processing      media     VidCourse        18
```

Figure 4-33 The data base DBSORT. This data base was created when the command SORT TO DBSORT ON SOURCE, ID was applied to the COURSE data base

A display of the results of the sort operation is shown in Figure 4-33. Notice that the SOURCE field entries are in alphabetical order and the three "Staff" records (records 4, 5, and 6) are in sequence by ID (100, 201, 310). If the need arises, Edwina can perform sorts that require the identification of primary, secondary, and tertiary key fields.

The issuing of a sort command results in the compilation of a another data base. The sorted version of the data base is stored on disk under another name. After the sort operation, the sorted version of the data base contains the records in the order described in the sort command (see Figure 4-8). Sorting is considered to be static. That is any future changes to the original data base will not be reflected in the sorted data base unless a new sort command is issued.

- Edwina uses the sorted version of the COURSE data base of Figure 4-33 to produce the listing of Figure 4-34. To do this she issues the following command.

* **LIST SOURCE, ID FOR TYPE= "vendor" .OR. TYPE = "media"** ↵

```
. list source, id for type = "vendor" .or. type = "media"
Record#  source       id
      1  HAL Inc      EX15
      7  Takdel Inc   2535
      8  Takdel Inc   3223
      9  Takdel Inc   7771
     10  VidCourse    VC10
     11  VidCourse    VC44
     12  VidCourse    VC88
```

Figure 4-34 Because the entries in the SOURCE field are alphabetized in Figure 4-33, the selected SOURCE entries in this figure are also alphabetized

Step 2: Indexing

When a data base is indexed, an index file is created. Unlike a sort file, the index file is never viewed by the user. Instead it is used as a reference to temporarily reorder the records in the data base file.

The index file contains two fields: a key field and a record number field. The key field is an ascending listing based on an expression entered as part of the INDEX command. The record number is the record's numerical position within the data file. When you list an indexed data base, dBASE III PLUS refers to the index file to list the original records in the indexed order (see Figure 4-35). The display appears in the indexed order but the original data base remains unchanged.

To understand the usefulness of an index, it is necessary to understand how records are accessed. When you activate the TRAINING data base and enter the command, LIST FOR EMPLOYEE = 'Targa, Phil', the database program begins at the first record and compares the contents of the EMPLOYEE field to the character string, "Targa, Phil". If there is no match, the program checks the next record, and so on, until a match is found. The match is noted and the search continues to the end of the file. At the end of the search the "Targa, Phil" records are displayed. For a large file this record-by-record comparison can be time consuming, even at computer speeds.

Indexing a file speeds up the search. A request for a particular record is first directed to the index file, which points, via the record number, directly to the memory location of the desired record. This data and index file approach to accessing a record is much faster than searching the entire data file.

For example, to display Phil Targa's records, the data base must first be indexed on the field EMPLOYEE (ex. INDEX ON EMPLOYEE TO TR-EMP). Then the FIND command is used to position the record pointer at the first "Targa, Phil" record (ex. FIND Targa, Phil). Finally, the LIST WHILE command is used to list all of Mr. Targa's records (ex. LIST WHILE EMPLOYEE = "Targa, Phil").

To summarize, indexing permits the display of sorted records without creating a separate sorted version of the data base. Indexing also allows rapid random access of records in a data base. Indexing is considered dynamic. When an index is open and a change is made to the original data base, the index file is automatically updated.

☐ Activate the TRAINING data base.

* USE TRAINING ↵

☐ Index the data base on the key EMPLOYEE. The index file will be named TR-EMP (TRaining-EMPloyee index).

* INDEX ON EMPLOYEE TO TR-EMP ↵

☐ The TR-EMP index file is now active and the data base will be displayed in alphabetical order based on the EMPLOYEE field. Use a LIST command with a scope parameter to display the first 17 records.

* LIST NEXT 17 ↵

☐ After looking at the display, tap the up arrow key to recall the previous command and view the remaining records in the data base.

* ↑ ↵

Notice that Phil Targa's records are grouped together (see Figure 1-35).

☐ Use the FIND command to position the record pointer at the first "Targa, Phil" record. Notice that quotes are not required in the next command.

```
. list next 17
Record#  ID      EMPLOYEE          DEPARTMENT  START     STATUS
    10   100     Klein, Ellen      Accounting  01/10/91  C
    14   SC445   Lewis, Barbara    Management  03/04/91  I
    21   VC10    Lewis, Barbara    Management  01/12/91  C
    22   MGT10   Lewis, Barbara    Management  01/15/91  C
    30   SC445   McGill, Annie     Marketing   03/04/91  I
     6   MGT10   Mendez, Carlos    Accounting  01/15/91  I
    19   SC445   Mendez, Carlos    Accounting  03/04/91  I
    28   MGT10   Molone, Maggie    Personnel   01/15/91  C
    27   3451F   Pfau, Amy         Management  03/20/91  I
    12   SC445   Pickford, Andrea  Sales       03/04/91  I
    29   100     Reyes, Fernando   Sales       01/04/91  C
     3   VC10    Targa, Phil       Finance     01/12/91  C
     8   100     Targa, Phil       Finance     01/04/91  C
    23   SC445   Targa, Phil       Finance     03/04/91  I
    32   3223    Washington, Armindo Finance   02/23/91  W
    16   YL877   Yodashkin, Peter  Finance     01/23/91  C
```

Figure 4-35 The final 16 records of the TRAINING data base indexed on EMPLOYEE

* **FIND Targa, Phil** ↵

Look at the status bar to see that the record pointer has moved.

☐ List all of Phil Targa's records.

* **LIST WHILE EMPLOYEE = "Targa, Phil"** ↵

The last command displays three indexed records beginning with the first "Targa, Phil" record. To remove an index either reactivate the data base (USE TRAINING) or enter the command SET INDEX TO.

Step 3: Practice

Activate the AUDIO data base created in Session One, Step 7 and complete the following tasks.

* List and print the entire data base ordered alphabetically by title
* List and print the entire data base ordered by playing time
* List and print any CD, TAPE or RECORD that is longer than 40 minutes in order by playing time
* List and print the entire data base ordered by format

* List and print the entire data base ordered by number of songs
* Use the INDEX, FIND and LIST WHILE commands to list all Depeche Mode recordings. Write the commands that you used on the print out. (Alternative: enter the command SET PRINT ON, enter the INDEX, FIND and LIST WHILE commands, then enter the command SET PRINT OFF)

Step 4: Terminating the Session

The QUIT command closes all dBASE files and returns the user to the DOS prompt.

☐ If you do not plan to continue to the next Session now, enter the QUIT command to terminate the current session.

* **QUIT** ↵

☐ When the DOS prompt appears, you may remove your data diskette from drive A and turn off the computer.

Session Four

Reports

(and More on Indexing)

Database software provides the ability to create customized or formatted reports. This capability allows you to design the layout of the report. This means that you have some flexibility in spacing and can include titles, subtitles, column headings, separation lines, and other elements that make a report more readable. The user describes the layout of the customized report interactively, and then stores it for later recall. The result of the description, called a report form, is recalled from disk storage and merged with a data base to create the customized report. Managers often use this capability to generate periodic reports (for example, Weekly Training Status Report).

Brad and Terri Suttor want to keep track of their credit card purchases so that they can monitor their spending habits. They use their computer expertise to create a data base. Then they index the data base and generate two reports. This session demonstrates the creation and use of a credit card data base. Also demonstrated is an index based on a complex expression and the creation and modification of a report form.

If dBASE III PLUS is not currently running, load the program to memory (refer to Session One, Step 1). Progress to the dot prompt, insert your data diskette in drive A and enter the command SET DEFAULT TO A.

In this session you will learn to:

- ◆ Understand and use logic fields
- ◆ Use a complex expression to index a data base
- ◆ Create a summary report
- ◆ Modify a report form
- ◆ Create a detailed report
- ◆ Copy a file's structure to another file
- ◆ Use logic fields in a FOR condition
- ◆ Delete records

Step 1: Creating a Data Base and Adding Data Base Records

Create the structure of the CARDS data base (see Figure 4-36). If needed, refer to Session One, Step 2: Creating a Data Base.

The PAID field in Figure 4-36 is a logical field. Logical fields are unique because the display of the data is slightly different from the data. When Logical is chosen as the field type, dBASE III PLUS automatically assigns a width of 1 position and limits valid entries to the letters T and F (true and false). However, when a logical field is displayed, periods appear on both sides of the T or F (.T.). Logical fields are also treated differently when they appear in FOR and WHILE expressions (see Session Two). This use of logical fields is explained later.

❑ Create the structure of the data base file named CARDS using the data shown in Figure 4-36. Enter the first field name as shown below.

* **CREATE CARDS** ↵
* **CARDNAME** ↵
* **C**
* **8** ↵

Field	Field Name	Type	Width	Dec
1	CARDNAME	Character	8	
2	LOCATION	Character	15	
3	USER	Character	5	
4	DATE	Date	8	
5	AMOUNT	Numeric	8	2
6	PAID	Logical	1	
7	REMINDERS	Character	16	

Figure 4-36 The CARDS data base structure

❑ Enter the remainder of the data in Figure 4-36.

❑ You should have tapped ENTER after entering the seventh field width (16). Now tap ENTER with the cursor at the eighth Field Name prompt to signify the end of the record definition for the CARDS data base, and tap ENTER again to confirm that the definition is correct.

* ↵ ↵

❑ Respond affirmatively to the input prompt.

* **Y**

dBASE: Session Four 217

☐ Add the records as shown in Figure 4-37. Enter the first record as illustrated below. Remember that tapping ENTER is not necessary when the data fills the field.

* **AMEX** ↵
* **HIS CLOTHIERS** ↵
* **BRAD** ↵
* **012491** *(Jan. 24, 1991)*
* **127.85**
* **F**
* **PANTS & 4 SHIRTS**

```
. list
Record#  CARDNAME  LOCATION       USER  DATE      AMOUNT PAID  REMINDERS
     1   AMEX      HIS CLOTHIERS  BRAD  01/24/91  127.85  .F.  PANTS & 4 SHIRTS
     2   VISA      HARRY'S FIX-IT TERRI 02/03/91   74.65  .F.  CAR TUNE-UP
     3   MASTER    ALL SPORTS     TERRI 02/11/91   87.40  .F.  WARM-UPS
     4   VISA      LEE'S CHINESE  BRAD  02/04/91   67.50  .F.  DINNER W/ RADERS
     5   DISCOVER  SEARS          TERRI 02/18/91  159.95  .F.  PAINT & MISC
     6   DISCOVER  SEARS          BRAD  02/18/91  110.25  .F.  FLOOR TILES
     7   VISA      DOYLE'S        TERRI 02/25/91   65.00  .F.  HAIR RE-DO
     8   AMEX      RHONDA'S TRAVEL TERRI 02/25/91 525.00  .F.  FAMILY REUNION
     9   VISA      SAULS'S SOUNDS BRAD  02/23/91   45.95  .F.  3 CD'S
    10   VISA      PLUMP'S EATERY BRAD  02/14/91   34.70  .F.  VALENTINE DINNER
    11   AMEX      TELTICKETS     BRAD  01/20/91   80.00  .F.  THEATER FOR 2
```

Figure 4-37   Records to be entered into the CARDS data base

☐ Enter records 2 through 11 of the CARDS data base. As you can see, no payment has been made for any of the newly entered purchases.

☐ After entering the last record, you should be at the end of file and record 11 (EOF/11). Return to the dot prompt.

* ↵

Step 2: Single Field Indexing and Creating a Summary Report

Terri generates a report that lists the amount owed on each credit card. She organizes the data base by using the INDEX command.

☐ Index the CARDS file on CARDNAME to an index file called CDINDEX and list the data base.

* **INDEX ON CARDNAME TO CDINDEX** ↵
* **LIST** ↵

The records are now listed in alphabetical order by credit card name. Notice that each record retains its original number.

☐ Create a report that lists the amount owed for each credit card. Figure 4-38 displays the report generation screen.

* **CREATE REPORT CDREPORT** ↵

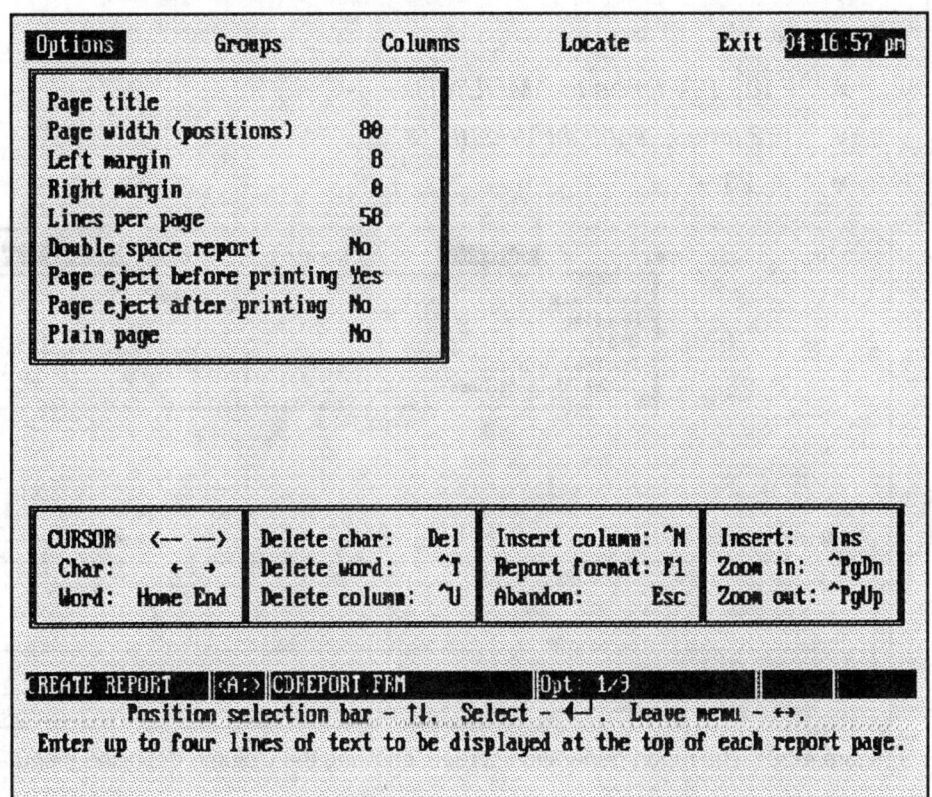

Figure 4-38   Report generation screen

☐ Move directly to the Group menu when the report screen appears.

* →

☐ Group the records according to credit card name.

* ↵
* F10
* ↵ ↵ *(select CARDNAME)*
* ↓ *(highlight Group heading)*
* ↵ **Credit Card:** ↵
* ↓ *(highlight Summary report only)*
* ↵ *(change to Yes)*

☐ Move to the Column menu. Select the column contents (see Figure 4-39).

* →
* ↵
* F10 ↓ *(4 times to AMOUNT)* ↵ ↵
* ↓ *(2 times, highlight Width)*
* ↵ **23** ↵

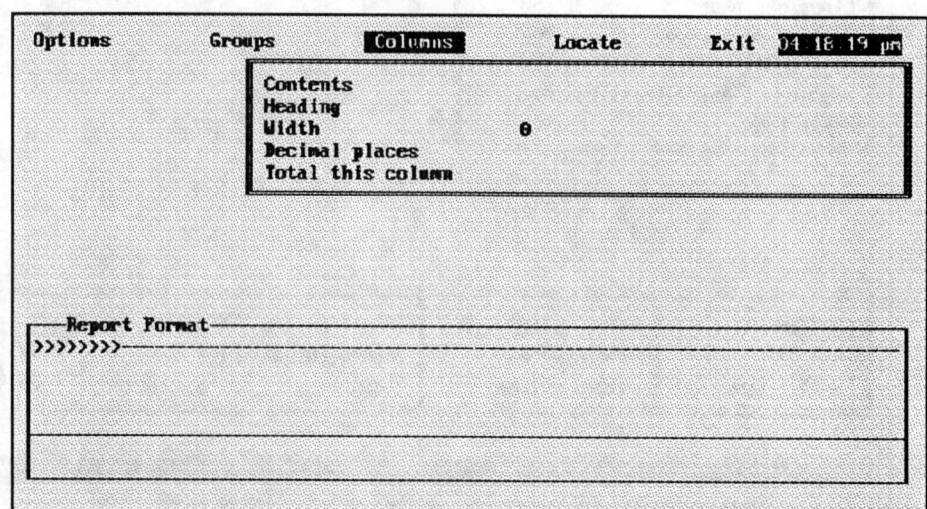

Figure 4-39 The report generation screen, showing the Column definition menu

☐ Retain the other default values and save the report format.

* E
* ↵

☐ Display the report on the screen (see Figure 4-40).

* **REPORT FORM CDREPORT** ↵

Changing the column width to 23 causes the subtotals and the total to be positioned to the right, resulting in a better visual display.

```
** Credit Card: AMEX
** Subtotal **
                    732.85

** Credit Card: DISCOVER
** Subtotal **
                    270.20

** Credit Card: MASTER
** Subtotal **
                     87.40

** Credit Card: VISA
** Subtotal **
                    287.80
*** Total ***
                   1378.25
```

Figure 4-40   CDREPORT output

Step 3: Multiple Field Indexing and Modifying a Report

As explained in Session Two, multiple field names may be included within an expression. Therefore, since the index key is an expression, a data base may be indexed on multiple fields. As is true of all expressions, if the fields to be included in the expression are of different data types, data transformation functions must be used.

For example, Brad and Terri decided to include information on individual purchases and list the purchases in chronological order. To obtain a chronological listing of purchases for each credit card, Terri uses the multiple field indexing feature. She creates an index expression that includes the CARDNAME field, a character field, and the DATE field, a date field. To avoid the error message "DATA TYPE MISMATCH," she uses the DTOC (date-to-character) function to convert the data in the DATE field to a string of characters. Since the CARDNAME field appears first in the index expression, it is the primary index field and the DATE field is the secondary index field.

☐ Use a multiple field index expression [CARDNAME + DTOC(DATE)] to generate a chronological listing of purchases for each credit card.

* **INDEX ON CARDNAME + DTOC(DATE) TO CDINDEX** ↵

Since the index was created earlier, dBASE III PLUS asks if you want to erase the old file and create a new one. Respond "y"es to the prompt.

* **Y**
* **LIST** ↵

☐ Modify the existing report by adding a title, column headings, and individual records. In the Options menu, add the title.

* **MODIFY REPORT CDREPORT** ↵
* ↵
* **AMOUNT OWED ON EACH CREDIT CARD**
* **CTRL** - **END**

☐ In the Group menu, change the "Summary report only" selection to "No" so that individual records will be included.

* →
* ↓ *(2 times)*
* ↵ *(change to No)*
* →

☐ In the Column menu, select the data fields to be included in the report.

* **CTRL**-**U** *(erase current selection)*
* ↵ **F10** ↓ *(highlight LOCATION)* ↵ ↵
* ↓
* ↵ **SPACE** *(4 times)* **LOCATION** **CTRL** - **END**
* **PGDN** *(select the next field)*

By inserting four spaces the column heading LOCATION is centered over its field.

☐ Repeat the procedure to add these column headings to the report: USER, DATE, and AMOUNT. Insert two spaces to center DATE over its field. It is not necessary to center USER or AMOUNT.

☐ Call the Exit menu and save the report format. You will be returned to the dot prompt.

* **E**
* ↵

☐ List the report (see Figure 4-41).

* **REPORT FORM CDREPORT** ↵

□ Print the report.

* **REPORT TO PRINT** ↵
* **CDREPORT** ↵

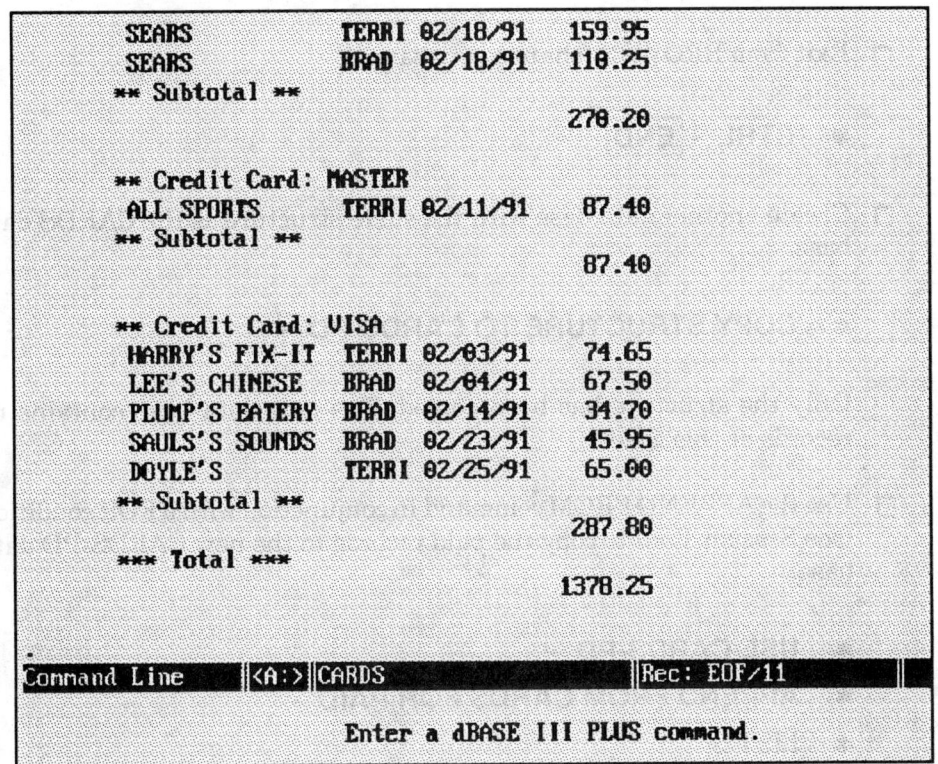

Figure 4-41 Partial display of the revised report CDREPORT

Step 4: Copying a File's Structure and Appending Selected Records to a New File

After paying a few of the charges, Brad and Terri want to alter the data base to reflect the payments. They change the PAID field to T (true) in the affected records. Terri retains the CARDS data base for unpaid charges and creates another identical data base called CARDS-PD to store the records for which charges have been paid.

□ Change the PAID field from F (unpaid) to T (paid) for the paid charges. The addition of "FREEZE PAID" to the BROWSE command prevents the cursor from being moved to any field other than the PAID field.

dBASE: Session Four **223**

* **BROWSE FREEZE PAID** ↵
* PGUP
* T
* T

Change HARRY'S, LEE'S and PLUMP'S from F to T to reflect payment of charges.

☐ Exit from BROWSE (changes are saved).

* CTRL - END

☐ Create another data base with the same structure as the CARDS data base.

* **COPY STRUCTURE TO CARDS-PD** ↵

Only the structure has been copied. The new data base contains no records at this time.

☐ Use the APPEND FROM command in conjunction with a FOR condition (see Session Two) to copy the paid records to the new CARDS-PD data base.

* **USE CARDS-PD** ↵
* **APPEND FROM CARDS FOR PAID** ↵
* **LIST** ↵

Logical fields are handled differently from other fields in FOR and WHILE expressions. To test for the presence of .T. or .F. in the field, you might expect to enter FOR PAID='T' or WHILE PAID='F', but the correct statement is FOR PAID or FOR .NOT. PAID.

Step 5: Deleting Records from a Data Base

Deleting records from a data base is a two step process. First the records to be deleted must be marked as candidates for deletion using the DELETE command. Then the records are physically removed from the data base with the PACK command. If a data base's index file(s) is(are) open they will be updated after the packing. Terri completes her electronic housekeeping by deleting all the paid charges from the CARDS data base.

☐ Use one command to open the CARDS data base and its index, CDINDEX. When an index is open, it will automatically be updated any time a change occurs to the data base.

* **USE CARDS INDEX CDINDEX** ↵

☐ In the CARDS data base, mark all paid records for deletion (see Figure 4-42).

* **DELETE FOR PAID** ↵
* **LIST** ↵

```
. delete for paid
     5 records deleted
. list
Record#  CARDNAME  LOCATION        USER  DATE      AMOUNT PAID  REMINDERS
    11  *AMEX     TELTICKETS      BRAD  01/20/91   80.00  .T.   THEATER FOR 2
     1  *AMEX     HIS CLOTHIERS   BRAD  01/24/91  127.85  .T.   PANTS & 4 SHIRTS
     8   AMEX     RHONDA'S TRAVEL TERRI 02/25/91  525.00  .F.   FAMILY REUNION
     5   DISCOVER SEARS           TERRI 02/18/91  159.95  .F.   PAINT & MISC
     6   DISCOVER SEARS           BRAD  02/18/91  110.25  .F.   FLOOR TILES
     3   MASTER   ALL SPORTS      TERRI 02/11/91   87.40  .F.   WARM-UPS
     2  *VISA     HARRY'S FIX-IT  TERRI 02/03/91   74.65  .T.   CAR TUNE-UP
     4  *VISA     LEE'S CHINESE   BRAD  02/04/91   67.50  .T.   DINNER W/ RADERS
    10  *VISA     PLUMP'S EATERY  BRAD  02/14/91   34.70  .T.   VALENTINE DINNER
     9   VISA     SAULS'S SOUNDS  BRAD  02/23/91   45.95  .F.   3 CD'S
     7   VISA     DOYLE'S         TERRI 02/25/91   65.00  .F.   HAIR RE-DO
```

Figure 4-42 Five records are marked as candidates for deletion

Records 1, 2, 4, 10 and 11 should be marked with an asterisk to denote that they are candidates for deletion. At this point any or all marked records may be unmarked using the RECALL command. Like other dBASE commands, RECALL accepts scope, for conditions and while conditions.

☐ Use the PACK command to physically remove the marked records from the data base.

* **PACK** ↵
* **LIST** ↵

The data base should now contain six records. This two step deletion process helps prevent the accidental deletion of records.

Step 6: Practice

Use the AUDIO data base created in Session Two, Step 11 to produce and print a formatted report that contains all entries in the data base, is sorted alphabetically by artist, and has subtotals for playing time for each artist. The report should be in the form displayed in Figure 4-43.

```
Page No.      1
03/12/91


        TITLE                PLAYING TIME


     ** Artist: Depeche Mode
      Some Great Reward        38.59
      Black Celebration        41.19
      People Are People        32.37
     ** Subtotal **
                              112.15

     ** Artist: Des Voix Bulgares
      Le Mystere               35.60
     ** Subtotal **
```

Figure 4-43 Partial display of the report to be created in Step 6: Practice

Step 7: Terminating the Session

If you do not plan to continue to the next Session now, enter the QUIT command to terminate the current session.

* **QUIT** ↵

When the DOS prompt appears, you may remove your data diskette from drive A and turn off the computer.

Session Five

Introduction to Programming

Our discussions up to this point on database software have assumed that the user enters one instruction or selects one menu option at a time. Database software provides the capability to combine these instructions in the form of a **program**. A database software program, like any other computer program, is made up of a sequence of instructions that are executed one after another. These instructions are executed in sequence unless the order of execution is altered by a test-on-condition instruction or a branch instruction.

An Example Database Program

Typically, a program will accept **input** (from the keyboard or a file), access disk **storage**, accomplish some **processing** activity, and provide some kind of **output** (to a disk file, a printer, or the monitor). To illustrate database programming, we use an example program that:

- Allows the user to make an inquiry to the TRAINING database (**storage**) in Figure 4-4.
- Allows the user to enter (**input**) the name of an employee (for example, "Targa, Phil").
- Searches the file and identifies all records that involve the employee in question (**processing**).
- Displays a "Training History Report" (**output**) that contains all records that apply to the employee in question.

A dBASE III PLUS program that accomplishes these tasks is shown in Figure 4-44. The comment instructions [those that begin with an asterisk (*)] embedded in the program of Figure 4-44 describe the purpose and function of the instructions that follow. An interactive session resulting from the execution of the program in Figure 4-44 is shown in Figures 4-45 and 4-46.

You could, of course, extract and display the information shown in Figure 4-46 by issuing a series of individual database software instructions. However, without a program, you would have to reenter the instructions each time you made a similar inquiry.

Writing Programs

Each program is a project. The following steps are followed for each programming project.

```
******* HISTORY.PRG *******
* This program allows the user to make an inquiry to the
* TRAINING data base. The user enters an employee name to
* generate an "EMPLOYEE TRAINING HISTORY" report for that
* employee.
*****************************************************************
* Activate the TRAINING data base
USE TRAINING
* Clear the screen
CLEAR
* Position cursor at row 4, column 20 and display title.
@ 4, 20 SAY "EMPLOYEE TRAINING HISTORY"
* Insert 2 blank lines.
?
?
* Display an input prompt (inside quotes) with leading and
* trailing spaces. "Accept" employee name into the variable NAME.
ACCEPT "  Enter employee's name (Last, First): " TO NAME
CLEAR
* Position cursor at row 4, column 8 and display heading.
@ 4, 8 SAY "Training History Report for: " + NAME
* Display the column headings for the report. A "?" at the
* beginning of a line causes the output cursor to be positioned
* at the beginning of the next line. The character string within
* the quotes is displayed. When nothing follows the "?", a blank
* line is inserted.
?
? "Department            Course         ID          Status"
? "========================================="
* Suppress dBASE confirmation messages.
SET TALK OFF
```

Figure 4-44 The HISTORY.PRG program code with embedded comments. The program continues on the next page

Describe the problem. Describing the problem involves identifying exactly what needs to be done.

Analyze the problem. Break the problem into its basic components for analysis. Remember: "Divide and conquer." Although different programs have different components, a good place to start with most programs is to analyze the output, input, processing, and file-interaction components.

Design the logic of the program. Next, you have to put the pieces together in the form of a logical program design (for example, a flowchart).

Code the program. The design of the program is translated into instructions, or a program. If the logic is sound and the design documentation

```
      * Set the record pointer to the first record in the file.
      GO TOP
      * In the following loop, the EMPLOYEE name for each record in the
      * data base is compared to the name entered to NAME. If a match
      * occurs, then the instructions between the IF and ENDIF are
      * executed. Do the loop WHILE the record being read is NOT the
      * EOF (end-of-file).
      DO WHILE .NOT. EOF()
           IF EMPLOYEE = NAME
               * The following instructions define the format of the output
               * displayed. A "?" at the beginning of a line causes the output
               * cursor to be positioned at the the beginning of the next line.
               * The character string within the quotes and the contents of the
               * field indicated (e.g., EMPLOYEE) are displayed. The "+"
               * indicates that the character string and the value of the field
               * are to be concatenated (joined together).
               ?
               ? DEPARTMENT + "   " + ID + "    " + STATUS   ENDIF
           * Advance the record pointer to the next record.
           SKIP
      ENDDO
      * Display a legend for the status codes.
      @ 18, 1 SAY "Status codes: C=complete; I=incomplete; and W=withdrawn"
      * Restore the default display setting.
      SET TALK ON
```

Figure 4-44 (cont.) The continuation of the HISTORY.PRG program code

(narrative description, logic diagram, and so on) is thorough, the coding process is relatively straightforward.

Test and debug the program. Once the program has been entered into the system, it is likely that you will encounter at least one **bug**. A bug is either a **syntax error** (violation of one of the rules for writing instructions) or a **logic error**. Ridding a program of bugs is the process of **debugging**.

Document the program. Over the life of the program, procedures and information requirements change. Updating programs to reflect these changes is much easier with good documentation (narrative description, logic diagram, embedded comments, and so on).

The programming capability of database software allows you to combine instructions in a logical sequence instead of entering them one at a time. The program in this session allows the user to make an inquiry to the TRAINING data base (see Figures 4-45 and 4-46).

If dBASE III PLUS is not currently running, load the program to memory (refer to Session One, Step 1). Progress to the dot prompt, insert your data diskette in drive A and enter the command SET DEFAULT TO A.

```
                    EMPLOYEE TRAINING HISTORY


Enter employee's name (Last, First): Targa, Phil
```

Figure 4-45   HISTORY.PRG data input screen. The program displays the heading and the input prompt. The user supplies the employee's name

```
             Training History Report for: Targa, Phil

Department      Course ID    Status
===================================

Finance         VC10         C

Finance         100          C

Finance         SC445        I




Status codes: C=complete; I=incomplete; and W=withdrawn
```

Figure 4-46   HISTORY.PRG output screen generated entirely by the program based on the employee's name entered at the input prompt

In this session you will learn to:

- Activate the program editing screen
- Enter dBASE commands into a program
- Use the @ SAY command to display messages during program execution
- Create a programming loop that examines each data base record in succession and quits automatically when it reaches the end of the data base

Step 1: Creating a Program

Since any frequently executed database task is usually turned into a program, dBASE III PLUS includes a program editing screen. Use CREATE COMMAND <Program Name> to create a new program.

☐ Prepare to create a program called HISTORY.

* **CREATE COMMAND HISTORY** ↵

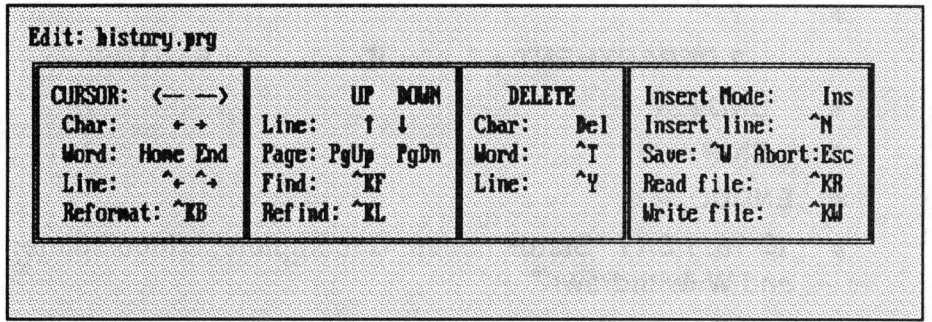

Figure 4-47 The edit instructions which appear at the top of the program editing screen

Observe the edit window at the top of the screen (see Figure 4-47).

☐ Tap F1 to toggle the edit window display on and off.

* **F1** **F1**

☐ Enter the program. The annotated comments (lines beginning with asterisks) in Figure 4-44 explain the purpose of program instructions. The comment lines do not effect the program and can be omitted to save entry time. The format of an interactive session is illustrated in Figures 4-45 and 4-46.

* **USE TRAINING** ↵
* **CLEAR** ↵
* **@ 4, 20 SAY "EMPLOYEE TRAINING HISTORY"** ↵
* **?** ↵
* **?** ↵
* **ACCEPT " Enter employee's name (Last, First): " TO NAME** ↵

* **CLEAR** ↵
* **@ 4, 8 SAY "Training History Report for: " + NAME** ↵
* **?** ↵
* **? "Department   Course   ID   Status"** ↵
* **? "=="** ↵
* **SET TALK OFF** ↵
* **DO WHILE .NOT. EOF ()** ↵
* **IF EMPLOYEE = NAME** ↵
* **?** ↵
* **? DEPARTMENT + "   " + ID + "   " + STATUS** ↵
* **ENDIF** ↵
* **SKIP** ↵
* **ENDDO** ↵
* **@ 18, 1 SAY "Status codes: C=complete; I=incomplete; and W=withdrawn"** ↵
* **SET TALK ON** ↵

Look over the program carefully and correct any keying errors.

☐ Save your program.

* **CTRL - W**

The save command returns you to the dot prompt.

Step 2: Running a Program

Use the DO <Program Name> command to run an existing program.

☐ Run the HISTORY program (see Figures 4-45 and 4-46).

* **DO HISTORY** ↵

* **Targa, Phil** ↵

Programs rarely run correctly the first time. If the program has bugs in it, you will need to modify it.

Step 3: Modifying a Program

Use MODIFY COMMAND <Program Name> to edit an existing program.

☐ Use the following command to recall and edit the HISTORY program file.

* **MODI COMM HISTORY** ↵
* *(make needed corrections)*
* **CTRL**-W *(save program)*

Step 4: Practice

Use the AUDIO data base created in Session Two, Step 11. Create a program that allows you to make an inquiry to the data base.

* The program first displays the heading "AUDIO LIBRARY" and the input request "Enter artist's name: "
* After the artist's name is entered, the program searches each record of the data base and displays any recordings by the artist entered
* Use the following display format:

    Artist's Name:

TITLE   FORMAT   PLAYING TIME
==

Step 5: Terminating the Session

The QUIT command closes all dBASE files and returns the user to the DOS prompt.

☐ If you do not plan to continue to the next Session now, enter the QUIT command to terminate the current session.

* **QUIT** ↵

☐ When the DOS prompt appears, you may remove your data diskette from drive A and turn off the computer.

Session Six

More Programming

This session demonstrates the creation and use of a program that displays customer account information for the telemarketing group at R & G. The program opens two data bases into two separate work areas and extracts and combines data from both data bases to create an output screen. In this session you will create two new data bases, study programming logic, be introduced to several new programming concepts and commands, and create a program that involves three nested loops.

Gram Mertz, manager of R & G's Programming Department, was asked by Sally Marcio, vice-president in charge of Sales and Marketing, to develop a dBASE III PLUS application for her department. Sally wants her telemarketing group (telephone sales) to be able to call up a display of pertinent customer account information. She asked that the information be displayed in invoice form and retrieved by customer account number. This session follows Gram's steps as he plans and creates Sally's program.

If dBASE III PLUS is not currently running, load the program to memory (refer to Session One, Step 1). Progress to the dot prompt, insert your data diskette in drive A and enter the command SET DEFAULT TO A.

In this session you will learn to:

◆ Plan a program

◆ Use the REPLACE command to enter repetitive data

◆ Use multiple field indexing

◆ Use nested functions

◆ Validate data input

◆ Use the STR and SPACE functions

◆ Use nested DO WHILE loops

◆ Use IF...ENDIF statements

Step 1: Creating Data Bases and Adding Data Base Records

The program to be created in this session requires two data bases. The ACCOUNTS data base contains the name and addresses of each of R & G's accounts. The ORDERS data base contains a separate record for each purchase made by one of R & G's accounts. Keeping the name and address data in a separate data base prevents redundant entries each time an account places an order.

Refer to Figures 4-48 through 4-51 to create the ACCOUNTS and ORDERS data bases (Alternative: copy ACCOUNTS.DBF and ORDERS.DBF from the Example Files Diskette to your data diskette)

- [ ] Use the structure presented in Figure 4-48 to create the data base named ACCOUNTS.

- [ ] Enter the data for records 1 through 5 as shown in Figure 4-49.

- [ ] Create the ORDERS data base from the structure presented in Figure 4-50.

- [ ] Enter the records listed in Figure 4-51. Data for the UPRICE (unit price) field will be entered in a later tutorial.

```
Field  Field Name  Type       Width  Dec
  1    ACCNO       Character    5
  2    ACCTNAME    Character   15
  3    ADDRESS     Character   15
  4    CITY        Character   10
  5    ST          Character    2
  6    ZIP         Character    5
  7    PHONE       Character   12
```

Figure 4-48 The structure of the ACCOUNTS data base

```
. list
Record#  ACCNO  ACCTNAME        ADDRESS         CITY       ST ZIP    PHONE
   1     21001  ALL HERE SHOP   GRAND CENTRAL   NEW YORK   NY 10016  212-673-2365
   2     21006  MAXI MARKET     321 HOLMES      SUNNYVALE  CA 94087  408-689-2387
   3     21004  SWEET'S SWEETS  378 W. MAIN     CHAMPAIGN  IL 60820  217-487-9537
   4     21008  HARD WEAR       6389 HARBOR CT  ARLINGTON  VA 22043  703-476-2231
   5     21007  THE LAIR        8642 N. MAY     OKLA. CITY OK 73108  405-986-3467
```

Figure 4-49 Records to be entered into the ACCOUNTS data base

```
Field  Field Name  Type        Width  Dec
  1    ACCNO       Character     5
  2    ORDNUMBER   Character     7
  3    DATE        Date          8
  4    PRODUCT     Character     7
  5    QTY         Numeric       5
  6    UPRICE      Numeric       6     2
```

Figure 4-50   The structure of the ORDERS data base

```
Record#  ACCNO  ORDNUMBER  DATE      PRODUCT  QTY UPRICE
    1    Z1001  8823561    12/03/90  FARKLE   1000
    2    Z1008  8901467    01/28/91  FARKLE   2000
    3    Z1004  8900245    01/15/91  TEGLER    600
    4    Z1001  8902405    02/14/91  FARKLE   1000
    5    Z1007  8900023    01/08/91  TEGLER    150
    6    Z1001  8900145    01/14/91  FARKLE   1200
    7    Z1006  8901356    01/24/91  QWERT     350
    8    Z1008  8902078    02/04/91  STIB      500
    9    Z1001  8900012    01/07/91  FARKLE   1000
   10    Z1008  8824597    12/15/90  QWERT     140
   11    Z1006  8823489    12/06/90  STIB     2400
```

Figure 4-51   Records to be entered into the ORDERS data base

Step 2: Entering Repetitive Data

Use the REPLACE command in conjunction with a FOR condition to enter repeated data.

❏ If necessary, make ORDERS the active data base (ORDERS should be displayed in the status bar).

* **USE ORDERS** ↵

❏ Enter the unit price for Farkles.

* **REPLACE UPRICE WITH 2.12 FOR PRODUCT = "FARKLE"** ↵

Five records are updated.

☐ Enter the unit prices for the other products. Save time by tapping the up-arrow cursor-control key to recall previous commands. Edit the old commands with the use of the cursor, INS, and DEL keys to enter the following data.

* **REPLACE UPRICE WITH .63 FOR PRODUCT = "TEGLER"** ↵
* **REPLACE UPRICE WITH 3.85 FOR PRODUCT = "STIB"** ↵
* **REPLACE UPRICE WITH 8.03 FOR PRODUCT = "QWERT"** ↵

☐ List the data base to see that all prices are entered correctly (see Figure 4-52).

* **LIST** ↵

```
. list
Record#  ACCNO  ORDNUMBER  DATE      PRODUCT  QTY   UPRICE
     1  21001  8823561    12/03/90  FARKLE   1000   2.12
     2  21008  8901467    01/28/91  FARKLE   2000   2.12
     3  21004  8900245    01/15/91  TEGLER    600   0.63
     4  21001  8902405    02/14/91  FARKLE   1000   2.12
     5  21007  8900023    01/08/91  TEGLER    150   0.63
     6  21001  8900145    01/14/91  FARKLE   1200   2.12
     7  21006  8901356    01/24/91  QWERT     350   8.03
     8  21008  8902078    02/04/91  STIB      500   3.85
     9  21001  8900012    01/07/91  FARKLE   1000   2.12
    10  21008  8824597    12/15/90  QWERT     140   8.03
    11  21006  8823489    12/06/90  STIB     2400   3.85
```

Figure 4-52 The ORDERS data base after entering each product's unit price

Step 3: Building a Multiple Field Index Expression Using Nested Functions

Use the INDEX command to group the orders chronologically by account number. The INVOICE program written later in this session uses the ORDINDEX index file created here.

As explained earlier (see Session Four, Step 3) all elements in an index key expression must be of the same type. This requirement means that multiple field indexing may involve the use of conversion functions. Converting date fields to character strings has additional considerations.

During indexing, dBASE III PLUS treats the first character of a string as the most significant, the second as the next most significant, and so on. Therefore, when dates are converted to character strings, dates that span several years may not be ordered correctly. For example, the string 02/23/91 would come before the string 12/15/90 in an index file because the first character 0 of the first date comes before the first character 1 of the second date. One solution to this situation is to subdivide date strings into two elements: a year string and a month/day string. That is, index for year first, then index for month and day. Use the function RIGHT(string, number) to create the year string.

The function RIGHT(string, number) operates only on character strings. It is used when the data in the DATE field has been converted to a character string with the DTOC (date-to-character) function. For example, the command RIGHT(DTOC(DATE),2) converts the data in the current DATE field to a string and reads the two rightmost characters. Similarly, the command LEFT(DTOC(DATE),5) converts the data in the current DATE field to a character string and reads the five leftmost characters. The DTOC function is nested within the functions RIGHT and LEFT and is performed first. If the data in the current DATE field are 02/23/91, the function RIGHT(DTOC(DATE),2) returns the characters 91 and the function LEFT(DTOC(DATE),5) returns the characters 02/23.

☐ Perform a three-level index. Group the records by account number, year and month/day.

* **INDEX ON ACCNO + RIGHT(DTOC(DATE),2) + LEFT(DTOC(DATE),5) TO ORDINDEX** ↵

☐ List the indexed data base (see Figure 4-53).

* **LIST** ↵

```
. index on accno + right(dtoc(date),2) + left(dtoc(date),5) to ordindex
100% indexed          11 Records indexed
. list
Record#  ACCNO  ORDNUMBER  DATE      PRODUCT   QTY   UPRICE
      1  21001  8823561    12/03/90  FARKLE    1000  2.12
      9  21001  8900012    01/07/91  FARKLE    1000  2.12
      6  21001  8900145    01/14/91  FARKLE    1200  2.12
      4  21001  8902405    02/14/91  FARKLE    1000  2.12
      3  21004  8900245    01/15/91  TEGLER     600  0.63
     11  21006  8823489    12/06/90  STIB      2400  3.85
      7  21006  8901356    01/24/91  QWERT      350  8.03
      5  21007  8900023    01/08/91  TEGLER     150  0.63
     10  21008  8824597    12/15/90  QWERT      140  8.03
      2  21008  8901467    01/28/91  FARKLE    2000  2.12
      8  21008  8902078    02/04/91  STIB       500  3.85
```

Figure 4-53 The records are listed chronologically within account number

Step 4: Planning a Program

Before writing the program, Gram outlines the logic of the program with the use of pseudocode, a programming design tool (see Figure 4-54). Pseudocode represents the logic in programlike statements written in plain English. Since pseudocode does not have any syntax guidelines (that is, rules for formulating instructions), you can concentrate on developing the logic of your program. Once you feel that the logic is sound, the pseudocode is easily translated to a program that can be executed.

Gram also develops a flowchart of the program (see Figure 4-55). The program has three loops, two of which are nested within the third. The body of the program is a loop named "View Another Account?" After all the data for an account are displayed, the question "View Another?" appears. If the user responds "Y" (yes), the user is prompted for another account number.

Within the large loop are two smaller loops: one tests the validity of the account number entered by the user; the other searches the ORDERS data base for records that contain the validated account number. In the first loop, a valid account number must be entered for the program to continue. In the second loop, however, program flow continues when the end-of-file marker is encountered.

Gram's final step is to key in the actual dBASE III PLUS commands. Look at the program code in Figure 4-56 and note that several new functions are introduced.

- **SPACE()** inserts a specified number of blank spaces.
- **TRIM()** deletes any leading or trailing blank spaces from the data in a character field.
- **STR()** converts numerical data into a character string.
- **UPPER()** converts a string of characters to upper case.
- **FOUND()** returns a logical .T. if a FIND or a SEEK makes a successful match.

New commands are also introduced (see Figure 4-56).

- **WAIT** displays a prompt and assigns a one-character response to a memory variable.
- **ACCEPT** displays a prompt and assigns a response of varied length to a memory variable.
- **DO WHILE .T.** will cause the loop to be repeated while the EXIT command is not in effect.

Invoice program (for Sally Marcio)

Initialization
    index the ORDERS data base
    DOWHILE user responds YES
        set the variables to zero
        ACCOUNTS is the active data base
        DOWHILE account number is not valid
            display the input prompt
            validate the account number
            IF not valid, display error message
        ENDDO
        display header information
        display customer name and address
        display account number
        display separator bar
        display column headings
        ORDERS is the active data base
        read first record
        DOWHILE end-of-file is NOT detected
            IF account number = ACCNO
                compute the amount
                accumulate to grand total
                display record and computed amount
            ENDIF
            read next record
        ENDDO
        display grand total
        display "VIEW ANOTHER?" prompt
        IF answer = YES, clear screen
        ENDIF
    ENDDO

Figure 4-54 Gram Mertz's pseudocode

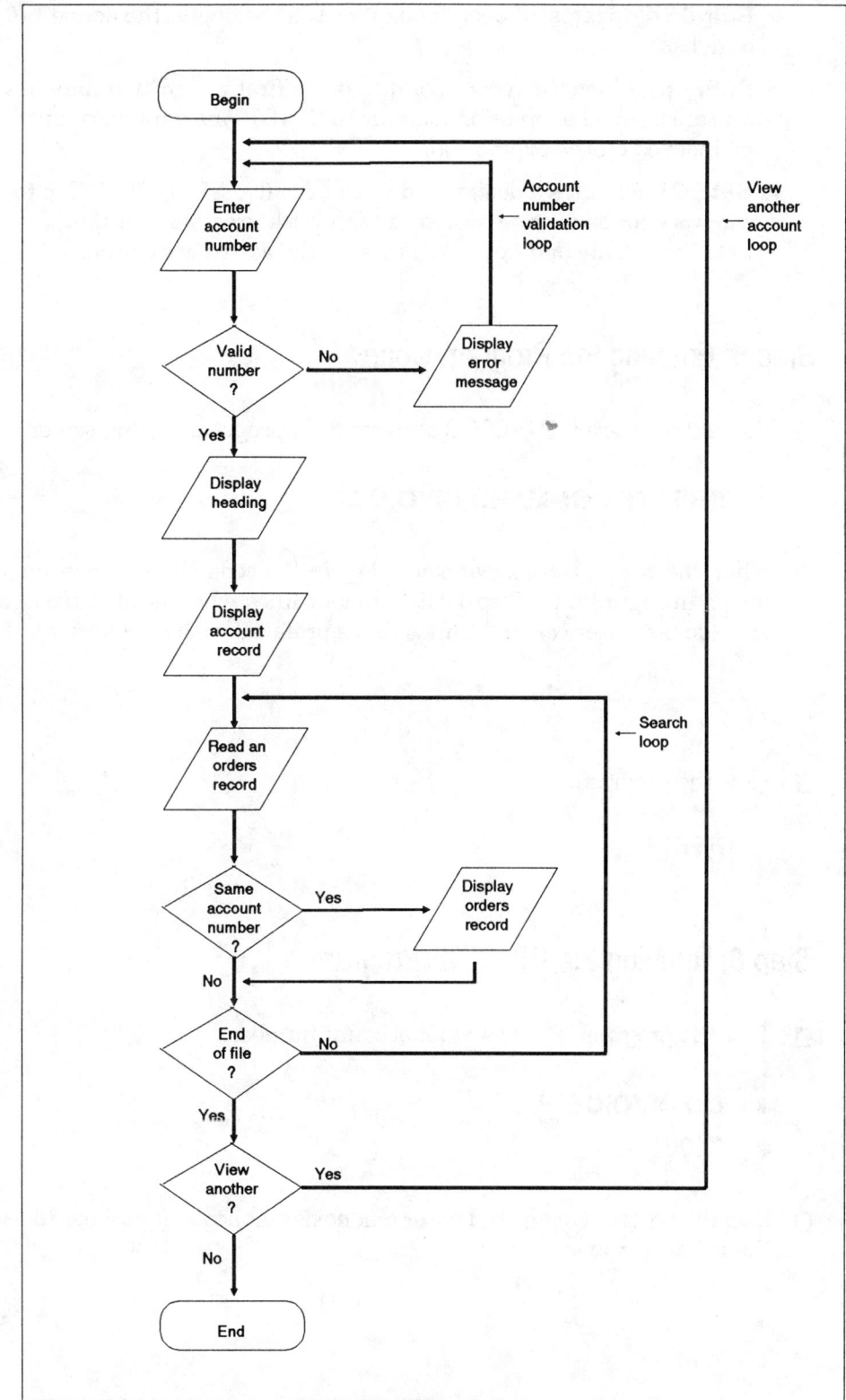

Figure 4-55 Gram Mertz's flow chart for the INVOICE program

- **REINDEX** updates all open index files that belong to the active data base.
- **SEEK** positions the record pointer at the first record that matches a user supplied expression (similar to FIND). The data base must be indexed on the expression.
- **SELECT** activates a designated work area (ex. SELECT 2). Up to ten work areas may be open and each work area may contain a data base. Only one work area may be the active work area.

Step 5: Entering the Program Code

☐ Name the program INVOICE and open the program editing screen.

* **CREATE COMMAND INVOICE** ↵

☐ When the word processor appears, key in the code for the program as shown in Figure 4-56. Tap TAB to indent lines when needed. To save time, do not enter comment lines (lines prefaced with an asterisk).

☐ Save the program.

* CTRL -W

Step 6: Running the INVOICE Program

☐ Test the program. Enter a valid account number.

* **DO INVOICE** ↵
* **Z1001** ↵

☐ Run the program again and enter a nonexistent account number to test the validation loop.

* **Y**
* **A14** ↵

☐ Now enter a correct account number.

```
* invoice program
*
* displays a selected customer's orders in invoice form
* variables list
*       ACCTNUMBER    - user input
*       LINETOTAL     - total sales for one order
*       GRANDTOTAL    - total sales for one account
*
*     initialization
*     turn off responses
SET ECHO OFF
SET TALK OFF
*     turn off status bar
SET STATUS OFF
*     clear all work areas and close all files
CLEAR ALL
*     load accounts.dbf and orders.dbf to work areas 1 and 2
USE ACCOUNTS
SELECT 2
*     activate the index file ORDINDEX created in Step 3
USE ORDERS INDEX ORDINDEX
*     omit the following command to speed program execution
*     if you are sure that ORDINDEX reflects any recent changes
*     made to the ORDERS.DBF file
REINDEX
*
*     begin "view another account" loop
*     do while user responds yes
DO WHILE .T.
   *     set memory variables to zero
   LINETOTAL = 0
   GRANDTOTAL = 0
   *     make accounts.dbf the active data base
   SELECT 1
   *
   *     begin "account number validation" loop
   *     do while account number is not valid
   DO WHILE .T.
      *     display input prompt
      @3,1 SAY " "
      ACCEPT "ACCOUNT NUMBER:  " TO ACCTNUMBER
      *     check the data base for a match
      SEEK UPPER(ACCTNUMBER)
      *     if no match, display error message and display prompt
      IF .NOT. FOUND()
         CLEAR
         @12,20 SAY "INVALID ACCOUNT NUMBER, PLEASE RE-ENTER"
         LOOP
      *     if there is a match, exit the validation loop
      ELSE
```

Figure 4-56 The INVOICE program (first frame)

```
        EXIT
ENDDO
    *    end "account number validation" loop
    *
    *    clear the screen and display invoice heading
CLEAR
@1,21 SAY "* * * * R & G ENTERPRISES * * * *"
@3,28 SAY "CUSTOMER INFORMATION"
@5,1 SAY "SOLD TO:"
@5,52 SAY "ACCT. NO.: " + ACCNO
    *    display the customer's name and address
? SPACE(4) + ACCTNAME
? SPACE(4) + ADDRESS
? SPACE(4) + TRIM(CITY) + ", " + ST + SPACE (3) + ZIP
    *    display the separator bar
? "======================================="
??"======================================="
    *    ---------------------------- 40 --------------------------
    *    display column headings
? SPACE(4) + "ORDER" + SPACE(42) + "UNIT"'
?  SPACE(4) + "NUMBER" + SPACE(6) + "DATE" + SPACE(6)
?? "ITEM" + SPACE(9) + "QTY" + SPACE(9) + "PRICE"
?? SPACE(9) + "AMOUNT"
    *    insert one blank line
?
    *    make orders.dbf the active data base
SELECT 2
GO TOP
    *    begin "search" loop
    *    do while the end of the data base is not encountered
DO WHILE .NOT. EOF()
   *    display any record that has the same account
   *    number as the validated account number
   IF ACCTNUMBER = ACCNO
        * computer the line amount and the grand total
      LINETOTAL = QTY * UPRICE
      GRANDTOTAL = GRANDTOTAL + LINETOTAL
        *    display the information for one order
      ? SPACE(4) + ORDNUMBER + SPACE(3) +
DTOC(DATE)
      ?? SPACE(3) + PRODUCT + SPACE(4) + STR(QTY,6)
      ?? SPACE(8) + STR(UPRICE,6,2) + SPACE(8)
      ?? STR(LINETOTAL,7,2)
   ENDIF
   SKIP
   *    continue search of data base
   LOOP
ENDDO
* end "search" loop
*
```

Figure 4-56 The INVOICE program (second frame)

```
*       insert three blank lines
?
?
?
*       display the grand total
?  SPACE(32) + "TOTAL AMOUNT OWED" + SPACE(14) + "$"
?? STR(GRANDTOTAL,7,2)
*       display the "view another" prompt
@23,12 SAY " "
WAIT "VIEW ANOTHER?  (Y/N)   " TO ANSWER
*       if the answer is yes, clear the screen, run the program again
IF UPPER(ANSWER) = "Y"
   CLEAR
   LOOP
*       if the answer is no, exit "view another account" loop
   ELSE
      EXIT
   ENDIF
ENDDO
*    end "view another account" loop
*
*    turn on status bar and responses
SET STATUS ON
SET TALK ON
SET ECHO ON
```

Figure 4-56 The INVOICE program (third frame)

* **Z1008** ↵

☐ Exit the program.

* **N**

If the program does not run successfully, check your program code. A common mistake is inserting ENTER when it should not be inserted. Another common error is forgetting to open or close character strings with quotes.

☐ If necessary, enter the following to recall and modify the program.

* **MODIFY COMMAND INVOICE** ↵

Remember to tap CTRL-W to save the modified code.

Step 7: Practice

Dorothy Grant owns a jewelry store named D. Grant's Jewelers. She has six employees (George Grant, Pat Grant, Audrey Grant, Greg Grant, Larry Grant and Valerie Grant). Dorothy asks Valerie to create a dBASE program to track sales. Valerie creates two data bases, GRANTS.DBF and G-SALES.DBF (see Figures 4-57 through 4-60). Valerie also outlines the program in pseudocode as follows:

```
Initialization
    index the G-SALES data base
    DOWHILE user responds YES
        set the variables to zero
        GRANTS is the active data base
        DOWHIILE employee name is not valid
            display the input prompt
            validate the employee's name
            IF not valid, display error message
        ENDDO
        display header information
        display the employee's name
        display the employee's number
        display separator bar
        display column headings
        G-SALES is the active data base
        read the first record
        DOWHILE end-of-file is not detected
            IF employee number = EMPNO
                compute the amount
                accumulate to grand total
                display record and computed amount
            ENDIF
            read next record
        ENDDO
        display grand total
        display "View Another" prompt
        IF answer = YES, clear screen
        ENDIF
    ENDDO
```

Create the two data bases displayed in Figures 4-57 through 4-60 (Alternative: copy GRANTS.DBF and G-SALES.DBF from the Example Files Diskette). Use Valerie's pseudo code as a basis for creating the program. The input screen should request the employee's first name (everyone's last name is Grant). The output screen should list all sales by the selected employee, compute and list a total sales amount, compute and list the employee's commission (total sales * commission percentage) and compute and list the total amount earned by the selected employee (commission + 4*base wages).

```
Field  Field Name  Type       Width  Dec
   1   EMPNUM      Numeric        3
   2   LASTNAME    Character      8
   3   FIRSTNAME   Character      9
   4   COMM        Numeric        5    2
   5   BASE        Numeric        4
```

Figure 4-57   The structure of the GRANTS data base

```
. list
Record#  EMPNUM  LASTNAME  FIRSTNAME  COMM  BASE
     1        1  GRANT     GEORGE     0.12  375
     2        2  GRANT     PAT        0.14  450
     3        3  GRANT     AUDREY     0.12  400
     4        4  GRANT     GREG       0.12  400
     5        5  GRANT     LARRY      0.12  400
     6        6  GRANT     VALERIE    0.15  475
```

Figure 4-58   The records to be entered into the GRANTS data base

```
Field  Field Name  Type       Width  Dec
   1   EMPNUM      Numeric        3
   2   DATE        Date           8
   3   ITEM        Character     10
   4   PRICE       Numeric        8    2
```

Figure 4-59   The structure of the G-SALES data base

```
. list
Record#  EMPNUM DATE     ITEM         PRICE
     1       6 12/27/90  RING         1230.00
     2       2 12/30/90  WATCH         400.00
     3       1 12/22/90  RING          876.00
     4       6 12/26/90  BRACELET     2460.00
     5       5 12/27/90  WATCH         870.00
     6       3 12/28/90  NECKLACE     3200.00
     7       4 01/04/91  BRACELET      699.00
     8       6 01/04/91  RING         2490.00
     9       2 01/05/91  RING         1400.00
    10       6 12/23/90  WATCH         475.00
    11       5 01/07/91  EAR RINGS     320.00
    12       2 11/30/90  NECKLACE     2300.00
    13       6 11/29/90  NECKLACE     1799.00
    14       3 12/15/90  WATCH         380.00
    15       1 01/12/91  BRACELET     1450.00
    16       2 11/21/90  NECKLACE     1460.00
    17       6 12/12/90  RING         3800.00
    18       2 01/05/91  WATCH         890.00
```

Figure 4-60 The records to be entered into the G-SALES data base

Step 8: Terminating the Session

The QUIT command closes all dBASE files and returns the user to the DOS prompt.

☐ If you do not plan to continue to the next Session now, enter the QUIT command to terminate the current session.

* **QUIT** ↵

☐ When the DOS prompt appears, you may remove your data diskette from drive A and turn off the computer.

Chapter 5

Lotus 1-2-3

Session One

Creating a Spreadsheet

Lotus 1-2-3, a product of Lotus Development Corporation, is a high-performance, integrated software package that provides electronic spreadsheet, graphics, and data management capabilities. The focus of this Lotus 1-2-3 session is on its spreadsheet capabilities. Later sessions explore the data management and graphics capabilities of Lotus 1-2-3.

In the summer of 1989, Lotus Development Corporation introduced two new versions of Lotus 1-2-3, Release 2.2 and Release 3. Both of the new versions are upgrades of the older version, Release 2.01. Release 2.2 is an intermediate upgrade for computers that do not have enough RAM or a powerful enough CPU to run Release 3 (see Session Nine).

Sessions One through Eight in this chapter focus on features that are common to all three releases (2.01, 2.2 and 3). Unless otherwise stated, the keystrokes presented in each step are appropriate for all three releases. All figures in Sessions One through Eight are based on Release 2.01. Session Nine is reserved for new features that appear in Release 3 but are not available in Release 2.01 or 2.2. The figures in Session Nine are based on Release 3.

The name electronic spreadsheet describes Lotus 1-2-3's fundamental application. The spreadsheet has been a common business tool for centuries. Before computers, the ledger (a spreadsheet) was the accountant's primary tool for keeping the books. Electronic spreadsheets are simply an electronic alternative to thousands of traditionally manual tasks. In this session, we will create two spreadsheets. First we will create a simple spreadsheet to demonstrate fundamental electronic spreadsheet concepts (see Figure 5-3). Then we will create a more complex spreadsheet, the R & G Enterprises income statement, to demonstrate more advanced spreadsheet concepts (see Figure 5-6).

In this session you will learn how to:

- ❖ Load and run Lotus 1-2-3
- ❖ Select commands from the command line
- ❖ Enter labels
- ❖ Enter values
- ❖ Enter formulas
- ❖ Save a spreadsheet
- ❖ Reset the column width
- ❖ Use repeated text to create separator lines
- ❖ Use the COPY command

- Use predefined functions
- Format cell entries
- Retrieve a spreadsheet
- Print a document
- Terminate a session

Step 1: Using Lotus 1-2-3

☐ Boot the system (see DOS, Session One).

☐ Change to the Lotus directory and load Lotus 1-2-3 to memory. In the next command, use the name of your Lotus 1-2-3 directory in place of "lotus" if it is different. For example, if the name of your lotus directory is lotus123, the next command would be cd \lotus123.

* **cd \lotus** ↵
* **123** ↵

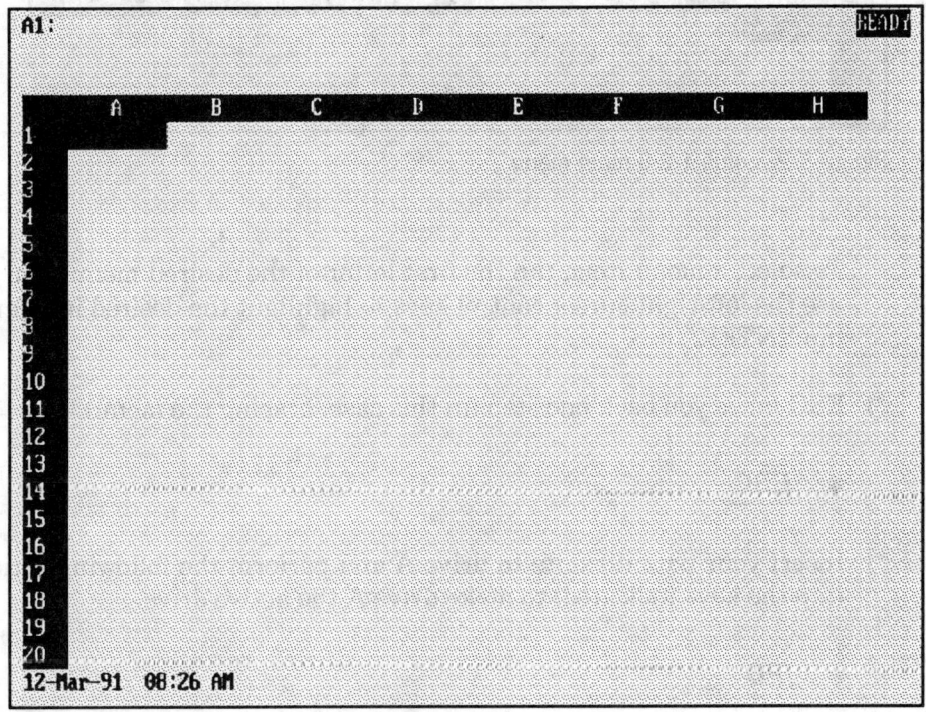

Figure 5-1 Lotus 1-2-3's blank workscreen

Figure 5-1 displays Lotus 1-2-3's work screen. The display includes a spreadsheet with rows and columns and a user interface. The user interface (control panel) consists of the three lines at the top of the screen. The first line contains status information for the current (highlighted) cell cursor (location, format, column width, location and contents) and the mode indicator (ready, point, menu, edit, wait, and so on). In the second line, you select commands and edit data. The third line displays a submenu or a brief description of a highlighted command.

☐ Use your cursor control keys to move the cell pointer around the screen and then return it to A1.

* → ↓ ← ↑

☐ Display the main menu in the user interface by tapping the forward slash key (/) (see Figure 5-2).

* /

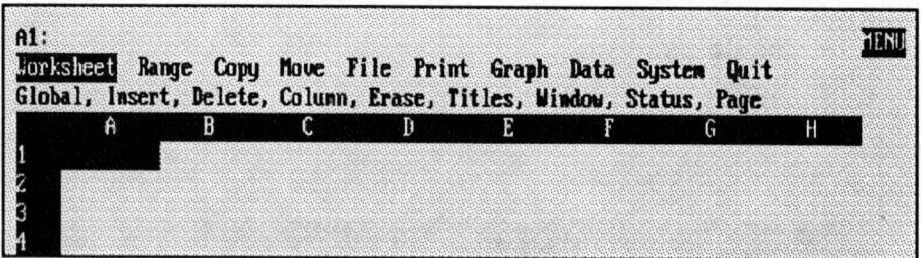

Figure 5-2 Lotus 1-2-3 main menu

To select a menu item, tap the first letter of the desired menu item or use the left/right cursor control keys to highlight the desired item and tap ENTER.

☐ ESC takes you back one step (in this case, erasing the menu).

* ESC

☐ Insert your data diskette in drive A and perform the following action (tap the keys indicated) to make drive A the active drive.

* /FD
* a: ↵

The forward slash displayed the main menu. The "F" selected the File submenu. The "D" selected the Directory option, and "a:" defined the active drive during the current session.

You are now ready to begin your Lotus 1-2-3 session. Three function key commands may prove helpful as you work through the following tutorials.

- F1 Context-sensitive Help key.
- F2 Permits editing of the contents of the current cell.
- F5 Move pointer to or "GoTo" a user-specified cell.

Step 2: Creating a Simple Income Statement

In this step we will create "The World's Most Concise Income Statement" (see Figure 5-3). Though small, this spreadsheet contains all three of the basic elements that may be entered into a Lotus 1-2-3 cell: a label, a value or a formula.

```
A1: 'Income

        A        B        C        D        E        F
1   Income     7400
2   Expenses   5200
3   Profit     2200
4
```

Figure 5-3 "The World's Most Concise Income Statement." Created to demonstrate label, value and formula entry

- **Label Entries.** A label entry is a word, phrase, or string of alphanumeric text (spaces included) that occupies a particular cell. In Figure 5-3, label entries occur in cells A1, A2 and A3. Unless otherwise specified, label entries are left justified.

- **Value Entries.** A value entry is any number. In Figure 5-3, value entries occur in B1 and B2. Value entries are automatically right justified.

- **Formula Entries.** Cell B3 contains a formula, but it is the numeric result (2200) that is displayed in the spreadsheet. Spreadsheet formulas use standard programming notation for **arithmetic operators**: + (add), - (subtract), * (multiply), / (divide), ^ (raise to a power, or exponentiation).

☐ Tap the HOME key to position the cell pointer in A1 (from this point forward, we will leave out the word "cell" when referring to a cell's address) and enter the "Income" label.

* HOME
* Income ↵

Notice that the user interface displays "A1: 'Income." A1 is the current cell pointer position. The apostrophe (') in front of Income was added by Lotus to designate a label entry. Lotus assumes that any entry that begins with a letter is a label.

> **Problem Solving**
>
> If you mistyped "Income", you have two solutions:
>
> 1. Merely type it again, the new entry will replace the old entry.
> 2. Tap function key F2 (the EDIT key). The contents of the current cell will appear on line two of the user interface. You are now in EDIT (or wordprocessing) mode. Use the BKSP, INS and cursor keys to edit the cell's contents, then tap the ENTER key to return to READY mode. The edited version will replace the unedited version.

☐ Complete the following keystrokes to position the cell pointer in A2 and enter the label "Expenses." After typing the first letter of "Expenses", stop and look at the status indicator in the upper right corner. It will indicate "LABEL".

* ↓
* E
* *(look at the status indicator)*
* **xpenses** ↵

Repeat this activity to enter "Profit" in A3.

☐ Use function key F5 to reposition the cell pointer to B1, then enter the value 7400. Function key F5 is the "GoTo" key.

* F5
* **B1** ↵
* **7400** ↵

Also enter the value 5200 in B2. Notice that value entries are not preceded by an apostrophe. Also notice that value entries are right aligned whereas the default alignment for label entries is left aligned.

☐ Profit is defined as income minus expenses. To calculate profit in our spreadsheet, we enter a formula in cell B3 that subtracts the value in B2 from the value in B1. The formula entered below includes cell addresses. Lotus replaces each cell address with the value stored at that address when calculating the result.

* F5

* B3 ↵
* +B1-B2 ↵

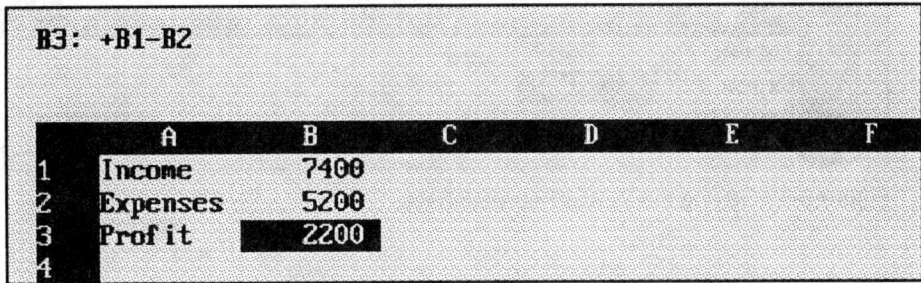

Figure 5-4 Cell B3 contains the formula +B1-B2. The formula's result is displayed in B3

Formula entries begin with an arithmetic expression (+, -, etc.). Notice in Figure 5-4 that the calculated result (2200) is displayed in the spreadsheet (B3) and the formula is displayed in the user interface (B3: +B1-B2).

Authors' Note
Moving the Cell Pointer

Throughout this chapter, you will be asked to use function key F5 to move the cell pointer. In everyday spreadsheet use, this method is most often used to move the cell pointer from one large area of the spreadsheet to another. For instance, we would always use F5 to jump from cell B14 to cell AG2400.

Our use of F5 to move the pointer small distances (i.e., from B2 to B3) is employed to assure that the cell pointer is correctly placed when entering data. Please use the cursor control keys (i.e., the down arrow key) instead of F5 if it is more efficient.

❏ Change the value in B2 to demonstrate the spreadsheet's recalculation feature.

* [F5]
* B2 ↵
* 8000 ↵

The calculated value in B3 should be -600 (see Figure 5-5).

❏ Select commands from the command line to save the spreadsheet. When prompted, enter the name WMCIS (for World's Most Concise Income Statement).

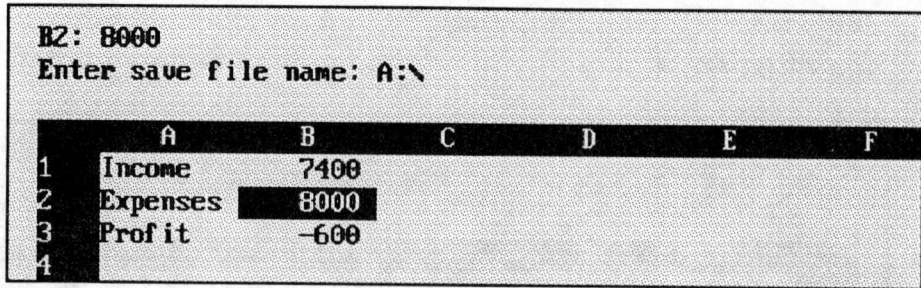

Figure 5-5 Saving the WMCIS spreadsheet

* /FS
* WMCIS ↵

Tapping the slash key called the main menu. Tapping "F" selected the File submenu. Tapping "S" selected the Save command.

☐ The next steps explain labels, values, formulas and command usage in greater detail as we construct a more complicated spreadsheet. Clear the worksheet before continuing.

* /WEY

In the remainder of this session, we will create the R & G Income Statement displayed in Figure 5-6. An income statement is one of the primary documents that describe a business's financial position. An income statement, also called a **profit and loss statement** or an **earnings report**, is the origin of the phrase "the bottom line," which has come to mean the final result. The bottom line in the income statement of Figure 5-6 is "NET PROFIT FOR THE YEAR" (row 20). R & G's past and current profits are all positive, but profits can also be negative (losses).

The income statement is essentially a record of a company's operating activities over an entire year. Some companies compile quarterly income statements to determine profit during a three month period. The income statement reflects the amount of money received from the sale of goods and services ("Net sales" in row 4) and other incomes ("Dividends and interest" in row 12) against all costs ("Cost of goods sold" and so forth in rows 6, 7, and 8) and other outlays ("Interest on bonds" in row 15 and "Provision for income tax" in row 18). Income statements are formatted differently for different types of companies; however, the R & G income statement in Figure 5-6 is representative for manufacturing companies.

```
A2: [W30] 'R & G INCOME STATEMENT ($1000)                              READY

         A                         B              C              D
1    ================================================================
2    R & G INCOME STATEMENT ($1000)  This Year      Last Year
3
4    Net sales                    $153,000       $144,780
5    Cost of sales & op. expenses
6      Cost of goods sold         115,260        117,345
7      Depreciation                 4,125          1,500
8      Selling &Admin. expenses    19,875         15,000
9                                 --------       --------
10       Operating profit         $13,740        $10,935
11   Other income
12     Dividends and interest         405            300
13                                 --------       --------
14       TOTAL INCOME             $14,145        $11,235
15   Less: interest on bonds        2,025          2,025
16                                 --------       --------
17   INcome before tax             12,120          9,210
18   Provision for income tax       5,475          4,160
19                                 --------       --------
20       NET PROFIT FOR YEAR       $6,645         $5,050
12-Mar-91  08:28 AM
```

Figure 5-6 The R & G income statement spreadsheet

Step 3: Formatting the Column Width

The standard or default column width for Lotus 1-2-3 is nine positions. The column width, however, does not limit the length of the entry. Lotus 1-2-3 permits entries of up to 240 character positions. An entry that exceeds the column width will spill over into any blank cell(s) to the immediate right. If the adjacent cell(s) already contains an entry, that portion of the entry that extends past the original cell is hidden from view. Lotus permits the user to vary the column width to improve readability.

The planned spreadsheet template (see Figure 5-6) has three columns. To make the most effective use of the display screen, revise the column width from the default of 9 positions to 30, 14 and 14 positions for columns A, B and C.

☐ Change column A to width 30. HOME positions the pointer at A1.

* HOME
* /WCS
* 30 ↵

☐ Use the global column width command to change columns B and C to width 14.

* /WGC 14 ↵

Release 2.2 users: notice the Global Settings screen that appears after tapping /WG.

All users: column widths that are set using /Worksheet Column Setwidth override those set using /Worksheet Global Columnwidth. In this case, column A will remain at a width of 30 and all other columns will be changed to width 14.

Step 4: Entering Labels

A special form of label entry is the **repeating text** entry. For example, in Figure 5-6 the entries in rows A1 and A3 are repeated text. To create this type of entry, the user taps the backslash key (\), and then enters a character string that is repeated in that cell. In Figure 5-6, the text string repeated in A1 is = (an equals sign) and the string repeated in A3 is a - (a hyphen). Repeating text entries are used primarily to enhance the appearance and readability of the spreadsheet.

In this step we enter all of the label entries needed for the spreadsheet of Figure 5-6.

First, enter all repeating text (such as the lines created by = and -) to provide some form to the spreadsheet template.

* HOME
* \= → \= → \= ↵

Tapping the right arrow cursor control key completed the cell entry and automatically positioned the cursor in the next cell to the right.

☐ Follow the foregoing procedure to add the repeated text as illustrated in Figure 5-6 to rows 3, 9, 13, 16, 19. Notice that on certain rows the repeated text entries begin at column B. For example, the keystroke sequence for row 9 is

* F5
* B9 ↵
* \- → \- ↵

☐ Now enter the labels for column A and row 2, beginning with the entry in A2. Remember, if you make an entry error, tap F2 to switch to edit mode. Edit the entry as you would text in a word processing document.

* [F5]
* A2 ↵
* **R & G INCOME STATEMENT ($1000)** ↵

☐ Complete the following to enter the column headings in row 2.

* [F5]
* B2 ↵
* **"This Year → "Last Year** ↵

Prefacing a label with a double quote (") causes it to be right justified.

☐ Next, make the other label entries (all in column A) for the spreadsheet as illustrated in Figure 5-7. Notice that some entries, such as those in A6 and A10, have either two or four leading spaces.

```
             A                          B            C
1   ========================================================
2   R & G INCOME STATEMENT ($1000)   This Year    Last Year
3   --------------------------------------------------------
4   Net sales                          153000       144700
5   Cost of sales & op. expenses
6     Cost of goods sold               115260       117345
7     Depreciation                       4125         1500
8     Selling & admin. expenses        19875         15000
9                                     ----------   ----------
10      Operating profit           +B4-B6-B7-B8  +C4-C6-C7-C8
11  Other income
12      Dividends and interest             405          300
13                                     ----------   ----------
14      TOTAL INCOME                   +B10+B12     +C10+C12
15  Less: interest on bonds               2025         2025
16                                     ----------   ----------
17  Income before tax                  +B14-B15     +C14-C15
18  Provision for income tax              5475         4160
19                                     ----------   ----------
20      NET PROFIT FOR YEAR            +B17-B18     +C17-C18
```

Figure 5-7 Actual cell entries to the R & G Income Statement spreadsheet

Step 5: Entering Values

Continue the development of the spreadsheet template of Figure 5-6 by entering the values.

☐ Enter the numeric values in rows 4, 6, 7, 8, 12, 15, and 18 of columns B and C. The other values in columns B and C are the results of formulas. The actual content of the spreadsheet cells is shown in Figure 5-7. Formulas are entered in the next step. For B4, B6, B7, and B8, enter

* ⎕F5⎕
* B4 ↵
* 153000 ↓ ↓ 115260 ↓ 4125 ↓ 19875 ↓

Notice that the values you entered are not formatted with a dollar sign ($) and a comma (,) as shown in Figure 5-6. We will format these entries later.

☐ Enter the other nonformula numeric values (identified above) as shown in Figure 5-7.

Step 6: Entering Formulas

Include the calculation capability to the spreadsheet template of Figure 5-6 by entering the formulas.

☐ Complete the following to enter the formulas as illustrated in Figure 5-7 (the actual content of the spreadsheet of Figure 5-6). For B10, enter

* ⎕F5⎕
* B10 ↵
* +B4-B6-B7-B8 ↵

Notice that the result, and not the formula, is displayed in cell B10. Validate your entry by comparing the result to the value displayed in B10 in Figure 5-6. Remember that your display does not include formatting yet. We will format in a later step.

☐ Instead of entering the formula for cell C10, we can copy the formula from cell B10. B10 is the "copy from" range and C10 is the "copy to" range. Your cell pointer should be in B10.

- ** /C
- ** ↵
- ** C10 ↵

☐ Move the pointer to C10 and notice that the formula copied to column C applies to column C, not column B.

☐ Refer to Figure 5-7 and enter all of the other formulas in column B (B14, B17 and B20). Use the copy command to enter like formulas in column C, just as you did for B10 and C10.

Step 7: Saving a Spreadsheet

Always save your work several times during a session. Never wait until the spreadsheet is "finished" before saving. Saving as you work allows you to return to a recently saved version should disaster strike. We will save the current spreadsheet under the name R&G.

- ** /FS
- ** R&G ↵

Step 8: Using Predefined Functions

Lotus 1-2-3 offers users a wide variety of predefined operations called **functions**. These functions can be used to create formulas that perform mathematical, logical, statistical, financial, and character-string operations on spreadsheet data. To use a function, simply enter the function prefix symbol (@) followed by the desired function name (@AVG for average) and the function **argument [@AVG(B6..B8)]**. The argument, which is placed in parentheses, identifies the data to be operated on. The argument can be one or several numbers, character strings, or ranges that represent data. In Figure 5-7, the operating profit (B10) is calculated by subtracting the individual cell values under the "cost of sales and operating expenses" heading (B6, B7, and B8) from the net sales (B4).

Or, the total of the "cost of sales and operating expenses" items can be computed with a function and its argument.

    +B4-@SUM(B6..B8)

The use of predefined functions can save a lot of time. What if the range to be summed was B6..B600? In this step, we will edit the formulas in B10 and C10 to demonstrate the use of predefined functions.

☐ Edit the "operating profit" cells to use the SUM function.

* ⬚F5⬚
* ⬚B10⬚ ↵
* ⬚F2⬚ *(edit cell)*
* ⬚BKSP⬚ *(8 times)*
* ⬚@SUM(B6.B8)⬚ ↵

Notice that a range may be entered with one period (B6.B8).

☐ Copy B10 to C10. You can enter C10 directly as illustrated in Step 6, or you can use the "point and shoot" selection method. To do this, move the cell pointer to the "copy to:" cell and tap ENTER.

* /C
* ↵
* → ↵

The results of these cells are, of course, unchanged.

Step 9: Formatting the Cell Entries

Values and formula calculations may be formatted to improve readability. Adding a format changes the cell's appearance but does not change its value. The procedure usually involves identifying the range to be formatted then selecting the appropriate format (percent in the example) from a menu of formatting options.

Currency amounts can be formatted so that commas and a dollar sign will be inserted. For example, in Figure 5-7 the value of "Net sales" for "This Year" was entered as 153000 in B4. Figure 5-6 shows the display of B4 when it is formatted for currency ($153,000).

Values can be formatted so that they will be displayed with a fixed number of places to the right of the decimal point. In Figure 5-6, the format of the "Net sales" data in the range B4..C4 is formatted to currency with zero decimal places. Numbers with more decimal digits than specified in the format are rounded when displayed.

Complete the spreadsheet template of Figure 5-6 by formatting the cell entries to improve appearance and readability. Two formats are used in the R & G Income Statement, currency with no decimals (ex. B4..C4) and comma with no decimals (ex. B6..C8). In this step, you will be shown how to format the range B4..C4 to currency with no decimals, and the range B6..C8 to comma with no decimals. Then you will format the remainder of the values in columns B and C.

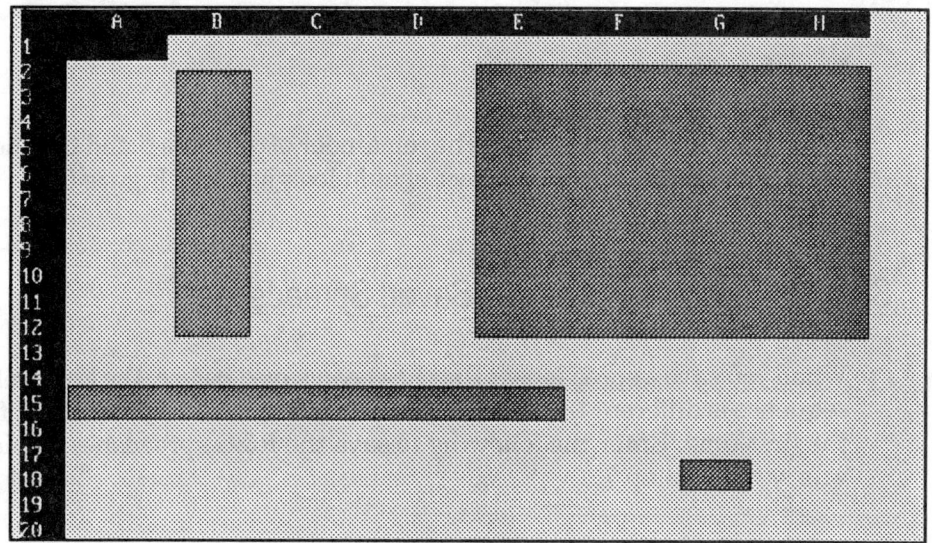

Figure 5-8 Electronic Spreadsheet: Ranges

Spreadsheet Ranges

Many electronic spreadsheet operations ask you to designate a **range** of cells. The four types of ranges are highlighted in Figure 5-8.

* A single cell (example range is G18)
* All or part of a column of adjacent cells (example range is B2..B12)
* All or part of a row of adjacent cells (example range is A15..E15)
* A rectangular block of cells (example range is E2..H12)

A particular range is depicted by the addresses of the endpoint cells and separated by two periods. Any cell can comprise a single cell range. The range for the total income amounts in Figure 5-6 is B14..C14 and the range for the row labels is A4..A20. The range of the dollar amounts in the two income statements for "This Year" and "Last Year" data is depicted by any two opposite corner cell addresses (B4..C20 or C4..B20).

☐ Format the entries in B4..C4 to "currency" with no decimal places.

* **/RFC**
* **0** ↵
* **B4.C4** ↵

☐ Format the entries in B6..C8 to "," (comma) format with no decimals.

* **/RF ,** *(the comma key)*

Lotus: Session One 263

* 0 ↵
* B6.C20 ↵

Refer to Figure 5-6 and format the remainder of columns B and C. When you are finished, the spreadsheet should look just like Figure 5-6.

Step 10: Saving a Previously Saved Spreadsheet

☐ When you save a spreadsheet that has been saved before, the keystroke sequence is different from the sequence used to save a spreadsheet for the first time. Enter the following to save the R&G spreadsheet which was saved in Step 7.

* /FS
* ↵
* R

After /FS, Lotus displays the file's name. Tapping the ENTER key tells Lotus to save the file using the same name. Tapping "R" to replace erases the old version on secondary storage and replaces it with the current version.

Step 11: Printing a Document

☐ Define the range to be printed and print the current spreadsheet. The range to be printed is A1..C20. In the following sequence, the range is entered with one period (A1.C20). Ranges may be entered with one or two periods.

* /PPR
* A1.C20 ↵

Release 2.2 users: notice the Print Settings screen that appears after tapping /PP.

☐ Turn on your printer, adjust the paper. The "A"lign command resets the printer to the top of the page. The "G"o command prints the spreadsheet and the "P"age command sends a form feed to the printer to eject the page after printing.

* AGP

* **Q** *(to return to the spreadsheet)*

Step 12: Retrieving a Spreadsheet

The work area does not have to be cleared before retrieving another spreadsheet. When the /File Retrieve command is entered, Lotus displays the names of all saved lotus spreadsheets in the current directory. To retrieve a named file, move the highlight bar to the name and tap the ENTER key. Lotus then clears the work area and calls up the desired spreadsheet. Retrieve the WMCIS spreadsheet created in Step 2.

* **/FR**
* *(highlight "WMCIS")*
* ↵

Step 13: Practice

If necessary, retrieve the WMCIS spreadsheet created in Step 2.

* Print the current spreadsheet.
* Format the range B1.B3 as currency with no decimals.
* Enter 8700 in B1 and 5622 in B2.
* Save the revised version.
* Print the revised version of the spreadsheet.

Step 14: Terminating a Session

If you do not want to continue to the next session now, complete the following to turn off your computer. Remember that you should always return to the DOS prompt before turning off the computer.

☐ To exit Lotus 1-2-3, first make sure that your work is saved (see Step 10), then issue the Quit command.

* *(if necessary, save your work)*
* **/QY**

☐ Remove your data diskette from drive A and turn off the computer.

Session Two

What if... Analysis

The real beauty of an electronic spreadsheet is that if you change the value of a cell in a spreadsheet, all other affected cells are revised accordingly. This capability makes spreadsheet software the perfect tool for "what if" analysis.

Monroe Green decides to modify the R & G Income Statement spreadsheet to add a pro rata "Next Year" column. The new column will allow him to perform "what if" analysis to forecast next year's performance.

In this session, we add a column to the existing R&G spreadsheet. Then we will create an additional section of the spreadsheet in rows 21 through 27 that includes "what if" forecast variables. These variables will be referenced in the new "Next Year" column. Finally, we will enter "best case" and "worst case" variables to see their effect on next year's bottom line.

If necessary, see Session One, Step 1 to start Lotus 1-2-3. Insert your data diskette in drive A and retrieve the "R&G" spreadsheet created in the previous session (refer to Session One, Step 12).

In this session you will learn how to:

- Insert a column
- Add a template to an existing spreadsheet
- Save incremental versions of a spreadsheet
- Create "What if ..." formulas
- Perform "What if ..." calculations

Step 1: Inserting a Column

Monroe Green wants to add a Next Year column to his spreadsheet. To do this, he inserts an empty column and copies all labels, values and formulas from the "This Year" column to the new column. Then he edits the new column.

☐ Insert a new column at column B (see Figure 5-9).

* `HOME`
* `F5`
* `B1` ↵
* `/WIC` ↵

	A	B	C	D
1	=================================		=================================	=================================
2	R & G INCOME STATEMENT ($1000)		This Year	Last Year
3	_____			
4	Net sales		$153,000	$144,700
5	Cost of sales & op. expenses			
6	Cost of goods sold		115,260	117,345
7	Depreciation		4,125	1,500
8	Selling &Admin. expenses		19,875	15,000
9			_____	_____
10	Operating profit		$13,740	$10,935
11	Other income			
12	Dividends and interest		405	300
13			_____	_____
14	TOTAL INCOME		$14,145	$11,235
15	Less: interest on bonds		2,025	2,025
16			_____	_____
17	INcome before tax		12,120	9,210
18	Provision for income tax		5,475	4,160
19			_____	_____
20	NET PROFIT FOR YEAR		$6,645	$5,050

12-Mar-91 05:40 AM

Figure 5-9 A new column has just been inserted at column B

☐ Copy column C to column B (see Figure 5-9).

* *(the cell pointer should be in B1)*
* /C
* C1.C20 ↵
* ↵

Notice that the "copy to" range was a single cell. When copying a range of cells, only the upper left cell needs to be designated as the "copy to" range.

☐ Enter a new label in B2, "Next Year."

* [F5]
* B2 ↵
* "Next Year ↵

Before editing the remainder of column B to add "what if" formulas, we must create the forecast variable template in rows 21 through 27 (see Step 2).

Step 2: Creating a Forecast Variable Template

Before Monroe can perform "what if" analysis, he must create a forecast variable template that defines each variable (see Figure 5-10).

☐ Tap the PGDN key to display rows 21 through 40.

* **PGDN**

☐ Refer to Figure 5-10 and enter the separator lines in rows 21, 23 and 27.

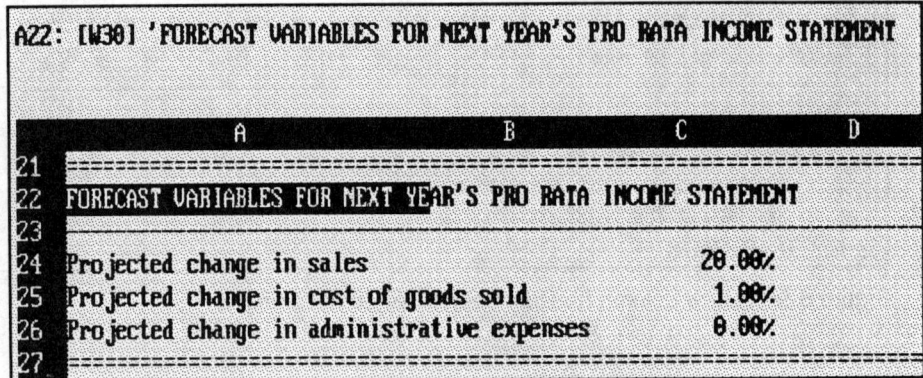

Figure 5-10 The Forecast Variables template added to the R & G Income Statement spreadsheet

☐ Enter the label in A22.

* **F5**
* **A22** ↵
* **FORECAST VARIABLES FOR NEXT YEAR'S PRO RATA INCOME STATEMENT** ↵

Notice that the label in A22 extends across columns B and C. If an entry were made in B22, only the first 30 positions, or the width of column A, would be visible on the spreadsheet ("FORECAST VARIABLES FOR NEXT YE").

☐ Refer to Figure 5-10 and follow the previous procedure to enter the labels in A24, A25 and A26. The numbers 20.00%, 1.00% and 0.00% will be entered and formatted next.

☐ Complete the following to enter the values in the range C24..C26.

- * F5
- * C24 ↵
- * .2 ↓
- * .01 ↓
- * 0 ↵

☐ Format the values in A24..A26 as percent with 2 decimal places.

- * /RFP
- * 2 ↵
- * C24.C26 ↵

Your template should now look the same as Figure 5-10.

Step 3: Adding "What if" Formulas to Column B

Now that we know each forecast variable's cell address, we can return to the Next Year column and enter "what if" formulas. For example, next year's net sales will be the product of this year's sales times the projected percentage change in sales. The formula to be placed in B4 will reference C4 (last year's sales) and C24 (the percentage change in sales forecast variable).

☐ Enter the formula that computes next year's projected net sales in B4.

- * PGUP
- * F5
- * B4 ↵
- * +C4*(1+C24) ↵

☐ Also enter the following:

Cell	Formula
B6	+C6*(1+C25)
B8	+C8*(1+C26)
B18	(C18/C17)*B17

The formula entered in B18 calculates next year's income tax provision based on the same percentage used to calculate this year's income tax provision (C18/C17). Notice that the formula in B18 did not require a

	A	B	C	D
1	===			
2	R & G INCOME STATEMENT ($1000)	Next Year	This Year	Last Year
3				
4	Net sales	$183,600	$153,000	$144,780
5	Cost of sales & op. expenses			
6	Cost of goods sold	116,413	115,260	117,345
7	Depreciation	4,125	4,125	1,500
8	Selling &Admin. expenses	19,875	19,875	15,000
9				
10	Operating profit	$43,187	$13,740	$10,935
11	Other income			
12	Dividends and interest	405	405	300
13				
14	TOTAL INCOME	$43,592	$14,145	$11,235
15	Less: interest on bonds	2,025	2,025	2,025
16				
17	INcome before tax	41,567	12,120	9,210
18	Provision for income tax	18,777	5,475	4,160
19				
20	NET PROFIT FOR YEAR	$22,790	$6,645	$5,050

12-Mar-91 08:30 AM

Figure 5-11 The R & G Income Statement after adding a "what if" calculation

leading plus sign (+) since it began with an open parens sign. Compare your display with Figure 5-11; they should be identical.

Step 4: Performing "What if ..." Analysis

Monroe Green, R & G's vice-president of Finance and Accounting, is now ready to create a variety of "what if" scenarios. The scenario illustrated in Figure 5-11 reflects the optimistic projections of two vice-presidents and the president--essentially the best-case scenario. The vice-president of the Operations Division has told Monroe that he is implementing a number of cost-cutting measures that will enable him to hold the cost of goods sold to a 1 percent increase, even though more products will be built and shipped. The vice-president of Sales and Marketing predicts that next year will be a great year and net sales will increase by 20 percent. The president of R & G, Preston Smith, asked all managers to hold the line on all selling and administrative expenses; therefore, Monroe expects these expenses to remain about the same. With spreadsheet software, Monroe was able to answer the question, "What if sales increased by 20 percent, cost-of-goods-sold increased by 1 percent, and everything else remained the same for the coming year?"

Monroe entered the three forecast variables in C24, C25, and C26 (see Figure 5-10) to get the pro rata income statement (the "Next Year" column of Figure 5-11). All calculations (sales with a 20 percent increase, net profit, earnings per share, taxes) are performed automatically because the appropriate formulas are built into the spreadsheet template. Some entries in the "Next Year" column are unchanged (depreciation, dividends, and interest); however, if Monroe wanted to reflect a change in depreciation, he would simply change the value of the "depreciation" entry in the "Next Year" column. The "provision for income tax" entry (B18) is extrapolated from the "This Year" column data by a formula that assumes the taxes will be paid at the same rate as the previous year [B18: (C18/C17)*B17]. The spreadsheet template of Figure 5-11 reflects the optimistic projections of R & G vice-presidents. Over the years R & G's president, Preston Smith, has learned to temper the optimistic projections of his vice-presidents with a touch of reality. To examine a worst-case scenario, Preston uses Monroe Green's spreadsheet template (Figures 5-10 and 5-11) to answer the following question:

> What if sales increased by 3 percent, cost-of-goods-sold increased by 2 percent, administrative expenses increased by 4 percent, and everything else remained the same for the coming year?

	A	B	C	D
1	==============================	==========	==========	==========
2	R & G INCOME STATEMENT ($1000)	Next Year	This Year	Last Year
3				
4	Net sales	$157,590	$153,000	$144,700
5	Cost of sales & op. expenses			
6	Cost of goods sold	117,565	115,260	117,345
7	Depreciation	4,125	4,125	1,500
8	Selling &Admin. expenses	20,670	19,875	15,000
9				
10	Operating profit	$15,230	$13,740	$10,935
11	Other income			
12	Dividends and interest	405	405	300
13				
14	TOTAL INCOME	$15,635	$14,145	$11,235
15	Less: interest on bonds	2,025	2,025	2,025
16				
17	Income before tax	13,610	12,120	9,210
18	Provision for income tax	6,148	5,475	4,160
19				
20	NET PROFIT FOR YEAR	$7,462	$6,645	$5,050

12-Mar-91 08:31 AM

Figure 5-12 The R & G Income Statement displaying Preston Smith's "worst case"

Preston Smith needs only to change the three forecast variables (C24..C26) to get the worst-case results of Figure 5-12.

In this step, we answer the question "What if the forecast variables are changed?"

❑ Enter Preston Smith's "worst case" values (.03, .02 and .04) into C24, C25, and C26.

* ▫F5▫

* C24 ↵
* .03 ↓ .02 ↓ .04 ↵ HOME

Compare your results with those of Figure 5-12.

☐ Enter other values for the forecast variables and observe how net profit is affected. When you are finished, reenter the original values .2, .01 and 0 in C24, C25 and C26.

Step 5: Saving Incremental Versions of a Spreadsheet

Save the most recent changes, the inserted column and the forecast variable template, under a new name. This way, you will have two versions of the spreadsheet, the original and the new version.

* /FS
* R&G1 ↵

Step 6: Practice

Create a first quarter sales summary spreadsheet for Begonia's Clothing Store for Women. Figure 5-15 displays the completed template.

* If necessary, clear the workscreen.
* Reset the width of column A to 12 and the width of columns B through G to 10.
* Place a separator line in row 3, columns A through G.
* Enter the column heading DIVISION in A4.
* Right align the headings JANUARY, FEBRUARY, and MARCH in B4..D4.
* Place a second separator line in A5..G5.
* Enter each division's name in A6..A17.
* Format B6..D17 as currency with 0 decimals and enter the sales data (see Figure 5-13).
* Save the spreadsheet as BEGONIA1.

Add a column of formulas in column E.

* Right align the heading TOTAL in E4.

	A	B	C	D
1				
2				
3				
4	DIVISION	JANUARY	FEBRUARY	MARCH
5				
6	Coats	$6,780	$14,780	$12,700
7	Dresses	$12,600	$13,580	$15,794
8	New Ideas	$14,670	$16,871	$17,400
9	Swimwear	$1,260	$1,150	$2,140
10	Casual	$8,600	$9,890	$11,502
11	Designer's	$15,890	$18,274	$21,252
12	Junior's	$13,680	$15,732	$18,296
13	Handbags	$6,400	$7,360	$9,580
14	Accessories	$9,580	$11,017	$12,813
15	Shoes	$7,650	$8,798	$11,400
16	Fragrances	$4,200	$6,700	$7,792
17	Spec Sizes	$12,400	$14,260	$16,584
18				

Figure 5-13 The BEGONIA1 spreadsheet

* Use the @SUM function to total the amounts in each row for rows 6 through 17 (create the formula for row 6 and copy the formula to rows 7 through 17).

* Format E6..E17 as currency with 0 decimals.

* Save the spreadsheet as BEGONIA2.

Create a LAST YEAR column in column F.

* Right align the heading LAST YEAR (total sales for the past year) in F4.

* Enter the sales data displayed in Figure 5-14 into column F.

* Format F6..F17 as currency with 0 decimals. Save the spreadsheet as BEGONIA3.

Add column totals formulas in row 19.

* Add two more separator lines in row 18 and row 20 (copy A3..G3).

* Enter the row heading TOTALS in A19 and use the @SUM function to

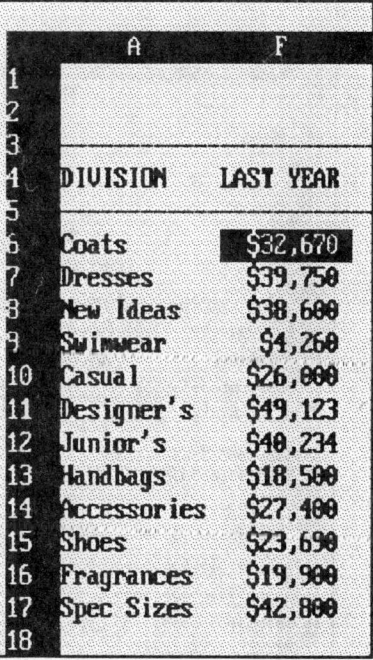

Figure 5-14 Last year's sales data to be entered into column F

total each of the columns B through F (create the formula for column B and copy the formula to C through F).

* Format B19..F19 as currency with 0 decimals.
* Save the spreadsheet as BEGONIA4.

Create the %CHG column in column G.

* Right align the column heading %CHG in G4.
* Create a formula to calculate the percentage change in sales from last year to this year (subtract last year's sales from this year's sales and divide the result by last year's sales).
* Enter the formula in G6 and copy the formula to G7..G17 and G19.
* Format G6..G17 and G19 as percent with 2 decimals.
* Enter the heading BEGONIA'S CLOTHING STORE FOR WOMEN with 6 leading spaces in B1.
* Enter the heading RETAIL SALES - FIRST QUARTER in C2.
* Compare your spreadsheet to Figure 5-15, then save the spreadsheet as BEGONIA5.
* Retrieve and print all five BEGONIA spreadsheets.

```
C2: 'RETAIL SALES - FIRST QUARTER                                          READY
```

	A	B	C	D	E	F	G
1			BEGONIA'S CLOTHING STORE FOR WOMEN				
2			RETAIL SALES - FIRST QUARTER				
3							
4	DIVISION	JANUARY	FEBRUARY	MARCH	TOTAL	LAST YEAR	%CHG
5							
6	Coats	$6,780	$14,780	$12,700	$34,260	$32,670	4.87%
7	Dresses	$12,600	$13,580	$15,794	$41,974	$39,750	5.59%
8	New Ideas	$14,670	$16,871	$17,400	$48,941	$38,600	26.79%
9	Swimwear	$1,260	$1,150	$2,140	$4,550	$4,260	6.81%
10	Casual	$8,600	$9,890	$11,502	$29,992	$26,000	15.35%
11	Designer's	$15,890	$18,274	$21,252	$55,416	$49,123	12.81%
12	Junior's	$13,680	$15,732	$18,296	$47,708	$40,234	18.58%
13	Handbags	$6,400	$7,360	$9,580	$23,340	$18,500	26.16%
14	Accessories	$9,580	$11,017	$12,813	$33,410	$27,400	21.93%
15	Shoes	$7,650	$8,798	$11,400	$27,848	$23,690	17.55%
16	Fragrances	$4,200	$6,700	$7,792	$18,692	$19,900	-6.07%
17	Spec Sizes	$12,400	$14,260	$16,584	$43,244	$42,800	1.04%
18							
19	TOTALS	$113,710	$138,412	$157,253	$409,375	$362,927	12.80%
20							

Figure 5-15 Completed sales summary template (BEGONIA5)

Step 7: Terminating the Session

If you do not want to continue to the next session now, complete the following to turn off your computer. Remember that you should always return to the DOS prompt before turning off the computer.

☐ To exit Lotus 1-2-3, first make sure that your work is saved (see Session One, Step 10), then issue the Quit command.

* *(if necessary, save your work)*
* /QY

☐ Remove your data diskette from drive A and turn off the computer.

Session Three

Modifying a Spreadsheet

Preston Smith, R & G's CEO, was impressed with the what if capabilities in Monroe Green's spreadsheet. Mr. Smith asked Monroe if he could add yet another column, an After Next year column, which would project what if calculations an additional year forward.

Preston Smith also asked Monroe Green if a management summary could be created showing average, minimum and maximum values for Net Sales, Operating Profit, Total Income and Net Profit for the Year. Preston wanted the summary to include last year, this year and next year's projections. Preston also wanted the summary to be responsive to any changes made in what if calculations.

Monroe said that he was pretty sure he could modify the spreadsheet to match Preston's wishes. This session follows Monroe's steps as he adds an additional "After Next" column and creates the management summary template. To accomplish these tasks, Monroe must use absolute cell referencing, the copy command, global column width changes, predefined functions, and row deletion. Finally, Monroe shows Preston how to divide the spreadsheet using the windows command to view separate parts of the spreadsheet simultaneously.

If necessary, see Session One, Step 1 to start Lotus 1-2-3. Insert your data diskette in drive A, make drive A the active drive and retrieve the "R&G1" spreadsheet created in Session Two (refer to Session One, Step 12).

In this session you will learn how to:

- ◆ Use absolute cell references with the copy command
- ◆ Use @AVG, @MIN and @MAX
- ◆ Delete rows
- ◆ Copy a block
- ◆ Use windows

Step 1: Inserting a Column

The first step Monroe takes to create the After Next column requested by Preston Smith is to insert a blank column and readjust the column widths (see Figure 5-16). Before beginning, confirm that the values in C24, C25 and C26 are 20%, 1% and 0%.

☐ Insert a new column at column B.

* HOME
* F5
* B1 ↵
* /WIC
* ↵

☐ Adjust the width of columns B, C, D, and E to a width of 10 positions so that all columns are displayed on the screen.

* /WGC
* 10 ↵

```
                A                    B       C         D         E
1  ================================          ============================
2  R & G INCOME STATEMENT ($1000)            Next Year This Year Last Year
3                 ----------------
4  Net sales                                 $183,600  $153,000  $144,700
5  Cost of sales & op. expenses
6      Cost of goods sold                     116,413   115,260   117,345
7      Depreciation                             4,125     4,125     1,500
8      Selling & Admin. expenses               19,875    19,875    15,000
9                                             -------   -------   -------
10     Operating profit                       $43,187   $13,740   $10,935
11 Other income
12     Dividends and interest                     405       405       300
13                                            -------   -------   -------
14     TOTAL INCOME                           $43,592   $14,145   $11,235
15 Less: interest on bonds                      2,825     2,825     2,825
16                                            -------   -------   -------
17 Income before tax                           41,567    12,120     9,210
18 Provision for income tax                    18,777     5,475     4,160
19                                            -------   -------   -------
20     NET PROFIT FOR YEAR                    $22,790    $6,645    $5,050
12-Mar-91  08:33 AM
```

Figure 5-16 The appearance of the R & G Income Statement after adding a blank column and adjusting the global column width

Step 2: Creating Absolute Cell Addresses

Monroe plans to copy the Next Year column (column C) to the blank column (column B) to create the After Next column (see Figure 5-15). Before doing so, each reference to a what if variable (D24, D25 and D26) in column C must be converted into an absolute cell reference. Otherwise the new formula will not be accurate. To understand why, we must talk about absolute and relative cell addresses.

- ◆ A **relative cell address** is based on its position relative to the cell containing the formula. When you copy a formula to another cell, the relative cell addresses in the formula are revised so that they retain the same position relative to the new location of the formula.

- ◆ An **absolute cell address** remains unchanged when a formula is copied. The dollar signs ($), which preface the column and/or the row in an absolute cell address, distinguish it from a relative cell address (for example, D4 is a relative address whereas $D$24 is an absolute address).

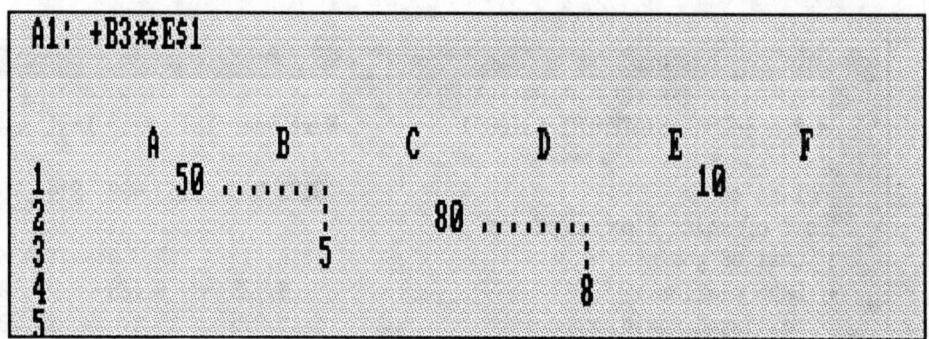

Figure 5-17 The formula in A1 contains both a relative and an absolute cell address

The two types of cell addressing are illustrated in the spreadsheet in Figure 5-17. Suppose that the formula B3*$E$1 is in cell A1. In the formula, B3 is a relative cell address that is one column to the right of and two rows down from A1, the location of the formula. If the formula, B3*$E$1, is copied to C2, the formula in C2 is D4*$E$1. Notice that D4 has the same relative position to the formula in cell C2: one column to the right and two rows down. The absolute cell address ($E$1) remains the same in both formulas.

In Monroe's current spreadsheet, the formulas in C4, C6 and C8 must be modified. For example if the unmodified formula C4 were to be copied to column B, all cell references would be adjusted and the formula would not refer to the what if variable in D24. The formula would be incorrect.

Copied formula Column B	Original formula Column C
+C4*(1+C24)	+D4*(1+D24)
+C4*(1+$D$24)	+D4*(1+$D$24)

However, change the relative reference, D24, into an absolute reference, $D$24, and the formula copies correctly. Use function key F4 to change cell references from relative to absolute.

❑ Use function key F4 to change the D24 relative cell reference in the formula in C4 to an absolute cell reference (see Figure 5-18).

* F5
* B4 ↵
* F2
* F4
* ↵

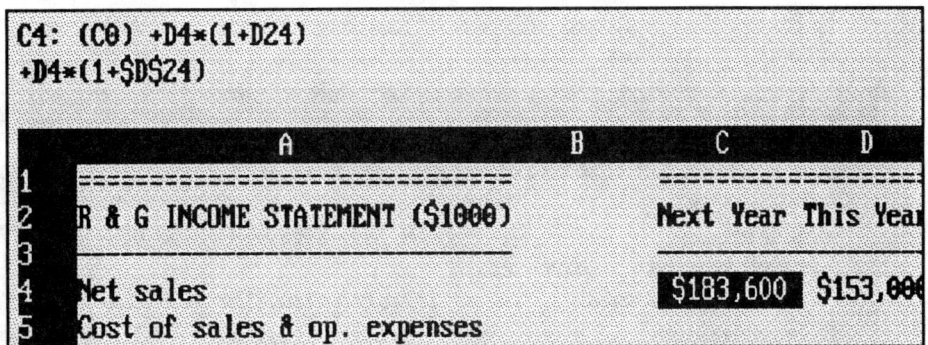

Figure 5-18 Using the EDIT key (F2) and the ABSOLUTE VALUE key (F4) to change the relative reference (D24) to an absolute reference ($D$24)

Follow the same procedure to modify the formulas in C6 and C8.

Step 3: Using Absolute Cell Addresses

Now Monroe is ready to copy column C to column B.

❑ Copy the range C1.C30 to B1.B30. Copying rows 1 through 30 also copies the separator lines in the Forecast Variables Template in rows 21 through 27.

* F5
* B1 ↵
* /C
* C1.C30 ↵
* ↵

Notice how the projected "Net Sales" in the new column is increased by the value of the forecast variable (projected change in sales) over the amount in the "Next Year" column.

☐ Edit the column heading in column B.

* F5
* B2 ↵
* "After Next ↵

Switch the pointer between B4 and C4. Notice that the relative addresses were revised during the copy operation, and the absolute addresses remained the same. Your spreadsheet should look like Figure 5-19.

	A	B	C	D	E
1	==
2	R & G INCOME STATEMENT ($1000)	AFTER NEXT	Next Year	This Year	Last Year
3					
4	Net sales	$220,320	$183,600	$153,000	$144,780
5	Cost of sales & op. expenses				
6	Cost of goods sold	117,577	116,413	115,260	117,345
7	Depreciation	4,125	4,125	4,125	1,500
8	Selling & Admin. expenses	19,875	19,875	19,875	15,000
9					
10	Operating profit	$78,743	$43,187	$13,740	$10,935
11	Other income				
12	Dividends and interest	405	405	405	300
13					
14	TOTAL INCOME	$79,148	$43,592	$14,145	$11,235
15	Less: interest on bonds	2,025	2,025	2,025	2,025
16					
17	Income before tax	77,123	41,567	12,120	9,210
18	Provision for income tax	34,839	18,777	5,475	4,160
19					
20	NET PROFIT FOR YEAR	$42,284	$22,790	$6,645	$5,050

Figure 5-19 The R & G Income Statement after adding an additional "what if" column

☐ Save the spreadsheet as R&G2.

* /FS
* R&G2 ↵

☐ Print only rows 1 through 20 of the current spreadsheet (see Session One, Step 11). Identify the range as A1.E20 so that all the columns that appear on the screen are printed.

* /PPR
* A1.E20 ↵
* AGPQ

Step 4: Adding a Template to an Existing Template

Since Preston Smith wants the management summary template to include only Last Year, This Year and Next Year, Monroe decides to create the manager's summary template in his first "what if.." spreadsheet (R&G1.WK1). Monroe would not have this option if he had not saved each incremental version of his spreadsheet.

Monroe retrieves the "R&G1" file created in Session Two and creates the "Three-Year Summary Data" template in the range A41..D60 (see Figure 5-20).

	A	B	C	D
41	==			
42	THREE-YEAR SUMMARY DATA	Average	Minimum	Maximum
43				
44	Net sales	$160,460	$144,700	$183,600
45	Operating profit	$22,621	$10,935	$43,187
46	TOTAL INCOME	$22,991	$11,235	$43,592
47	NET PROFIT FOR YEAR	$11,495	$5,050	$22,790

Figure 5-20 The Three-Year Summary template added to the R & G Income Statement spreadsheet

☐ Retrieve the spreadsheet "R&G1.WK1" and position the pointer at "home".

* /FR
* *(highlight "R&G1.WK1")* ↵
* HOME

☐ Copy A1..D20 to A41..D60.

* /C
* A1.D20 ↵
* A41 ↵

Step 5: Modifying the "R&G1" Template to Create Another Template

Monroe is ready to modify the copied template in A41.D60 to become the THREE-YEAR SUMMARY template. Monroe sees the new template hiding within the copied template. Like a sculptor starting with a new piece of stone, Monroe chips away the unneeded portions until the desired result appears (see Figure 5-20).

First Monroe changes the column headings, then notices that the four items requested by Preston Smith are in rows 44, 50, 54 and 60. Monroe enters formulas in row 44 (net sales) that use functions to calculate the three year average (column B), display the minimum three year value (column C) and display the maximum three year value (column D). Monroe then copies these functions to rows 50, 54 and 60, letting the relative addresses automatically change to refer to the desired rows in the original template. Finally, Monroe deletes the unneeded rows from the SUMMARY template.

- ☐ Move the pointer to the template copy.

  * F5
  * A41 ↵

- ☐ Key in the appropriate template title and column headings.

  * F5
  * A42 ↵
  * THREE-YEAR SUMMARY DATA →
  * "Average → "Minimum → "Maximum ↵

Entering a new label replaces the existing label. Preceding a label with a double quote (") right justifies the label.

- ☐ Use functions to determine the average, minimum, and maximum values in each category.

  * F5
  * B44 ↵
  * @AVG(B4.D4) → @MIN(B4.D4) → @MAX(B4.D4) ↵

- ☐ Copy the functions to the other ranges.

* **/C**
* **B44.D44** ↵
* **B50** ↵

☐ Use the same procedure to copy range B44..D44 to B54 and B60. Notice that the relative cell addresses in the ranges are automatically adjusted. For example, the functions in row 50 refer to the range B10..D10.

☐ Delete any unneeded rows in the template copy. Delete rows 55 through 59.

* **/WDR**
* **A55.A59** ↵

☐ Repeat this procedure to delete rows 51 through 53 and then rows 45 through 49. Each time rows are deleted, the remaining rows are moved up to fill the space.

Step 6: Using Windows

Use the window feature to view the newly created summary template in the lower window and the original template in the upper window (see Figure 5-21).

☐ Split the screen into horizontal windows.

* **F5**
* **A30** ↵ *(move template to the bottom of screen)*
* **F5**
* **A41** ↵ *(position pointer at window division)*
* **/WWH**

☐ Move the pointer to the Forecast Variables template and change the variables. Notice the immediate changes that occur in the Three-Year Summary template.

* **F5**
* **A21** ↵
* **F5**

* C24 ↵
* .05 ↓
* .03 ↓
* .02 ↵

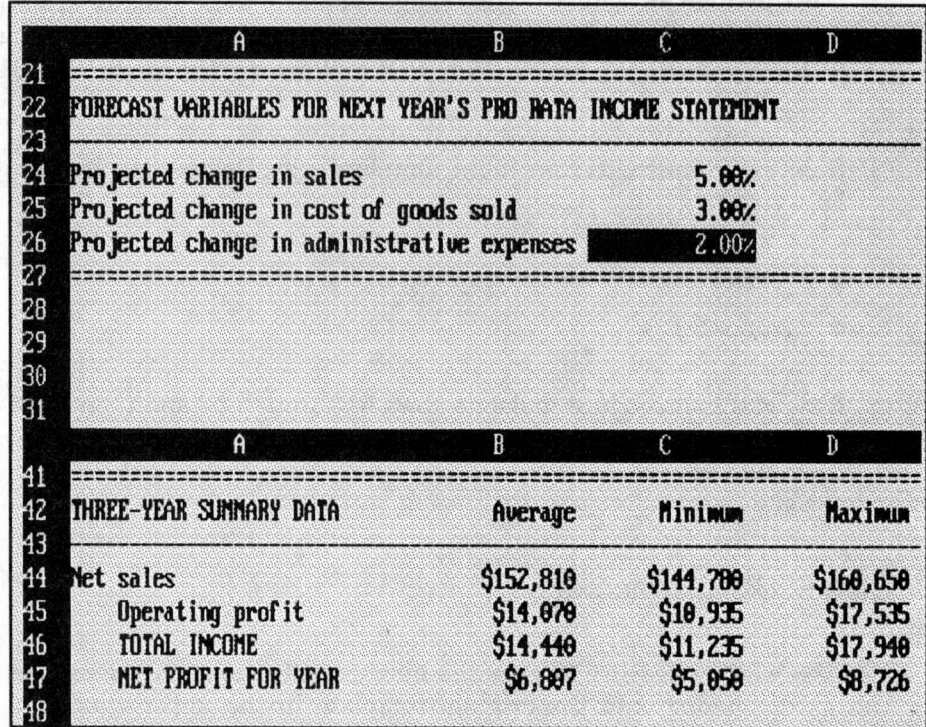

Figure 5-21 The R & G Income Statement as it appears in two windows

☐ Also move the pointer to A1 in the top window to view the original template. Move the pointer up and down to scroll through the income statements.

* **HOME**

The window feature enables you to scan simultaneously the actual entries in the income statements while viewing summary data. Move the pointer about in the upper window to view different portions of the spreadsheet without affecting the lower window. Tap F6 to move the pointer from window to window. Only one window is active at a time.

☐ After you have practiced manipulating the windows, clear the window.

* /WWC

☐ Save the revised spreadsheet under the name R&G3.

* /FS
* R&G3 ↵

Step 7: Practice

Retrieve the BEGONIA5 spreadsheet created in Session Two, Step 6. Use absolute cell referencing to calculate the percentage of total sales for each division.

* Insert a new column at column F.
* Enter connecting separator lines in F3, F5, F18, and F20.
* Reset the width of column F to 18.
* Right align the column heading % TOTAL SALES in F4.
* Enter a formula in F6 that calculates the sales for the Coats Division as a percentage of total sales for the store (divide the Division's sales total in E6 by the store's sales total in E19).

	A	B	C	D	E	F
1		BEGONIA'S CLOTHING STORE FOR WOMEN				
2		RETAIL SALES - FIRST QUARTER				
3						
4	DIVISION	JANUARY	FEBRUARY	MARCH	TOTAL	% TOTAL SALES
5						
6	Coats	$6,780	$14,780	$12,700	$34,260	8.37%
7	Dresses	$12,600	$13,580	$15,794	$41,974	10.25%
8	New Ideas	$14,670	$16,871	$17,400	$48,941	11.96%
9	Swimwear	$1,260	$1,150	$2,140	$4,550	1.11%
10	Casual	$8,600	$9,890	$11,502	$29,992	7.33%
11	Designer's	$15,890	$18,274	$21,252	$55,416	13.54%
12	Junior's	$13,680	$15,732	$18,296	$47,708	11.65%
13	Handbags	$6,400	$7,360	$9,580	$23,340	5.70%
14	Accessories	$9,580	$11,017	$12,813	$33,410	8.16%
15	Shoes	$7,650	$8,798	$11,400	$27,848	6.80%
16	Fragrances	$4,200	$6,700	$7,792	$18,692	4.57%
17	Spec Sizes	$12,400	$14,260	$16,584	$43,244	10.56%
18						
19	TOTALS	$113,710	$138,412	$157,253	$409,375	
20						

Figure 5-22 The completed spreadsheet, BEGONIA6

* Edit the formula that you entered in F6 so that the reference to total sales (E19) is an absolute cell address. (Hint: F2 is the edit key and F4 is the absolute key.)
* Copy the revised formula in F6 to F7..F17.
* Format F6..F17 as percent with 2 decimals.
* Save the spreadsheet as BEGONIA6.
* Print the range A1..F20.

Figure 5-22 displays the completed template.

Step 8: Terminating the Session

If you do not want to continue to the next session now, complete the following to turn off your computer. Remember that you should always return to the DOS prompt before turning off the computer.

☐ To exit Lotus 1-2-3, first make sure that your work is saved (see Session One, Step 10), then issue the Quit command.

  * *(if necessary, save your work)*
  * */QY*

☐ Remove your data diskette from drive A and turn off the computer.

Session Four

The Database Side of Spreadsheets

Lotus 1-2-3 is actually an integrated package that includes database (data management) and graphics capabilities. Sessions One through Three emphasized spreadsheet capabilities; that is, those aspects of spreadsheet software that are computer-based extensions of applications for lined paper (spreadsheets). Before reading this session, you should have acquired at least a fundamental understanding of the spreadsheet concepts.

This session focuses on the database (data management) capabilities of integrated spreadsheet software packages. It discusses and illustrates how spreadsheet rows and columns can be conceptualized as a data base and applied to data base applications.

If necessary, see Session One, Step 1 to start Lotus 1-2-3. Insert your data diskette in drive A and make drive A the active drive.

In this session you will learn how to:

- Explain how a database can be created within the context of a spreadsheet format
- Describe the database features of electronic spreadsheet software
- Create a spreadsheet data base
- Make inquiries to a spreadsheet data base
- Sort a spreadsheet data base

Step 1: Understanding Spreadsheet Data Bases

The tabular format of the spreadsheet work area provides a natural setting for the creation, maintenance, and manipulation of a data base.

Each row in a spreadsheet data base represents one record (related data about a particular event or thing). Each column in a spreadsheet database represents one field (the smallest logical unit of data).

The COURSE data base in Figure 5-23 is used to illustrate the database side of spreadsheet software. The concepts embodied in the database example of Figure 5-23 are introduced in Chapter 4. The common example will help you to contrast the spreadsheet software approach to data management with the database software approach.

Edwina Cool, ERI's education coordinator, uses spreadsheet software to help her with her record-keeping tasks. Her COURSE data base (see Figure 5-23) contains a record for each course that DEP offers to their employees and for several courses at the State University. The first row in a spreadsheet data base **always** contains the **labels** for the fields in the records (for example, ID, TITLE, and so on). The second and subsequent rows contain one **course record** each. Each row record in the COURSE data base contains the following fields:

* **ID**. Identification number (supplied by DEP for in-house courses, by vendors, and by State University).
* **TITLE**. Title of course.
* **TYPE**. Type of course (in-house seminar, multimedia, college course, or vendor seminar).
* **SOURCE**. Source of course (DEP staff or supplier of course).
* **DURATION**. Duration (number of hours required to complete course).

	A	B	C	D	E
1	ID	TITLE	TYPE	SOURCE	DURATION
2	100	MIS Orientation	in-house	Staff	24
3	201	Micro Overview	in-house	Staff	8
4	2535	Intro to Info. Proc.	media	Takdel Inc	40
5	310	Programming Stds.	in-house	Staff	6
6	3223	BASIC Programming	media	Takdel Inc	30
7	7771	Data Base Systems	media	Takdel Inc	30
8	CIS11	Business COBOL	college	St. Univ.	45
9	EX15	Local Area Networks	vendor	HAL Inc	30
10	MGT10	Mgt. Info. Systems	college	St. Univ.	45
11	VC10	Elec. Spreadsheet	media	VidCourse	20
12	VC44	4th Generation Lang.	media	VidCourse	30
13	VC88	Word Processing	media	VidCourse	18
14					

Figure 5-23 Electronic Spreadsheet: Database Format

To create a spreadsheet data base, there are a few basic rules that you must follow.

* The first row must contain the labels for the fields.
* The second and each subsequent row (to the end of the data base) must contain a record; that is, blank rows and divider lines are not permitted.
* A particular field can contain label or numeric entries, but not both.

The fundamental capabilities of integrated spreadsheet software and database software are similar.

- ◆ Create and maintain (add, delete, and revise records) a data base.
- ◆ Extract and list or find and highlight those records that meet certain conditions.
- ◆ Sort records in ascending or descending sequence by primary and secondary fields.

Software that is designed specifically for data management provides considerably more capabilities than spreadsheet software does. For example, database software permits sorting on three or more (not just two) fields and has a report generation feature. Database software also contains powerful commands that allow data in many different data bases to be related and manipulated. Spreadsheet database management works well with "flat file" data bases, where all the data are kept in one data base.

Step 2: Creating a Spreadsheet Data Base

In this step, we will create the spreadsheet data base template displayed in Figure 5-23.

☐ The planned spreadsheet data base template (see Figure 5-23) has five columns. Reset the width of column A to 6. HOME positions the pointer at A1.

* HOME
* /WCS
* 6 ↵

Use the preceding procedure to reset the width of column B to 22, D to 11, and E to 8. Do not change column C.

☐ Enter the labels for the fields in row 1.

* HOME
* ID → TITLE → TYPE → SOURCE → DURATION ↵

☐ Enter the first of the 12 records shown in Figure 5-23 in row 2. Enter all IDs and TITLEs (columns A and B) as labels; that is, begin any numeric ID (100) or TITLE (4th...) with an apostrophe (').

* F5
* A2 ↵

    ✱ '100 → MIS Orientation → in-house → Staff → 24 ↵

☐ Enter the remainder of the records in rows 3 through 13. At this point your spreadsheet should look just like Figure 5-23.

Step 3: Extracting Data

With spreadsheet software you can retrieve, view, and print records based on preset conditions. You set conditions for the selection of records by associating the desired condition with the appropriate field or fields in the **criterion range**. The user-defined criterion range (A19..E20 in Figure 5-24) contains a copy of the first row (the field label row) and the conditions (under the appropriate field label). For example, Figure 5-24 illustrates the procedure for **extracting** and displaying the course records that meet both of the following conditions:

       TYPE is "in-house" DURATION is less than or equal to (<=) 10 hours

Those records that meet both criteria are extracted and displayed in the user-defined output range (A15..E18).

This step demonstrates the extraction method of querying a spreadsheet data base.

```
E20: [W8] +E2<=10
Input  Criterion  Output  Find  Extract  Unique  Delete  Reset  Quit
Copy all records that match criteria to Output range
       A         B                  C          D            E           F
 1    ID        TITLE              TYPE       SOURCE       DURATION
 2    100       MIS Orientation    in-house   Staff        24
 3    201       Micro Overview     in-house   Staff         8
 4    2535      Intro to Info. Proc.  media   Takdel Inc   40
 5    310       Programming Stds.  in-house   Staff         6
 6    3223      BASIC Programming  media      Takdel Inc   30
 7    7771      Data Base Systems  media      Takdel Inc   30
 8    CIS11     Business COBOL     college    St. Univ.    45
 9    EX15      Local Area Networks vendor    HAL Inc      30
10    MGT10     Mgt. Info. Systems college    St. Univ.    45
11    VC10      Elec. Spreadsheet  media      VidCourse    20
12    VC44      4th Generation Lang. media    VidCourse    30
13    VC88      Word Processing    media      VidCourse    18
14
15    ID        TITLE              TYPE       SOURCE       DURATION
16    201       Micro Overview     in-house   Staff         8
17    310       Programming Stds.  in-house   Staff         6
18
19    ID        TITLE              TYPE       SOURCE       DURATION
20                                 in-house                  0
12-Mar-91  08:16 AM
```

Figure 5-24 Extracting information from a spreadsheet data base

☐ To use the Data-Query-Extract method, first copy the field labels into rows 15 and 19. These rows provide labels for the output range (A15..E18) and the criterion range (A19..A20).

* /C
* A1.E1 ↵
* A15 ↵

Repeat this procedure to copy the labels to row 19.

☐ Identify the conditions (the criteria) in row 20 (the TYPE is "in-house" and the DURATION is less than or equal to 10 hours).

* [F5]
* C20 ↵
* in-house ↵
* [F5]
* E20 ↵
* +E2<=10 ↵

The formula result shown in E20 is zero; however, the formula is displayed in the user interface (see Figure 5-24).

☐ Identify the following ranges: input, criterion, and output.

* /D Q I
* A1.E13 ↵
* C
* A19.E20 ↵
* O
* A15.E18 ↵

Release 2.2 users: notice the **Query Settings** screen that appears after tapping /DQ.

☐ Extract all the records that meet the criteria specified in row 20 to the output range (A15..E18).

* E
* Q

Records 201 and 310 should have been extracted.

Step 4: Finding Data

Another way to locate and display the records that meet certain conditions is to **find** them. When you issue the find command, the first record that meets the criteria is highlighted in reverse video (see Figure 5-25). To see other records that meet the criteria, simply tap the up or down cursor control keys.

You can use the cursor control keys to scan or "page" through the data base.

	A	B	C	D	E	F
1	ID	TITLE	TYPE	SOURCE	DURATION	
2	100	MIS Orientation	in-house	Staff	24	
3	201	Micro Overview	in-house	Staff	8	
4	2535	Intro to Info. Proc.	media	Takdel Inc	40	
5	310	Programming Stds.	in-house	Staff	6	
6	3223	BASIC Programming	media	Takdel Inc	30	
7	7771	Data Base Systems	media	Takdel Inc	30	
8	CIS11	Business COBOL	college	St. Univ.	45	
9	EX15	Local Area Networks	vendor	HAL Inc	30	
10	MGT10	Mgt. Info. Systems	college	St. Univ.	45	
11	VC10	Elec. Spreadsheet	media	VidCourse	20	
12	VC44	4th Generation Lang.	media	VidCourse	30	
13	VC88	Word Processing	media	VidCourse	18	
14						
15						
16						
17						
18						
19	ID	TITLE	TYPE	SOURCE	DURATION	
20			in-house		0	

12-Mar-91 08:18 AM

Figure 5-25 Finding information in a spreadsheet data base

❐ Use the find command to highlight each record that matches the criteria in row 20. First, however, erase the output range so that your results will look like that of Figure 5-25.

* /RE
* A15.E18 ↵
* /DQF

Notice that record 201 is highlighted.

☐ Use your down cursor key to find additional records that meet the criteria.

* ↓

Use the up cursor key to search in reverse.

☐ Return to the worksheet when you have finished viewing the records.

* ESC
* Q

☐ Erase A19..E20 before proceeding to the next step. The criterion range is no longer needed. Delete it to remove visual clutter.

* /RE
* A19.E20 ↵

Step 5: Sorting a Spreadsheet Data Base

The records in a spreadsheet data base can be sorted for display in a variety of formats. The COURSE data base in Figure 5-23 is sorted by ID. Edwina Cool wanted a presentation of the COURSE data base that was sorted by ID within SOURCE (see Figure 5-26). This involves the selection of a **primary key field** and a **secondary key field**. Edwina selected SOURCE as the primary key field, but she wanted the courses offered by each source to be listed in ascending order by ID.

To achieve this record sequence, she selected ID as the secondary key field. You would normally define a secondary key when you expect duplicates in the primary key fields. For example, in Figure 5-23, the SOURCE or primary key field has three entries for Takdel Inc. Once the key fields are identified, the sort command can be issued to rearrange and display records in the desired sequence. Notice in Figure 5-26 that the SOURCE field entries (column D) are in alphabetical order and the three "Staff" records (rows 3, 4, and 5) are in sequence by ID (100, 201, 310).

☐ Identify the records to be sorted. Do not include the labels (row 1).

* /DSD
* A2.E13 ↵

Release 2.2 users, notice the Sort Settings screen that appears after /DS.

☐ Identify the primary key field as SOURCE and the order as ascending.

* *(in the sort menu)*
* **P**
* **D1** ↵
* **A** ↵

☐ Identify the secondary key field as ID and the order as ascending.

* *(in the sort menu)*
* **S**
* **A1** ↵
* **A** ↵

☐ Perform the sort and return to the worksheet.

* *(in the sort menu)*
* **G**

Compare your spreadsheet to Figure 5-26.

	A	B	C	D	E
1	ID	TITLE	TYPE	SOURCE	DURATION
2	EX15	Local Area Networks	vendor	HAL Inc	30
3	100	MIS Orientation	in-house	Staff	24
4	201	Micro Overview	in-house	Staff	8
5	310	Programming Stds.	in-house	Staff	6
6	CIS11	Business COBOL	college	St. Univ.	45
7	MGT10	Mgt. Info. Systems	college	St. Univ.	45
8	2535	Intro to Info. Proc.	media	Takdel Inc	40
9	3223	BASIC Programming	media	Takdel Inc	30
10	7771	Data Base Systems	media	Takdel Inc	30
11	VC10	Elec. Spreadsheet	media	VidCourse	20
12	VC44	4th Generation Lang.	media	VidCourse	30
13	VC88	Word Processing	media	VidCourse	18
14					

Figure 5-26 Sorting a spreadsheet data base

☐ Save the current spreadsheet under the name "coursedb".

* **/FS**

* **coursedb** ↵
* *(if saved earlier)* **R**

☐ Print the course data base.

* **/PPR**
* **A1.E13** ↵
* **AGPQ**

☐ Clear the worksheet.

* **/WEY**

Step 6: Practice

Create a name and address data base. Sort the data base and extract various records from the data base.

* Start with a blank spreadsheet.
* Set the width of columns A and B to 12, columns C and D to 17, and column E to 4.
* Enter the data displayed in Figure 5-27.
* Prepare the spreadsheet for data query by copying A1..F1 to both A14..F14 and A17..F17.

	A	B	C	D	E	F
1	First Name	Last Name	Address	City	ST	ZIP
2	Phil	Cline	1915 N.W. 25th	Oklahoma City	OK	73107
3	Sherry	Howard	3587 Lee Dr.	Jackson	MS	39208
4	Bill	Allred	630 W. Call	Tallahassee	FL	32308
5	Warren	Sherman	3745 Rogers	Ft. Worth	TX	76109
6	Malcolm	Haney	642 Tulane Av	Little Rock	AR	72204
7	Sharon	Bias	125 Lake View	Gainesville	GA	30501
8	Janet	Roche	432 Oak St.	Nashville	TN	37203
9	Joyce	Phinney	345 Pratt Dr.	New Orleans	LA	70122
10	Michael	Howard	3587 Lee Dr.	Jackson	MS	39208
11	Alison	Haney	933 Hilltop	Little Rock	AR	72204
12	Kristine	Haney	3216 West End	Nashville	TN	37203
13						

Figure 5-27 Data to be entered into a name and address data base

* Define the data query ranges: Input (A1..F12), Criterion (A14..F15), and Output (A17..F20).
* Extract the records of those people who live in Arkansas.
* Use SHIFT-PRTSC to print the current display.
* Extract the records of those people who have the last name "Haney".
* Use SHIFT-PRTSC to print the current display.
* Sort the data base alphabetically in ascending sequence by last name.
* Use SHIFT-PRTSC to print the current display.
* Sort the data base alphabetically in ascending sequence by state.
* Use SHIFT-PRTSC to print the current display.
* Sort the data base alphabetically in ascending sequence using Lastname as the primary field and Firstname as the secondary field.
* Use SHIFT-PRTSC to print the current display.
* Save the spreadsheet as FRIENDS.

Step 7: Terminating the Session

If you do not want to continue to the next session now, complete the following to turn off your computer. Remember that you should always return to the DOS prompt before turning off the computer.

☐ To exit Lotus 1-2-3, first make sure that your work is saved (see Session One, Step 10), then issue the Quit command.

* *(if necessary, save your work)*
* */QY*

☐ Remove your data diskette from drive A and turn off the computer.

Session Five

Graphics Capabilities

As stated in Session Four, Lotus 1-2-3 is actually an integrated package that includes database (data management) and graphics capabilities. Session Four focused on the database side of Lotus 1-2-3. This session focuses on Lotus's graphics capabilities. Before reading the following session, you should have acquired at least a fundamental understanding of spreadsheet concepts.

With the graphics component of this integrated software package, you can create a variety of presentation graphics from data in an electronic spreadsheet. The use of graphics software has become synonymous with polished presentation. Among the most popular presentation graphics are bar graphs, pie graphs, and line graphs (seen in Figures 5-30, 5-33, and 5-34, respectively). Other types of graphs are possible. Each of these graphs can be annotated with graph titles, labels for axes, and legends.

Graphic representations of data have proven to be an effective means of communication. It is easier to recognize problem areas and trends in a graph than it is in a tabular summary of the same data. Compare the data in the spreadsheet of Figure 5-29 to the graphic representation of that data in Figures 5-31 and 5-32.

A number of studies confirm the power of presentation graphics. These studies uniformly support the following conclusions:

- ◆ People who use presentation graphics to get their message across are perceived as better prepared and more professional than those who do not.

- ◆ Presentation graphics can help to persuade attendees or readers to adopt a particular point of view.

- ◆ Judicious use of presentation graphics tends to make meetings shorter. Perhaps it's true that a picture is worth a thousand words!

For many years, the presentation of tabular data was the preferred approach to communicating tabular information. However, this approach was preferred by default: it was simply too expensive and time consuming to produce presentation graphics manually. Today, you can use graphics software to produce perfectly proportioned, accurate graphs in a matter of seconds. Prior to the introduction of graphics software, the turnaround time for producing a graph was at least a day, and often a week.

One of the real advantages of this integrated package is that any changes made to data in a spreadsheet can be reflected in the graphs as well.

In this session you will learn how to:

- ◆ Explain how bar graphs, pie graphs, and line graphs are created from spreadsheet data.
- ◆ Discuss graphics features of electronic spreadsheet software
- ◆ Use the Lotus Access System
- ◆ Use spreadsheet graphics capabilities
- ◆ Produce a bar graph
- ◆ Save and print/plot a graph
- ◆ Produce stacked-bar and clustered-bar graphs
- ◆ Produce a pie graph
- ◆ Produce a line graph
- ◆ Add labels and subheadings to graphs
- ◆ Change fonts

Step 1: Starting the Lotus Access System

The Lotus Access System is a shell that provides "point and shoot" (highlight and tap ENTER) starting capability for the various programs in the Lotus family. In previous sessions, we used the "123" command to by-pass the Access System and start the spreadsheet directly. In this session, we will use both the spreadsheet and PrintGraph capabilities. The Access System allows us to run either program.

☐ At this point, if necessary, boot your system. If Lotus is currently running, quit the program and return to the DOS prompt.

☐ Follow the procedure outlined below to start Lotus. In this session we will not use the "123" command to start Lotus. Instead, use the "lotus" command which calls the Lotus Access System (see Figure 5-28). In the next command, use the name of your Lotus 1-2-3 directory in place of "lotus" if it is different. For example, if the name of your lotus directory is lotus123, the next command would be cd \lotus123.

* **cd \lotus** ↵
* **lotus** ↵

☐ Run the 1-2-3 spreadsheet by highlighting and selecting "1-2-3" in the Lotus Access System menu.

* *(highlight "1-2-3")*
* ↵

```
1-2-3  PrintGraph  Translate  Install  View  Exit
Enter 1-2-3 -- Lotus Worksheet/Graphics/Database program

                    1-2-3 Access System
                     Copyright 1986
                  Lotus Development Corporation
                     All Rights Reserved
                       Release 2.01

The Access System lets you choose 1-2-3, PrintGraph, the Translate utility,
the Install program, and A View of 1-2-3 from the menu at the top of this
screen. If you're using a diskette system, the Access System may prompt
you to change disks. Follow the instructions below to start a program.

o Use [RIGHT] or [LEFT] to move the menu pointer (the highlight bar at
  the top of the screen) to the program you want to use.

o Press [RETURN] to start the program.

You can also start a program by typing the first letter of the menu
choice. Press [HELP] for more information.
```

Figure 5-28 Lotus Access System menu

Step 2: Entering the Data

The data needed to produce a graph must already exist in a spreadsheet. You create a graph by selecting a series of commands. The first command usually chosen selects the type of graph to be produced: bar graph, pie graph, line graph, and so on. Other commands identify the ranges of spreadsheet data to be printed or plotted and also choose spreadsheet ranges that will be printed as labels on the graph. Once you have identified the source of the data and labels, and perhaps added a title, you can display, print, or plot the graph.

Sally Marcio, the vice-president of Sales and Marketing at R & G, is an avid user of spreadsheet and graphics software. The spreadsheet of Figure 5-29 is an annual summary of the sales for each of R & G's four products by sales region. The data from this spreadsheet provide the basis for demonstrating the compilation of bar, pie, and line graphs.

Use the Lotus 1-2-3 procedures and techniques that you learned in Session One to create the sales summary spreadsheet of Figure 5-29.

☐ Set the width of column A to 15 positions and the width of columns B through F to 11 positions.

☐ Enter all labels (except rows 14 through 17), including repeating text (rows 4 and 9) and values as shown in Figure 5-29. Notice that the labels in B3..F3 and A10 are right justified. The numbers in column F and in row 10 are the results of formulas.

☐ Enter the formulas to sum sales by product (rows), by region (columns), and overall. Enter the formula @SUM(B5..E5) in F5 and copy it to F6..F8. Enter the formula @SUM(B5..B8) in B10 and copy it to C10..F10.

☐ Format all value and formula entries (B5..F10) as shown. Format the entries as currency with 0 decimal places.

☐ Save the spreadsheet template as "sales".

	A	B	C	D	E	F
1	ANNUAL SALES FOR R & G BY REGION					
2						
3	Product	Southern	Western	Northern	Eastern	Total
4						
5	Science Fiction	$7,140	$14,790	$13,260	$15,810	$51,000
6	Romance	$5,460	$11,310	$10,140	$12,090	$39,000
7	Biography	$3,150	$6,525	$5,850	$6,975	$22,500
8	Non-fiction	$5,250	$11,875	$10,750	$12,625	$40,500
9						
10	Totals	$21,000	$44,500	$40,000	$47,500	$153,000
11						

Figure 5-29 R & G's annual sales data to be used to create various graphs

Step 3: Producing a Bar Graph

A bar graph contains vertical bars of varying heights. The height of the bars is proportional to a range of numeric values in an electronic spreadsheet. To prepare the bar graph of Figure 5-30, Sally first had to specify appropriate ranges; that is, the values in the "Totals" row (range B10..E10 of Figure 5-29) are to be plotted and the region names (range B3..E3 of Figure 5-29) are to be inserted as labels along the horizontal or **X** axis. Sally also added a title for the graph, "Sales Summary by Region", and titles for X axis, "Region", and the vertical or **Y** axis, "Sales ($1000)".

The **origin**, or the point at which the **X** and **Y** axes meet, is automatically set at zero. Sally accepted this default; however, you may want to set the origin at other than zero when you want to highlight the differences between the bars. If Sally had set the origin at $20,000, the bar in Figure 5-30 illustrating the sales for the Eastern Region ($47,500) would be over 27 times the height of the bar illustrating the sales for the Southern Region sales ($21,000); that is, a net of $27,500 would be compared to a net of $1,000. Setting the origin at $20,000 would make the differences between

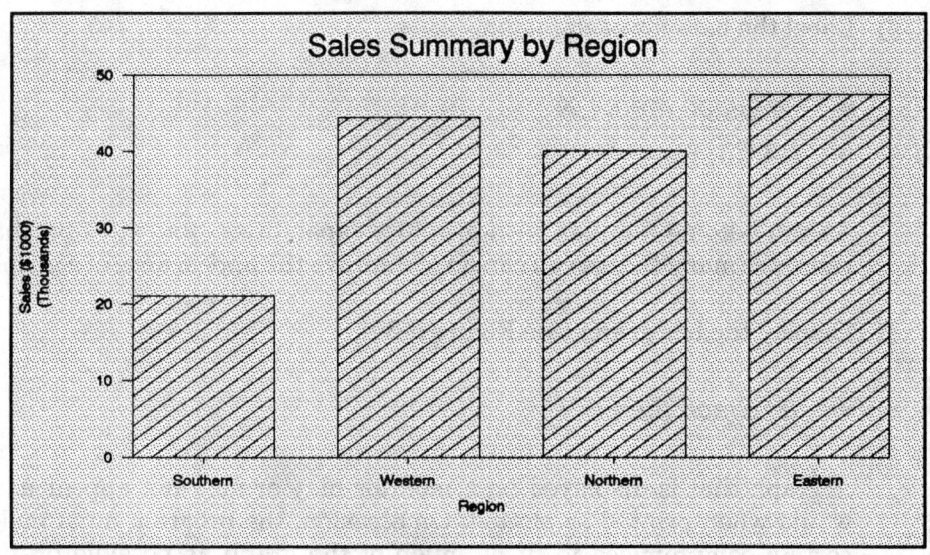

Figure 5-30 Bar graph based on the data in the Figure 5-29 spreadsheet

the regional sales figures more apparent--perhaps too apparent for the sales manager for the Southern Region.

In this step we will produce the bar graph illustrated in Figure 5-30.

- ☐ Identify the data to be graphed.

    * /GA *(define first data range)* **B10.E10** ↵

    Release 2.2 users: notice the Graph Settings screen that appears after tapping /G.

- ☐ Select "Bar" graph.

    * *(in Graph menu)* **TB**

- ☐ Add the main heading and labels for the X-axis and Y-axis.

    * *(in Graph menu)* **OTF**
    * **Sales Summary by Region** ↵
    * *(in Graph/Options menu)* **TX**
    * **Region** ↵
    * *(in Graph/Options menu)* **TY**
    * **Sales ($1000)** ↵
    * **Q** *(to return to Graph menu)*

Lotus: Session Five 301

❏ Label the bars for each region.

* *(in Graph menu)* **X**
* **B3.E3** ↵

As you become familiar with graphics capabilities, you will find that there are many things you can do to improve the appearance of a graph.

❏ Display the bar graph (see Figure 5-30).

* *(in Graph menu)* **V**

A graph that is displayed on a monitor may or may not appear as it would when printed or plotted. On occasion, the program must make certain compromises to fit as much of the graph as possible on the display (for example, labels written vertically rather than horizontally).

❏ Tap SPACE or any key to return to the spreadsheet.

* **SPACE**

Lotus 1-2-3 saves the settings for the current graph when the spreadsheet is saved.

❏ If you wish to create and then recall more than one graph from the spreadsheet data, you will need to name each graph.

* *(in Graph menu)* **NC**
* **bargraph** ↵
* **Q**

To recall the settings for a particular graph (make it the current graph), select "Graph" (from the main menu), "Name," and "Use," and then highlight and select the name of the desired graph.

Step 4: Saving and Printing/Plotting a Graph

The actual physical presentation of a graph is dependent on the available hardware (matrix printer, laser printer, plotter, and so on). Computer-generated graphic images can be recreated on paper, transparency acetates, 35 mm slides, or they can be displayed on a monitor or projected onto a large screen. The use of sophisticated and colorful graphics adds an aura of professionalism to any report or presentation. Some of the more common approaches to presenting a graph are discussed below.

- ◆ Dot-matrix and ink-jet printers, both black on white and color, can be used to reproduce the graphic image on either paper or transparency acetates.
- ◆ Multi-pen plotters can be used to produce professional-quality presentation graphics (in color) on either paper or transparency acetates.
- ◆ Laser printers enable very-high resolution (close to typeset quality) black on white graphs.
- ◆ Desktop film recorders reproduce a high-resolution graphic image on 35 mm film in either black and white or color. Some models provide the facility for users to process and mount their own slides. Others require outside processing.
- ◆ A less expensive alternative to a desktop film recorder is the hood, lens, and mounting brackets that enable the users to photograph the graphic image with an ordinary 35 mm camera. The quality of the resulting 35 mm slide is, of course, dependent on the resolution of the monitor.
- ◆ Screen-image projectors project the graphic image to a large screen, similar to the way television programs are projected to a large TV screen. Another device transfers the graphic image that is displayed on the monitor to a large screen with the use of an ordinary overhead projector.

In this step, we will save and print the current graph.

☐ In Lotus 1-2-3, the current graph settings are saved when the spreadsheet is saved.

- ∗ **/FS**
- ∗ **sales** ↵
- ∗ *(if "sales" is an existing file)* **R**

☐ If you plan to print/plot a particular graph, you will need to create a separate PrintGraph file. The bar graph is the current graph.

- ∗ **/GS**
- ∗ **bar** ↵
- ∗ **Q**

The commands above create a file, called BAR.PIC (Lotus 1-2-3 adds the PIC extension), from which the bar graph can be printed.

- Use Lotus's PrintGraph program to print the bar graph (like Figure 5-30). Before loading Lotus's PrintGraph program, we must first exit the 1-2-3 spreadsheet.

  * **/QY**

  Since we used the Access System to start the 1-2-3 spreadsheet, we return to the Access System when we exit.

- Highlight and select "PrintGraph" to run Lotus's graph printing program.

  * *(highlight "PrintGraph")*
  * ↵

- Change the default PrintGraph settings so that the program searches drive A for BAR.PIC and identify the device on which the graph will be printed/plotted.

  * **SHG**
  * **a:** ↵
  * **P**
  * *(highlight the output device)*
  * `SPACE` ↵
  * **QQ**

- Select the image that will be printed.

  * **I**
  * *(highlight BAR)*
  * `SPACE` ↵
  * **AG P**

  More than one image may be marked. Lotus will print each graph in the order it was marked. Printing/plotting a graph may take a few minutes.

- Exit PrintGraph.

* **E**
* **Y**

☐ Use the Access System to return to the 1-2-3 program and retrieve the "sales" spreadsheet.

* *(highlight "1-2-3")*
* ↵
* **/FR**
* *(highlight "sales")*
* ↵

Step 5: Producing Stacked-Bar and Clustered-Bar Graphs

The sales figures for each region in Figure 5-29 (range B5..E8) can be plotted in a **stacked-bar graph**. Each bar is made up of the sales figures for each of the four products. Because of this, a legend is needed to distinguish which parts of the stacked bar for a particular region apply to which product. Sally specified that the range A5..A8 be the range for the legend labels (the names of the products). The resultant graph, shown in Figure 5-31, helps Sally to better understand the distribution of product sales within the four regions. The **clustered-bar graph** in Figure 5-32 is an alternative presentation to the stacked-bar graph. These graphs visually highlight the relative contribution that each product made to the total sales for each region.

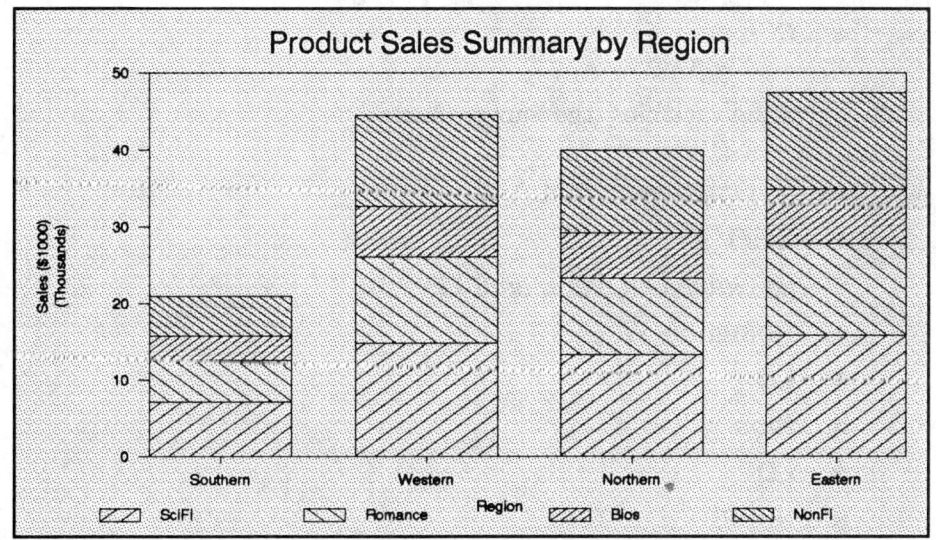

Figure 5-31 Stacked-bar graph based on the data in the Figure 5-29 spreadsheet

In this step we will first produce a stacked-bar graph, then we will use the same data to produce a clustered bar graph.

☐ Identify the range of the data to be graphed.

* **/GA**
* **B5.E5** ↵
* *(in Graph menu)*
* **B**
* **B6.E6** ↵
* **C**
* **B7.E7** ↵
* **D**
* **B8.E8** ↵

☐ Select "Stacked-Bar" graph.

* *(in Graph menu)* **TS**

☐ Add the main heading and labels for the X-axis and Y-axis. The heading and labels for the bar graph are still current in Lotus 1-2-3, and so the labels for the X-axis and Y-axis are unchanged. Enter a new title.

* *(in Graph menu)* **OTF**
* **ESC**
* **Product Sales Summary by Region** ↵
* **Q**

☐ Label the variables (the four products).

* *(in Graph menu)* **OLA**
* **SciFi** ↵
* *(in Graph/Options menu)* **LB**
* **Romance** ↵
* **LC**
* **Bios** ↵
* **LD**
* **NonFi** ↵
* **Q** *(to return to Graph menu)*

☐ Display the stacked-bar graph on the screen.

* *(in Graph menu)* **V**
* SPACE

☐ Produce and display the clustered-bar chart illustrated in Figure 5-32. All of the specifications are the same for the stacked-bar and the clustered-bar charts except for the selection of type of graph.

* *(in Graph menu)* **TBV**
* SPACE

Because the data range (B5..E8) has both rows and columns, the request for a "Bar" graph is interpreted as a request for a clustered-bar graph.

☐ Save the graph settings as "multibar".

* *(in Graph menu)* **NC**
* **multibar** ↵
* **Q**

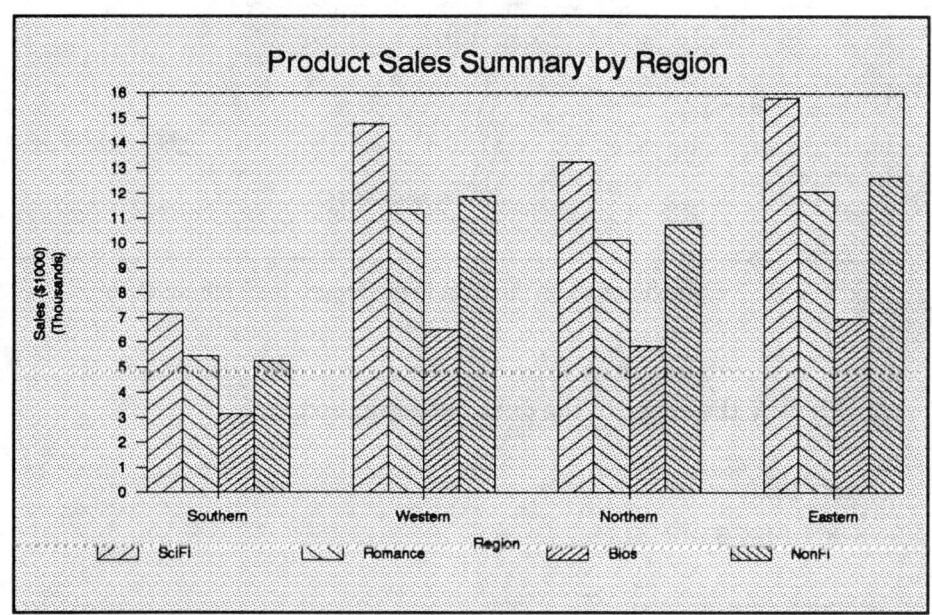

Figure 5-32 Clustered-bar graph based on the data in the Figure 5-29 spreadsheet

Step 6: Producing a Pie Graph

Pie graphs are the most basic of presentation graphics. A pie graph graphically illustrates each "piece" of data in its proper relationship to the whole "pie." To illustrate how a pie graph is constructed and used, refer again to the "Annual Sales" spreadsheet in Figure 5-29.

Sally Marcio produced the sales-by-product pie graph in Figure 5-33 by specifying that the values in the "Total" column (range F5..F8 of Figure 5-29) be the pieces of the pie. She specified further that the product names (range A5..A8) be inserted as labels. She also added a title. The numbers in parentheses represent what percent each piece (total sales for a particular product) is of the whole (total sales, or the value in F10, $153,000). To emphasize the product with the greatest contribution to total sales, Sally decided to **explode** (or separate) the Science Fiction piece of the pie.

In this step we will produce the pie graph illustrated in Figure 5-33.

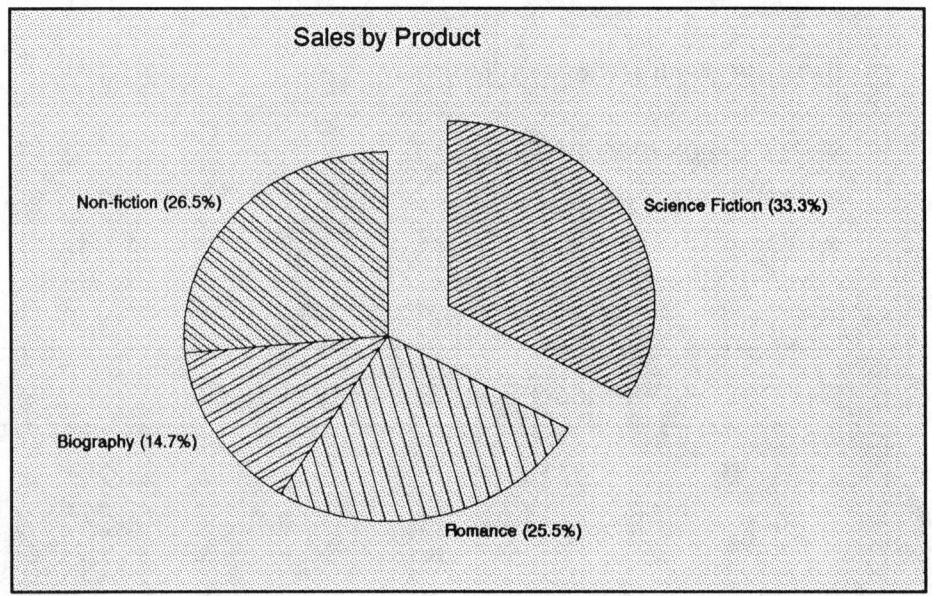

Figure 5-33 Pie graph based on the data in the Figure 5-29 spreadsheet

☐ Identify the range of the data to be graphed.

* /GA
* F5.F8 ↵

☐ Select "Pie" graph.

* *(in Graph menu)* **TP**

- Add the main heading and labels.

    * *(in Graph menu)* **OTF**
    * ESC
    * **Sales by Product** ↵
    * **Q**
    * *(in Graph menu)* **X**
    * **A5.A8** ↵
    * **Q**

- Explode the Science Fiction piece of the pie (segment 1). Add 100 to the shading code (0, 1, 2, 3, ... 7) for the piece that you wish to explode. These codes must be in adjacent cells of a row or column.

    * F5
    * **A18** ↵
    * **101 → 2 → 3 → 4** ↵
    * **/GB**
    * **A18.D18** ↵

- Display the pie graph.

    * *(in Graph menu)* **V**
    * SPACE

- Save the graph settings as "piegraph".

    * *(in Graph menu)* **NC**
    * **piegraph** ↵
    * **Q**

Step 7: Producing a Line Graph

A line graph connects similar points on a graph with one or more lines. Sally Marcio used the stacked-bar graph of Figure 5-31 to visually highlight relative product sales by region. She used the same data in the spreadsheet of Figure 5-29 to generate the line graph of Figure 5-34. The line graph makes it easy for Sally to compare sales between regions for a particular product.

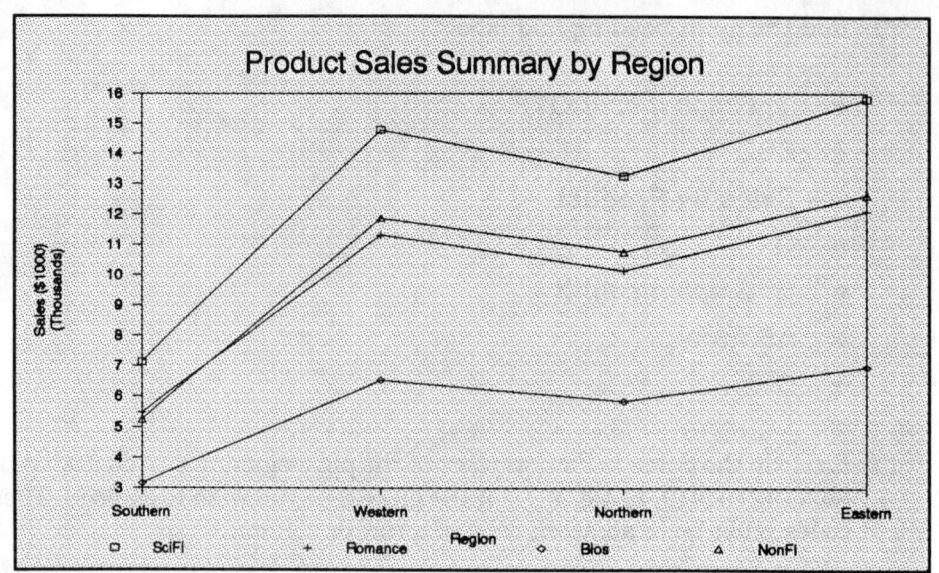

Figure 5-34 Line graph based on the data in the Figure 5-29 spreadsheet

In the line graph of Figure 5-34, four ranges of data from the spreadsheet of Figure 5-29 (B5..E5, B6..E6, B7..E7, and B8..E8) are plotted and each range connected by a line, one line for each product. The graph clearly indicates that the proportion of product sales is similar for each region.

In this step we will produce and display the line graph illustrated in Figure 5-34. The specifications for this line graph are the same as those for the stacked-bar and clustered-bar graphs of Step 5, except for the selection of graph type.

☐ Activate the "MULTIBAR" graph settings.

* **/GNU**
* *(highlight "MULTIBAR")* ↵
* SPACE
* *(in Graph menu)* **TLV**
* SPACE **Q**

☐ Save your work and clear the spreadsheet.

* **/FS**
* **sales** ↵
* *(if "sales" is an existing file)* **R**
* **/ WEY**

Step 8: Practice

Use the file BEGONIA5, created in Session Two, Step 6, as the basis for creating two bar graphs and a pie graph.

* Retrieve the file BEGONIA5.
* Create a bar graph that displays the total sales for each division (E6..E17).
* Make the first line of the graph's title BEGONIA'S CLOTHING STORE FOR WOMEN and the second line RETAIL SALES (QTR 1).
* Place the name of each division at the top of the bar representing the sales for that division.
* Use the Name-Create command to save the graph settings as BAR-SALES.
* Use the Save command to create a B-SALES.PIC file.
* Revise the current settings to create a second bar graph that displays the percentage change in sales for each division (G6..G17). Figure 5-35 displays the completed graph.
* Revise the second line of the heading to read %CHG FROM LAST YEAR'S SALES (QTR 1).

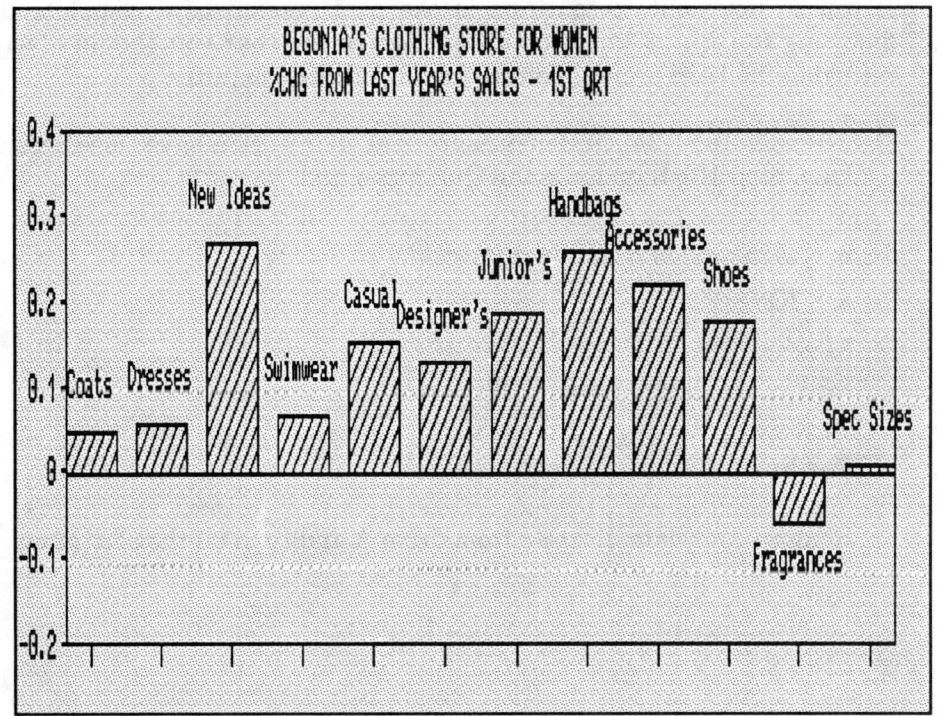

Figure 5-35 BAR-%CHG graph based on the BEGONIA5 spreadsheet

* Use the /Graph-Options-Scale command to set the Y axis scale to Manual, Lower = -.2 and Upper = .4.
* Use the Name-Create command to save the graph settings as BAR-%CHG.
* Use the Save command to create a BAR-%CHG.PIC file.
* Recall the settings for the initial graph BAR-SALES.
* Revise the graph-type selection to create a pie graph that displays each division's quarterly sales.
* Revise the graph settings to explode the pie segments for the Coats and New Ideas divisions.
* Use the Name-Create command to save the settings as PIE-SALES.
* Use the Save command to create a P-SALES.PIC file.
* Save the spreadsheet.
* Quit 1-2-3 and load PrintGraph.
* Print the B-SALES, P-SALES and BAR-%CHG graphs.

Step 9: Terminating the Session

If you do not want to continue to the next session now, complete the following to turn off your computer. Remember that you should always return to the DOS prompt before turning off the computer.

❒ To exit Lotus 1-2-3, first make sure that your work is saved (see Session One, Step 10), then issue the Quit command.

* *(if necessary, save your work)*
* */QY*

❒ Exit the Lotus Access System.

* **E**

❒ Remove your data diskette from drive A and turn off the computer.

Session Six

Introduction to Macros

Macros are a work-saving feature. A macro is a series of often-repeated keystrokes that are saved in a cell and invoked by tapping the ALT key in combination with a letter key.

For example, by now you know how important it is to save your work frequently. To save a Lotus spreadsheet that has been saved before involves five keystrokes (/FS ↵ R). If you store the five keystrokes in a macro (ALT-S), you need only tap two keystrokes to invoke the macro which, in turn, saves the spreadsheet. Invoking a macro requires no fuss and little thinking, just ALT and a letter key.

Another macro example that saves even more keystrokes is a print macro. For example, Monroe Green must print his R&G1 spreadsheet template many times (see Session Two). He creates a print macro that automatically selects and prints a designated range within the spreadsheet. Once created, Monroe never has to think about what range or what settings to use to print, he just invokes the correct macro. In fact, after Monroe created the print macro, he displayed the macro's name on the spreadsheet. This allowed Preston Smith, R & G's CEO (who is not an experienced Lotus user), to create printouts.

Creating a macro involves these steps:

- Decide what task you want to automate.
- Store a representation for each of the task's keystrokes in a cell or a series of cells.
- Assign a macro name to the first cell of the series.

Creating a macro varies depending on the Lotus release you are using. Releases 2.01 and earlier require that macro keystroke representations be entered manually. Releases 2.2 and 3 include a keystroke memorization feature that creates macro keystroke representations automatically.

This session demonstrates manual keystroke representation entry, which is possible in all Lotus releases. The next session demonstrates the keystroke memorization feature, which is only available with Release 2.2, 3 and certain versions of 2.01 that have been enhanced with the Lotus Value Pack. The Value Pack is also explained in the next session.

In this session we will discuss macro basics: how to create a macro, where to store macros, how to name and document macros, and how to create a macro menu. We will create three macros, a save macro, a print macro and a goto macro.

If necessary, see Session One, Step 1 to start Lotus 1-2-3. Insert your data diskette in drive A, make drive A the active drive and retrieve the "R&G1" spreadsheet created in Session Two (see Session One, Step 12).

In this session you will learn how to:

- Enter macro keystroke representations
- Name a macro
- Invoke a macro
- Create a macro menu
- Use range names

Step 1: Creating a Macro

The first macro we will create is the save macro. When macro keystroke representations must be entered manually, it is always a good idea to perform the task once and write down each keystroke.

☐ Perform the chosen task and write down each keystroke.

* /FS ↵ R

Five keystrokes are required to save the spreadsheet.

☐ Next, we must decide where to store the macro's keystrokes. Two general rules apply. First, all macros should be kept in the same location. When you need to find and edit a macro it helps if they are all in the same area. Second, the macro area should be below and to the right of the spreadsheet's general work area (see Figure 5-37). This rule's purpose is to prevent inadvertent changes to a macro when rows or columns are added or deleted from the spreadsheet work area. We will create our macros beginning in K80.

* [F5]
* K80 ↵

☐ Now it is time to enter the macro's keystrokes. The keystroke representations must be entered as a label. Since our macro begins with tapping the forward slash key, we must first tap the single quote key to enter the macro as a label (see Figure 5-36).

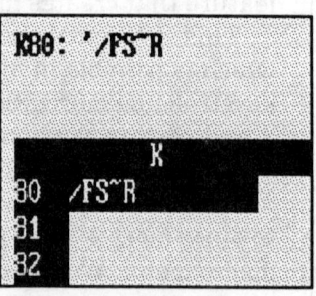

Figure 5-36 The "save" macro's keystrokes are entered in K80

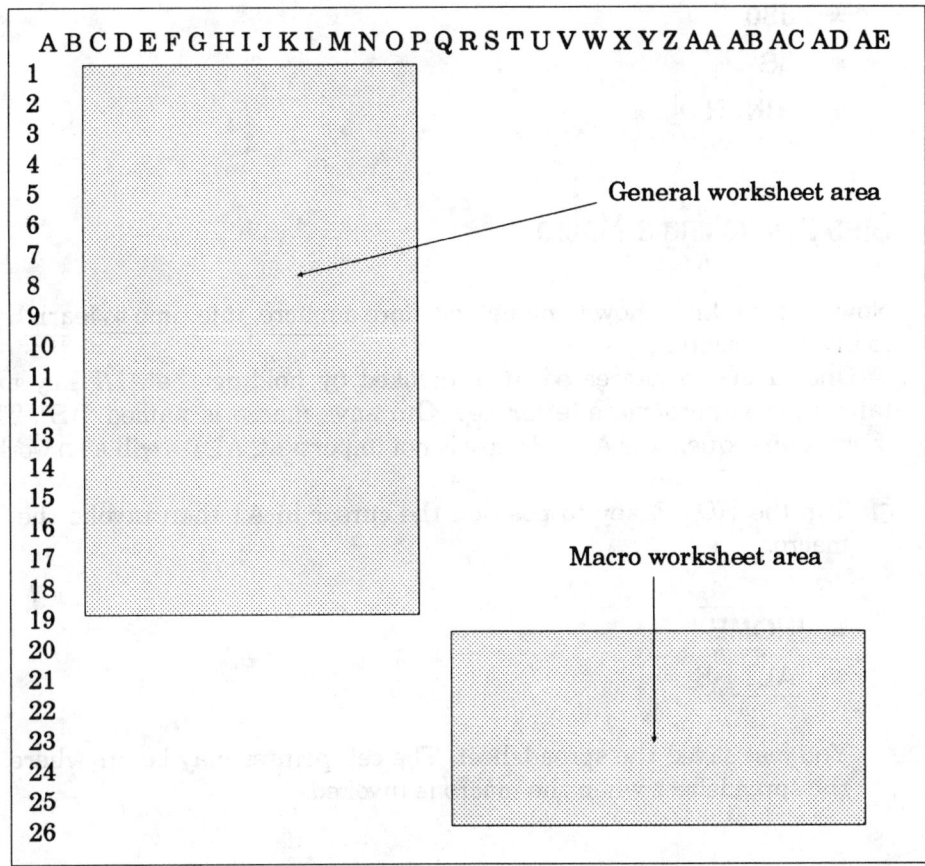

Figure 5-37 The macro worksheet area should be below and to the right of the general worksheet area

*   '/FS~R ↵

The fourth character in the macro is the tilde (~ rhymes with filled). In macros, a tilde represents the tapping of the ENTER key.

▢ Next, we assign a name to the macro. First we place the name in the cell immediately to the left of the macro (J80), then we use the Range-Name-Labels-Right command to assign the name to the cell containing the macro. A macro name has two elements: the backslash symbol and a letter. The name must be entered as a label, which means it must be prefaced with a single quote.

> **Problem Solving**
>
> If cell J80 has a series of SSSSSSSS's or sssssss's, you did not preface the macro name with a single quote. Enter the macro name again. Four keystrokes are required:
>
> 1. a single quote (')
> 2. a backslash symbol (\)
> 3. the letter S (uppercase or lowercase)
> 4. the ENTER key

*   `F5`

* J80 ↵
* '\S ↵
* /RNLR ↵

Step 2: Invoking a Macro

Now that you know how to name and store a macro, it is time to learn how to invoke a macro.

Once a macro is created, it is invoked by holding the ALT key and tapping the appropriate letter key. Our save macro is named "\S". The invocation sequence is ALT-S (case is not important, ALT-s will also work).

☐ Tap the HOME key to position the cursor in A1 then invoke the \S macro.

* [HOME]
* [ALT]-S

You just saved the spreadsheet. The cell pointer may be anywhere in the spreadsheet when the macro is invoked.

Step 3: Creating a Print Macro

Preston Smith asked Monroe Green to try several different "what if" scenarios in the spreadsheet Monroe developed. Preston also asked Monroe to print each scenario. Monroe decided to create a macro to print the spreadsheet. Once created, the macro will always be available to print future what if calculations. This step creates Monroe's print macro.

☐ Perform the task once and note the keystrokes required.

* /PPCAR
* A1.D20 ↵
* AGPQ

The third and fourth commands, Clear and All, reset all print settings to their default values.

☐ Store the keystroke representations in cells K82.K84 (see Figure 5-38).

* [F5]

* K82 ↵
* '/PPCAR ↓
* A1.D20~ ↓
* AGPQ ↵

Macro keystrokes may occupy more than one cell. Each successive cell must immediately follow the cell above. Macro execution begins in the first cell. The cell's keystrokes are read from left to right. Then execution moves to the next lower cell and its keystrokes are read from left to right. This continues until a blank cell is encountered. The macro stops at the first blank cell.

☐ Name a multiple cell macro by placing the name adjacent to the topmost cell and performing the Range-Name-Labels-Right command. Place the print macro's name, \P, in J82 (see Figure 5-38).

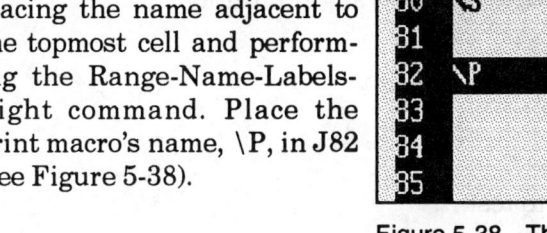

Figure 5-38 The "print" macro's keystrokes are entered in K82.K84

* [F5]
* J80 ↵
* [F5]
* J82 ↵
* '\P ↵
* /RNLR ↵

☐ Invoke the macro to test it.

* [ALT]-P

If your macro did not print the template, compare it with Figure 5-38. Refer to the next step to edit your macro.

☐ Use the ALT-S macro to save your spreadsheet.

Step 4: Editing a Macro

Macro keystrokes may be edited just like any Lotus label. Position the cell pointer on the portion of the macro that needs editing and either tap function key F2 to edit the cell's contents or enter a completely new label.

For example, Monroe noticed that his print macro does not print the Forecast Variable template. To include the Forecast Variable template in the printout he edits the range portion of the macro, changing it from A1.D20~ to A1.D27~. Monroe positions the cell pointer in K83 and uses the edit function to make the alteration. This step demonstrates Monroe's procedure to edit his print macro.

☐ Position the cell pointer in K83.

* F5
* K83 ↵

☐ Use function key F2 to edit the range definition.

* BKSP BKSP
* 7~ ↵

☐ Invoke the macro to test it.

* ALT -P

☐ Use the ALT-S macro to save your spreadsheet.

Step 5: Creating a Macro Menu

Monroe just created two macros. But will he remember them when he uses the spreadsheet four months hence? Assuming that he will forget about the macros, Monroe decides to create a macro menu (see Figure 5-39). He includes each macro's name and a brief description of the macro's function. He also creates a third macro (ALT-M) that allows him to jump to the macro work area.

☐ Monroe decides to place his macro menu in A30.A34. He positions the cell pointer in A30 and enters the menu heading.

* F5
* A30 ↵
* ^**** Macro Menu **** ↵

Prefacing the label with a carat (^) centers the label within the column.

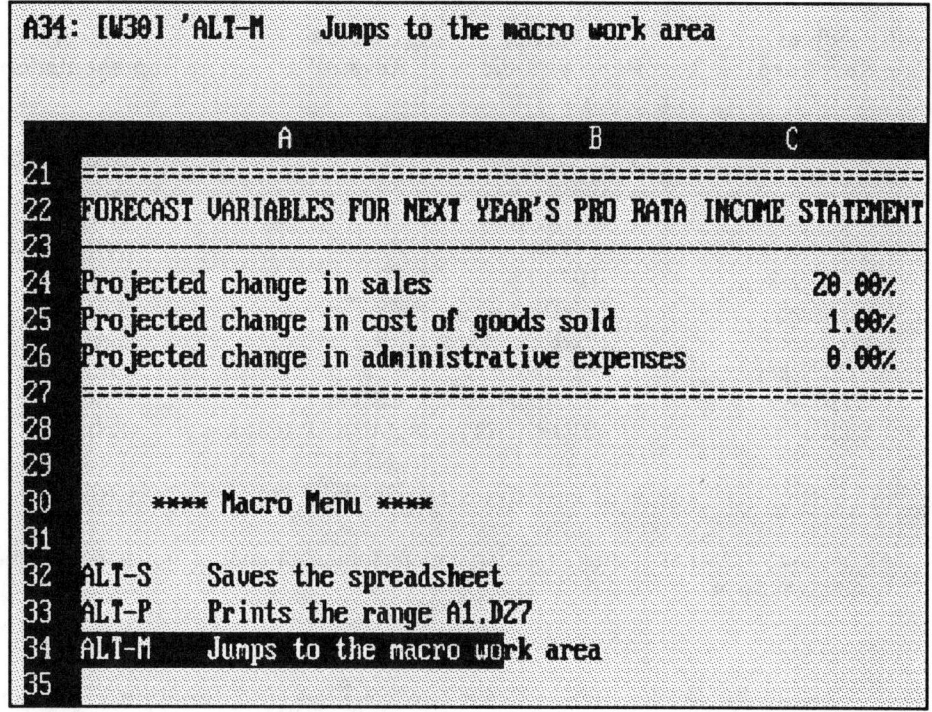

Figure 5-39   The macro menu is created A30.A34

❒ Enter the ALT-S macro definition.

* **F5**
* **A32** ↵
* **ALT-S**
* **SPACE** *(4 times)*
* **Saves the spreadsheet** ↵

Refer to Figure 5-39 and enter the ALT-P and ALT-M macro definitions (we will create the ALT-M macro next).

❒ Use the ALT-S macro to save your spreadsheet.

Step 6: Creating a Goto Macro

Monroe's final step in this procedure is to create the ALT-M macro that will allow him to jump to the macro work area. The goto macro includes two new macro elements, a function key reference and a range name.

Actual Keystroke	Macro Representation	Actual Keystroke	Macro Representation
↵	~	F2	{EDIT}
←	{LEFT}	F3	{NAME}
↑	{UP}	F4	{ABS}
→	{RIGHT}	F5	{GOTO}
↓	{DOWN}	F6	{WINDOW}
HOME key	{HOME}	F7	{QUERY}
END key	{END}	F8	{TABLE}
PGUP key	{PGUP}	F9	{CALC}
PGDN key	{PGDN}	F10	{GRAPH}
CTRL-←	{BIGLEFT}	ESC key	{ESC}
CTRL-→	{BIGRIGHT}	BACKSPACE key	{BS}
		INSERT key	{INSERT}
		DELETE key	{DEL}

Figure 5-40 Macro keystroke representations for cursor control, function and other specialized keys

Certain keystrokes (i.e., cursor control keys and function keys) have special macro keystroke representations. For instance, to represent tapping function key F5, the goto key, the representation {GOTO} is entered. To create a macro that jumps to the beginning of the macro area (J80), Monroe might enter the macro {GOTO}J80~. Other special keystrokes are listed in Figure 5-25.

Many commands require range designations (e.g., /Copy, /Move, /Range Format, etc.). Until now, we have used the range address method to enter ranges. That is, we have entered the two diagonally opposite cell addresses to define ranges. It is also possible to preassign a name to a designated range. Then when a range is requested, the name can be entered in place of the cell addresses. For example, Monroe uses the /Range Name Create command to assign the name MACROTOP to cell J80. Then he uses the name MACROTOP in place of the cell address in his ALT-M macro: {GOTO}MACROTOP~.

The benefit of using range names becomes apparent when rows are added or deleted from a spreadsheet. For instance, if rows 40 through 44 were deleted, the macro area would no longer begin at J80, it would begin at J75. If Monroe's ALT-M macro had been entered {GOTO}J80~, it would no longer point to the beginning of the macro area. However, if his macro is {GOTO}MACROTOP~ the range name is automatically adjusted when rows or columns are added and deleted. If Monroe's macro uses a range name, it will still work.

☐ Assign the name MACROTOP to cell J80.

* F5

* J80 ↵

Lotus: Session Six 320

* /RNC
* MACROTOP ↵
* ↵

☐ Create the ALT-M macro.

* F5
* K86 ↵
* {GOTO}MACROTOP~ ↵
* ←
* '\M ↵
* /RNLR ↵

☐ Test the ALT-M macro.

* HOME
* ALT -M

Cell J80 should be in the upper left corner.

Step 7: Practice

Create two macros. The first macro erases the active cell. The second macro displays a worksheet filename list.

* Begin with a clean worksheet.
* Create the first macro in K21.
* The cell erasing task involves four keystrokes: /RE ↵ . Enter the keystroke representations in K21.
* Enter the macro's name, \E, in J21.
* Assign the name to the macro.
* Test the macro by positioning the cell pointer in A1 and entering your name. Invoke the ALT-E macro to erase your name.

Create the second macro which displays a worksheet filename list. The task requires the keystrokes /FLW.

* Enter the keystroke representations in K23.

* Enter the macro name, \T, in J23.
* Assign the name to the macro.
* Save your spreadsheet as ET.
* Test the macro by invoking the ALT-T macro. When the file list appears, select ET by highlighting the name and tapping ENTER.

Create a macro menu that describes both macros.

* Enter the menu heading in A7.
* Enter the macro descriptions in A9 and A10.

Save and print.

* Print both the macro menu and the macro work area.
* Save the spreadsheet.

Step 8: Terminating a Session

If you do not want to continue to the next session now, complete the following to turn off your computer. Remember that you should always return to the DOS prompt before turning off the computer.

☐ To exit Lotus 1-2-3, first make sure that your work is saved, then issue the Quit command.

* *(if necessary, save your work)*
* **/QY**

☐ Remove your data diskette from drive A and turn off the computer.

Session Seven

Dates and More on Macros

In Lotus 1-2-3 releases 1, 2.0 and 2.01, macro keystroke representations must be entered manually (see Session Six). In 1988, Lotus Development Corporation published the Lotus Value Pack, which includes an automatic macro keystroke memorization feature named Lotus Learn. The Value Pack enhanced release 2.01.

In 1989, Lotus began selling Release 2.2 and Release 3. Both of these upgrades include Lotus Learn as a standard feature.

This session demonstrates Lotus Learn. If you are using Release 2.01, step 1 in this session confirms the existence of Lotus Learn and demonstrates how to invoke the feature. If you do not have the Learn feature, you may still work through this session but will have to enter all macro keystrokes representations manually.

Opie Rader, a System Analyst with the RANI Corporation, decides to create a product summary template. The template includes several horizontal separator lines, so he uses the Lotus Learn feature to create a macro to enter the lines. Opie also includes date calculations in the template. For instance, Opie wants to include an average week's sales calculation and must know how long each store has been selling each product. Opie subtracts the shipment receipt date from the report date to determine how long each store has been selling a product. This session follows Opie's steps as he creates the sales summary template (see Figure 5-42).

If necessary, see Session One, Step 1 to start Lotus 1-2-3. Insert your data diskette in drive A, make drive A the active drive and retrieve the "R&G1" spreadsheet created in Session Two (refer to Session One, Step 12).

In this session you will learn how to:

- Invoke an add-in feature
- Use Lotus Learn to memorize keystrokes
- Name a macro
- Invoke a macro
- Enter and format dates
- Use dates in formulas
- Use an absolute cell reference during the copy procedure

Step 1: Using Lotus Add-in Features with Release 2.01

This step is for users of Release 2.01 only. It confirms the existence of the Add-in Manager which must be present in order to use the Lotus Learn feature. Release 2.2 and Release 3 include Lotus Learn as a standard feature and do not require the Add-in Manager to run Lotus Learn.

An **add-in** is a program that adds additional capabilities to Lotus 1-2-3. Add-ins are monitored by the Add-in Manager which controls their addition, use and removal. An add-in must be attached (made available by adding to memory) before it may be invoked (called up via the Add-in Manager menu or by tapping its appropriate keystroke combination). When an add-in is no longer needed, it may be detached (removed from memory).

Add-ins are invoked from within Lotus 1-2-3 and should not be confused with add-*ons*, that can only be run outside Lotus 1-2-3 (i.e., one must quit Lotus before running the add-on).

- ☐ Confirm the existence of the Add-in Manager. Tap ALT-F10 to display the Add-in Manager main menu (see Figure 5-41).

* 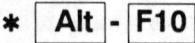 Alt - F10

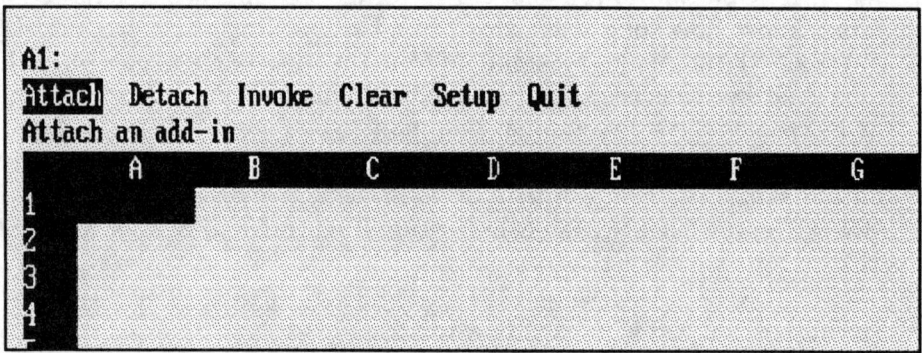

Figure 5.41 Lotus Add-in Manager main menu

If the Add-in Manager did not appear, the Lotus Learn feature is not available. You may still work through this session but will have to enter all macro keystroke representations manually (see Session Six).

- ☐ Attach Lotus Learn.

  * **A**
  * *(highlight "LEARN.ADN")* ↵
  * **N Q**

> **Problem Solving**
>
> Lotus may flash an error signal ("Add-in already attached"). The Add-in Manager often is set up to attach add-ins automatically when 1-2-3 is started. Once a feature is attached, it may not be attached again. Tap the ESC and Q keys to return to READY mode.

Opie Rader, a RANI Corporation System Analyst, wants to create a product sales summary template and knows that he will be entering horizontal separators (for example, the dashed line on row 2) several times throughout the template. He suspects that because he is performing a repetitive task, there must be a way to automate the procedure and let Lotus 1-2-3 do the work for him. He asks Rowina Marconi, the education coordinator at RANI, for help, and she suggests the following procedure when creating a macro:

- Decide what task you want to perform.
- Assign a cell range to store the macro keystroke representations
- Turn on Lotus Learn
- Perform the task once allowing Lotus to record the keystroke sequence
- Turn off Lotus Learn
- Assign a name (consisting of the backslash symbol followed by a letter) to the first cell that contains the macro keystroke text
- Reposition the cell cursor, if necessary
- Invoke the macro by tapping ALT and the letter in the macro name

Opie follows Rowina's advice to create his macro. He decides he wants a macro that creates a horizontal line across seven cells.

☐ (For **Release 2.01**) Invoke Lotus Learn.

* **Alt** - **F10**
* l
* *(highlight LEARN)* ↵

☐ (For **Release 2.2 and 3**) Activate the Learn feature.

* /WL

☐ Assign a cell range to store the macro keystroke representations. The assigned "learn range" should not overlap the proposed template.

* R J35.J40 ↵
* QQ *(Release 2.01 only)*

☐ Position the cell cursor to enter the first horizontal line (see Figure 5-42).

	A	B	C	D	E	F	G
1	RAM Corporation - Sales Summary					Date:	01-May-91
2							
3	Region	Style No.	Date Rcd	# Rcd	# Sld	Weeks	%/Week
4							
5	West	A234NG	21-Feb-91	436	215	9.9	5.00%
6		B421GF	20-Mar-91	563	410	6.0	12.14%
7		C298FR	05-Apr-91	210	50	3.7	6.41%
8							
9	Central	A234NG	10-Feb-91	678	597	11.4	7.70%
10		B421GF	17-Mar-91	325	256	6.4	12.25%
11		C298FR	25-Feb-91	289	178	9.3	6.63%
12							
13	East	A234NG	28-Feb-91	532	478	8.9	10.14%
14		B421GF	15-Mar-91	649	560	6.7	12.85%
15		C298FR	30-Mar-91	420	150	4.6	7.81%
16							
17	Totals	A234NG		1646	1290	10.0	7.88%
18		B421GF		1537	1226	6.4	12.58%
19		C298FR		919	378	5.9	7.02%
20							

12-Mar-91 08:59 AM

Figure 5-42 Opie Rader's product sales summary template

* **F5**
* **A2** ↵

☐ Use ALT-F5 to toggle Lotus Learn on.

* **Alt** - **F5**

The LEARN box appears at the bottom of the screen.

☐ Perform the task once.

* \- ↵ *(fill first cell with hyphens)*
* /C ↵
* → . → *(5 times to G2)* ↵

☐ Tap ALT-F5 again to toggle Lotus Learn off.

* **Alt** - **F5**

The LEARN indicator vanishes and the CALC indicator appears.

☐ Tap any key to recalculate the spreadsheet to enter the keystroke representations automatically.

Lotus: Session Seven **326**

* ↵

If you do not have the LEARN feature, refer to Figure 5-43 to enter the keystroke representations manually. Each keystroke is explained below.

☐ Move the pointer to J35 to see the macro.

* [F5]
* J35 ↵

The macro fills the cell containing the pointer with hyphens (\-~), invokes the copy command (/c), and copies the first cell (~) into the next six cells ({RIGHT}.{RIGHT}{RIGHT}{RIGHT}{RIGHT}{RIGHT}. The tilde (~) represents the ENTER key and the symbol {RIGHT} represents the right arrow key. All other keystrokes can be taken at face value; that is, a "c" represents the C key.

☐ Assign a name to the cell that contains the keystroke text. In the cell to the immediate left of the macro's first cell, enter the two-character name (backslash and a letter) as a label. In this case, the cell to the left is I35.

* ← *(position pointer at I35)*
* '\S *(S for separator line)* ↵

☐ Use the Range Name Labels Right command to assign the name to the top cell that contains macro keystrokes.

Figure 5-43 Macro keystroke representations

* /RNLR
* ↵

☐ Invoke the macro by tapping ALT and the letter in the macro name. Use the macro to insert the other separator lines of the sales summary template of Figure 5-42.

* [HOME] [F5]
* A4 ↵
* [ALT]-S

Also use the macro to insert separator lines in rows A8, A12, A16, A20.

☐ Before continuing to the next Step, set the column width of columns A, B, C and G to 11. The column width is necessary to view the dates that will be entered.

Step 2: Entering and Formatting Dates

Opie records the date each shipment was received (column C). Entering dates is a two-step process. First, calculate the date value or the number of days between January 1, 1900 and the desired date. The date value is used in formulas to calculate the number of days between two dates. Lotus 1-2-3 has functions that calculate the date value automatically. Second, use one of five date formats to display the date value in a format that can be easily interpreted.

The calculated date values are used in the column F formula to determine the number of weeks between the date each shipment was received and the date of the report. Opie follows the two-step process to enter the dates into column C.

☐ Use the function @DATE(year,month,day) to calculate and enter the date value into C5.

* F5
* C5 ↵
* @DATE(91,2,21) ↵

The date value 33290 (the number of days from January 1, 1900 to February 21, 1991) appears in the cell.

☐ Format the date value so that it is displayed in a more readable format.

* /RFD1
* ↵

☐ Refer to Figure 5-38 to enter and format the other dates in column C.

Step 3: Entering Spreadsheet Data and Aligning Column Headings

Opie's boss wants to know each product's average weekly sales percentage. This way he will know which products are "hot." The average weekly sales percentage equals the average number of goods sold per week (column E divided by column F) divided by the number of goods received (column D).

```
     A         B           C              D              E
 1  RANI Corporation - Sales Summary
 2
 3  Region    Style No.    Date Rcd       # Rcd          # Sld
 4
 5  West      A234NG       @DATE(91,2,21)    436            215
 6            B421GF       @DATE(91,3,20)    563            410
 7            C298FR       @DATE(91,4,5)     210             50
 8
 9  Central   A234NG       @DATE(91,2,10)    678            597
10            B421GF       @DATE(91,3,17)    325            256
11            C298FR       @DATE(91,2,25)    289            178
12
13  East      A234NG       @DATE(91,2,28)    532            478
14            B421GF       @DATE(91,3,15)    649            560
15            C298FR       @DATE(91,3,30)    420            150
16
17  Totals    A234NG                    @SUM(D5,D9,D13)  @SUM(E5,E9,E13)
18            B421GF                    @SUM(D6,D10,D14) @SUM(E6,E10,E14)
19            C298FR                    @SUM(D7,D11,D15) @SUM(E7,E11,E15)
20
```

Figure 5-44 Actual cell entries to Opie Rader's summary template (columns A..E)

☐ Enter the column F formulas to calculate the number of weeks between the date received (column C) and the report date (cell G1).

* **F5**
* **F5** ↵
* **(G$1-C5)/7**

The formula subtracts the column C date value from the report date value (G1), and divides the resultant number of days by 7. The dollar sign in the formula freezes the cell reference during the following copy procedure.

☐ Copy the formula to F6 and F7.

* **/C**
* ↵
* ↓ . ↓ ↵

Move the pointer to F6 and F7 and notice that the relative address (C5) changed but the absolute address (G$1) remained unchanged. Since the formula was copied within one column, only the row reference ($1) needed to be made absolute.

- Copy the range F5.F7 to F9 and F13.

- Refer to Figure 5-45 and enter the other formulas. Use the copy command to facilitate formula entry. For example, enter the formula in G5 and copy it to G6 and G7. Then copy the range G5.G7 to G9, G13 and G17. Next enter the formula into D17 and copy the formula to the range D17.F19. The D17 formula uses the @SUM function to add the contents of three cells [@SUM(D5,D9,D13)].

- Enter all labels. Right align the labels in range B3.G3 and the label in F1. All other labels are left aligned.

- Enter the values in columns D and E.

- Format column F as fixed with 1 decimal. Format column G as percent with 2 decimals.

- Save the spreadsheet as SUMMARY.

	F	G
1	Date:	@DATE(91,5,1)
2		
3	Weeks	%/Week
4		
5	(G$1-C5)/7	(E5/F5)/D5
6	(G$1-C6)/7	(E6/F6)/D6
7	(G$1-C7)/7	(E7/F7)/D7
8		
9	(G$1-C9)/7	(E9/F9)/D9
10	(G$1-C10)/7	(E10/F10)/D10
11	(G$1-C11)/7	(E11/F11)/D11
12		
13	(G$1-C13)/7	(E13/F13)/D13
14	(G$1-C14)/7	(E14/F14)/D14
15	(G$1-C15)/7	(E15/F15)/D15
16		
17	@AVG(F5,F9,F13)	(E17/F17)/D17
18	@AVG(F6,F10,F14)	(E18/F18)/D18
19	@AVG(F7,F11,F15)	(E19/F19)/D19
20		

Figure 5-45 Actual cell entries to Opie Rader's summary template (columns F and G)

Step 4: Practice

Create a macro that displays Opie Rader's sales summary template's macro keystroke area. Opie decides that since he would be jumping to the macro keystroke area often, he should create a macro that does the work for him.

* Use the /Range Name Create command to assign the name MACROS to cell I33 (see Session Six).

* Invoke Learn.

* Assign a single cell learn range (J33).

* Turn on learn.

* Perform the task (F5 MACROS ↵).

* Turn off learn.

* Tap ENTER to recalculate the spreadsheet. The keystroke representations will appear in J33.

* Enter the name (\M) in I33.

* Assign the name to J33.

* Test the macro by tapping HOME then ALT-M.

Create a macro that prints Opie's Sales Summary Template.

* Invoke Learn.
* Assign a single cell learn range (J40).
* Turn on learn.
* Make sure your printer is ready, then perform the task (/Print Printer Clear All Range A1.G20 ↵ Align Go Page Quit).
* Turn off learn.
* Tap ENTER to recalculate the spreadsheet. The keystroke representations will appear in J40. Use ALT-M to jump to the macro area.
* Enter the name (\P) in I40.
* Assign the name to J40.
* Test the macro by tapping ALT-P.
* Save the spreadsheet.

Step 5: Terminating the Session

If you do not want to continue to the next session now, complete the following to turn off your computer. Remember that you should always return to the DOS prompt before turning off the computer.

☐ To exit Lotus 1-2-3, first make sure that your work is saved, then issue the Quit command.

* *(if necessary, save your work)*
* /QY

☐ Remove your data diskette from drive A and turn off the computer.

Session Eight

Printing with Allways

Allways, subtitled the Spreadsheet Publisher, is an enhancement to Lotus 1-2-3 created by Funk SoftWare Inc. Allways is an add-in program and is controlled by Lotus's Add-in Manager (see Session Seven for a discussion of add-ins). In 1989, Lotus Development Corp began bundling Allways with Lotus 1-2-3 Release 2.01 and Release 2.2. This added sophisticated printing capabilities to these releases.

For example, once Opie completed his sales summary template (see Figure 5-42), he decided to format it with Allways before showing it to his boss. Opie has learned that first impressions are important and wants his work to look as professional as possible. Opie calls up the Add-in Manager and invokes Allways. He discovers that he must make several changes to the template before formatting with Allways. This session follows Opie's steps as he uses fonts, gray shading and cell outlining to create a polished printout of his sales summary template (see Figure 5-46).

This session assumes that Allways has been setup and is available through the Add-in Manager. The commands in this session are based on Allways Version 1.0.

If necessary, see Session One, Step 1 to start Lotus 1-2-3. Insert your data diskette in drive A, make drive A the active drive and retrieve the "SUMMARY" spreadsheet created in Session Seven (refer to Session One, Step 12). We will use Allways to modify the printed appearance of Opie Rader's product sales summary template.

In this session you will learn how to:

♦ Invoke Allways
♦ Change a display's point size
♦ Change a cell's font
♦ Add shadings to selected cells
♦ Outline selected cells
♦ Change print margins
♦ Print a graph on the same page as a spreadsheet template

Step 1: Preparing the SUMMARY Template

Changes need to be made to the SUMMARY template before invoking Allways. These changes are cosmetic and are usually discovered by experimentation, jumping back and forth between Lotus 1-2-3 and Allways as

RANI Corporation – Sales Summary   Date: 01–May–91

Region	Style No.	Date Rcd	# Rcd	# Sld	Weeks	%/Week
West	A234NG	21–Feb–91	436	215	9.9	5.00%
	B421GF	20–Mar–91	563	410	6.0	12.14%
	C298FR	05–Apr–91	210	50	3.7	6.41%
Central	A234NG	10–Feb–91	678	597	11.4	7.70%
	B421GF	17–Mar–91	325	256	6.4	12.25%
	C298FR	25–Feb–91	289	178	9.3	6.63%
East	A234NG	28–Feb–91	532	478	8.9	10.14%
	B421GF	15–Mar–91	649	560	6.7	12.85%
	C298FR	30–Mar–91	420	150	4.6	7.81%
Totals	A234NG		1646	1290	10.0	7.80%
	B421GF		1537	1226	6.4	12.50%
	C298FR		919	378	5.9	7.02%

Figure 5-46 Opie Rader's product sales summary template printed with Allways

the printout is refined. For example, when Opie printed the spreadsheet with Allways, he discovered that he did not want the separator lines. So he had to leave Allways and return to Lotus to remove the separator lines.

☐ Erase the separator line in row 2.

* /RE A2.G2 ↵

Use the above procedure to erase the other separator lines in rows 4, 8, 12, 16 and 20.

☐ Since Opie also wants to draw a box around the template (see Figure 5-46), he must add a column to the left of the template for the left side of the box and a row above the template for the top of the box.

* HOME
* /WIC ↵
* /WIR ↵

☐ Save the revised template as SUMMARY1 (see Figure 5-47).

* /FS SUMMARY1 ↵

```
      A       B       C       D       E       F       G
 1
 2        RANI Corporation - Sales Summary              Date:
 3
 4        Region  Style No.  Date Rcd    # Rcd   # Sld   Weeks
 5
 6        West    A234NG     21-Feb-91    436    215     9.9
 7                B4216F     20-Mar-91    563    410     6.0
 8                C298FR     05-Apr-91    210     50     3.7
 9
10        Central A234NG     10-Feb-91    678    597    11.4
11                B4216F     17-Mar-91    325    256     6.4
12                C298FR     25-Feb-91    289    178     9.3
13
14        East    A234NG     28-Feb-91    532    478     8.9
15                B4216F     15-Mar-91    649    560     6.7
16                C298FR     30-Mar-91    420    150     4.6
17
18        Totals  A234NG                 1646   1290    10.0
19                B4216F                 1537   1226     6.4
20                C298FR                  919    378     5.9
12-Mar-91  09:06 AM
```

Figure 5-47 Revised template, SUMMARY.1 Cosmetic changes have been made to the spreadsheet to prepare it for printing with ALLWAYS

Step 2: Invoking Allways and Formatting the Template

☐ Call up the Add-in Manager and invoke Allways.

* ALT - F10
* I
* *(highlight ALLWAYS)* ↵

Allways employs a graphical user interface (GUI) to display the SUMMARY1 template. Change the template heading's font setting to appreciate the benefit of this display. Move the pointer to B2 and use the forward slash (/) to call up the Allways main menu.

* → ↓
* /FF3 ↵ ↵

The previous series of commands changed the point size of the label in B2 from 10 pt to 14 pt. The GUI display allows us to view the template as it actually will appear when it is printed (What You See Is What You Get - WYSIWYG)

☐ Add light shading to the range B4.H5.

* **/FSL**
* **B4.H5** ↵

Also add light shading to B9.H9, B13.H13, and B17.H17.

☐ Change the font of the label in B6.B18 to Triumvirate Italic.

* **/FF2** ↵ **B6.B18** ↵

☐ Change the appearance of the label in B2 to boldface.

* **/FBS**
* **B2** ↵

Also assign boldface B6.B18.

☐ Draw a box around the template.

* **/FLO**
* **A1.I22** ↵

Step 3: Printing and Saving an Allways Version of the Template

Opie prints the completed template then returns to Lotus to save the current version of the template. The Allways settings are saved automatically.

☐ Reset the margins before printing the template.

* **/LML .5** ↵
* **R .5** ↵
* **QQ**

The margins are measured in inches (as in WordPerfect 5.0).

☐ Print the template.

* **/PRS**
* **A1.I22** ↵

* G

Allways lists each row as information is sent to the printer. Your printout should be similar to Figure 5-46.

☐ Return to Lotus 1-2-3.

* ESC

☐ Save the Lotus template to save the Allways format changes.

* /FS ↵ R

Step 4: Printing Graphs with Allways

Opie looks at the completed printout and realizes that the data would be easier to understand if it were presented in graphics format. Opie returns to Lotus 1-2-3 and creates a graph based on the data. Then he uses Allways to print the graph. Allways has several graphics features that Opie finds helpful.

- ❖ Allways allows graphs to be printed without leaving 1-2-3.
- ❖ Allways expands and contracts graphs to fit in a user defined range.
- ❖ Allways can print both templates and graphs on the same page.

In this step, we will create a bar graph in Lotus 1-2-3. Then we will invoke Allways and print the graph on the same page as the Sales Summary template (see Figure 5-48).

☐ Define the graph settings.

* /GTB
* A H6.H8 ↵
* B H10.H12 ↵
* C H14.H16 ↵

☐ Enter the graph titles.

* *(in the graph menu)*
* OTF

RANI Corporation – Sales Summary

Date: 01-May-91

Region	Style No.	Date Rcd	# Rcd	# Sld	Weeks	%/Week
West	A234NG	21-Feb-91	436	215	9.9	5.00%
	B421GF	20-Mar-91	563	410	6.0	12.14%
	C298FR	05-Apr-91	210	50	3.7	6.41%
Central	A234NG	10-Feb-91	678	597	11.4	7.70%
	B421GF	17-Mar-91	325	256	6.4	12.25%
	C298FR	25-Feb-91	289	178	9.3	6.63%
East	A234NG	28-Feb-91	532	478	8.9	10.14%
	B421GF	15-Mar-91	649	560	6.7	12.85%
	C298FR	30-Mar-91	420	150	4.6	7.81%
Totals	A234NG		1646	1290	10.0	7.80%
	B421GF		1537	1226	6.4	12.50%
	C298FR		919	378	5.9	7.02%

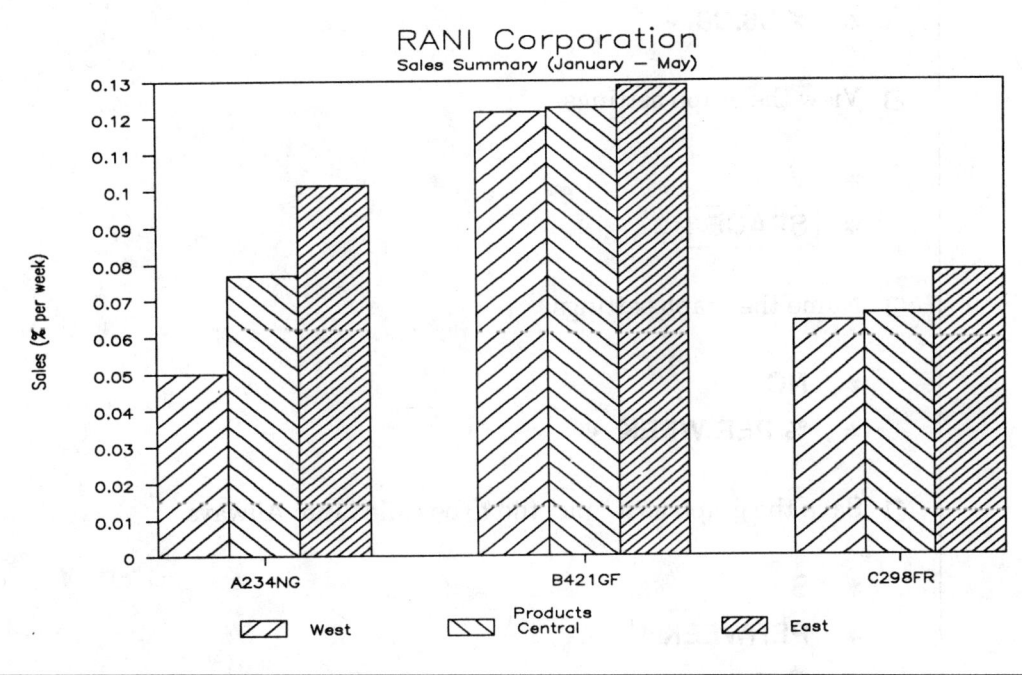

Figure 5-48 Product sales summary template and an associated graph printed on the same page with Allways

* **RANI Corporation** ↵
* **TS**
* **Sales Summary (January - May)** ↵
* **TX**
* **Products** ↵
* **TY**
* **Sales (% per week)** ↵

☐ Enter the legends.

* *(in the options menu)*
* **LA**
* **West** ↵
* **LB**
* **Central** ↵
* **LC**
* **East** ↵
* **Q**

☐ Enter the product names on the X-axis.

* **X C6.C8** ↵

☐ View the graph settings.

* **V**
* **SPACE**

☐ Name the graph settings.

* **NC**
* **% PER WEEK** ↵

☐ Save the graph as a ".pic" file to be called into Allways.

* **S**
* **PERWEEK** ↵
* **Q**

☐ Save the template to save the graph settings.

* /FS ↵ R

☐ Invoke Allways.

* ALT - F10
* /
* (highlight ALLWAYS) ↵

☐ Add the PERWEEK graph to the printout.

* /GA
* (highlight PERWEEK.PIC) ↵
* B25.H42 ↵
* Q

☐ Redefine the print range and print the graph and the template.

* /PRS
* A1.I42 ↵
* G

☐ Return to 1-2-3 and save the template.

* ESC
* /FS ↵ R

Step 5: Practice

Use Allways to print the SALES template created in Session Five.

* Retrieve the SALES template.
* Invoke Allways and format the template for printing (change fonts, add shading, outline cells, add columns or rows if necessary, etc.).
* Print the revised template.
* Include the graph BAR.PIC, also created in Session Five, in the printout.

ANNUAL SALES FOR R & G BY REGION

Product	Southern	Western	Northern	Eastern	Total
Science Fiction	$7,140	$14,790	$13,260	$15,810	$51,000
Romance	$5,460	$11,310	$10,140	$12,090	$39,000
Biography	$3,150	$6,525	$5,850	$6,975	$22,500
Non-fiction	$5,250	$11,875	$10,750	$12,625	$40,500
Totals	$21,000	$44,500	$40,000	$47,500	$153,000

Figure 5-49 Sample solution to the practice exercise

* Save the other graph settings (PIEGRAPH and MULTIBAR) as ".pic" files.
* Print the template and all three graphs on one page.

Step 6: Terminating the Session

If you do not want to continue to the next session now, complete the following to turn off your computer. Remember that you should always return to the DOS prompt before turning off the computer.

☐ To exit Lotus 1-2-3, first make sure that your work is saved, then issue the Quit command.

* *(if necessary, save your work)*
* **/QY**

☐ Remove your data diskette from drive A and turn off the computer.

Session Nine

New Features in Release 3

Lotus Development Corporation began selling Lotus 1-2-3, Release 3 in July, 1989 and Release 2.2 in August, 1989. To run Release 3, your computer must have at least 1Mb of RAM, a hard drive, and an 80286 processor or later. Release 3 will not run on computers with an 8088 or an 8086 processor. Release 2.2 is designed to run on 8088 and 8086 computers. It contains some of the new features found in Release 3.

New features included in both Release 2.2 and Release 3 that were not available in Release 2.01 are:

- File linking to spreadsheets stored on disk
- UNDO (erases the effects of the most recent command)
- Keystroke memorization is now a permanent feature rather than an add-in
- Enhanced (faster) recalculation
- Additional graphics capabilities
- Additional printing capabilities
- The ability to create macro libraries that can be used with any spreadsheet

New features included in Release 3 that are not available in any other release.

- File linking between several active spreadsheets
- Three-dimensional worksheets within a file
- The ability to access, query, and update external databases entirely within 1-2-3
- Search and replace
- Attaching notes to cells

This session demonstrates two new features unique to Release 3: file linking between active spreadsheets and querying an external data base. Also presented is the UNDO feature.

- **File linking** is the ability to use values stored in external spreadsheets in the current file. These values are referenced in formulas. Changes made to the referenced external cells will update the spreadsheet that contains the referencing formulas.

- ❖ The new /Data External command allows users to establish a connection between Lotus 1-2-3 and an externally managed data base (one that was created and is maintained by another program - such as dBASE III PLUS). This allows users to access, update and query an external data base.

- ❖ The **UNDO** command erases the effects of the most recently entered command. The command returns the spreadsheet to its condition before the most recent command was entered.

In this session, we will activate five files from the Example Files Diskette and link them together through formulas. Then we will change data in a referenced file and see the change reflected in the referencing file. Next, we will connect Lotus 1-2-3 to the CARDS data base created in Chapter Four and make queries to the data base from within Lotus. During the Query, we will demonstrate the UNDO feature.

Before beginning this session, make a backup copy of the Example Files Diskette. Use DOS's DISKCOPY command to create a duplicate of the Example Files Diskette.

In this session you will learn how to:

- ❖ Activate multiple spreadsheets simultaneously
- ❖ Display multiple spreadsheets in perspective
- ❖ Link multiple spreadsheets
- ❖ Copy data across multiple spreadsheets
- ❖ Refresh (update) all formulas in a linked file
- ❖ Connect to an external database
- ❖ Query an external database
- ❖ Enable and use the UNDO feature

Step 1: Activating Multiple Spreadsheets

Release 3 allows many spreadsheets to be open simultaneously. The number of open spreadsheets is limited only by available RAM. In this step, we will open five files: the RANI Headquarters Sales Summary file and a file for each of RANI's four sales regions (North, South, East and West). All five files exist on the newly made copy of the Example Files Diskette. Change to your Lotus Release 3 directory and load Lotus to memory. Insert the copy of the Example Files Diskette into drive A and make drive A the active drive.

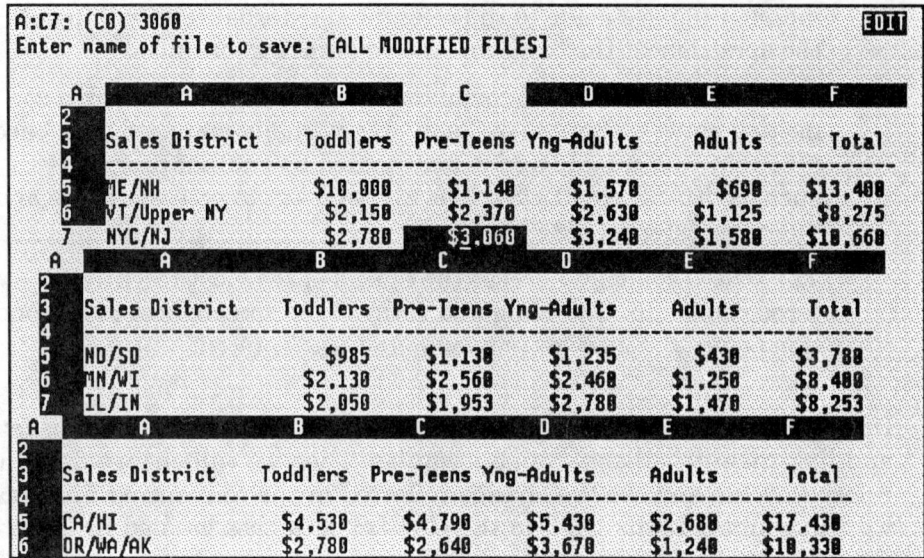

Figure 5-50 Lotus files displayed in "perspective"

☐ Retrieve the RANI Headquarter's Sales Summary file.

* /FR
* HQ ↵

☐ Save this file under another name to preserve the original file.

* /FS HEADQTRS ↵

☐ Open the Southern Region's Sales file.

* /FOA SOUTHERN ↵

Use the same commands to open the Western, Northern and Eastern Regions' files.

☐ Display the open files in perspective (see Figure 5-50).

* /WWP

☐ The last three files added appear in a layered display.

☐ Zoom in and out of perspective by tapping ALT-F6. Notice that "ZOOM" appears near the bottom of the screen.

* [ALT] - [F6]
* [ALT] - [F6]

❑ Move the pointer to the HEADQTRS template.

* [CTRL] - [PGDN] *(4 times)*

CTRL-PGDN and CTRL-PGUP move the cell pointer from open template to open template. If more than three templates are open, the display will scroll.

Step 2: Linking Multiple Files

Files may be linked together so that a change in one file will be reflected in another file. For example, if the headquarters file is linked to the regional files, any changes in the regional sales summaries will update the headquarters file automatically.

Files are linked by entering formulas that refer to cells or ranges in external files. External cells and ranges are referred to in the same three ways that cells and ranges are referred to in the current file (i.e., typing the address, using the range name, or highlighting the range).

Create an external reference by preceding the range name or address with the external file's path and name placed within double angle brackets. This special configuration is called a file reference. For example, Rhea Ruggiero creates a new 1991 Headquarters sales summary template (HEADQTRS). To save typing, she copies the product category names from the Southern Region sales summary template (SOUTHERN).

Rhea places the pointer in HEADQTRS and activates the copy command. When Lotus prompts her to enter the COPY FROM range, Rhea enters "<<SOUTHERN.WK3>>PRODUCT LIST" (see Figure 5-51). The file reference is the portion within double brackets, and PRODUCT LIST is the range name. Had the SOUTHERN file been in a different directory, Rhea would have included the path in the file reference (ex. <<C:\REGIONS\SOUTHERN.WK3>>).

Rhea used the range name method to copy data from one file to another. She decides to use a different method, highlighting the range, to link the two files. Rhea activates the HEADQTRS and SOUTHERN files (she reads both into memory with the /File Open command). Rhea is able to reference cells and ranges by moving the pointer to the correct file and highlighting the range. She uses the keystroke combinations CTRL-PGDN and CTRL-PGUP to move the pointer to the previous active file or the next active file.

❑ Use the named range method to copy the product category column headings from the SOUTHERN file to the HEADQTRS file. The range

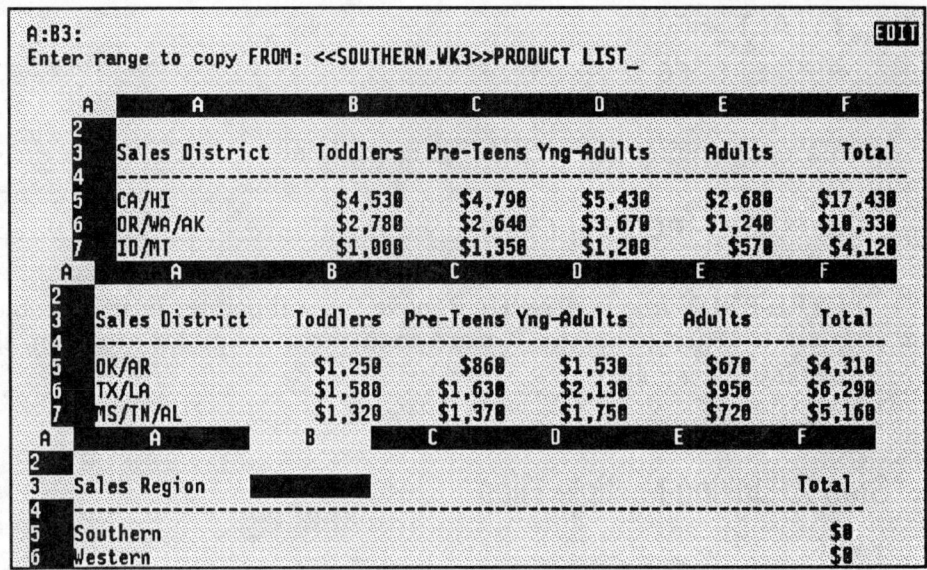

Figure 5-51 Entering a file reference during the COPY procedure

name PRODUCT LIST has been assigned to range B3.E3 in the Southern Region file.

* F5
* B3 ↵
* /C <<SOUTHERN.WK3>>PRODUCT LIST ↵ ↵

☐ Use the range highlight method to link B5 in the HEADQTRS file to B10 in the SOUTHERN file.

* F5
* B5 ↵
* +
* CTRL - PGUP
* ↓ *(5 times, to B10)* ↵

The two files are linked. Both cells now represent total Toddlers apparel sales and any change in the SOUTHERN file will be reflected in the HEADQTRS file. Notice that the formula contains a complete file reference that was entered automatically by Lotus.

☐ Copy the formula to the other product categories.

* /C ↵
* C5.E5 ↵

Move the pointer to the other cells in row 5 and notice that Lotus adjusts external references just like it adjusts internal references.

☐ Change the value of Toddlers sales in the OK/AR district to see the change reflected in the HEADQTRS files.

* CTRL-PGUP
* F5
* B5 ↵
* 1800 ↵
* CTRL-PGDN

Toddlers total sales changed from $5,460 to $6,010 in the HEADQTRS file.

☐ Link the HEADQTRS file to the Western Region's sales totals.

* F5
* B6 ↵
* +
* CTRL-PGUP CTRL-PGUP
* ↓ (6 times) ↵
* /C ↵ C6.E6 ↵

Use the same procedure to link HEADQTRS to the Northern Region and the Eastern Region. When the pointer is in B7 and B8, the template headings will not be visible. To determine the current file's name, watch the formula created in the status line.

☐ Save the current version of the files.

* /FS ↵ R

The save routine saves any open file that has been modified.

Step 3: Updating Linked Files

As demonstrated in the previous step, a change in an externally referenced range is immediately reflected in the cell containing the formula. If the formula was in a file that was not open, though, the formula would not be updated. Lotus solves this situation with the Link-Refresh command which updates all formulas with data from any referenced file, whether the external file is open or on disk.

In this step, we will clear all files from memory, then retrieve and modify the Eastern Region file. When the HEADQTRS file is subsequently opened it will not reflect the change made to the EASTERN file. After we issue the Link-Refresh command, the HEADQTRS file will be updated.

☐ Erase all files from memory.

* **/WEY**

☐ Retrieve the Eastern Region file.

* **/FR**
* **EASTERN** ↵

☐ Change the NYC/NJ Pre-Teens sales total from $3,060 to $3,550.

* **F5**
* **C7** ↵
* **3550** ↵
* **/FS** ↵ **R**

☐ Open the HEADQTRS file.

* **/FR**
* **HEADQTRS** ↵

The value in C8 (Eastern Pre-Teens) does not reflect the change made to the EASTERN file.

☐ Issue the Link-Refresh command to update the HEADQTRS file.

* **/FAL**

The HEADQTRS file had to be refreshed because both files (EASTERN and HEADQTRS) were not open at the time the EASTERN file was modified. The Link-Refresh command reads all referenced external files, whether they are open or not.

☐ Save the HEADQTRS file then clear memory.

* **/FS** ↵ **R**

* /WEY

Step 4: Connecting to an External Data Base

Release 3 contains a new command that allows direct access to external data bases created by other applications (e.g., dBASE III PLUS). The /Data External command allows data to be exchanged between Release 3 and external data bases. Lotus Release 3 can USE external data bases, LIST tables and fields, CREATE tables, DELETE tables, and even send a command to an external data base management program.

A **database table** is a collection of records that all share the same fields. A data base file usually consists of multiple tables that are related to one another through common index keys.

Release 3 requires a full table name before it can connect to an external table. The full table name includes the name of a data base driver, the name of the external data base and the name of a table within the external data base.

Release 3 is shipped with a database driver (SAMPLE) that allows Lotus to connect to data bases created by dBASE III PLUS. Other data base drivers are available but must be obtained separately from Lotus Development Corporation.

Connect Lotus to the CARDS data base created in Chapter Four, Session Four. Once connected, query the CARDS data base directly from a Lotus template. If necessary, copy the CARDS.DBF data base from your data diskette into the PRACTICE directory (use /System to temporarily enter DOS, enter COPY A:CARDS.DBF C:\PRACTICE, then enter EXIT to return).

☐ Connect Lotus to the CARDS data base.

* **/DEU**
* **SAMPLE \PRACTICE CARDS** ↵
* ↵

When the SAMPLE data base driver is used, the second element (the external data base name) is actually the path to the data base file.

☐ List the fields in the CARDS data base.

* HOME
* *(in the Data External menu)*
* **LF** ↵ ↵
* **Q**

Step 5: Using UNDO

When UNDO is enabled, you can erase the effect of the most recent Lotus command. To demonstrate the UNDO feature we will turn on UNDO then list all the records in the CARDS data base. Then we will activate UNDO to erase the list.

☐ Enable UNDO.

* **/WGDOUEQ**

UNDO is now enabled for this session.

☐ Set up a database query to list all the records in the CARDS database.

* **/RT**
* **A1.A7** ↵
* **A10** ↵
* **/WDR**
* **A1.A9** ↵
* **/C**
* **A1.G1** ↵ **A3** ↵
* **/DQI CARDS** ↵ **C A1.G2** ↵ **O A3.G20** ↵ **Q**

☐ Perform the query.

* **/DQEQ**

Notice that the INPUT range name was the external database CARDS. The records of the CARDS database should appear.

☐ Activate UNDO to erase the records list.

* **ALT**-**F4**
* **Y**

The worksheet returns to its pre-query status.

☐ Display selected records from the CARDS database.

* **/RE A4..G20** ↵

Lotus: Session Nine 350

- ✳ F5
- ✳ C2 ↵
- ✳ BRAD ↵
- ✳ /DQEQ

Only Brad's records appear.

☐ Widen column B to 15 to improve readability.

- ✳ /WCS 15 ↵

☐ Activate UNDO again to see which command is "undone."

- ✳ ALT - F4
- ✳ Y

The Undo command returns the spreadsheet to its most recent READY mode status.

Step 6: Practice

The owners of Begonia's Clothes for Women opened a new store, Orchid's Clothes for Women. Orchid's contains exactly the same departments as Begonia's. Create two new files: an ORCHID sales summary file and a sales summary file that is linked to the other files to total the sales of both stores (CORSAGE).

- ✳ Retrieve the BEGONIA5 file.
- ✳ Change the heading to ORCHID, enter new sales data (your choice) and save the file as ORCHID.
- ✳ Open the BEGONIA5 file after ORCHID.
- ✳ Activate perspective mode.
- ✳ Move the cursor to ORCHID.
- ✳ Open a new file, CORSAGE, before ORCHID.
- ✳ Copy department labels and column headings from ORCHID to CORSAGE.
- ✳ Link each sales summary cell in CORSAGE to the corresponding cells in ORCHID and BEGONIA. For example, use the formula @SUM(<<BEGONIA.WK3>>C5,<<ORCHID.WK3>>C5) to link A:C5 to the other files.

* Save and print all three files.

The training coordinator just rushed in and asked to see a listing of the TRAINING database. Can you display the records without leaving Lotus 1-2-3?

* Clear the worksheet.
* Connect to the TRAINING database (it should be in your PRACTICE directory).
* List the fields in the TRAINING database.
* Set up a data query.
* Extract all records.
* Ask the training coordinator for a raise based on your superior understanding of Lotus 1-2-3.

Step 7: Terminating the Session

Complete the following to turn off your computer. Remember that you should always return to the DOS prompt before turning off the computer.

☐ To exit Lotus 1-2-3, first make sure that your work is saved, then issue the Quit command.

* *(if necessary, save your work)*
* /QY

☐ Remove your data diskette from drive A and turn off the computer.

Lotus: Session Nine 352

Appendices

Appendix A.   MS-DOS Command Summary

Appendix B.   WordPerfect 5.0 Command Summary

Appendix C.   dBASE III PLUS Command Summary

Appendix D.   Lotus 1-2-3 Command Summary (Release 2.01)

Appendix A:

MS-DOS Command Summary

Internal Commands

The following commands are loaded into RAM when the computer is booted up. An internal command may be activated anytime the DOS prompt is present.

- **break** When break is off, DOS checks for CTRL-C entry during screen, keyboard, and printer reads and writes. When break is on, CTRL-C entry is also checked during other activities such as disk reads and writes.

    Ex: **BREAK ON**

- **chdir (cd)** Change to a different directory.

    Ex: **CD **

- **cls** Clears the screen and places the DOS prompt in the upper left corner.

    Ex: **CLS**

- **copy** Copies one or more files to a new location.

    Ex: **COPY MEMO.TXT A:**

- **date** Displays the current system date and prompts for new date entry.

    Ex: **DATE**

- **del (erase)** Deletes one or more files.

    Ex: **DEL EXTRA.FIL**

- **dir** Displays the contents of the current or a named directory.

    Ex: **DIR**

- **exit** Terminates current command.com processing and returns to the previous level.

    Ex: **EXIT**

- **mkdir (md)** Creates a new directory.
    Ex: **MD PRACTICE**

- **path** Creates a new path, or, when entered alone, displays the current path.
    Ex: **PATH C:\DOS;C:\WP50**

- **prompt** Changes the appearance of the DOS prompt.
    Ex: **PROMPT PG**

- **ren (rename)** Changes the name of a file.
    Ex: **REN TEMP.TXT CHPT1.WP**

- **rmdir (rd)** Removes a named directory (the directory must be empty).
    Ex: **RD PRACTICE**

- **set** Makes one character string equal to another character string. In the following example, the character string "W5" can be used to start WordPerfect because it is equivalent to the string "C:\WP50\WP /R".
    Ex: **SET W5=C:\WP50\WP /R**

- **time** Displays the current system time and prompts the user to enter a new time.
    Ex: **TIME**

- **type** Displays the contents of DOS text files.
    Ex: **TYPE FILE.TXT**

- **ver** Displays the current DOS version number.
    Ex: **VER**

- **verify** Turns the verify switch on when writing to a disk.
    Ex: **VERIFY ON**

- **vol** Displays the disk volume label.
    Ex: **VOL**

Internal Commands Used in Batch Files

- **echo** Turns the batch echo feature on and off. ECHO OFF suppresses command display during batch file processing. Also used to display screen messages during batch file processing.

    Ex: **ECHO OFF**

- **goto** Jumps batch file processing to the line after a specified label.

    Ex: **GOTO END**

- **if** Performs a command based on the result of a condition.

    Ex: **IF STRING1 == STRING2 COPY *.* A:**

- **pause** Suspends batch file execution and waits for the user to tap a key.

    Ex: **PAUSE**

- **rem** Displays remarks that appear on the same line as the REM command.

    Ex: **REM Insert a diskette in drive A.**

External Commands

Each of the following commands is contained in its own separate file. These files are usually found in the \DOS directory. These commands are not loaded into RAM during boot up. They may only be activated if their execution file is in the current directory or a path command has been entered that points to the directory containing the execution file.

- **append** Creates a search path for data files.

    Ex: **APPEND C:\LOTUS\FILES**

- **attrib** Sets or displays file read-only and archive attributes.

    Ex: **ATTRIB +R THISFILE.TXT**

- **backup** Backs up one or more files from one disk to another.

    Ex: **BACKUP C:\DBASE\FILES*.* A:**

- **command** Executes the command processor.

    Ex: **COMMAND**

- **comp** Compares the contents of two sets of files.
    Ex: **COMP C:\DATA C:\BACKUP**

- **diskcomp** Compares the contents of two named diskettes.
    Ex: **DISKCOMP A: B:**

- **diskcopy** Makes an exact copy of a diskette.
    Ex: **DISKCOPY A: A:**

- **find** Searches for a character string in a file or set of files.
    Ex: **FIND "Arbuckle" C:\WP50\MEMOS**

- **graphics** Allows SHIFT-PRTSCR to print graphics screens to certain printers.
    Ex: **GRAPHICS**

- **keyb** Changes the keyboard's country designation. For example, to type French characters, enter:
    Ex: **KEYB FR**

- **label** Creates, changes or deletes a disk's volume label.
    Ex: **LABEL A:**

- **mode** Sets operation modes for input/output devices.
    Ex: **MODE COM1:48,E,,,P**

- **more** Displays output one screen at a time.
    Ex: **TYPE FILE.TXT | MORE**

- **print** Background prints one or more files.
    Ex: **PRINT *.WP**

- **restore** Restores files that were backed up using the BACKUP command.
    Ex: **RESTORE A: C:\DBASE\FILES*.***

- **sort** Sorts and displays data.
    Ex: **DIR | SORT**

- **sys** Places the DOS system files on a disk.
    Ex: **SYS A:**

- **tree** Displays a directory listing of a given drive.

    Ex: **TREE C:**

- **xcopy** Copies files and directories, including lower level directories, if they exist.

    Ex: **XCOPY A: B:**

Dangerous External Commands (Handle with Care)

Each of the following two commands are dangerous because they may erase all the data on your hard drive. Do not use either command unless you know exactly what you are doing.

- **fdisk** Displays a series of menus to help you configure a hard disk for use with MS-DOS.

    Ex: **FDISK**

- **format** Totally erases a disk, then prepares the disk in the specified drive to store files.

    Ex: **FORMAT A:**

Appendix A 358

Appendix B:

WordPerfect 5.0 Command Summary

```
WordPerfect 5.0 Template (IBM Layout)

           ┌─────────────────────┬─────────────────────┐
           │       Shell         │       Spell         │
       F1  │       SETUP         │     <-SEARCH        │  F2
           │     Thesaurus       │      Replace        │
           │      Cancel         │     Search->        │
           ├─────────────────────┼─────────────────────┤
           │       Screen        │        Move         │
       F3  │       SWITCH        │    ->INDENT<-       │  F4
           │    Reveal Codes     │       Block         │
           │        Help         │      ->Indent       │
           ├─────────────────────┼─────────────────────┤
           │    Text In/Out      │     Tab Align       │
       F5  │    DATE/OUTLINE     │       CENTER        │  F6
           │     Mark Text       │    Flush Right      │
           │     List Files      │        Bold         │
           ├─────────────────────┼─────────────────────┤
           │      Footnote       │        Font         │
       F7  │        PRINT        │       FORMAT        │  F8
           │    Math/Columns     │        Style        │
           │        Exit         │      Underline      │
           ├─────────────────────┼─────────────────────┤
           │     Merge/Sort      │    Macro Define     │
       F9  │    MERGE CODES      │      RETRIEVE       │  F10
           │      Graphics       │        Macro        │
           │      Merge R        │        Save         │
           └─────────────────────┴─────────────────────┘

                         Legend:

                   Ctrl + Function Key
                   SHIFT + FUNCTION KEY
                    Alt + Function Key
                    Function Key alone
```

Command Listing

Keystroke(s)	Command
Ctrl-F5	Add Password
Shft-F8	Advance (Printer's Platen)
Ctrl-PgUp	Advanced Macros (Command Selection)
Ctrl-F10	Advanced Macros (Access)
Shft-F8	Align/Decimal Character
Ctrl-F6	Align Text on Tabs
Ctrl-F9	Alphabetize text
Ctrl-F8	Appearance of Printed Text
Ctrl-F1	Append to Clipboard (Block On)
Ctrl-F4	Append Text to a File (Block On)
Ctrl-F5	ASCII Text File
Shft-F1	Assign Keys
Shft-F1	Attributes, On-screen
Ctrl-F8	Attributes, Printed
Alt-F5	Authorities, Table of
Shft-F8	Auto Hyphenation
Shft-F5	Auto Paragraph Numbering
Alt-F5	Auto Reference
Shft-F1	Automatically Format and Rewrite
Shft-F1	Auxiliary Files Location
Backspace	Backspace (Delete)
Shft-F1	Backup Files, Automatic
Shft-F1	Backup Directory Location
Shft-F2	Backward Search
Ctrl-F8	Base Font
Shft-F1	Beep Options
Shft-F7	Binding Width
Shft-F1	Black and White, View Doc. In
Alt-F4	Block
Ctrl-F4	Block, Append (Block On)
Shft-F6	Block, Center (Block On)
Ctrl-F5	Block, Comment (Block On)
Del	Block, Delete (Block On)
Ctrl-F4	Block, Move (Block On)
Shft-F7	Block, Print (Block On)
Shft-F8	Block, Protect (Block On)
Ctrl-F8; F6	Bold
Alt-F9	Box (Figure, Table, Text, Users)
F1	Cancel
Home"/"	Cancel Hyphenation Code
Shft-F7	Cancel Print Job(s)

Shft-F3	Capitalize Block (Block On)
Shft-F7	Cartridges and Fonts
Shft-F3	Case Conversion (Block On)
Shft-F6	Center Block (Block On)
Shft-F8	Center Page (Top to Bottom)
Shft-F8	Center Tabs
Shft-F6	Center Text
Shft-F1	Centimeters, Units of Measure
F5	Change Default Directory
Ctrl-F5	Change Comment to Text
Ctrl-F8	Change Font
Shft-F5	Change Text to Comment (Block On)
Ctrl-v	Character Set (International)
Shft-F8	Character Spacing
F7	Clear Screen
Ctrl-F1	Clipboard
Shft-F1	Codes, Default
Shft-F9	Codes, Merge
Alt-F3	Codes, Reveal
Ctrl-F8	Color Print
Shft-F1	Colors/Fonts/Attributes
Alt-F7	Columns
Alt-F7	Columns, Define
Shft-F1	Columns, Side-by-side Display
Ctrl-PgUp	Commands, Programming
Shft-F1	Comment Display
Ctrl-F5	Comment in Document
Alt-F5	Compare Screen and Disk Documents
Ctrl-F5	Comment to Text
Ctrl-v	Compose
Alt-F5	Concordance
Alt-F5	Condense Master Document
Shft-F8	Conditional End of Page
Shft-F9	Control Characters
Shft-F7	Control Printer
Ctrl-F5	Convert Documents (5.0 to 4.2)
Ctrl-F4	Copy a Block (Block On)
F5	Copy File(s)
Ctrl-/F4	Copy Text (Block On or Off)
Ctrl-F2	Count Words
Alt-F5	Cross Referencing
Shft-F1	Cursor Speed
Ctrl-F4	Cut text (Block On or Off)
Shft-F8	Date of File Creation
Shft-F1	Date Format, Default
Shft-F5	Date/Time
Shft-F8	Decimal/Align Character
Shft-F8	Decimal Tabs, Define

Shft-F1	Default Codes
F5	Default Directory
Shft-F1	Default Settings
Ctrl-F10	Define Macros
Shft-F5	Define Paragraph/Outline Numbering
Shft-F7	Define Printer
Alt-F4	Define Text (highlight)
Alt-F5	Define ToC,Lists,ToA,Index (Block) M
Bksp, Del	Delete
F5	Delete File
Ctrl-End	Delete to End of Line
Ctrl-PgDn	Delete to End of Page
Ctrl-F4	Delete Text (Block On or Off)
Home, Bk/Del	Delete to Word Boundary
Ctrl-Backsp	Delete Word
Ctrl-v	Diacriticals/Digraphs
Ctrl-F2	Dictionary
F5	Directories
Shft-F1	Display and Entry of Numbers
Shft-F1	Display Attributes
F5	Display Disk Space
Shft-F1	Display Document Comments
Shft-F8	Display Pitch
Shft-F1	Display Setup
Shft-F1	Document Backup
Alt-F5	Document Compare
Shft-F8	Document Format
Shft-F7	Document Preview
Shft-F10	Document Retrieve
F5	Document Search
Shft-F8	Document Summary, Create/Edit
Shft-F1	Document Summary, on Save/Exit
Ctrl-F5	DOS Text File
Shft-F8	Dot Leaders
Shft-F7	Downloadable Fonts
Shft-F7	Downloadable Fonts Path
Shft-F7	Download Fonts to Printer
Ctrl-F3	Draw Lines
Shft-F3	Dual Document Editing
Ctrl-F5	Encrypt a Document
F9	End of Field
End	End of Line
Ctrl-End	End of Line, Delete to
Ctrl-PgDn	End of Page, Delete to
Shft-F9	End of Record
Ctrl-F7	Endnote
Ctrl-F7	Endnote Placement
Alt-F5	Endnotes, Generate

Shft-F1	Enhanced Keyboard Definition
Alt-F10	Execute Macro
F7	Exit WordPerfect
Alt-F5	Expand Master Document
Ctrl-v	Extended Characters
Home Alt-F2	Extended Replace
Home F2	Extended Search
Shft-F1	Fast Save (unformatted)
Shft-F1	Fast Text Display
Alt-F9	Figure Box, Define and Edit
Ctrl-F5	File, DOS text
F5	File, Mark
Shft-F1	File Location, Auxiliary
F5	File Management
F5	File Search
Shft-F1	Filename on Status Line
Shft-F1	Files, Backup
Alt-F6	Flush Right
Ctrl-F8	Font Appearance
Ctrl-F8	Font Attributes
Ctrl-F8	Font, Base
Ctrl-F8	Font Color
Shft-F8	Font, Initial (Document)
Shft-F7	Font, Initial (Printer)
Ctrl-F8	Font Size
Shft-F7	Fonts, Downloadable
Shft-F7	Fonts, Download to Printer
Shft-F8	Footers
Ctrl-F7	Footnote
Shft-F8	Force Odd/Even Page
Hm,Hm,Ins	Forced Insert
Hm,Ins	Forced Typeover
Shft-F7	Foreign Languages (International)
Ctrl-v	Foreign Characters (")
Shft-F8	Format Line/Page/Doc./Other
Ctrl-F3	Format Screen
Setup	Format Screen, Automatically
Shft-F7	Forms, Define
F2	Forward Search
Alt-F5	Generate Tables, Indexes, etc.
Ctrl-F5	Generic Word Processor Format
Alt-F2	Global Search and Replace
Ctrl-Home	Go To
Ctrl-F1	Go to DOS/Shell
Alt-F9	Graphics
Alt-F9	Graphics Box Options
Shft-F7	Graphics Quality

Shft-F1	Graphics Screen Type
Shft-F8	H-Zone
F4,Shft-Tab	Hanging Indent
"-"	Hard Hyphen
Ctrl-Enter	Hard Page Break
Shft-F1	Hard Return Display Character
Home-Space	Hard Space
Shft-F8	Headers
F3	Help
Shft-F7	Help, Printer
Alt-F3	Hidden Codes
"-"	Hyphen, Hard
Ctrl "-"	Hyphen, Soft
Home "-"	Hyphen Character
Shft-F8	Hyphenation
Shft-F1	Hyphenation Module(s) Location
Shft-F8	Hyphenation Zone
Shft-F1	Inches
F4	Indent Left Only
Shft-F4	Indent Left and Right
Alt-F5	Index (define or generate)
Alt-F5	Index, Mark text for (Block On)
Shft-F1	Initial Codes, Default
Shft-F8	Initial Codes, Document
Shft-F7	Initial Font, Printer
Shft-F8	Initial Font, Document
Shft-F1	Initial Settings, Default
Shft-F7	Initialize Printer
Hm,Hm,Ins	Insert, Forced
Ins	Insert/Replace mode
Ctrl-v	Insert Any Character
Alt-F5	Insert Subdocument
Ctrl-v	International Characters
Shft-F7	Interrupt Print Job
Home, Enter	Invisible Soft Return
Ctrl-F8	Italics Print
Shft-F8	Justification
Shft-F8	Justification Limits
Shft-F8	Keep Lines Together
Shft-F8	Kerning
Shft-F1	Keyboard Definitions/Layout
Shft-F7	Landscape Fonts
Shft-F7	Landscape Forms
Shft-F8	Landscape Paper Size/Type

Shft-F8	Languages
Ctrl-F8	Large Print
Shft-F8	Left and Right Margins
Shft-Tab	Left Margin Release
Shft-F8	Letter/Word Spacing
Alt-F9	Line, Graphics
Ctrl-F3	Line Draw
Shft-F8	Line Format
Shft-F8	Line Height/Numbering/Spacing
F5	List Files
Alt-F5	Lists, Mark text for (Block On)
Shft-F1	Location of Auxiliary Files
Shft-F7	Location of Forms
Ctrl-F5	Locked Document(s)
Alt-F5	Long Form, Table of Auth.
F5	Look at a File
Shft-F3	Lower/Upper Case (Block On)
Ctrl-PgUp	Macro Commands
Ctrl-F10	Macro Commands, Help on
Ctrl-F10	Macro Editor
Ctrl-F10	Macros, Define
Alt-F10	Macros, Execute
Shft-F1	Macros, Keyboard Definition
Ctrl-F9	Mail Merge
Shft-F8	Manual Hyphenation
Shft-Tab	Margin Release
Shft-F8	Margins Left and Right
Shft-F8	Margins - Top and Bottom
Alt-F5	Mark Text (ToC, Index, ToA, List)
Alt-F5	Master Document
Alt-F7	Math
Shft-F1	Menu Letter Display
Ctrl-F9	Merge
Shft-F9	Merge Codes
F9	Merge R
Shft-F1	Mnemonics
Ctrl-F4	Move Text (Block On or Off)
F5	Move/Rename File
Esc	n= (set temporarily)
Shft-F1	n= (default)
Ctrl-Enter	New Page
Shft-F8	New Page Number
Alt-F7	Newspaper Columns
Ctrl-F8	Normal Font
Shft-F8	Number Lines
Shft-F7	Number of Copies
Shft-F8	Number Pages

Shft-F8	Odd/Even Page
Shft-F7	Offsets, Page
Shft-F7	Orientation, Fonts
Shft-F7	Orientation, Forms
Shft-F8	Orientation, Paper Size\Type
Shft-F1	Original Document Backup
Shft-F1	Original Keyboard
Shft-F8	Orphan/Widow
Shft-F8	Other Format
Shft-F5	Outline
Shft-F8	Overstrike
Ctrl-Enter	Page Break, Hard
PgDn	Page Down
Shft-F8	Page Format
Shft-F8	Page Format, Suppress
Shft-F8	Page Length
Ctrl-Home	Page Number, Go To
Shft-F8	Page Number, New
Ctrl-B	Page Number in Text
Shft-F8	Page Numbering
Shft-F7	Page Offsets
PgUp	Page Up
Shft-F7	Page View
Shft-F7	Paper Location
Shft-F8	Paper Size/Type
Shft-F7	Paper Trays
Shft-F5	Paragraph Numbering, Auto
Alt-F7	Parallel Columns
Ctrl-F5	Password
Shft-F7	Path for Downloadable Fonts
Shft-F7	Path for Printer Command Files
Shft-F8	Percent of Optimal Spacing
Shft-F8	Pitch, Display
Shft-F7	Port, Printer
Shft-F7	Portrait Fonts
Shft-F7	Portrait Forms
Shft-F8	Portrait Paper Size\Type
Shft-F7	Preview
Ctrl-F9	Primary File, Merge
Shft-F7	Print
Shft-F7	Print Block (Block On)
Ctrl-F8	Print Color
Shft-F7	Print Document on Disk
Shft-F7;F5	Print from Disk
Shft-F7	Print Full Document
Shft-F7	Print (Cancel,Display,Rush,Stop)
F5,Shft-F7	Print List Files

Shft-F1	Print Options, Default
Shft-F7	Print Options, Document
Shft-F7	Print Page
Shft-F7	Print Preview
Shft-F7	Print Quality
Ctrl-F8	Printed Attributes
Shft-F7	Printer, Initialize
Shft-F7	Printer, Select
Shft-F8	Printer Command
Shft-F7	Printer Command Files Path
Shft-F7	Printer Control
Shft-F1	Printer Files Location
Shft-F7	Printer Fonts
Shft-F8	Printer Function
Shft-F7	Printer Port
Ctrl-PgUp	Program Macros (Command Display)
Ctrl-F10	Program Macros, (Access)
Shft-F1	Prompt for Summary
Ctrl-F5	Protect a Document
Shft-F8	Protect Block
Shft-F7	.PRS file, Edit
Shft-F7	.PRS files, View
Shft-F7	Quality of Text, Graphics
F7	Quit WordPerfect
Shft-F1	Reassign Keys
F1	Recover Text
Ctrl-F4	Rectangle, Move/Copy (Block On)
Shft-F8	Redline Method
Ctrl-F8	Redline Print
Alt-F5	Redline, Remove
Alt-F5	Reference, Auto
Alt-F5	References, Generate
Ctrl-F3	Reformat Screen
Ctrl-F5	Remove Password
Alt-F5	Remove Redline and Strikeout
F5	Rename/Move File
Shft-F1	Repeat Value
Esc	Repetition Number (n)
Alt-F2	Replace
Hm, Alt-F2	Replace, Extended
Shft-F7	Report Printer Status
F1	Restore Deleted Text
Ctrl-F1	Retrieve Clipboard
Ctrl-F4	Retrieve Column
Shft-F10	Retrieve Document
Ctrl-F5;F5	Retrieve DOS Text File
Shft-F10;F5	Retrieve a File

Ctrl-F4	Retrieve Text (Move key)
Alt-F3	Reveal Codes
Ctrl-F3	Rewrite Screen
Shft-F8	Right Justification
Shft-F8	Right Justification Limits
Shft-F8	Right Margin
Ctrl-F3	Ruler
F10	Save Text
Shft-F1	Save, Fast (unformatted)
Ctrl-F3	Screen
Shft-F1	Screen Display
+(Num Pad)	Screen Down
-(Num Pad)	Screen Up
Ctrl-F3	Screen Rewrite
Shft-F1	Screen Setup
Ctrl-F3	Screen Split
Shft-F1	Scrolling Speed
F2	Search
Alt-F2	Search and Replace
F5	Search for File(s)
Ctrl-F9	Secondary File, Merge
Alt-F3	See Codes
Shft-F7	Select Printer(s)
Shft-F7	Send Printer a "GO"
Shft-F8	Set Pitch (Letter/Word Spacing)
Shft-F8	Set Tabs
Shft-F1	Settings, Initial (Default)
Ctrl-F8	Shadow Print
Shft-F7	Sheet Feeder
Ctrl-F1	Shell, Go to
Alt-F5	Short Form, Table of Auth.
Shft-F1	Side-by-side Columns Display
Ctrl-F8	Size of Print (Attributes)
Ctrl-F8	Small Capitalized Print
Ctrl-F8	Small Print
Ctrl "-"	Soft Hyphen
Ctrl-F9	Sort
Hm, Space	Space, Hard
Shft-F8	Spacing Lines
Shft-F8	Spacing Justification Limits
Ctrl-F2	Spell
Ctrl-F3	Split Screen
Shft-F1	Status Line Display
Shft-F7	Stop Printer
Ctrl-F8	Strike-out
Alt-F8	Style
Shft-F1	Style Library File Location
Alt-F5	Subdocument

Shft-F1	Subject Search Text
Ctrl-F8	Subscript Print
Shft-F8	Summary, Document
Shft-F1	Summary Prompt
Ctrl-F8	Superscript Print
Shft-F8	Suppress Page Format
Shft-F7	Swappable Fonts & Cartridges
Shft-F3	Switch Documents
Tab	Tab
Ctrl-F6	Tab Align
Ctrl-F3	Tab Ruler
Shft-F8	Tab Set
Alt-F5	Table of Authorities (Block On)
Shft-F1	Table of Authorities, Default
Alt-F5	Table of Contents, Mark (Block On)
Alt-F5	Target
Alt-F9	Text Box
Alt-F7	Text Columns
Ctrl-F5	Text In/Out
Shft-F7	Text Quality
Ctrl-F5	Text to Comment (Block On)
Alt-F1	Thesaurus
Shft-F8	Thousands' Separator
Shft-F5	Time/Date
Shft-F1	Timed Document Backup
Shft-F8	Top and Bottom Margin
Shft-F7	Type Through (to printer)
Hm, Ins	Typeover, Forced
Ins	Typeover mode
F1	Undelete
Shft-F8	Underline Spaces and Tabs
Ctrl-F8;F8	Underline Text
Shft-F1	Units of Measure
Ctrl-F5	Unlock a Document
Alt-F5	Update References
Shft-F3	Upper/Lower Case
Alt-F9	User-defined Box
Alt-F3	View Codes
Shft-F7	View Document
Shft-F8	Widow/Orphan Protection
Ctrl-F3	Window
Ctrl-F3	Word Count
Ctrl-Left	Word Left, Move
Ctrl-Rt	Word Right, Move
F5	Word Search

Shft-F8	Word/Letter Spacing	
Shft-F8	Word Spacing Justification Limits	
Ctrl-F5	WP 4.2 format	

Appendix C:
dBASE III PLUS Command Summary

Starter Set

?	DELETE FILE	LABEL	REPORT
APPEND	DIR	LIST	SCREEN
AVERAGE	DISPLAY	LOCATE	SEEK
BROWSE	DO	MODIFY	SET
CHANGE	EDIT	PACK	SKIP
CLEAR	ERASE	QUERY	SORT
CONTINUE	EXPORT	QUIT	STORE
COPY	FIND	RECALL	SUM
COUNT	GO/GOTO	RELEASE	TOTAL
CREATE	IMPORT	RENAME	TYPE
DELETE	INDEX	REPLACE	USE

Advanced Set

ACCEPT	INPUT	PARAMETERS	RUN/!
CANCEL	INSERT	PRIVATE	SAVE
CALL	JOIN	PROCEDURE	SELECT
CLOSE	LOAD	PUBLIC	SUSPEND
COPY FILE	LIST CMDS	READ	TEXT
DISPLAY CMDS	LOOP	REINDEX	UPDATE
DO CASE	MACRO/&	RESTORE	VIEW
DO WHILE	MODIFY CMDS	RESUME	WAIT
EJECT	NOTE/*	RETRY	ZAP
EXIT			

dBASE III PLUS Functions and Set Commands

Database Functions

Function	Return Value
BOF()	.T. if the record pointer is before the first logical record of the file.
DBF()	The name of the database file if one is open. Null string if there isn't one open.
DELETED()	.T. if record is marked for deletion.
EOF()	.T. if the record pointer is after the last logical record in the file.
FIELD(#)	The name of the field in the database corresponding to #. Valid numbers are 1...128. Invalid numbers return a null string.

Date Functions

Function	Return Value
CDOW(Date)	The name of the day of the week used in "Date".
CMONTH(Date)	The name of the month used in "Date".
CTOD(Str)	Date of the "Str".
DATE()	The system date in the SET DATE format.
DAY(Date)	Number indicating the day of the month.
DOW(Date)	Number of the day of the week used in "Date".
DTOC(Date)	Character string in the SET DATE format of "Date".
MONTH(Date)	Number of the month used in "Date".
YEAR(Date)	Number of the year used in "Date".

Numeric Functions

Function	Return Value
ABS(#)	The absolute value of the #.
EXP(#)	The value of e to the # power.
IIF(.L.,E1,E2)	"E1" if ".L." is evaluated to be .T., "E2" if ".L." is .F. (E1 and E2 must be the same data type.)
INT(#)	The integer portion of #.
LOG(#)	The natural logarithm of #.

String Functions

Function	Return Value
ASC(Str)	The number representing the ASCII equivalent of the leftmost character of the Str.
AT(Str1,Str2)	A number indicating the position of Str1 inside Str2. Zero if Str1 isn't there.
CHR(#)	A character string indicating the ASCII equivalent of the #.
ISALPHA(Str)	.T. if the first character of Str is a letter.
ISLOWER(Str)	.T. if the first character of Str is a lowercase letter.

SET TO Commands

SET ALTERNATE	SET FIELDS	SET MESSAGE
SET CATALOG	SET FILTER	SET ORDER
SET COLOR	SET FUNCTION	SET PATH
SET DATE	SET FORMAT	SET PRINT
SET DECIMALS	SET HISTORY	SET PROCEDURE
SET DEFAULT	SET INDEX	SET RELATION
SET DELIMITERS	SET MARGIN	SET TYPEAHEAD
SET DEVICE	SET MEMOWIDTH	SET VIEW

SET ON/OFF Commands

SET (switch)	**When option is ON:**
SET BELL ON/off	Enables the console bell.
SET CARRY on/OFF	Brings information from the last record into the next record.
SET CENTURY on/OFF	Makes all dates display with a 4 digit year (e.g., 1985).
SET CONFIRM on/OFF	Requires the user to press the Enter key before dBASE III PLUS continues to the next GET.
SET CONSOLE ON/off	Makes sure all information is displayed on the screen.
SET DEBUG on/OFF	Routes output of SET ECHO to the printer.

Appendix C 374

Appendix D:

Lotus 1-2-3 Command Summary (Release 2.01)

The Main Menu

/
Worksheet Range Copy Move File Print Graph Data System Quit

The Worksheet Menu

/Worksheet
Global Insert Delete Column Erase Titles Window Status Page

/Worksheet Global
Format Label-Prefix Column-Width Recalculation Protection Default Zero

/Worksheet Insert
Column Row

/Worksheet Delete
Column Row

/Worksheet Column
Set-Width Reset-Width Hide Display

/Worksheet Erase
No Yes

/Worksheet Titles
Both Horizontal Vertical Clear

/Worksheet Window
Horizontal Vertical Sync Unsync Clear

/Worksheet Status
Displays current settings

/Worksheet Page
Inserts printer page break symbol

The Worksheet Global Menu

/Worksheet Global
Format Label-Prefix Column-Width Recalculation Protection Default Zero

/Worksheet Global Format
Fixed Scientific Currency , General +/- Percent Date Text Hidden

/Worksheet Global Label-Prefix
Left Right Center

/Worksheet Global Column-Width
Enter global column width

/Worksheet Global Recalculation
Natural Columnwise Rowwise Automatic Manual Iteration

/Worksheet Global Protection
Enable Disable

/Worksheet Global Default
Printer Directory Status Update Other Quit

/Worksheet Global Zero
No Yes

The Range Menu

/Range
Format Label Erase Name Justify Protect Unprotect Input Value Transpose

/Range Format
Fixed Scientific Currency , General +/- Percent Date Text Hidden Reset

/Range Label
Left Right Center

/Range Erase
Enter range to erase: A1..A1

/Range Name
Create Delete Labels Reset Table

/Range Justify
Enter justify range: A1..A1

/Range Protect
Enter range to protect: A1..A1

/Range Unprotect
Enter range to unprotect: A1..A1

/Range Input
Enter data input range: A1..A1

/Range Value
Copy a range, converting formulas to values

/Range Transpose
Copy a range, switching columns to rows

The Copy Command

/Copy
Copy a cell or a range of cells

The Move Command

/Move
Move a cell or a range of cells

The File Menu

/File
Retrieve Save Combine Xtract Erase List Import Directory

/File Retrieve
Select a file to retrieve

/File Save
Save the current file

/File Combine
Copy Add Subtract

/File Xtract
Formulas Values

/File Erase
Worksheet Print Graph Other

Appendix D 377

/File List
Worksheet Print Graph Other

/File Import
Text Numbers

/File Directory
Define the default directory for the current session

The Print Menu

/Print
Printer File

/Print File
Send print output to a named file

/Print Printer
Range Line Page Options Clear Align Go Quit

/Print Printer Range
Define the range to be printed

/Print Printer Line
Advance the printer one line

/Print Printer Page
Advance the printer to the top of the next page

/Print Printer Options
Header Footer Margins Borders Setup Pg-Length Other Quit

/Print Printer Clear
Reset some or all print setting

/Print Printer Align
Define the current printer head location as the top of the page

/Print Printer Go
Use current print settings and begin printing

/Print Printer Quit
Exit the print menu

/Print Printer Options Header
Enter the header

/Print Printer Options **Footer**
Enter the footer

/Print Printer Options **Margins**
Left Right Top Bottom

/Print Printer Options **Borders**
Columns Rows

/Print Printer Options **Setup**
Enter ASCII codes to initialize the printer

/Print Printer Options **Pg-length**
Define the number of lines each page will contain

/Print Printer Options **Other**
As-Displayed Cell-Formulas Formatted Unformatted

/Print Printer Options **Quit**
Quit the options menu and return to the printer menu

The Graph Menu

/Graph
Type X A B C D E F Reset View Save Options Name Quit

/Graph **Type**
Line Bar XY Stacked-Bar Pie

/Graph **X**
Define the label range to be displayed on the X-axis

/Graph **A** (B, C, D, E and F)
Define the A data range

/Graph **Reset**
Graph X A B C D E F Quit

/Graph **View**
Display the current graph setting

/Graph **Save**
Save the current graph setting in a .PIC file to be printed

/Graph **Options**
Legend Format Titles Grid Scale Color B&W Data-Labels Quit

/Graph **Name**
Use Create Delete Reset

Appendix D 379

The Data Menu

/Data
Fill Table Sort Query Distribution Matrix Regression Parse

/Data Fill
Fill a range with numbers

/Data Table
1 2 Reset

/Data Sort
Data-Range Primary-Key Secondary-Key Reset Go Quit

/Data Query
Input Criterion Output Find Extract Unique Delete Reset Quit

/Data Distribution
Calculate the frequency distribution of a range

/Data Matrix
Invert Multiply

/Data Regression
X-Range Y-Range Output-Range Intercept Reset Go Quit

/Data Parse
Format-Line Input-Column Output-Range Reset Go Quit

The System Command

/System
Begin an additional DOS session on top of the current session

The Quit Command

/Quit
No Yes

Index

A

Active drive:
   changing, 44
   defined, 29
Add-on card, 17
Address (memory), 7
Allways (*see*
   Lotus 1-2-3, Allways)
Alphanumeric characters, 6
Arithmetic and logic unit
   (ALU), 8

B

Batch file, 54, 74
   %1 parameter, 77
   use, 76
Binary numbering system, 6
Bit, 6
Bus, 16

C

Computer system, 4
Configuration, 16
Control unit, 8
Coprocessor, 17
Cylinders (*see*
   Tracks)

D

Daisy-wheel, 11
Data base:
   creation, 182
   field, 182
   field definition, 185
   fields, 185-86
   record, 183
   retrieving, 194
   saving, 193
Database, 3
   defined, 180
Database table, 349
dBASE:
   command parameters, 196
   command structure, 194
   constant, 197

   expression list, 196
   FOR condition, 202
   function, 197, 238-39
   function key settings, 182
   loading, 180
   OFF, 205
   operator, 197
   programming, 227
   programming (creating), 231
   programming (example code), 243
   programming (planning), 239
   programming (writing), 227
   reports, 216
   running a program, 232
   SCOPE, 200
   WHILE conditions, 205
dBASE commands:
   ACCEPT, 239
   APPEND, 187
   APPEND FROM, 199, 224
   AVERAGE, 208
   BROWSE, 188-89, 224
   CLEAR, 206
   CLOSE DATABASE, 193
   COPY STRUCTURE, 224
   COUNT, 208
   CREATE, 185
   CREATE COMMAND, 231
   CREATE REPORT, 219
   DELETE, 224-25
   DO, 232
   DO WHILE, 239
   EDIT, 188, 190
   FIND, 214
   HELP, 195
   INDEX, 213
   LIST, 196
   LIST TO PRINT, 191
   MODIFY COMMAND, 233
   MODIFY REPORT, 222
   PACK, 224-25
   QUIT, 193
   REINDEX, 242
   REPLACE, 236
   REPORT FORM, 220
   REPORT TO PRINT, 223
   SEEK, 242
   SELECT, 242

SORT, 211
SUM, 208
USE, 193
WAIT, 239
dBASE command summary, 371
Default options, 21
Digitizing tablet, 10
Directory:
   changing, 47
   creation, 46
   defined, 29
   removing, 47
Disk drive, 13
Diskette, 13
   components, 41
   labeling, 44
DOS:
   booting the system, 27
   date entry, 32
   defined, 26
   loading DOS, 31
   running an application, 28
   switch, 37
   time entry, 32
DOS commands:
   CD (CHDIR), 47
   CLS, 33
   COPY, 50
   COPY + CON, 57
   COPY CON, 55, 63
   DATE, 34
   defined, 32
   DIR, 37, 64
   DISKCOPY, 43
   EDLIN, 68-70, 74
   ERASE, 66
   FORMAT, 42
   MD (MKDIR), 46
   PATH, 68
   PROMPT, 34
   RD (RMDIR), 47
   TIME, 34
DOS command summary, 354
DOS prompt, 27, 33
Dot-matrix, 11

E

Electronic spreadsheet, 3, 250
   absolute cell address, 277-80
   database management, 287
   graphics, 297
   macro creation, 325
   macros (defined), 313
   profit and loss statement, 256
   range names, 320
   ranges, 263
   relative cell address, 278, 280
   what if analysis, 266, 270
Expansion boards (*see*
   Add-on card)
Expansion slots, 17
Extension (filename), 28

F

File, 28, 36
Filename, 28
Font, 165
Function key, 18

G

Graph presentation, 303

H

Hard copy, 4

I

Icons, 23
Indexing, 212, 218, 221
Ink-jet, 11
Input, 4
Input/Output devices, 10
Input/Output operations, 5
Insert text mode, 89
Integrated electronic spreadsheet
   (*see* Electronic spreadsheet)

J

Joystick, 10

K

Keyboard, 4, 10, 18

L

Laser printer, 12
Logical operators, 202
Lotus access system, 298
Lotus add-in manager, 324, 332
Lotus learn, 323
Lotus 1-2-3:
   absolute cell address, 329
   activating multiple spreadsheets, 343
   add-in, 324

Allways, 332
Allways (invoking), 334
Allways (printing), 335
column width, 257
criterion range, 290
data base creation, 289
database driver, 349
data external, 349
data external command, 343
data extraction, 290
data find, 292
data query, 291
data sort, 293
date entry, 328
file linking, 342, 345
formatting cell entries, 262
formula entry, 253, 255, 260
functions, 261, 282
graphs (bar), 300
graphs (clustered-bar), 305
graphs (line), 309
graphs (pie), 308
graphs (saving and printing), 302
graphs (stacked-bar), 305
inserting a column, 266
label entry, 253-54, 258
link-refresh, 348
loading, 251
macro keystrokes, 320
macro menu, 318
macros (creation), 313-14
macros (editing), 317
macros (invoking), 316
main menu, 252
printing a spreadsheet, 264
quitting Lotus, 265
relative cell address, 329
release 2.2 (new features), 342
release 3 (new features), 342
repeating text entry, 258
retrieving a spreadsheet, 265
row insertion, 333
saving a spreadsheet, 261, 264, 272
undo, 343, 350
value entry, 253-54, 260
window, 283
work screen, 251
Lotus 1-2-3 command summary, 375
Lotus value pack, 313, 323

M

Macro, 22
Macro worksheet placement, 315

Menu:
  bar, 20
  pop-up, 20
  pull-down, 20
Menus, 20
Microcomputer, 2, 4
Microdisk, 13
Microprocessor, 4
Modem, 17
Monitor, 4, 11, 32
Motherboard, 4-5
Mouse, 10

O

Optical scanners, 10
Output, 4

P

Parallel port, 16
Path, 29
  defined, 30
Peripherals (*see*
  Input/Output devices)
Personal computer (*see*
  Microcomputer)
Personal computing, 2
Pixel, 11
Plotter, 11
Port, 16
Printer, 4, 11
Printer/plotter driver, 12
Print spooler, 17
Processing, 4
Processing operations, 5
Programming, 22

R

RAM, 6, 8, 13
Random access memory (*see*
  RAM)
Read-only memory (ROM), 7
Read/write head, 14
Relational operators, 202
Rootname, 28

S

Scrolling, 18
Search string, 203
Sector, 14
Serial port, 16
Software, 2

Sorting, 210
Source diskette, 43
Speech synthesizers, 12
Storage, 4
    primary storage, 7
    secondary storage, 7, 13
Switch (*see*
    DOS)

T

Target diskette, 43
Tracks, 14
Typeover text mode, 89

V

Voice recognition, 10

W

Wildcard character, 60
    asterisk (*), 60
    defined, 29
    question mark (?), 61
    use, 62
Window, 21, 24
WordPerfect:
    adding text, 89
    block operations, 86
    clean Screen, 81
    clip-art, 173
    columns, 126, 128
    combining files, 139
    default settings, 82
    document retrieval, 96
    endnote, 114
    ESC repeat feature, 101
    exiting, 100
    footnote, 112-14
    format menu, 104
    graphics text box, 168
    help, 82
    in-line boldface, 94
    letter merge file, 119
    line draw, 103
    loading, 80
    macro (ALT-letter), 144
    macro (chaining), 158
    macro (defined), 143
    macro (editing), 149
    macro (interactive), 153
    macro (named), 147
    macro (temporary), 148
    margin setting, 106
    marked text underline, 95
    marking text, 95
    math, 126, 130
    merging, 117
    moving text, 86
    name and address merge file, 117
    printing, 97, 108
    reveal codes, 91
    saving a document, 86, 90, 107
    search, 92
    search and replace, 92-93, 106
    sorting, 126, 134
    spell-check, 109-11
    styles, 162, 164, 166-67
    tab settings, 104-5
    thesaurus, 111
    user-defined box, 169
    view document, 97
WordPerfect command summary, 359
Word Processing, 3
    defined, 80
Word wrap, 85